Spirituality, Ethics, and Relationship in Adulthood: Clinical and Theoretical Explorations

Spirituality, Ethics, and Relationship in Adulthood: Clinical and Theoretical Explorations

Edited by

Melvin E. Miller

&

Alan N. West

PSYCHOSOCIAL PRESS
Madison Connecticut

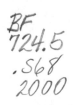

Library of Congress Cataloging-in-Publication Data

Spirituality, ethics, and relationship in adulthood : clinical and theoretical explorations / edited by Melvin E. Miller & Alan N. West.

p. cm.

Chiefly papers presented at the Society for Research in Adult Development Symposia, 1994 to 1996.

Includes bibliographical references and indexes.

ISBN 1-887841-29-6

1. Adulthood—Psychological aspects—Congresses. 2. Maturation (Psychology)—Congresses. I. Miller, Melvin E. II. West, Alan N.

BF724.5.S68 1999

155.6—dc21 99-39480

CIP

Manufactured in the United States of America

To our wives and children:
Loren and Priscilla, Melissa and Abigail,
Aaron and Brendan

Table of Contents

Contributors and Editors

Leslie P. Fairfield, Ph.D., is Professor of Church History at the Trinity Episcopal School for Ministry in Ambridge, Pennsylvania.

Carol Hren Hoare, Ph.D., is Professor of Human Development and Human Resource Development at George Washington University, Washington, DC.

Ronald R. Irwin, Ph.D., is a developmental psychologist. He has been involved with the Society for Research in Adult Development for over 10 years and is an editorial board member of the *Journal of Adult Development.*

Lene Arnett Jensen, Ph.D., is a postdoctoral student with the Department of Sociology at the University of California-Berkeley. The chapter included here draws upon her dissertation work, for which she has received the 1997 Dissertation Award from the Association for Moral Education and the William Henry Prize from the University of Chicago.

Ruthellen Josselson, Ph.D., is Professor of Psychology at Fielding Institute, Santa Barbara, CA, and Towson University, Baltimore. Recipient of the APA Henry Murray Award (1994) and a Fulbright Research Fellowship (1989-1990), she has also recently been Visiting Professor at the Harvard Graduate School of Education and Forchheimer Professor of Psychology at the Hebrew University in Jerusalem.

Jackson Kytle, Ph.D., has been on the faculty of Columbia University's Department of Psychiatry, and Antioch University. After founding the McGregor School on the Antioch campus in Ohio, he left as Provost and Vice President to become President of Goddard College from 1990 to 1994. After a sabbatical at the Harvard Graduate School of Education, he was appointed Dean of Vermont College, Norwich University's center for innovation and distance education in Montpelier, VT.

John J. McKenna, Ph.D., has been affiliated with Trinity College of Vermont in Burlington, VT, for more than 23 years; he currently holds an appointment of Associate Professor of Psychology. After 12 years as a monk of the Cistercian Order, he obtained a Master's degree in Psychology and Religion from Andover Newton Theological School in Newton Center, MA. Following doctoral studies in clinical psychology at the University of Vermont, he began a part-time clinical practice for adolescents, adults, and couples.

Melvin E. Miller, Ph.D., has twice been a Visiting Scholar at Harvard Divinity School. He is now Professor of Psychology and Director of Psychological Services at Norwich University, Northfield, VT.

Elena Mustakova-Possardt, Ph.D., is Assistant Professor of Psychology at the University of West Georgia.

Andrés G. Niño, Ph.D., lectures in psychology at Merrimack College, and works as a staff clinician in the Arbour Health System, Boston. He began research in the area of psychotherapy and spirituality as a Visiting Scholar at Harvard University in 1988. He is currently a Research Scholar at the Center for Research on Women at Wellesley College, MA.

Jennifer L. Rike, Ph.D., is Assistant Professor of Religious Studies at the University of Detroit Mercy, where she teaches theology. She is an ordained minister in the Presbyterian Church (U.S.A.).

Pano Rodis is a doctoral candidate in the Department of School and Counseling Psychology at the University of Massachusetts, Amherst and a Visiting Assistant Professor in the Department of Education at Dartmouth College, NH.

Kevin F. Ryan, M.A., J.D., is an associate professor in the Department of Justice Studies and Sociology at Norwich University, Northfield, VT. He is at work on a book on the origins and persistence of American drug policy.

Jan Sinnott, Ph.D., is a Professor of Psychology at Towson University, Baltimore. She did postdoctoral study at the National Institutes of Health. Her private practice is in Baltimore and in Washington, DC.

Alan N. West, Ph.D., is Project Director for an alcohol treatment outcomes study for the State of New Hampshire and is in private practice in New London, NH.

Preface

The chapters in this book are unified around three thematic groupings: Spirituality, Morality, and Ethics; Interrelationship, Intimacy, and Involvement; and the Self in Transformation. The authors of this interdisciplinary work are psychologists, social scientists, and theologians who feel strongly, even passionately, about the spiritual, emotional, and relational demands of adulthood. These thoughtful scholars write from various perspectives about matters of ultimate concern. They integrate theory, empirical research, clinical data, and personal experience and belief. The interdisciplinary approach means that theologians write about psychological and relational concerns, and sociologists and an array of psychologists write about religious and spiritual matters.

Approximately half of the chapters evolved from papers presented at the Society for Research in Adult Development (SRAD) Symposia from 1994 through 1996. The remaining chapters were invited.

A project of this magnitude cannot be completed without considerable help from many sources. We thank Jackson Kytle, Loren Miller, Ken Smith, and Ernest Zebrowski for their editorial assistance and guidance, and Sharon Dickinson for her dedicated administrative and clerical support throughout this process. Finally, we thank the editorial staff at International Universities Press/Psychosocial Press for its support and guidance. Their foresight, support, and untiring effort helped bring this project to fruition. They had the vision and integrity to see it through until the end.

Melvin E. Miller
Alan N. West

Introduction: New Visions for Adulthood in the Postmodern Era

Melvin E. Miller

A few contemporary scholars have attempted to address the perplexing concerns of our era. The philosopher Charles Taylor describes our epoch, and the circumstances of the modern self, in terms of the interplay of numerous complex conflicts and a vast array of competing internal forces. For example, Taylor (1989) describes the late 20th century individual (and culture) as caught in the tension between the perspectives of the disengaged instrumentalists (those believers in the exclusive role of science, reason, and atomistic reductionism), and that of the romantic expressionists, those who believe wholeheartedly in the importance of self-fulfillment and personal expression. Thus, modern people are caught between these two philosophical perspectives, often believing in the truth value of both (or more), and thus experience difficulty in finding their bearings.

Describing common responses to the complex demands of the postmodern era, Robert Jay Lifton (1993) has called our epoch the age of uncertainty. It is also an age of fragmentation, i.e., fragmentation of the self. Nevertheless, Lifton is optimistic about our "adaptive capacity," referring to the image of the Greek god Proteus. Proteus could change himself into various shapes in response to the demands of any crisis. Lifton champions the contemporary Proteus, whose flexibility and resilience promote adaptation to current crises.

Bob Kegan (1994) enumerates the varied demands confronting contemporary people in his book, *In Over Our Heads*. Kegan argues that most people are, in fact, "in over their heads," given today's high-level demands and the high level of abstraction required to meet them. Kegan speaks of the interpersonal changes required for mature adult living, and, in addition, believes people must become better able to deal with psychological complexity, both cognitively and emotionally, to meet the demands of the 21st century and the challenges of life's later years.

Another major demand addressed in this volume is that of the ethical challenges confronting the modern person (cf. Habermas, 1993; Rawls, 1971; Rorty, 1991; Stout, 1988; Vasudev, 1994). We see (along with Kegan) many individuals fighting to keep their heads above water. Ethical questions remain illusory and irrelevant for them because they are too busy surviving to be in a position to address the complexity of ethical considerations. Yet there are some who consciously strive to become better persons, more ethical in business transactions and interpersonal relationships. There are those who endeavor to become more skilled at ethical decision making. There are those who struggle to become more conscientious, sensitive, and aware as they attempt to overcome the beguiling draw of egoism and narcissism. These individuals not only yearn to realize better ways of behavior, but strive to comprehend and actualize universal ethical truths. Jurgen Habermas (1993) is one contemporary thinker seeking a language and forum for discussing the moral and ethical requirements of modern life. He believes there must be a more openly accessible dialogue about important ethical issues. Habermas enjoins us to find a way to bring everyone—representatives and issues from all cultures—to the table of debate. He poses a method of discourse ethics, an approach which privileges the ideals of freedom, altruism, and universalism. In this vein, Habermas advocates for both a vehicle and a venue that will help promulgate universal justice, freedom, and ethical behavior.

While these ethicists consider the precarious human condition in global terms, another group of thinkers has focused on the relationship needs of individuals in contemporary society. Authors in this domain write about the felt need for deeper intimacy in contemporary relationships. To date, most have been women focusing on women's issues (Anderson and Hopkins, 1991; Gilligan, 1982; Josselson, 1992, 1996; Miller, 1976), but recently we have begun to see men writing about the relationship needs and desires of men (Bly, 1990; Goldberg, 1987; Keen, 1991). We find both men and women expressing a need for autonomy, individuation, actualization, and relationship (interpersonal intimacy and connectedness). Both men and women have needs for close friendship, intimate dialogue, and interpersonal connectedness.

Much of adult life seems geared to finding such relational involvement. Some of the debate in the professional literature on contemporary adulthood focuses on the related controversy over whether the majority of adults yearn to escape from the demands of the world or enhance their level of worldly involvement. This debate is often characterized as one between the wish for "increased interiority" (a greater focus on one's inner life), and the desire for an increased level of activity and heightened engagement with the activities of the world.

Several academics have discussed the urge or press toward increased interiority (Ryff, 1986, 1991; Shafranske, 1996; Thomas & Eisenhandler, 1994). The idea has also found voice in the popular press. For example, *Time* (Kaplan, 1996) boasted a lead article on spirituality and healing, the *Los Angeles Times* (Healy, 1996) included an article declaring spirituality a central concern to people in the middle years, and the *New York Times* (Niebuhr, 1996) and the *Washington Post* (LaBier, 1995) discussed the rise in spiritual questions and quests in midlife adults, along with the increased need for ritual among even the most liberal of churchgoers.

Given the increased attention to the religious dimension of life reflected in both the general academic and lay press, it would be appropriate to turn our attention to the responses engendered by this cry for spirituality, by this increased interest in religion and the spiritual, within the discipline of psychology in particular, and within the social sciences in general.

THE SOCIAL SCIENCE RESPONSE TO THE SPIRITUAL QUEST

The American Psychological Association published a book on *Religion and the Clinical Practice of Psychology* (Shafranske,

1996). The APA, in supporting and promoting this volume, has sanctioned an effort to meet the demands of the times. Likewise, a number of authors (Fowler, 1996; Fuller, 1994; Meissner, 1996; Seeber, 1990; Thomas & Eisenhandler, 1994; Wulff, 1996) have begun to respond to the call for a thoughtful, in-depth inquiry into religious and spiritual issues. These writers have begun to take seriously, from a social science perspective, the need to investigate religious and spiritual matters in the mature years.

Despite such compelling recent developments, the social sciences in general (and psychology in particular) historically have been predisposed to playing down such needs, goals, and strivings. This has been the case from Freud to Skinner, from Wundt to Watson. We have tended to dismiss such motivations and life objectives in favor of those that are more quantifiable and less controversial. This has been true despite the efforts of theorists like James (1902/1958), Allport (1950), and Maslow (1970) who have not only attempted to direct our thinking to religious matters, but have sanctioned and encouraged their study as well. We might wonder why there has been so much resistance to studying the religious and the spiritual. In partial response to such a query, we find, as James Birren (1990) aptly notes, that those in the social sciences have been felt more comfortable researching and writing about "how life *is lived* rather than . . . how it *should be* lived" (p. 41). In light of Birren's theoretical dichotimization and implicit criticism of modern-day psychology, in this volume we will be speculating about both *what is* and *what ought* to be in adult psychology in general, and in adult spiritual development in particular.

How did psychology arrive at a place where it could begin to look at the oughts of development? How did this become permissible? Perhaps it has been the advent of a more comprehensive life span approach to development, versus a piecemeal, unintegrated approach, that has paved the way for the exploration of such essential dynamics. The introduction of longitudinal and cross-sectional longitudinal procedures has enabled and actually encouraged in-depth research with more mature adult populations. Likewise, these new life span approaches have promoted an additional mode of adult development studies, i.e., simply listening to people talk and narrate their life stories. Through such strategies we have begun to get a sense of the necessity of looking at spiritual needs, spiritual talk, and spiritual narrative. The Spiritual Well-Being Section of the 1971 White House Conference on Aging seemed to make such discussions permissible on a larger scale (Seeber, 1990, p. 6). The 1987 Claremont conference on Spiritual Maturity and Wholeness in the Later Years brought a number of creative thinkers and researchers together to discuss such matters (Seeber, 1990, p. 5), as have the ongoing activities of Division 36 (Psychology of Religion) of the APA and the Society for Research in Adult Development (SRAD). At its annual Adult Development Symposium, the SRAD fosters a spirited dialogue on all dimensions of adult development—covering every age-stage period in adulthood. Topics addressed at these symposia include, but are not limited to: cognitive development, ethical and moral development, social–emotional development, and the religious dimension. These crucial meetings, along with the emergence of a more pervasive, open, and inclusive approach to qualitative and narrative lifespan research, helped break the inertia. Through new investigative procedures, sanctioned by both our government and academia, we began to talk honestly with adults and listen to them with open ears and minds. We began to ask them more questions about their personal development, their spiritual development, and the evolution of their ideas and values. In short, we began to ask them what was on their minds. We found that many people longed to have the needs of the soul addressed; we found that adults yearned to talk about spiritual issues. We also discovered that more than a few were willing to risk talking about such needs and interests. For those willing participants, we are grateful.

THE CHALLENGE

This book will identify, address, and explore the emotional, relational, and philosophical demands of the adult years. These issues are addressed here in a way that respects the complexity of the matters at hand, and honors the inner worlds—the thoughts and emotions—of the people we study. Furthermore, the essays in this volume ideally will assist professional psychologists, social workers, and therapists—regardless of theoretical persuasion—in becoming further attuned to the spiritual needs and longings of their clients. Likewise, they should enhance the clinician's awareness of how such spiritual strivings interface with related interpersonal and psychodynamic issues.

This book is about the woman and man interested in talking about spiritual, ethical, and relational matters. This book is about their struggles to doubt and to believe; to create meaningful lives and workable relationships. This book is about adults who are still trying to develop and actualize themselves. It is about those who are striving to become makers of meaning; it is about those engaged in a spiritual quest. It is also about those who are attempting to become spiritually enlivened. Similarly, this volume concerns individual struggles—those of the subjects (the research participants) and the clients or patients of the contributors. Indeed, it is also about the contributors themselves—academicians and clinicians from various theoretical and religious orientations. This book is written by and about people involved in similar interests, engaged in similar struggles, and with similar passions.

This book is about matters of ultimate concern. It is about striving toward a new moral way, a new ethic, and new ways of relating. It is about an effort to bring the spiritual back into everyday life; it entails an attempt to quicken, enliven, and animate lives, as both participants and authors alike endeavor to meet the emotional and philosophical challenges of the adult years.

OVERVIEW OF THE CHAPTERS

The chapters in this volume are arranged thematically, with each topical group reflecting critical themes in adult development. Part I, "Spirituality, Morality, and Ethics," highlights the ethical and moral concerns of adult development. This section begins with Andres Nino's "Spiritual Quests and the Life Structure in Adulthood: A Psychological Perspective." Nino's chapter provides a fitting way to begin this journey in that he highlights both the necessity of studying spiritual development in adulthood, and the need for individual spiritual quests and their role in shaping life structures. Nino also carefully emphasizes the relationship between spirituality and clinical practice, and briefly discusses the implications of spiritual development for the practicing psychologist or clinician.

In chapter 2, Carol Hoare next takes us on an exciting exploration into little known aspects of Erikson's intellectual career in her chapter, "Morality, Ethics, Spirituality, and Prejudice in the Writings of Erik H. Erikson." Hoare invites us to look at the historical backdrop of Erikson's focus on morality, ethics, and spirituality, and the formative influences on his thinking made by writers such as Kierkegaard, Goethe, and Freud. Not only does Carol Hoare aptly highlight Erikson's special contributions to the ethical and spiritual literature, she emphasizes the crucial role that his wife Joan played in Erikson's own spiritual and ethical development.

Pano Rodis, in chapter 3, presents "An Ethicospiritual Analysis of Postmodernism." Rodis begins with an attempt to clarify the two major ethicospiritual traditions in postmodern thought, one originating in the philosophy of Friederich Nietzsche, and the other evolving from the writings of the Russian theorist, Mikhail Bakhtin. In addition to his analysis of these two traditions, Rodis offers a provocative discussion of the range of postmodern thinking and theorizing, especially as related to ethical and spiritual concerns. Rodis brings the chapter to a conclusion by exploring how postmodern ethical thought can be translated into a greater sense of ethical responsibility. Finally, he discusses how ethical thinking might ultimately result in faithful, right action.

In chapter 4, "Critical Consciousness and Its Ontogeny in the Life Span," Elena Mustakova-Possardt invites us to explore with her a particular version of ethical and social consciousness that she calls critical consciousness. Mustakova-Possardt acknowledges the roots of her project in the writings of Freire, originator of the critical consciousness concept, and then describes the development of her own research and theorizing. There is an implicit and perhaps explicit moral imperative in Mustakova-Possardt's chapter. She enjoins all individuals to develop the capacity to enter into a moral dialogue with their environments, to develop a global sensitivity and awareness, to know what is ethically right and responsible, and to develop the capacity to act in accordance with such a global ethical awareness. Mustakova-Possardt contends that the future of humankind may be contingent upon the development of critical consciousness in all persons.

In Part II, "Interrelationship, Intimacy, and Involvement," we explore the dynamics of relationship in adulthood, the fundamental necessity of human growth through interconnectedness, and the ways in which relationships and intimate connectedness interface with the ethical and spiritual. This set of chapters begins with "Relationship and Connection in Women's Identity from College to Midlife," by Ruthellen Josselson, in which the author reviews her research on women's relationships over the life span. Excerpts and vignettes from the lives of her research participants give additional color and texture to the central points of her study. In brief, Josselson found that the core component of a woman's sense of self is inextricably embedded in her relationships. "Identity in women is fundamentally relational," according to Josselson. Relationships, connections, and religious commitments, as it turns out, were much more predictive of a woman's overall identity than any decisions relating to vocational or political ideology. Josselson concludes her chapter with some critical insights related to women's spirituality, relationships, and adult development.

The next chapters in Part II are more theoretical in orientation and highlight the essential interconnectedness of spirituality and relationship. In chapter 6, "Loving with Integrity: A Feminist Spirituality of Wholeness," Jennifer Rike presents an original look at the familiar concepts of Christian love and care, approaching this topic from a combined theoretical and practical perspective. Rike criticizes the more traditional understanding of Christian love and care, as well as the positions taken on such matters by some contemporary feminist theologians and therapists. She asserts that most who write about these constructs neglect one essential element, i.e., the role of integrity. According to Rike, integrity must become a criterion of care; integrity must guide the application of both love and care. Rike believes that the old theories must be reconstructed within the context of new working models that include the primacy of the integrative processes of human development, and an enhanced awareness of the importance of moral integrity.

In chapter 7, "Cognitive Aspects of Unitative States: Spiritual Self-Realization, Intimacy, and Knowing the Unknowable," Jan Sinnott offers an intriguing analysis of the challenges of processing and integrating mystical experiences. Sinnott draws upon ideas set forth in her postformal development theory to help explain how humans might understand such experiences and use them creatively to their advantage. Sinnott also explores the interpersonal side of the experience of unitative states. She discusses the newfound awareness of the other experienced in these states, as well as the emerging capacity of the mystic to relate to the other in love. For those interested in clinical applications, Sinnott discusses the role the therapist or guide might play in helping someone come to understand, assimilate, and integrate such experiences.

Leslie Fairfield, a theologian and historian, discusses the primacy of human interpersonal connectedness in chapter 8, "Fifth Order Consciousness and Early Greek Christianity." Here Fairfield promotes the foundational nature of interpersonal connection and interdependence and anchors this interdependence—especially the mutual interdependence of men and women—in the concept of the Trinity, and in the writings of the early Greek Christians. Fairfield also draws upon the writings of Robert Kegan, Martin Buber, and Karl Barth to clarify his compelling theoretical stance.

In chapter 9, "On Constructing an Engaged Life," Jackson Kytle invites the reader to consider what is involved in creating an engaged and meaningful life. Kytle, in this interdisciplinary investigation, draws upon an array of existential theorists, developmental and social psychologists, and the real-life example of the Canadian pianist Glenn Gould to enlist our attention to the question: How to make the best use of a life? In addition to offering a typology of levels of engagement, Kytle assists our understanding through a review of Maslow's concept of peak experiences and Csikszentmihalyi's notion of flow. After an excursion through the vicissitudes of attention and mood, Kytle returns the reader once again to the personal challenge of constructing one's own "engaged life."

Part III, "The Self in Transformation," features the individual struggling with the process of personal change and transformation. Although the authors approach this phenomenon from a variety of perspectives, the self in transformation remains a common focus throughout.

In chapter 10, "On Being at Both Center and Circumference: The Role of Personal Discipline and Collective Wisdom in the Recovery of Soul," John McKenna discusses the importance of personal practice in a spiritual discipline as an aid to self-transformation. McKenna begins with a brief review of the notions of soul, spirit, and spirituality. He then takes the reader through an overview of three personal practice disciplines and four collective wisdom traditions. Throughout his chapter, McKenna invites the reader to ponder the almost paradoxical tension existing between living at both the center and circumference —the tension between discovery of soul and personal enlightenment, and the practice of being in the world, being purposefully engaged in good works and deeds. McKenna concludes by reviewing the commonalities of the world's major religions and collective wisdom paths.

In chapter 11, "Meditation and the Evolution of Consciousness: Theoretical and Practical Solutions to Midlife Angst," Ron Irwin writes about the emotional discomfort and confusion that sometimes occur during the midlife years. In this chapter, Irwin offers a theoretical foundation for his approach based upon the seminal ideas espoused by a variety of contemporary postformal thinkers. He eventually moves into a discussion of the ways in which modern adults have attempted to struggle with and resolve their midlife angst, while privileging meditation as a premiere vehicle for assisting with this process.

Chapter 12, by Mel Miller, "The Interplay of Object Relations and Cognitive Development: Implications for Spiritual Growth and the Transformation of Images," integrates object relations theory with more traditional models of religious faith development in an effort to understand individual spiritual strivings. In doing so, he draws upon both clinical vignettes and research protocols to elucidate his position. He concludes by offering a model of spiritual development which is sensitive to both clinical and research findings. Some thoughts on the selection of religious images and ultimate points of reference are also offered.

Kevin Ryan, in chapter 13, "Conversion and the Self," outlines the various forms of conversion experiences and the multiplicity of motivations that may lie behind them. As a social theorist, Ryan is interested in both true, deep, or veridical change, as well as with claims of change and transformation that may be feigned. He offers the reader a typology of conversion experiences, and relates each type back to the pivotal concept of self. Throughout this chapter, Ryan continues to invite the reader to question the psychological dynamics and individual meanings of conversion experiences and personal transformations, and to appreciate their inextricable connection with the construct of self.

In chapter 14, Lene Jensen writes about "Conversions across the Culture War Divide: Two Case Studies." Jensen compares the conversion experiences of two men, one of whom converts from a religiously liberal to a more conservative or orthodox position, while the other converts from a conservative religion to a more liberal one. She includes excerpts from interviews conducted with these men, and grounds her discussion in the current sociological debate regarding the cultural and class differences typically manifested by those championing the orthodox vis-à-vis the progressivist positions.

REFERENCES

Allport, G. W. (1950). *The individual and his religion: A psychological interpretation.* New York: Macmillan.

Anderson, R., & Hopkins, P. (1991). *The feminine face of God: The unfolding of the sacred in women.* New York: Bantam.

Birren, J. E., (1990). Spiritual maturity in psychological development. In J. J. Seeber (Ed.), *Spiritual maturity in the later years* (pp. 41–53). Binghamton, NY: Haworth.

Bly, R. (1990). *Iron John: A book about men.* Reading, MA: Addison-Wesley.

Fowler, J. (1996). Pluralism and oneness in religious experience: William James, faith development theory, and clinical practice. In E. P. Shafranske (Ed.), *Religion and the clinical practice of psychology* (pp. 165–186). Washington, DC: American Psychological Association.

Fuller, A. R. (1994). *Psychology and religion: Eight points of view.* Lanham, MD: Rowman & Littlefield.

Gilligan, C. (1982). *In a different voice.* Cambridge, MA: Harvard University Press.

Goldberg, H. (1987). *The inner male: Overcoming roadblocks to intimacy.* New York: New American Library.

Habermas, J. (1993). *Justification and application: Remarks on discourse ethics.* Cambridge, MA: MIT Press.

Healy, M. (1996, November 17). "Seekers" find churches fill spiritual void. *The Los Angeles Times,* p. A1.

James, W. (1958). *The varieties of religious experience.* New York: New American Library. (Original work published 1902).

Josselson, R. (1992). *The space between us: Exploring the dimensions of human relationships.* San Francisco: Jossey-Bass.

Josselson, R. (1996). *Ethics and process in the narrative study of lives.* Thousand Oaks, CA: Sage.

Kaplan, M. (1996, June 24). Ambushed by spirituality. *Time, 147,* 62.

Keen, S. (1991). *Fire in the belly: On being a man.* New York: Bantam.

Kegan, R. (1994). *In over our heads: The mental demands of modern life.* Cambridge, MA: Harvard University Press.

LaBier, D. (1995, February 20). The '60s generation confronts itself. *The Washington Post,* p. B5.

Lifton, R. J. (1993). *The protean self: Human resilience in an age of fragmentation.* New York: Basic.

Maslow, A. H. (1970). *Religion, values, and peak-experiences.* New York: Viking Press.

Meissner, W. W. (1996). The pathology of beliefs and the beliefs of pathology. In E. P. Shafranske (Ed.), *Religion and the clinical practice of psychology* (pp. 241–267). Washington, DC: American Psychological Association.

Miller, J. B. (1976). *Toward a new psychology of women.* Boston: Beacon Press.

Niebuhr, G. (1996, December 8). Unitarians striking chords of spirituality. *The New York Times,* p. A28.

Rawls, J. (1971). *A theory of justice.* Cambridge, MA: Harvard University Press.

Rorty, R. (1991). *Objectivity, relativism, and truth.* New York: Cambridge University Press.

Ryff, C. (1986). The subjective construction of self and society: An agenda for life-span research. In V. W. Marshall (Ed.), *Late life: The social psychology of aging.* Beverly Hills, CA: Sage.

Ryff, C. D. (1991). Possible selves in adulthood and old age: A tale of shifting horizons. *Psychology and Aging, 6,* 286–295.

Seeber, J. J. (1990). (Ed.). *Spiritual maturity in the later years.* Binghamton, NY: Haworth Press.

Shafranske, E. P. (1996). (Ed.). *Religion and the clinical practice of psychology.* Washington, DC: American Psychological Association.

Stout, J. (1988). *Ethics after Babel: The language of morals and their discontent.* Boston: Beacon Press.

Taylor, C. (1989). *Sources of the self: The making of the modern identity.* Boston, MA: Harvard University Press.

Thomas, L. E., & Eisenhandler, S. E. (Eds.). (1994). *Aging and the religious dimension.* Westport, CT: Auburn House.

Vasudev, J. (1994). *Ahimsa,* justice, and the unity of life: Postconventional morality from an Indian perspective. In M. E. Miller & S. Cook-Greuter (Eds.), *Transcendence and mature thought in adulthood* (pp. 237–255). Lanham, MD: Rowman & Littlefield.

Wulff, D. M. (1996). The psychology of religion: An overview. In E. P. Shafranske (Ed.), *Religion and the clinical practice of psychology* (pp. 241–267). Washington, DC: American Psychological Association.

PART I

Spirituality, Morality, and Ethics

1.

Spiritual Quests in the Life Structure of Adulthood: A Psychological Perspective

Andrés G. Niño

In the last two decades, scholars in diverse disciplines have written widely on the characteristics of the modern self. Largely, they offer a rather gloomy view of widespread inner emptiness, isolation, and unfulfillment (Kohut, 1977), and the lack of an interior life (Dupre, 1976; Taylor, 1989; Tillich, 1988). Similarly, Gergen (1991) and Levin (1987) discuss the notable increase in a variety of well-known psychopathologies and self-disturbances, e.g., depression, hopelessness, narcissism, social saturation, and the fragmentation of self. Explanations for such alienation and psychological distress vary, but the loss of some form of transcendence and the inability to find coherence in life are commonly articulated themes (Brewster, 1994; Dupre, 1976).

At the approach of a new millennium, we have begun to see an eagerness for the spiritual reflected in narratives of personal journeys and other self-explorative accounts. After a long

---

An extended version of this chapter, "Assessment of Spiritual Quests in Clinical Practice," 1997, appeared in the *International Journal of Psychotherapy, 2,* 193–212.

exodus through new ideologies and technological wonders, interest has returned to that "care of the self" principle which has been characteristic of Western culture since Roman times (Foucault, 1988). Perhaps such spiritual striving has been present always, but we grasp the nuances and problems of our own times with a greater sense of immediacy and relevance.

Over the last decade especially, spiritual issues previously confined to the cloister of traditional religion have been raised defiantly in the noisy and confused arena of the secular community. Spiritual concerns have been voiced in several new books and journals and a flurry of media events. Marwick (1995) cites George Gallup's impressions of this growing phenomenon: "We have been negligent about exploring this spiritual area of life. But this is changing rapidly. The public is being increasingly drawn to the nonmaterial aspects of existence" (p. 1561).

These developments have encouraged psychologists to reevaluate theoretical positions. In an early response to the widespread interest, the American Psychological Association (APA) Division of Psychotherapy dedicated a special journal issue (Bradford & Spero, 1990) that stimulated a fruitful line of inquiry. Recently, a valuable collection of papers on religion, spirituality, and clinical practice (Shafranske, 1996) has appeared. There is a new awareness of the theoretical issues involved in spirituality as well as its practical applications for professional care.

The most recent diagnostic manual of the American Psychiatric Association (DSM-IV, 1994) includes a new category which mentions spiritual and religious problems as the focus of clinical attention. This new category is called Religious or Spiritual Problem (Code: V62.89), and includes examples such as: "distressing experiences that involve loss or questioning of faith, problems associated with conversion to a new faith, or questioning of spiritual values that may not necessarily be related to an organized church or religious institution" (p. 685). The momentum and trajectory manifest in this new classification—and in the related developments noted above—are encouraging.

TOWARD COMMON GROUND

Measures of "religion" (either extrinsic or intrinsic), and "spirituality" have been used interchangeably as basic variables in psychological research. Despite their commonalities, the distinctions among these concepts have been recognized throughout centuries of cultural discourse. What appears, at first glance, to be a broad, homogeneous reference, is in fact a multidimensional expression of human creativity, simultaneously public and intimate, universal and unique, accessible to all, yet a mystery beyond grasp. No wonder there have been so many doctrines, techniques, and schools of knowledge in this complex domain. Nor is it surprising that psychology has often produced inconclusive results in traditional religious studies (Kirkpatrick & Hood, 1990). In our modern pluralism, tradition has been fragmented. Many individuals either do not identify with traditional religious sources of meaning or cannot integrate them with their own experiences. The religious factor has been diffused through an unprecedented diversity. Even among groups previously considered homogeneous within their own faith, substantial numbers of people have modified their tenets and adopted unorthodox forms of religious expression. The spiritual life is cultivated in myriad ways.

Religious diversity and alternative modes of spiritual exploration have been at the center of my professional work and research interests for some time now. I believe they must be incorporated into a broader psychological perspective of spirituality. The main question is this: Is there a common ground for the fundamental strivings of the self toward internal coherence and transcendence regardless of whether people adhere to more traditional religious principles and beliefs?

If the answer is yes, we should consider as basic the human capacity to see and search beyond the material and impermanent aspects of life. A modest and assumption-free attitude will help us observe closely the unfolding of meaning-making activity throughout adulthood, as each person formulates spiritual questions and answers of his or her own. For years, this perspective has guided my reflections on psychological theory and therapy toward a deeper understanding of the role of spirituality.

SPIRITUAL QUESTS IN THE CONTEXT OF THE LIFE STRUCTURE

A few years ago I took part in a seminar where a group of postgraduates grappled with the nature of spiritual concerns in adulthood (Nino, 1992). The question I put to them was: "What do we mean by spiritual?"[1] The group concluded that there are many different meanings attached to terms such as *religion* or *spirituality,* and that explaining them properly would require an in-depth exploration of one's life story. Other researchers have come to the same conclusion, pointing out that this definitional problem has made it difficult to establish frames of reference for dialogue across professions or to conduct systematic investigation (Gorsuch, 1988; Pargament, Sullivan, Balzer, Van Haitsma, & Raymark, 1995).

Notwithstanding problems of definition, when the issue of "the spiritual" is mentioned, most people react as if they understand the domain and can draw upon their personal experience. Although religious affiliations or adherence to specific faith and beliefs are mentioned, the emphasis is often placed on one's unique perspective, the efforts that have been made to make sense out of disparate experiences, and the attempts made to arrive at a valued purpose in life. The seminar participants distinguished the striving that runs deep in one's core from "religiousness," "peak experiences," and "state of doubt," emphasizing a process of creating purpose, meaning, and direction in life—well beyond the framework of organized religion. Participants seemed to be looking beyond themselves, piercing the unknown and returning with their own insights,

[1] The seminar was offered in 1992 by Professor Robert Kegan of Harvard University. Kegan, in one of his earlier essays, discussed the "religious power" contained in the constructive-developmental (meaning-making) approach to adulthood. Kegan (1980) based his thoughts concerning religious development on the dynamics of self in relation to a Ground of Being or ultimate environment as discussed in the works of Tillich, Whitehead, and Fowler (pp. 409–416).

trying to make sense of their daily lives. They also seemed to cherish many of the situations in which they were involved, even the struggles, fears, and confusion that often go along with feelings of strength and confidence. Some individuals discovered something that was not in their lives before. Others reexamined what they already knew was truly important beyond ordinary concerns of daily living. Some adopted a certain position as if facing the unavoidable depth of mystery in life. In the words of one participant: "I am unfinished in some ways without living inwardly. . . . By nourishing this activity, one feels more whole."

The ideas voiced at this seminar were limited but poignant examples of how people actually bind together experiences and events into an overarching structure of meaning and purpose with a sense of transcendence. I call this subjective experience *spiritual quest,* a time-honored term used here as a framework for understanding personal narratives. Its underlying impetus is not a transitional state of doubt or conflict, but a longstanding yearning which, once realized, persists through life. The salient characteristics of spiritual quests are these:

1. A spiritual quest is rooted in a normal developmental process in which a person negotiates fundamental questions, tasks, and events of adulthood, and by so doing finds meaning and purpose. Professional therapists see many adults involved in the search, evaluation, and reinterpretation of important experiences throughout life. Clients are often introspective about questions of personal destiny, happiness, the ethical reference for one's behavior, God, the meaning of life, suffering, and death. These questions involve conceptions of human nature, fulfillment, harmony, and redemption, all invested with profound meanings and implications for the individual and society. The way in which these concerns are formulated and expressed constitutes, in Kohut's terms,[2] the fundamental striving of a person toward the realization of values, ambitions, and ideals identified as central to the core self (Kohut, 1985, p. 9).

---

[2] I use Kohut's approach to illustrate how psychological theory that emphasizes introspection and empathy can help explore the dimension of spirituality. Randall (1984) explains Kohut's views in more detail. More recently, Heimbrock (1991) offers a psychoanalytic perspective on this matter.

The capacity for spiritual quest emerges in adolescence and continues to develop throughout adulthood. It is sustained through the primacy of reflection and the power of engagements with life experiences. Questions arise from myriad situations and encounters confronting the individual for which more than a momentary solution and transitional meaning must be found. The individual must become engaged despite efforts to remain, psychologically, at a distance. The process acquires its own trajectory and grows in importance as the individual invests meaning into the objects, themes, and concerns predominant at different stages of the life cycle.

2. *From a developmental perspective, the spiritual quest is an important component of a person's life structure.* Spiritual quests are especially relevant in what Levinson calls the *life structure* (Howenstein, Silberstein, Newton, & Newton, 1992; Levinson, 1986, 1996), which is defined as "the underlying pattern or design of a person's life at a given time" (Levinson, 1996, p. 22), based on the reflective stance of the individual facing the unavoidable questions emerging principally from relationships to others, politics, religion, community, leisure, and the body. Its components include "external aspects—events, social contexts, roles, influences of all kinds—as well as internal aspects, subjective meanings, motives, conflicts, personal qualities. The life structure is the framework within which these aspects are interwoven" (Levinson, 1996, p. 24).

Spirituality is often set apart, disconnected from other engagements of the adult self, and treated as an event with a life of its own. Partly because of the vagueness of conceptual boundaries, it has also been identified with powers of perception and expansion of consciousness or as a peculiar humanistic interest appealing to certain sensitive people. But the concerns of a spiritual quest are central to the core self and cannot be resolved in a vacuum of abstraction. They take their shape and relevance within the complex interaction of components of the life structure.

For example, attitudes toward members of one's family, particularly the very old, or those suffering from impairments and chronic illness, are subtly and deeply influenced by humanistic, ethical, religious, and other considerations about the value of life, concepts of dignity and responsibility, and perspectives on death. The practical ways in which a person negotiates the demands of the life course, such as helping and caring for the elderly, become engagements of one's spiritual quest. They influence other aspects of one's life structure as well, such as family or career priorities. Through life events, personal values are refined and a moral space is formed that forges internal coherence and direction.

3. The spiritual quest is pursued by a self embedded in a physical and sociocultural context. The term *spiritual quest* invokes the image of a private concern, generated in the core self as a response to inner needs and motivations. Yet, confronted with questions of ultimacy, people often seek sustenance from proximal cultural contexts such as family and community support groups. For many people, the spiritual quest appears to be nourished principally by a particular religion or faith community. Interactions between normal developmental processes and longstanding beliefs supported by the wisdom, authority, and adherence of many other people, may become powerful, synergistic sources of behavioral motivation.

Religious organizations tend to define acceptable interpretations and practices, expecting acquiescence from adherents. Many individuals, on the other hand, often forego such certainty for the sake of working through their own formulations. Images, stories, and precepts acquired through religious instruction early in childhood may change dramatically with the cognitive and affective experiences of adulthood.

Observers from different disciplines have noted increasing complexity in the dynamic interplay between societal transformations and the changing life courses of individuals (Buchmann, 1989). This fact has a bearing on our understanding of the "human condition" (Pruyser, 1987) and the gradual shifts of positions and tenets that influence the different ways individuals, groups, and generations confront spiritual issues. A compelling illustration of this phenomenon is offered by Williams and Davidson's (1996) detailed generational analysis of American Catholics.

4. Active engagement in the spiritual quest builds internal coherence and strength in the individual. Recent interdisciplinary clinical research using "religion and spirituality" as a single variable reveals positive correlations with good mental and physical health (Bergin, 1991; Koenig, 1990; Levin, Larson, & Puchalski, 1997; Schumaker, 1992). I believe that when the spiritual quest is effectively integrated in the individual's life structure, the resulting internal coherence is a basic determinant of physical and emotional health.

Kohut (1977) refers to the full assertion of innermost goals and ideals as a major step toward the cohesiveness of the self. The majority of adults avoid the demands of such a task. The tendency for most of us, as Kohut points out, is "to withdraw, dilute or falsify those ideals" (p. 39). As one of my fellow seminar participants put it: "At first I hated the questions because they forced me to face myself, but then I am glad I had the chance to reflect on them for the first time in my life."

Such engagement requires a realistic appraisal of one's life structure at a particular time. It implies revisions and modifications directed at the complex network of cognitions and affects that regulate a person's way of being, views and interpretations of the world, forms of relating, and priorities and goals. This may be considered as a common ground for basic "spiritual survival" (Kohut, 1977, p. 516).

Kohut (1985, p. 30) also affirms that the exploration of one's nuclear self often reveals inconsistencies and conflicts. DSM-IV's recognition of "religious and spiritual problems" affirms that spiritual quests may involve transient instability and disequilibrium (American Psychiatric Association, 1994). But the effort may also be the precursor to a major developmental gain, since the psychological work that is required in the process opens the way to creative resolutions. The lessons learned can be brought to bear as a coping resource when the individual confronts critical situations in life or experiences forms of psychological fragmentation.

5. *Engagement of the self in the spiritual quest finds adequate expression in a life narrative.* Every person needs to be listened to and understood with regard to one's unfinished and fragile narratives. Different motives may fuel the sharing of one's experience, but the act of sharing appears to be a common need during adulthood. From the point of view of spiritual quests,

the full extent of an individual's active engagement becomes clear in the telling of important personal experiences. Narrative offers the most adequate context for the issues and concerns that shape the interior life.

Exploring a personal narrative and the spiritual quest within it, however, is a delicate and difficult task. The psychological perspective proposed in this paper offers a practical guide to such a task through the personal narrative project described in the following section. It takes into consideration the particular historical period in which the individual grew up, as well as the impact of major trends in various aspects of living during the years the person obtained an education, worked, and established a family. Beyond that, it also considers the unique individual differences associated with family, developmental history, gender, ethnicity and living conditions.

Gender, in particular, is a major factor to be considered when exploring spiritual quests. Women's experiences have been subjected to the impact of the patriarchal social, political, and religious structures in Western culture. Until recently, women typically have played a less visible and vocal role, one that did not include equality in power sharing and authority, personal growth and independence. As this situation takes a dramatic turn, their experiences in spiritual quests become more cogent and relevant than ever.[3]

PERSONAL NARRATIVE PROJECT

In light of these five dimensions to spiritual quests, I have become increasingly interested in exploring these and related spiritual issues in the psychotherapy process. I am particularly interested in working from psychological theory and research that emphasizes a developmental and clinical understanding of human experience through narrative (Bruner, 1990; Kotre,

[3] Awareness of this fact and its far-reaching implications has motivated feminist scholars and writers to articulate their own perspective on spirituality. For example, Anderson and Hopkins (1991) write about the religious and spiritual experiences of women as they highlight the characteristic ways women relate, establish commitments, and accept (and promote) the interdependence of all living things.

1984; Rabin, Zuker, Emmons, & Frank, 1990). In therapy and research I ask questions of people that lead the dialogue into the elusive depth of experience where one is usually alone pondering issues of ultimacy and value in one's life. Some of these dialogues have also taken place in ordinary conversations or have become available to me in the form of personal notes and written stories.

To engage a person with the topic in a way that allows a progressive build-up of trust and ease for self-expression, I

TABLE 1.1
Spiritual Quest Form (SQF)

Instructions: After you have completed these sentences you may expand on any one of them, describing how events or people have influenced your personal experience on that issue.

1. I see myself now . . .
2. I think the spiritual . . .
3. The people I have met . . .
4. Thinking about my past . . .
5. When I feel fragmented . . .
6. My relation to God . . .
7. The world around me . . .
8. A meaningful life . . .
9. The best I have ever done . . .
10. What I really would like to do . . .

Source: SQF developed by Andres G. Nino, Ph.D., 1992.

developed the *Spiritual Quest Form* (see Table 1.1). It is a sentence completion exercise that elicits a projection of the *élan vital* of the core self, and focuses on three areas of inner life within which people attempt to integrate their experience of themselves and others. These three dimensions are: (1) inwardness—a capacity that emerges in the adult self from a sustained effort of introspection and the frequent appraisal of the meaning and value one creates through experience; (2) relatedness—the context in which the experience of empathy nourishes and transforms the self, offering also the possibility to transcend the boundaries of significant others toward an ultimate other; (3) generativity—a fundamental engagement that enables the individual to construct an enduring narrative in a historical context, despite the inevitable impermanence of self and others.[4]

Attentive listening to personal narratives reveals that activity in these interrelated areas has different shades of intensity and sense of direction at different periods in an individual's life. Taken together, they offer a vision of a person's engagement with self and the world and a way to gradually construct a particular form of individual meaning. A dialogue follows in which the inquirer and research participant (or therapist and patient) join efforts to coexplore the issues with the purpose of giving expression to inner subjective experience.

After administering the Spiritual Quest Form (SQF), I usually suggest a follow-up interview to expand upon and evaluate the responses. This can be considered a form of life review which, for the purpose of this inquiry, is a task oriented toward identification, integration, and resolution of issues of importance in a person's life. I point out that a narrative project describing one's predicament in this regard helps the individual to gain a broader vision of one's self. There is always a certain redemptive value in recapturing one's self at a given time to create something new out of the past and heal or consolidate experiences.

These sessions concentrate on a few basic objectives: (1) engaging the person in articulating the meanings and values attached to particular events; (2) encouraging the person to take new perspectives, to disentangle, reevaluate, and emphasize matters which the person might pursue further; and (3) leading the person gradually toward an active process of resolution that will expand the depth and quality of generative engagements.

CONCLUSION AND DIRECTIONS FOR FUTURE RESEARCH

The integration of a dimension of spirituality in the psychotherapeutic process is a difficult task that requires a clearly defined

[4] I first discussed these areas of activity from the point of view of spiritual quests in adulthood in an analysis of Augustine's autobiographical narrative *Confessions* (Nino, 1990). In Nino (1994), I further elaborated on their relevance to the exploration of the spiritual dimension in the therapeutic process.

frame of reference. This paper discusses the concept of spiritual quest and attempts to articulate one possible frame of reference. It also offers suggestions relating to the exploration of spiritual quests through the use of personal narratives. Some questions for future research with the SQF are: How do people express their spirituality within and outside of organized religion? What cultural factors, changes, and problems currently influence views or experiences of spirituality? Are there different characteristics in spiritual quests in the experience of women and men? Are there specific aspects to be considered when dealing with certain clinical problems such as the addictions, traumatic conditions, or chronic illness? Answers to these questions will help broaden our perspectives on the human religious experience and life structure in adulthood.

REFERENCES

American Psychiatric Association (1994). *Diagnostic and statistical manual of mental disorders.* (4th ed.). Washington, DC: Author.

Anderson, R., & Hopkins, P. (1991). *The feminine face of God: The unfolding of the sacred in women.* New York: Bantam.

Bergin, A. E. (1991). Values and religious issues in psychotherapy and mental health. *American Psychologist, 46,* 394–403.

Bradford, D. T., & Spero, M. H. (Eds.). (1990). Psychotherapy and Religion [Special Issue]. *Psychotherapy, 27.*

Brewster, M. (1994). Selfhood at risk. Postmodern perils and the perils of modernism. *American Psychologist, 49,* 405–411.

Bruner, J. (1990). *Acts of meaning.* Cambridge, MA: Harvard University Press.

Buchmann, M. (1989). *The script of life in modern society. Entry into adulthood in a changing world.* Chicago: University of Chicago Press.

Dupre, L. (1976). *Transcendent selfhood.* New York: Seabury.

Foucault, M. (1988). Technologies of the self. In L. Martin, H. Gutman, & P. Hutton (Eds.), *Technologies of the self* (pp. 16–49). Amherst: University of Massachusetts Press.

Gergen, K. J. (1991). *The saturated self.* New York: Basic.

Gorsuch, R. L. (1988). Psychology of religion. *Annual Review of Psychology, 39,* 201–221.

Hembrock, H. G. (1991). Psychoanalytic understanding of religion. *The International Journal for the Psychology of Religion, 1,* 71–89.

Howenstein, R. A., Silberstein, L. R., Newton, D. S., & Newton, P. M. (1992). Life structure revitalization: An adult developmental approach to psychodynamic psychotherapy. *Psychiatry, 55,* 194–206.

Kegan, R. (1980). Where the dance is: Religious dimensions of a developmental framework. In J. Fowler & A. Vergote (Eds.), *Toward a moral and religious maturity* (pp. 404–440). Morristown, NJ: Silver Burdett.

Kirkpatrick, L. A., & Hood, R. W., Jr. (1990). Intrinsic-extrinsic religious orientation: The boon or bane of contemporary psychology of religion? *Journal for the Scientific Study of Religion, 29,* 442–462.

Koenig, H. G. (1990). Research on religion and mental health in later life: A review and commentary. *Journal of Geriatric Psychiatry, 23,* 23–53.

Kohut, H. (1977). *The restoration of the self.* New York: International Universities Press.

Kohut, H. (1985). On the continuity of the self and cultural selfobjects. In C. Strozier (Ed.), *Self psychology and the humanities. Reflections on a new psychoanalytic approach* (pp. 232–243). New York: Norton.

Kotre, J. (1984). *Outliving the self: Generativity and the interpretation of lives.* Baltimore, MD: Johns Hopkins University Press.

Levinson, D. J. (1986). A conception of adult development. *American Psychologist, 41,* 3–14.

Levinson, D. J. (1996). *The seasons of a woman's life.* New York: Knopf.

Levin, D. M. (Ed.). (1987). *Pathologies of the modern self. Postmodern studies on narcissism, schizophrenia, and depression.* New York: New York University Press.

Levin, J. S., Larson, D. B., & Puchalski, C. M. (1997). Religion and spirituality in medicine: Research and education. *Journal of the American Medical Association, 278,* 792–793.

Marwick, C. (1995). Should a physician prescribe prayer for health? Spiritual aspects of well-being considered. *Journal of the American Medical Association, 273,* 1561–1562.

Nino, A. G. (1990). Restoration of the self: A therapeutic paradigm from Augustine's *Confessions. Psychotherapy, 1,* 8–18.

Nino, A. G. (1992, April). *Spiritual quests in adulthood.* Paper presented at Adult Development Seminar, Harvard Graduate School of Education, Cambridge, MA.

Nino, A. G. (1994). *The assessment of spiritual quests in clinical practice.* Paper presented at the Sixth European Symposium for the Psychology of Religion, University of Lund, Sweden.

Pargament, K. I., Sullivan, M. S., Balzer, W. K., Van Haitsma, K. S., & Raymark, P. H. (1995). The many meanings of religiousness: A policy capturing approach. *Journal of Personality, 63,* 953–983.

Pruyser, P. W. (1987). Where do we go from here? Scenarios for the psychology of religion. *Journal for the Scientific Study of Religion, 26,* 173–181.

Rabin, A. I., Zuker, R. A., Emmons, R. A., & Frank, S. (Eds.). (1990). *Studying persons and lives.* New York: Springer.

Randall, R. L. (1984). The legacy of Kohut for religion and psychiatry. *Journal of Religion and Health, 23,* 106–114.

Schumaker, J. F. (1992). *Religion and mental health.* New York: Oxford University Press.

Shafranske, E. (Ed.). (1996). *Religion and the clinical practice of psychology.* Washington, DC: American Psychological Association.

Taylor, C. (1989). *Sources of the self. The making of the modern identity.* Cambridge, MA: Harvard University Press.

Tillich, P. (1988). *The spiritual situation in our technical society.* Macon, GA: Mercer University Press.

Williams, A. S., & Davidson, J. D. (1996). Catholic conceptions of faith: A generational analysis. *Sociology of Religion, 57,* 273–289.

2.

Morality, Ethics, Spirituality, and Prejudice in the Writings of Erik H. Erikson

Carol H. Hoare

Ethical, principled behavior, or its incomplete development, defines personal identity in mature adulthood, according to Erik Erikson. Erikson recognized three intermingled attributes, morality, ethics, and spirit, as characteristic of a highly developed adult identity. As many know, Erikson first created the concept *psychosocial identity* to explain the self-in-vocation-and-ideology crisis of adolescents. It was born of Erikson's own identity confusion in his youth, a confusion that resurfaced when he immigrated to the United States. After showing how identity develops and can be thwarted, Erikson elaborated on the ways in which identity unfolds throughout adulthood. This chapter summarizes key concepts of Erik H. Erikson on moral, spiritual, and ethical development, particularly as his thinking pertains to adults in their potential for ethical growth.

More than any other transformer of 20th century thought, Erikson is inseparable from the concepts he created. His ideas about the way identity moves from intimacy-isolation in young adulthood to generativity-stagnation in middle adulthood were based, in part, on his expanding knowledge and his insight into himself and others as he traversed his own young and middle adult years. Increasingly, he wrote of the connection between identity and spirituality in the midlife stage of generativity. After his own adult life led beyond identity-generativity, and he had begun to envision how adults approach the ego's twilight in the waning years of life, Erikson wrote increasingly about the connection he saw between identity and the "Ultimate Other."

First, so that we can locate him in 20th century developmental thought, I will briefly explore Erikson's overall contributions to lifespan thinking, and then discuss his key ideas about ethics and spirituality. It is important to understand that Erikson's lifespan theory is now taken for granted. To many practitioners in psychoanalysis, counseling, and human development, Erikson's concepts are fundamental. Erikson wrote from within a socially based psychoanalytic framework. His concepts were broad brush in that he charted the major ego investments and the way these play out in developmental stages. Studying the ways in which society and the personal resources of family and individual talents interpenetrate one another to shape each ego and its evolution, he wrote largely about the human potential for healthy personality, social, and moral development. Less so, he conceptualized the pathology that results from failing to achieve intimacy, care of others, and acceptance of mortality. Erikson's is a hierarchical theory. He specified the content of the eight life stages he conceptualized and posited an invariant sequence for those stages. The fact that Erikson posed exact psychodynamic content and psychosocial resolutions for each of the three stages of adult development, and the fact that he suggested what adults need to do to insure their own ethical development, has led some to cast him as prescriptive and a moralist. Such criticism seems unfair; yet it has been directed against every theorist who has been so bold as to detail content for healthy behavior and to position human development against eternity.

Because key experiences in his youth and young adulthood shaped his ethical–spiritual views, we will touch on Erikson's own identity confusion and the relationship of that confusion to his concepts about spirituality. Erikson was an existential and a border thinker. He wrote on the hazy periphery where one discipline meets another, where, for instance, psychology joins history, where sociology joins psychology, and where psychiatry joins religion. It was natural for him to write on the temporal and existential boundary as well. This is the meeting ground where psyche meets a sense of theos, where adult psyches soften their denial of death, sense their future nonexistence, and perceive themselves as living in a spiritual form beyond the time- and space-bound location of earth.

The second area, that of Erikson's writings on morality and spirituality, illustrates his thinking about the moral to ideological to ethical development that many humans experience. He conceptualized this development using his clinical work with patients and his conceptual linkages between psychoanalytic theory and history, philosophy, literature, anthropology, and scripture. As a principal transformer of 20th century psychoanalytic and social science thought, Erikson was a holistic, nonreductionistic thinker. In some respects, he stood on the shoulders of his identity model, Sigmund Freud, but he stood as well on the concepts of Kierkegaard, Goethe, Schopenhauer, Nietzsche, Lao Tse, Silesius, and St. Augustine. This chapter presents Erikson's main tenets with the hope that interested readers will find their way to his writings (e.g., 1963, 1964b, 1981) in the original.

BIOGRAPHICAL FACTORS AFFECTING ERIKSON'S RELIGIOUS, ETHICAL, AND SPIRITUAL THOUGHT

Erik Erikson's life spanned nearly the entire 20th century (he was born in 1902 and died in 1994). Erikson himself made much of this fact and noted that many of his youthful experiences were linked to dramatic changes in human and scientific understandings and to forces that would forever change the course of history. These experiences contributed to his theoretical formulations. For example, Erikson's youth in Germany coincided with Einstein's discovery of relativity and Freud's systematization of mechanisms in the unconscious. He experienced firsthand Hitler's rise to power and the growing threat of Nazism. By birth both Jew and Gentile, he came to understand that, by virtue of genetics, he was a potential candidate for Hitler's extermination plan. In 1933, Erikson fled Austria just as Hitler was threatening in the north and Mussolini from the south (Coles, 1970). In the mid-1960s in the United States, Erikson was so moved by witnessing racial discord and the plight of those seeking equality that he dedicated a significant portion of his later writing to concepts of pseudospecies thinking, or prejudice, and to ethical behavior (among these writings *Gandhi's Truth* [1969] is prominent). To Erikson, the racism of Hitler's Germany and the Ku Klux Klan in America were far distant in time, but very close in their origin and meanings. They led him to write, over and over again, that no person could gain or keep a viable identity by forcing others to lose theirs. Prejudiced behavior, in its deprivation of opportunities for others, augurs against ethical development.

In his youth, Erikson felt ostracized and alienated from traditional institutions, community, and occupational roles. The illegitimate offspring of a mother who was a Danish Jew and a father who was a Danish gentile artist, he was later adopted by a prominent Karlsruhe pediatrician, Dr. Theodor Homburger, whom his mother married when young Erik was 4 years old. Growing up, Erik was tall and blond and did not fit into local institutions. He was castigated as a "goy" in the temple and a "Jew" in school, an outcast throughout (Erikson, 1970, 1975). Disinterested in the instructional rigors of traditional German curricula, and believing himself artistically gifted, he left academics behind immediately upon graduation from Das Humanitische Gymnasium, a classical secondary school. He then roamed the Black Forest with friends and worked as a wandering artist. Entering art school, and then dropping out, he found his way to Florence where he suffered a moderately serious depression upon seeing that his artistic ambitions aimed toward failure. Confused and despondent, he went home to Karlsruhe, Germany and from there to Vienna where his friend Peter Blos had obtained a position for him. That position was tutoring in the small school Anna Freud, Dorothy Burlingham, and Eva Rosenfeld had established for children undergoing psychoanalysis. There, Anna Freud discerned Erikson's sensitivity to children. She invited him to enter the Freud Institute to study psychoanalysis.

In 1933, Erikson completed his psychoanalytic studies. By then he had obtained a psychoanalytic diploma from Freud's Institute and a Montessori certificate, two vouchers that would serve as his only academic credentials throughout his clinical, teaching, and writing life. Upon his immigration to the United States in 1933, he rose to prominence almost at once as Boston's first child psychoanalyst. Nonetheless, his earlier identity confusion, a condition he later described as being on the borderline between neurosis and psychosis, and his resurgent confusion on immigrating to a country where he was unsure of his ability to obtain work, led to two main outcomes. First, he connected content and sage insights from many different fields and thinkers, most of whom lived in the 17th through 19th centuries, and he updated them using contemporary psychoanalysis. In this way, he remained a border thinker. Second, he contributed original thought about society's role in fostering or thwarting identity and other forms of development. His sense of alienation, born partly of his childhood experiences and partly because he found no place for his adolescent identity ambitions, remained alive in his psyche. Various autobiographic accounts testify to this alienation, and to the theorist who, throughout his life, kept alive his sense of identification with the plight of adolescents and young adults who searched for a fit in society.[1]

Erikson gave his adopted country its first full theory of healthy life span development. He shifted Freudian thought from geologic-type structures and narrow instincts to a focus on the social world and its contributions to a developing, changing, biopsychosocial person. Resisting emphasis on the dark forces that Freud saw controlling the person, Erikson looked instead to the healthy developmental potentials of children and adults. He took Freud's five stages of psychosexual development, converted these to a theory of psychosocial development, and added intimacy, care, and personal integration as the three stages of adulthood. In directing his spotlight on culture and society, Erikson (1937, 1942, 1943, 1950) was the

[1] This information is found, in part, in Erikson's publications of 1970 and 1975. It is supplemented by Erikson's autobiographic notes and letters found in the unpublished papers of Erik and Joan Erikson in the Harvard College Library, Cambridge, MA.

first psychoanalyst in the United States to illustrate how these external forces exist within the psyche. For example, he showed that young children absorb the norms, mores, outlooks, and habits of their families and cultures. By the time children become preadolescents, they perceive life from within a psychological lens that has been crafted by this imprinting. Erikson's especially significant contribution—the construct of the identity crisis—now popularized beyond its original meaning, connects the biopsyche of youth with a society that is absorbed by youth and, conversely, offers a vocational place for the young person as she or he projects an ideological sense of self into a future work role, space, and time. By the time youth become adolescents, many of them understand their social position to be that of social opportunity or deprivation.

Many latter-day psychologists, counselors, and developmentalists know Erikson's theory only by its eight-stage grid and the nuclear crises that he posed for each of those stages. Some also know him as the influential writer of *Childhood and Society* (1950, 1963), one of 12 books and more than 100 published articles that represent the body of his thought. However, little has been written about Erikson's view that ethical responsibility is integral to the adult's identity development. In *Insight and Responsibility* (1964b), Erikson illustrated that insight is worthless if it does not lead to more responsible behavior. Just as Kohlberg (1971) knew cognitive development as necessary but, in and of itself, inadequate for the attainment of higher levels of moral development, Erikson believed that insight alone was but a way station to heightened moral behavior. Thus he disagreed with Kohlberg that one can assess moral development using inferential tests of moral reasoning. To Erikson, morals and principles are only real when they operate behaviorally. Further, only when the adult develops beyond young adulthood's investments in vocational development, sexual intimacy, and other forms of self-gratification, can insight ripen into the conscious obligations of actively, generatively caring for others. Principled behavior, doing that which helps both others and the self to grow, leads adults to the upper reaches of identity development. Thus, responsible, ethical action is the telos toward which Erikson's theory points. Writing about ethical responsibility, Erikson linked his thought with the precepts of

Soren Kierkegaard and Sigmund Freud, with psychohistorical observations of Martin Luther and Mahatma Gandhi, with scripture from the Old and New Testaments, with the sayings of Jesus, and with thought from ancient philosophers and mystics. In his psychohistorical books, articles, and essays, Erikson wrote mainly about those he believed to have been both moral, spiritual leaders and, at the same time, identity leaders; that is, those who led the way through their own behavior in their historical eras. In *Young Man Luther* (1958), he wrote of the identity–intimacy crisis of Martin Luther and Luther's role in changing religious history. In *Gandhi's Truth* (1969), he portrayed the identity–generativity crisis of Mahatma Gandhi and Gandhi's role in demonstrating ways in which nonviolent strategies can alter oppressive regimes. At the end of his writing years, Erikson published, in 1981, a remarkable article titled "The Galilean Sayings and the Sense of 'I'." This essay is about Jesus of Galilee, and the relationship between the human identity and a sense of a numinous, eternal, other "I," experienced as the Almighty. In this article and in related books, Erikson used identity icons to show how some originators moved beyond the legalities of society (Gandhi), beyond the institutional church (Luther), and beyond Old Testament scripture (Jesus). If the mind grows by the content on which it feeds, Erikson fed on the ideas, principles, and strategies of those very few whom, for a variety of reasons, history has called great. He consistently wrote about giant egos, superegos, and forceful personalities whose strength of will and intentional disobedience wrought historical changes in ways of seeing, believing, and behaving. The persons he chose to study were teaching vehicles. Predominantly, Erikson's messages were subtle ones that said rules, structures, and laws of society should not be construed as morally binding artifacts that required obedience. Instead, moral obligations had to be determined by that which is fair, liberating, and socially just for all.

MORALITY AND ETHICS

In the 1950s, 1960s, and 1970s, many in caregiving and teaching roles believed there was an endpoint toward which one's moral life and mature behavior aimed. Examples of the theory that guided such thought include Maslow's notions about self-actualization, Kohlberg's concepts about postconventional reasoning, and Erikson's concepts about ethics. These are of a piece, conceptualized differently by each theorist, but uniform in terms of the telos, or endpoint, to which development was seen as directed. Erikson thought that a person can and should stretch toward an advanced state of commitments and principled behavior. These attributes grow in conjunction with increased introspective knowledge of a spiritual self, one that insightful adults increasingly understand as a magnetic force they cannot evade. Erikson wrote during what some have called the dusk of utopian thought (Manuel & Manuel, 1979). In that era, theorists and practitioners were less wary than today about defining adult behavior in terms of its obligations. In the last two decades, relativism has supplanted such telos thinking to the extent that theorists, counselors, psychologists, and teachers seem ever more wary of proffering principles as guidelines for behavior. In so doing, they might be accused of being prescriptive, illiberal, rigid, or otherworldly. Erikson himself was a relativistic thinker. He wrote about the ways in which history, culture, and position in society shape the psyche. Yet he placed his work in the context of ethics and spirituality. Each being was a human temple to the Ultimate. No one should treat another as an object of personal gain because each person is a created being, a product of suprahuman design. He believed that morally developed adults were those who stood in fundamental awe and humility before the powers that created them. These views were, in fact, significant reasons for Erikson's declining popularity among members of mainstream psychiatric and psychoanalytic circles, while they simultaneously expanded his appeal to social science and theological audiences.

Erikson knew that he was a utopian thinker, a stereotype that concerned him. Yet he remained convinced, to the end of his working life, that adults are obliged to liberate their inner selves from the material world in order to move to the level of personal ethics, authenticity, and spirituality. This is an evolution in which adults conjure their identity in terms of transpersonal, transphysical, becoming. Framing development in those terms, Erikson said he had incorporated the Hindu worldview. His thinking also modeled many of the concepts of the existential philosopher Soren Kierkegaard, his Danish compatriot. As did Erikson, Kierkegaard had positioned the ethical above the aesthetic, developmentally. The attractive physical world gives way to the ethical. This is a disciplined form of heightened subjectivity in which adults who search for the Ultimate eclipse their material needs, interests, and gains in the process. Like Kierkegaard, Erikson wrote abstractly, revealing his topic bit by bit, sometimes teaching through visual images. Both thinkers wrote for the ages. They were concerned that specific details would lead readers to prematurely discard their concepts.

Just as Erikson would not permit himself to be captive of any one discipline, profession, or identity, he stayed beyond the boundary of institutional religions as well. Wright (1982), Zock (1990), and others have tied Erikson's concepts directly to religion. This is problematic because it brands Erikson as a pseudoreligious writer and locks him narrowly to institutionalized practices. Erikson remained apart from adherence to form and rites; he believed that such behaviors lead too easily to form for the sake of form. Such behavioral habituations, once they are institutionalized and ingrained, tend toward routinization and narrow tendencies of patterning and thought. In collective groups, Erikson found that the narrow lock of institutions led readily to what he called the pseudospecies propensity. Adherents to firm religious groups seem to say: "Our way of seeing and finding the Ultimate and eternity is the best or only way." A student history, Erikson knew the myriad ways religions had been used to murder, pillage, make war, and exclude, all in the name of the Divine.

Erikson's most unique contributions to developmental thought relating to ethics and spirituality, are, first, his broad brush concepts of the developmental path that humans travel from moralistic thinking and behavior to ethical acts; second, his theoretical view of the negative identity as it is portrayed in his concept pseudospeciation; and third, his revision of the Golden Rule. His writings on spirituality stand apart and will complete this chapter. Together these four aspects constitute a unique developmental view, one that is normative for the moral-to-ideological development of youth, while, for the adult years, it portrays a potential of adults to move to the ethical, spiritual level. It was Erikson's view that not everyone is inclined to proceed to the final stage. Achievement of the last stage can be thwarted by the absence of positive role models or by rigid superego development in youth, and, in adulthood, by denial, rigidity, serious mental disorders, or cognitive decline.

THE HUMAN DEVELOPMENTAL PATHWAY: FROM CHILDHOOD MORALITY, THROUGH ADOLESCENT IDEOLOGY, TO ADULT BEHAVIORAL ETHICS

Erikson was an admirer of children. To him, children possessed a glowing intelligence that was his resource just as dreams had been Freud's resource. Erikson knew that many persons, if not most, lose their childhood vitality on their way to adulthood. This is partly a result of living within adult roles and responsibilities that necessarily narrow one's choices and options. Erikson believed that the adult basis of ethics is found in childhood. As concrete thinkers, children adopt moral behavior by learning right versus wrong and a rule-driven orientation. This is their foundation for later principles. In such learning, children adopt their parents' or key caregivers' superegos, sometimes adopting a strict governing system of rights and wrongs, do's and don'ts. Children first learn these behaviors as legalisms that become childhood restraints imposed by the parents on the child, then by the child on the self and others. These righteous legalisms represent children's needs to see others abide by those restraints to which they themselves must adhere. We see this first in children's play, when toddlers tell their dolls and toys what they should and should not do. Later, learned rules are taken to the playground and ball field where they are transformed to quid pro quo reciprocity through the rules of the game. Erikson observed that every culture has its own established values. These values and the rules based on them are inculcated in children as cultural norms.

There are two important elements here. First, it is self-evident that every child is groomed by parents or key caregivers to adopt the structures and controls that are offered, unless these are unavailable or are withheld. Erikson did not specify these structures and prohibitions because they vary from family to family, culture to culture, and nation to nation. He did write that part of such structures originate in habits that are imprinted through the rituals of daily life, such as mealtime, bedtime, and toilet rituals. Although the ways these rituals become established and ingrained are different, Erikson observed that this imprinting and ritualization is as much a fact for the psychosocial human as it is for numerous lower-order creatures. Erikson was concerned about the harsh restraints that some parents impose on children, in effect making their children pay for the difficulties of their own earlier childhoods. He felt that too tightly developed superegos are the basis for later adult rigidity and judgmental attitudes toward other persons who adopt different, perhaps less formidable, controls.

Second, Erikson believed that children should learn more about what they can and should do, within bounds, instead of learning what they had better *not* do in the form of punishment vendettas. Today, we frequently hear parents who say to their children, "You had better *not* do this or that or you will go to jail." Or: "If you behave like that, your parents will have to appear in court." Such fear induction occurs among the more affluent as well as in less advantaged families, partially compelled, it seems, by an increasingly legalistic U.S. society. Erikson believed there are dangers in a world in which moral development is led by what one had better *not* do, as compared with what one needs *to do,* to provide optimal development for self and others. Whenever possible, Erikson attempted to change negatives into positives. He was mainly concerned about improving the care and development of children. He was also concerned about the ongoing development of the child in the now grown adult. To him, development in all humans meant overriding the guilt and negative inclinations that each person possesses so as to build more consciously on positive tendencies.

In the second major stage of his system of moral development, that of adolescence, Erikson observed that youth do not leave their learned morality behind. Instead they wrap it into ideological thinking. As they begin to think abstractly, adolescents, at least in Western societies, contemplate their autonomous definition of self as separate from the nuclear family. Adolescents become members of a future envisioning, reality-constructing peer group. In doing so, they share in the need for and privilege of criticizing the existence of pressing social problems that their parents' generation did not solve. They pose such criticism against ideas about their own future contributions and begin to establish an operating philosophy of life, an ideology. Previously patterned behavior is not abandoned. Rather, early childhood moralisms are partly superseded by the ability to engage in utopian thinking. Commitment to ideals develops because of an expanded cognitive apparatus and wider experience in the world. The adolescent, now on the cusp of adulthood, develops a sense of solidarity with his or her like-kind, the chosen group. However, he observed the link between the development of prejudice and identity in the teen years. He feared that prejudice, the pseudospecies tendency, was especially prevalent among those late adolescents and young adults who, for a variety of reasons, had failed to achieve viable, positive identities. There are preferred groups and shunned groups throughout our secondary schools and colleges and, in fact, some of the excluded are parents and elders who are omnipresent members of the out-group. Two empirical studies (Bushkoff, 1992; Streitmatter & Pate, 1989) found that advanced identity development entails operating within a moral centering of values that are based on group, social, and cultural norms, while avoiding the exclusion of those who seem most unlike the self (see also Hoare, 1991, 1994). As Erikson (Erikson & Newton, 1973) said, "you cannot be fully yourself if your identity depends on somebody else's identity loss, a potentially vicious symbiosis in the sense that each lives—and dies—off the other" (pp. 85–86).

The culmination of childhood morality and adolescent ideology, to Erikson, is the ethics of adulthood. In adulthood, ethics are learned through commitments that, once established, become abiding obligations. The care or generativity theme is now prominent, the adult asking: "How do I care for the progeny, products, and ideas I have produced, those that responsible behavior requires I not abandon but nourish and sustain?" "How do I engage myself in a generative way in the work of this world?" Here the Hindu idea of "householding" as a steward who insures the survival of the world, figures prominently in Erikson's work. His thinking is that of a "cogwheeling" intergenerational set of responsibilities in which he asks adults to consider what each generation owes and can contribute to the others. In this, he saw children as vital resources for adult learning and development:

> [A]ny adult who has managed to train a child's will must admit that he has learned much about himself and about will that he never knew before, something that cannot be learned in any other way. Thus each growing individual's strength "dovetails" with the strengths of an increasing number of persons arranged about him in the social orders of family, school, community, and society. (1964a, p. 422)

There are three points about Erikson's stage of caring, ethical adulthood that command attention. First, Erikson equated ethics with the caritas of Christianity, believing with St. Paul that the acts of love define the highest level. Thus, Erikson's position is at variance with the justice orientation that is fundamental to Kohlberg's theory. The voice of "care," which Gilligan (1982) and her followers principally attribute to a female form of morality, corresponds to Erikson's idea of generativity for both genders.[2] Second, learned morality and developed ideology are enfolded into the active adult work of

---

[2] Erikson's complete life-span theory is based on a male-normed view of development. Thus, he has been variously criticized by women theorists (e.g., Gilligan) who have held that he did not differentiate between equal, but different, ways of being in the world and thus cast women in dependent roles. In various writings, Erikson said that the species would be limited in transcending its aggressive tendencies until women held a greater share of leadership; further, he placed *care* (to Gilligan, the female moral "voice") above *justice* in his hierarchy of moral behavior. In various gatherings, he also said that he could not speak for women but wondered why they were not included on those occasions. Consequently, at least part of the criticism of Erikson is groundless.

commitments. One does not outgrow the moralistic superego that was developed in childhood, nor does one replace the ideology gained in adolescence. Instead all three, morality-ideology-ethics, now exist in a new set of relationships one to another. The person, as seen by Erikson, is an organic, integrated being who cannot be removed from his or her previous development and its resolutions. Prior accomplishments and deprivations are always part of developmental advancement; they are forever contemporary. Here we see one of the dilemmas Erikson's thought poses. For one reason or another, some adults cannot move up the cognitive ladder to engage in metapsychological thought. Some remain riveted to the reciprocity level of rules and morality. Other regress downwards to concrete cognitive levels due to senility or to some other mentally debilitating disease. In such persons, there may well be a tendency to maintain, or to return to, the isms that emerge from moralistic guilt. Ritualism and moralism and its resultant dogmatism can focus behavior so narrowly and compulsively that we must wonder, with Erikson, whether this is dangerous to faith, to further individual development, and to peaceful coexistence with others. As Erikson wrote:

> The "lowest" in man thus is apt to reappear in the guise of the "highest": irrational and prerational combinations of goodness, doubt, and rage can re-emerge in the adult in those malignant forms of righteousness and prejudice which we may call moralism. In the name of high moral principles it can employ all the vindictiveness of derision, of torture, and of mass-extinction. (1964a, p. 416)

Erikson's provocative points focus on the ways that a harshly shaped superego, bred in childhood, can combine with the internalized rage at being held down, and with a sense of personal guilt. These can come to the fore in adulthood as the need to find others incorrect so as to bolster one's own sense of morality, ideology, identity, and claim to the Kingdom. Needing to assuage a sense of being wrong or bad, negative personal inclinations are projected onto others. In religious beliefs, moralizing occurs as prejudice against those who hold different beliefs or live out what are seen to be deviant variations of the one true way of being in the world.

Third, like Sigmund Freud, Erikson was markedly concerned about the effects of technology on the species. He expressed grave concern about human tendencies to exert hyperrational, objectified, machinelike thinking with respect to every person and thing. The age had become one of disembodied technology and technique. Heightened rational thought, he felt, comes at the cost of feeling. This is particularly the case when social systems engender isolates who work and live apart from shared community life. As Erikson saw the 20th century unfold, he noted a deterioration in ethical conscience and principled behavior among adults. He associated some of this with the machinations of tool-advanced industrialization and with the ways objectivity and objective reasoning are glorified. To him, intellect alone, when devoid of empathy, is a cold and mindless deterioration from the subjective, feeling person who cares about others and, thereby, nurtures the ethical self. Since Erikson associated what children and youth see in the adults of their day with the kind of adults such youth will become, we might share his fear for U.S. society and the world.

PSEUDOSPECIES MENTALITIES: THE NEGATIVE IDENTITY AND PREJUDICE

In adopting their parents' superegos, children adopt ideas of what Erikson called the "negative identity." This takes different forms depending on the family, society, culture, and historical period. Each of us can probably hear some of those voices now: "You'd better not be. . . ." Fill in the blanks: "Lazy, dirty, sloppy, a bum, an alcoholic like your Uncle Harry. . . ." In learning what they had better *not* be, children incorporate images as their negative identity elements. These become identity models and attributes children learn to avoid and, paradoxically, in the deepest reaches of their psyches, may fear they really are or are in danger of becoming. By some point in late youth, this human tendency is deeply established. Youth may reject those who exhibit such negative identity models and traits, using them as a screen onto which they project their fears, anxieties, and antipathies. Or, if they lack positive identity models and beliefs that they can succeed in their worthwhile identity ambitions, they may readily adopt the negative identity as their own, becoming just like the model they were expressly warned to avoid emulating. One identity idea or another, positive or negative, *will* take hold.

At the group level, Erikson termed the negative identity the pseudospecies "mentality." It is the tendency to be prejudiced against other persons or entire groups. He explained this tendency in *Gandhi's Truth:*

> The term denotes the fact that while man is obviously one species, he appears and continues on the scene split up into groups (from tribes to nations, from castes to classes, from religions to ideologies) which provide their members with a firm sense of distinct and superior identity—and immortality. This demands, however, that each group must invent for itself a place and a moment in the very center of the universe where and when an especially provident deity caused it to be created superior to all others, the mere mortals. (1969, p. 431)

In this, Erikson found a "human propensity" in each of us, traceable to the tribal origins of the species, and the family origins of contemporary humans, to lift one's own confidence in identity, competence, and uniqueness by prejudging, stereotyping, and excluding entire groups of people. This early human evolutionary need to believe that all who were not members of their group must be a "gratuitous invention" or some "irrelevant deity" makes outsiders minimally useful as a "screen" onto which the in group or tribe could project their antipathic tendencies and negative identities (Erikson, 1968, p. 41).

As is true of each of Erikson's constructs, prejudice holds both positive and negative elements. Throughout human evolution, the development of cohesive group identities has enabled groups, and therefore the species, to survive. The belief in being chosen makes people feel capable of survival. It becomes a self-fulfilling prophecy insofar as groups work to insure survival. Yet some collectives take their need for group cohesion to the extreme of belief in their superiority over all other groups. Erikson's principal concerns about these pseudospecies beliefs were threefold: First, he perceived that excluded persons and groups tend to absorb negative appraisals of themselves from others and build these into their own self-images. This leads to depression, self-hate, rage, and, eventually, vented aggression. Second, he observed that those who were held down could be fully excluded, devalued, and deprived of opportunities to develop positive identities. He understood his own youthful exclusion as that of someone who was unacceptable both in the Jewish temple his family attended in Karlsruhe, Germany, and in the non-Jewish, German community as well. He reminded America what its society had done to Native Americans and to African Americans. Further, he was clear in stating that exclusion leads to deprivations for both the excluded and the excluding persons. Humans cannot develop if their identity gain depends on another person's or group's identity loss. A genuine identity can never be obtained by depriving others of their rights to identity, for a vicious cycle develops in which the deprived and those who deprive feed off each other. Third, there are enormous dangers to the entire human species in a nuclear age when one pseudogroup or another can use its aggression to claim rights denied, or to keep its dominion intact.

Beyond the power of Erikson's pseudospecies idea to advance thought about how adults have systematically deprived outsiders from participation in a full species-identity, this concept changes another negative into a positive. Erikson asked adults to consider ways in which they might work toward inclusion of all. Typical of Erikson, he attempted to pull blame and guilt out of the equation. He wanted persons to learn from past errors, to develop the insight to see that, for historical, psychosocial, and biosurvival reasons, every person is prejudiced. His hope was that adults would recognize the prejudice tendency, and learn to place it empathically and intellectually aside as they worked toward a fully inclusive identity in one species-wide humankind. He believed that the end point of this would be a system of international ethics that was held together by human values held in common and affirmed.

CHANGING THE GOLDEN RULE

Few theorists have been so bold as to suggest that the Golden Rule be changed. "Do unto others as you would have others do unto you," was, to Erikson, written at the developmental level of a child, at a reciprocity level of moral development:

> . . . the rule alternately employs the method of warning, "Do not as you would not be done by," and of exhortation, "Do as you would be done by." . . . it must be admitted that the formula, "Do not to others what if done to you would cause you pain," does not presuppose much more than the mental level of the small child who desists from pinching when he gets pinched in return. (1964a, p. 414)

Erikson proposed an alternate, higher level Rule for adults: "Do unto others what will help them even as it helps you to grow." This is congruent with his concept of the goal that humans can, at their best, attain: moral development and moralizing in childhood, ideological development and the beginnings of a philosophy of life in adolescence, and ethical development through ideals and behaviors that nurture it in adulthood. Thus, the learned morality of childhood and the ideology of adolescence, blend into principles concerning how adults might aim toward improving the one life they were given. Here again, the pseudospecies tendency comes into play. "Children," he wrote, "can be made to feel evil and . . . adults continue to project evil on one another and on their children, far beyond the call of rational judgment" (1964a, p. 415). He felt that too many parents do not bring their children along in positive moral development, respecting them at each step in the process. Instead, they treat their own progeny as one or another form of pseudospecies.

Beginning with his firsthand experiences of World Wars I and II, and the belief that someone like Hitler was always a lurking possibility in the future of humanity, Erikson used psychoanalytic methods and artistic writing to attempt to enlighten his audiences. As has been said, he troubles us. He forces us to view the fact of prejudice in each and every person; he tells adults that they are called, by the best of what their identity development can be, to grow up; he illustrates the human need to believe in a power and Great Spirit beyond, within, and between humans. Writing on the border of psychology, sociology, religion, history, and the group-based origins of the species, he believed he could not shirk his own ethical responsibility to alert those who might be able "to see," through insight and meta-analytic thought, the very real tendencies of humans to destroy all of creation. As a result of moving farther and farther afield of any discrete location within psychoanalysis, Erikson risked and found greater professional marginalization.

SPIRITUALITY AND THE ULTIMATE OTHER

Intertwined with his concepts of moral and ethical development are Erikson's sometimes amorphous ideas on spirituality. In some ways these fit well within psychoanalysis and within Erikson's developmental theory. In other respects they take him outside both. Three remarkably different writers influenced his conceptualization of the earth-transcending adult. These are Soren Kierkegaard, Martin Luther, and Sigmund Freud. In Erikson's later years, the presumably "authentic sayings" of Jesus of Nazareth were included. Joan Mowat Erikson, Erik Erikson's wife of more than 60 years, also influenced Erikson's views. As a devout daughter of an Episcopalian minister, Joan Erikson's role in her husband's thinking and writing has been vastly underestimated.[3]

Issues of spirituality began in earnest with Erikson's writing of *Young Man Luther* (1958). Ethics, moral responsibility, and

[3] Knowledge of Joan Erikson's role in Erik Erikson's writing comes from my studies of the Eriksons' respective and collaborative writings, and from interviews of Joan Erikson, colleagues, friends, and students who knew the couple.

diffuse writings about eternity are imbedded in nearly every paper and book thereafter. By his 71st year of life, he had become explicit: "one pole of any identity, in any historical period, relates man to what is forever contemporary, namely, eternity" (1974, p. 41). By eternity, Erikson meant that which is beyond human physical life. However, he also positioned the Kingdom and spirit within humans and between them. In coming to this, he had examined the sayings of Jesus in Luther's translation:

> [I]f the Kingdom is so vague in its temporal boundaries, *where* is it? This question Jesus answers in another context: "Behold, the kingdom of God is in the midst of you" (Luke 17:21). The Greek original, *entos hymon,* presumably can mean "between you" as well as "within you," for Luther's translation, "inwendig in Euch," claims just that. (Erikson, 1981, p. 347)

In this same source of the Galilean sayings, Erikson used one of the favorite terms of his mid- and later life, that of "actualization." Used in both the intra- and interpersonal sense, Erikson meant finding the best within one's adult being that will be self and other activating. This includes an awareness of the Spirit and of human potential. It entails an inclusion of others and a concern that others are cared about and freely permitted to be their genuine selves.

By 1981, Erikson was writing about the need to be aware of the presence of evil and sin, and the need to repent. But by repentance he did not mean the breast-beating, guilt-feeling confession of an evil self. He held repentance to be a positive affirmation in which the adult alters his or her position with respect to the self and to the Almighty. Adults take the idea of sin and place it behind them in time, working instead to do good works for and with others. Erikson saw this spatially. Persons turn back to look at the past of the self, and then turn around to look toward the future of a new self who elects ethical actions. It is a positive anticipation. Again, he used Luther's translation:

> Thus, repentance as an active choice (and the Greek word for it is *metanoia,* translated by Luther as "Umkehr"—"turnabout")

> makes one central to one's life-space. With all the pain of penitence inherent in the word, one need not be inactivated by bad conscience, nor banned by divine judgment; and this seems to be a step toward the alertness of the sense of *I*, which is also implied in that repeated encouragement: "Be aware! Be wakeful! Watch!" (Erikson, 1981, p. 348)

From his early years as an artist, Erikson had been interested in the way humans thought about and used spatial concepts. Once a psychoanalyst, these ideas first appeared in print when Erikson connected anthropology and psychology to show how individual psyches and group ideas are infiltrated by space and time. He wrote:

> Perhaps there are no deeper differences between peoples than their feeling for space and time. This contains all that a nation has learned from its history, and therefore characterize concepts of reality and ideals of conduct which no nation can afford to have questioned by another without experiencing a threat to its very existence. (1937, p. 104)

Erikson found that the psyches of Sioux people were shaped by the expansive prairie land they roamed and the language that told about it. Ideas of wide-reaching "centrifugal" existence infused their ideas as they hunted buffalo and wandered about in groups (1937, p. 104). Diametrically opposite the Sioux, the Yurok lived in ideas of a restricted "centripetal" world (1943, p. 257). They held no concepts of east, west, north, or south, but lived amidst ideas of space in which salmon, deer, and the rivers provided principal coordinates that focused their lives and thought. Industrialized peoples as well harbored psychological notions based on geography and space. For example, early 20th century Germans held restricted notions of freedom that were due, in part, to their country's "lack of natural frontiers" (1942, p. 484). Germans felt "encircled" and "vulnerable to sweeping invasions" (p. 483). This overwhelmed and rigidified their thinking, a paralysis that made room for Hitler.

When Erikson brought matters of the spirit into the psychological equation, he found significance in humans' upright posture, their tendencies to visually scan fore and aft through space and time, their use of symbols to convey spiritual meanings, and the paradox of the space that exists between humans. To Erikson, the very "core" of adult being was found in its upward stance, a position that he found useful to express his ideas of connections with others and with a God image:

> As a Navajo medicine man recently put it when asked by a friend for a definition of what is human: indicating the figure of a cross, he said that a person was most human where the (vertical) connection between the ground of creation and the Great Spirit met the (horizontal) one between the individual and all other human beings. (1976, p. 18)

Erikson was trying to show how, although the space between persons and the space between humans and their creator, could not be given concrete physical form, it was useful to imagine it somehow could. He believed this was useful for two primary reasons. First, if adults could learn to think in such a way, diverse humans throughout the globe might understand that they share a specieswide human relationship and community. This was Erikson's way to infuse stone-cold reasoning with feeling so that nuclear annihilation of the species might be prevented.

Second, Erikson believed that adults needed faith. In their developmental transition from the joy, trust, and sensitivity of childhood to the highly cerebral, subjectively detached reasoning of controlling, tool-manipulating adulthood, 20th century adults had lost the primary bond to their God, the ability to experience the Ultimate as a subject. Here Erikson pointed readers spatially backward to their own childhoods and to the child that he hoped each adult would be able to locate within his or her being. It was not childishness, but childlikeness, that Erikson believed adults needed to emulate. Joy, attachment, animation, playfulness, and trust were qualities Erikson observed as those which adults needed to find in the child inside them. These same qualities would also connect them with their creator.

Searching through Erikson's many writings on ethics, morality, and spirituality, readers find themselves asking what Erikson himself believed about the existence of eternity and God. Did he align himself with Sigmund Freud, seeing these as an illusion? Did he envision the Ultimate as a singular creator, as a trinity of three, or as a committee of many more? It is a feature of believing, doubting adults that they—we—are interested in learning what others believe about the creator. In particular, we wish to know how those human originators such as Erik Erikson, an individual whose own era has called gifted, positioned themselves against faith and held images of God—if, in fact, they did. Erikson himself searched through the writings of Kierkegaard, Freud, and Einstein to learn what they had believed. In Kierkegaard, he found a disturbed, faith-filled, irreligious isolate. In Freud, he found a not so atheistic man. In Einstein, he found a pondering, questioning believer. But what about Erikson himself?

Here Joan Erikson's hand comes decidedly to the fore. The positive outcome of both the first and the last stage of the Eriksonian, life-stage developmental theory that the Eriksons created together eventually became that of *hope.* The infant's repetitive experience of trust in the caregiver leads to hope in the future, while the elder's trust that his or her life was worthy, that progeny and the species will continue to live on, lends hope. These resources also result in the tendency to hope for continuity in some spiritual form. Trust is subsumed in the word *integrality,* the term the Eriksons eventually used instead of integrity to describe adults' completion in the last stage of life as elders come to accept that their lives will soon end (1984, p. 163). Trust, in all of the Erikson writings, leads to hope. Hope expresses itself in the last stage as faith, for wisdom includes faith.

In Erik Erikson's writing, there were some changes from his early years. As a young psychoanalyst, Erikson did not dismiss Freud's belief that God is the image the human projects forward as an eternal father, a wish fulfillment that substitutes for the earthly father who had abandoned him or her. In his later writings, Erikson cast this aside to agree with Joan Erikson:

The mother is the eye-to-eye trusted being, an essential resource through which the child first comes to see a God-image. In later life, this earlier mother-resource and her remembered affirmation permit the elder to contemplate God in an otherworldly, spiritual way as a reality (compare, for example, Erikson, 1981, and J. M. Erikson, 1988).

It is difficult to discern how much of Erikson's early God image was based on his relative youth, how much was based on his full belief in what he wrote, how much was due to his need to be accepted as a writing psychoanalyst, and how much was due to a need to maintain his lineage with Freud. Throughout his active writing years, Erikson changed. At first he was more clinical and detached. Later, whether attracted by the eternal or by his own need to believe in the eternal, or perhaps because his feminine, nurturant self came to the fore, his writing shows greater affect. In publications, he implied but did not explicitly say what it was that he believed. In his unpublished Harvard papers, he said he was a Christian follower.

Erikson thought that psychoanalysis would eventually have to accept the burden it had imposed by keeping itself so apart from the spiritual beliefs that religions fostered. It was his great hope that psychoanalysis could free humans from mental suffering so that they could engage themselves in positive, self- and life-affirming ways with the Ultimate concerns that each person has. Therefore, developmental principles and psychoanalysis had to connect with theos in order to take the person beyond mere adjustment to reality and the narrow experiences of one physical, psychosocial life. Throughout his writing, Erikson searched for the commonalities that bonded all persons in one shared species. He found two of these commonalities in the love adults have for children and in adults' search for connections with the great Spirit. He dismissed the view that the eternal begins where life ends, believing instead that it began at the beginning. And he believed in one specieswide community that needed to consider its future jointly, spiritually. As he said, "a community of I's may well be able to believe in a common fund of grace or destiny only to the extent that all acknowledge a super-I that each I partakes in: A Being that Is" (1975, p. 108).

REFERENCES

Bushkoff, T. G. (1992). *The relationship between late adolescents' attitudes towards persons with disabilities and identity formation.* Unpublished doctoral dissertation, The George Washington University, Washington, DC.

Coles, R. (1970). *Erik H. Erikson: The growth of his work.* Boston: Atlantic/Little, Brown.

Erikson, E. H. (1937). Observations on Sioux education. *The Journal of Psychology, 7,* 101–156.

Erikson, E. H. (1942). Hitler's imagery and German youth. *Psychiatry, 5,* 475–493.

Erikson, E. H. (1943). *Observations on the Yurok: Childhood and world image.* Monograph. University of California Publications in American Archeological Ethnology. Berkeley, CA: University of California Press.

Erikson, E. H. (1950). *Childhood and society.* New York: Norton.

Erikson, E. H. (1958). *Young man Luther.* New York: Norton.

Erikson, E. H. (1963). *Childhood and society* (2nd ed., enlarged). New York: Norton.

Erikson, E. H. (1964a). The golden rule and the cycle of life. (The George W. Gay Lecture on Medical Ethics, Harvard University, 1963). In R. W. White (Ed.), *The study of lives* (pp. 412–428). New York: Atherton Press.

Erikson, E. H. (1964b). *Insight and responsibility.* New York: Norton.

Erikson, E. H. (1968). *Identity: Youth and crisis.* New York: Norton.

Erikson, E. H. (1969). *Gandhi's truth.* New York: Norton.

Erikson, E. H. (1970). Autobiographic notes on the identity crisis. *Daedalus, 99,* 730–759.

Erikson, E. H. (1974). *Dimensions of a new identity: The Jefferson lectures in the humanities.* New York: Norton.

Erikson, E. H. (1975). *Life history and the historical moment.* New York: Norton.

Erikson, E. H. (1976). Reflections on Dr. Borg's life cycle. *Daedalus, 105,* 1–28.

Erikson, E. H. (1981). The Galilean sayings and a sense of "I." *The Yale Review, 70,* 321–362.

Erikson, E. H. (1984). Reflections on the last stage—and the first. In *The Psychoanalytic Study of the Child, 39,* 155–165. New Haven, CT: Yale University Press.

Erikson, J. M. (1988). *Wisdom and the senses: The way of creativity.* New York: Norton.

Erikson, E. H., & Newton, H. (1973). *In search of common ground.* New York: Norton.

Gilligan, C. (1982). *In a different voice.* Cambridge, MA: Harvard University Press.

Hoare, C. H. (1991). Psychosocial identity development and cultural others. *Journal of Counseling and Development, 70,* 45–53.

Hoare, C. H. (1994). Psychosocial identity development in United States society: Its role in fostering exclusion of cultural others. In E. Salett & D. Koslow (Eds.), *Race, ethnicity, and self: Identity in multicultural perspective* (pp. 24–41). Washington, DC: NMCI Publications of the National Multi-Cultural Institute.

Kohlberg, L. (1971). From is to ought: How to commit the naturalistic fallacy and get away with it in the study of moral development. In T. Mischel (Ed.), *Cognitive development and epistemology* (pp. 151–235). New York: Academic Press.

Manuel, F. E., & Manuel, F. P. (1979). *Utopian thought in the western world.* Cambridge, MA: Belknap Press of Harvard University Press.

Streitmatter, J. L., & Pate, G. S. (1989). Identity status development and cognitive prejudice in early adolescents. *Journal of Early Adolescence, 9,* 142–152.

Wright, J. E., Jr. (1982). *Erikson: Identity and religion.* New York: Seabury Press.

Zock, H. (1990). *A psychology of ultimate concern.* Atlanta, GA: Rodopi Press.

3.

An Ethicospiritual Analysis of Postmodernism

Pano T. Rodis

The influence of an ethicospiritual analysis within psychology seems to grow every year (Kvale, 1992; Prilleltensky, 1997). Such an analysis connects a concern with ethics, defined by Aristotle as the study of "right" action versus "wrong" action, to a concern with spirit, the essential, animating attitude or character of a person, event, or product (e.g., a text, an action) of a person (Aristotle, 1991). Naturally, it is in most cases impossible to talk about either spirit or ethics in isolation from each other; for just as whatever we do is done with a certain spirit, the spirit with which we approach any portion of our lives has direct ethical implications.

The major endeavor of this chapter is to identify and then amplify the tensions between two, broad ethicospiritual traditions in postmodern thought. The first of these is the humanistic, optimistic, and "cheerful" form of postmodernism, which is associated foremost with the Russian theorist, Mikhail Bakhtin (1975/1981, 1965/1984a, 1929/1984b); the second is the notably grimmer, even apocalyptic, version of postmodernism which is associated foremost with Friedrich Nietzsche (1887/1969, 1888/1988) and Michel Foucault (1978, 1979, 1990, 1994). Although both traditions are inveterately ironic, or, as the historian Hayden White masterfully expresses it, marked by "skepticism in thought and relativism in ethics" (White, 1973/1990), they nonetheless yield markedly different spiritual worldviews, both of which, if applied with discernment and discipline, can be truly useful to psychology. In this essay, I call the Bakhtinian form of postmodernism *parodic*, as it uses dialectical play to resolve conflicts and encourage tolerance. The Nietzschean-Foucaultian postmodernism I call *satiric*, because it sees conflict as omnipresent and inextinguishable, thus leading to actions emphasizing power relations. In describing these two ethicospiritual positions, I hope to provide a basis for evaluating the wisdom and the utility of the theories, modes of investigation, and options for action that postmodernism has made available to psychologists and other persons.

WHAT IS POSTMODERNISM?

Over the last two decades, the word *postmodernism* has appeared with increasing frequency in the discourses of both popular culture and the academic disciplines, touching off a number of provocative discussions (Allen & Baber, 1992; Denner, 1995; Fenn & Capps, 1992; Gergen, 1995; Hoesterey, 1991; Held, 1995). This wildfire expansion of the postmodern idea—an expansion which suggests that this idea is somehow salient, that it speaks to our experience—has stimulated many writers to consider the era we are currently living in the "postmodern era" (Kvale, 1992). Nonetheless, postmodernism is elusive of easy definition. As Steven Best and Douglas Kellner (1991) have aptly written:

> . . . there is no unified postmodern theory, or even a coherent set of positions. Rather one is struck by the diversities between theories often lumped together as "postmodern" and the plurality—often conflictual—of postmodern positions. One is also struck by the inadequate and undertheorized notion of the "postmodern" in theories which adopt, or are identified in, such terms. (Best & Kellner, 1991, p. 2)

Nonetheless, because of the influence of popular books in psychology (e.g., Kenneth Gergen's *The Saturated Self* [1991], Robert J. Lifton's *The Protean Self* [1993], and Camile Paglia's *Sexual Personae* [1990]) as well as more esoteric and scholarly works from philosophy and literary criticism (e.g., Jacques Lyotard's *The Postmodern Condition: A Report on Knowledge* [1984], Michel Foucault's *The History of Sexuality* [1990], and Jacques Baudrillard's *America* [1988]) many of us associate postmodernism with a challenge to moral positions widely held and epistemological practices previously regarded as foundational. Moreover, not only as "theory," but also as a force of ethical challenge, postmodernism seems to emanate from a confusing spectrum of positions, including, at one extreme, a species of nihilistic relativism that might seem to justify any expression of value or power, no matter how deviant, and at the other, a kind of fervent political and social radicalism centered in the critique of power. Postmodernism has been labeled by some as a massive cultural force unleashed by material shifts in the global economy, by others as a philosophical perspective brandished by a small party of intellectuals, and by a few others as the origin of a "new science," which has emerged during the late 20th century from the narrow ideological confines of the modernist science associated with Descartes and his intellectual descendants. Like numerous other "isms" in world history, postmodernism has its advocates and acolytes, as well as its critics and scoffers. Not surprisingly, even as postmodernism seems to be gaining in influence, entering since the 1980s into virtually all of the disciplines, both within the humanities and the sciences, it has also been increasingly the recipient of sharp attacks. It seems, then, that if we are to enter into a discussion about postmodernism, we must begin by trying to clarify what it is, accepting at the outset that all definitions ventured must lack total sufficiency.

Given these many cautions, I think it is all the same possible to say that at its very basis, and in nearly every aspect of its manifestation, postmodernism exists as a definable body of thought primarily through its efforts to articulate and make meaningful a number of previously unseen or devalued problems in our familiar ways of knowing and acting. And in order to express and explore these problems, postmodernism has invested in the creation of several new techniques of interpretation. These techniques, more than anything else, *are* postmodernism. That is, although postmodernism might be said to exist as a disposition or attitude, as a body of more-or-less coherent truth claims, or as the *weltgeist* of the contemporary era, postmodernism is probably first and foremost identified with the novel means of analyses by which it has come into being. This is not to say that postmodernism is nothing but a set of analyses—hardly so!—but it is by studying these practices that we can best prepare ourselves to clearly discuss postmodernism as spirit, aesthetic, and ethical force.

Edward Davenport identifies seven kinds of postmodern analysis (Davenport, 1985), each of which has influenced psychology in some fashion. (1) *Hermeneutics,* associated primarily with Hans-Georg Gadamer and Paul Ricouer, is centered in an investigation of the means by which humans approach interpretation, a process which is ubiquitous in mental and social life, and how humans succeed (or fail) in influencing each others' interpretations; (2) *Poststructuralism,* associated primarily with Michel Foucault and Jacques Derrida, aims to "deconstruct" artifacts of culture and consciousness (from texts to social institutions), seeking to expose the motives, persuasive devices, and histories concealed within them; poststructuralism is concerned foremost with issues of power; (3) *Marxist critical theory,* associated primarily with Adorno and Habermas, is also concerned primarily with issues of power, but it approaches the interpretation and the evaluation of social problems in terms consistent with the socialist tradition in Europe beginning with Marx; (4) *Linguistic philosophy,* associated primarily with Wittgenstein and Toulmin, attempts to understand all forms of human knowledge, ranging from the religious to the scientific to the everyday, as a series of "language games," in which the codes or modes of expression utilized dictate the play of possible meanings; (5) *Ethnomethodology,* associated primarily with Garfinkel, asserts that any "finding" elicited during the study of one human being by another is not objective, but the particular product of a variable, unfolding interaction between subject and observer; (6) *Tacit-knowledge theory,* associated primarily with Polanyi and Kuhn, examines the influences of both articulated intellectual assumptions and unarticulated social rules on the construction of scientific knowledge; and (7) *Critical rationalism*, associated primarily with Karl Popper, acknowledges the arbitrariness which can be found to some degree in all scientific theories, but, instead of rejecting science, assays to develop methods for coping with its epistemological weaknesses.

Even in my very brief synopses of these seven theories, it is easy to see why postmodernism has been accused of relativism and even nihilism (Bernstein, 1992; Fenn & Capps, 1992; Gergen, 1991; Held, 1995; Norris, 1990). Each theory treats as problematic the very practices of knowledge on which Western culture has largely depended, at least since Descartes. Moreover, Western culture is here challenged both in terms of the empirically oriented practices and beliefs that underlie its science, and in terms of the linguistically grounded practices and beliefs that drive all its endeavors, from the humanities to the social sciences to religion to the so-called hard sciences. Postmodernism, in other words, questions not just the truth-claims or conclusions made by one group of people or another (for such sociopolitical forms of critique are familiar enough), but the very methods of knowing which since the Enlightenment we have come to consider foundational: What, after all, is more foundational to us than the language we use to describe our worlds to ourselves and to others? Moreover, postmodernism often plies its questions in a curiously hungry way, feeding now on dearly held major propositions of science or faith and in the next moment on some apparently minor idiosyncrasy of language or attitude. Postmodern theory is generally critical and suspicious, accusatory and tireless. It is, it seems, in many ways a reembodiment of the relativizing and ironic sophist intellect which Socrates strove to crush with his own philosophy anchored in a vision of a unified, timeless realm of Truth. And what are sophists in the most pejorative sense but very clever barbarians—persons who undermine the moral order not through physical means, but through intellectual techniques which disconcert, mesmerize, and inspire uncertainty and paralysis?

In the new postmodern context, whether one wishes to call it barbarian or not, all attempts at knowledge, including those which strictly follow scientific rules of inquiry, can be construed as unable to rise above the status of interpretations shaped by assumptive biases. While this relativistic logic is problematic, and can even be dangerous, it is correct in reminding us of the power of our predispositions in determining our "truths." Postmodernism points us in the often unnerving direction of investigating our behaviors, convictions, and even our existences along a continuum that stretches from *creator* to *created.* That is, it compels us to consider the extent to which we construct and are constructed by the language we use, the environments in which we live, and the practices we utilize, these constructions forming a web beyond which it may be impossible to find objective perspective. If this is so—or even partly so—it radically accents the importance of our evaluative practices; for if we are indeed as radically constrained as *knowers* as postmodern theory asserts, we are, by no means, relieved of responsibility as moral actors. Indeed, postmodernism, although it has been associated with moral relativism and even nihilism, compels us to take much more seriously our capacities for affirmation (the positive valuation of a thing) and critique (the interrogation of a thing's value), for both play determining roles in the conceptual and social worlds in which we live.

ETHICS

As a glance at its voluminous literature suggests, ethics can be set apart from other subdisciplines in philosophy by its concentration on the sphere of *action* or doing. Ethical philosophy is especially interested in questions such as, What is "right" action, and, How do we decide amongst the range of possible actions open to us? To the extent that these questions capture what ethics are about, they suggest that ethics are concerned, on the one hand, with what *must* be done and, on the other, with what humans *will.* To restate this in somewhat more descriptive language, ethics are concerned, in one dimension, with the fulfillment and realization of certain "oughts" or imperatives (e.g., Kant's categorical imperative) which are not properly amenable to challenge, dilution, or rejection; and, in another dimension, with human agency, volition, and creativity. To integrate these two dimensions is to arrive at a familiar paradox: ethics is concerned simultaneously with what must be done (because it is true and good) and with our recognized capacity to act in novel or unsanctioned ways, including our ability to author new conceptions of truth and goodness and/or reject established ones.

Traditionally, ethical philosophy has been characterized by its efforts to define and demarcate the first of these dimensions. From Plato to Kant to many contemporary writers, there has been expressed the conviction that rightness and goodness have a firm, independent, and constant existence, and thus can be both known and actualized. Once the right and the good have been enunciated, it is possible to determine which actions ought to be performed and which ought not. Psychology has made many contributions to this tradition, including the very familiar practice in clinical settings of promoting "healthy" behavior and working to extinguish "pathological" behavior, a frame of reference saturated with unacknowledged ethical assumptions.

Beginning with Nietzsche, Western ethical philosophy has increasingly turned in the direction of investigating the latter of the two dimensions, which is concerned with "the manifestation of man as the maker of his own human existence" (Ricouer, 1992, p. 335). Generally considered an early postmodernist (and also the philosopher who proclaimed himself a "psychologist without equal" [*Ecce Homo,* p. 266]), Nietzsche developed a unique form of historical critique to show that human morality is, in every case, a contrivance, usually dreamed up to serve the purposes of some particular group or class. In *On the Genealogy of Morals,* Nietzsche (1887/1969) described the origin of his new methodology of ethical critique, one better able to understand issues of good and evil because it discarded the search for absolutes and replaced it with a study of human "prejudices" and their interactions with historical circumstances:

> Fortunately I learned early to separate theological prejudice from moral prejudice and ceased to look for the origin of evil *behind* the world. A certain amount of historical and philological schooling, together with an inborn fastidiousness of taste in respect to psychological questions in general, soon transformed my problem into another one: under what conditions did man devise these value judgments good and evil? *and what value do they themselves possess?*. . .
>
> Thereupon I discovered and ventured divers answers; I distinguished between ages, peoples, degrees of rank between individuals; I departmentalized my problem; out of my answers there grew new questions, inquiries, conjectures, probabilities—until at length I had a country of my own, a soil of my own, an entire discrete, thriving, flourishing world, like a secret garden the existence of which no one suspected. . . . (Nietzsche, 1887/1969, p. 43)

Nietzsche's "secret garden" eventually consisted of a thoroughgoing "revaluation of all values" in which, among other things, Christianity—the foundation of nearly two millennia of ethical philosophy in the West—was redescribed as a kind of ethico-cultural Trojan Horse whereby the Jews, conquered politically by the Romans, retaliated by creating a religion which subverted the value system on which Rome was founded. Religion, philosophy, political ideology: all of these were reinterpreted as fields wherein the really meaningful question was that of power. Hauntingly summarized in an opening section of his *The Antichrist,* Nietzsche (1888/1988) authored a new *realpolitik* conception of ethics centered in the assumption that power is what matters to people, whatever their protestations to the contrary:

> What is good?—Whatever augments the feeling of power, the will to power, power itself, in man.
>
> What is evil?—Whatever springs from weakness.
>
> What is happiness?—The feeling that power *increases*—that resistance is overcome.
>
> Not contentment, but more power; *not* peace at any price, but war; *not* virtue, but proficiency (virtue in the Renaissance sense, *virtu,* virtue free of moral acid). (Nietzsche, 1888/1988, p. 43)

Setting aside for a moment the question of whether or not this ethos should be adopted, we must first ask ourselves, Does this ethos seem to describe the way that most people actually feel, think, and behave? Does it capture some essential theme in the underlying psychology of individuals and groups as they negotiate their ways through a world that forces them to struggle for survival—if not dominance—on any number of different fronts? Moreover, might Nietzsche's formula be useful in thinking about the ways that psychologists and other scientists actually operate as they create theories, perform experiments, influence legal policies, found university programs, and so on?

What is generally important in Nietzsche's work is his insistence that ethics are the products of persons, engendered in order to achieve some purpose, to actualize some idea, or to alter power relations between groups and between individuals. As such, ethical systems are variable, inconstant, and subject to all the motley shaping forces of history. Accordingly, when asking questions like What is good? and What is right? we are best served by rooting our answers in two kinds of analysis: (1) a pragmatic psychological, sociological, and political analysis of the particular conditions in which persons find themselves, and (2) an open philosophical and psychological analysis of human creativity, desire, and imagination. Naturally, the answers that result from such lines of inquiry will be particular and relative, not absolute and universal.

If we now return for a moment to the seven theoretical positions enumerated by Davenport, we see that each of them, dealing from one perspective or another, takes up the question of power, often as a facet of the wider problem of *arbitrariness* in human "knowledge practices," or ways of constructing knowledge. If our knowledge practices differ, why do they differ? If none of them are purely necessitated by "reality," why do they exist at all? Some of the postmodern schools—like the Marxist and the poststructuralist—are explicitly interested in the role that the "will to power" plays in deciding what passes for knowledge in any given situation or culture. Is it the power interests of some ascendant political or social group that "arbitrarily" cause some kinds of research to be performed and others to be neglected? How much do the personal interests of individual psychologists figure in the choice of which therapy to utilize or whether or not to support managed care?

Indeed, such power dynamics penetrate even into the most subtle nuances of word usage. Foucault, for example, shows how the use of the word *ideology* in a public document encourages a very different response from the more neutral but otherwise equivalent word *idea,* exactly because it activates in the reader a concern with power issues (1990). And other postmodern theories, such as the linguistic philosophy of Wittgenstein, find that the very codes and communicative practices we utilize exert a kind of independent power, only accidentally of benefit or injury to living persons, to shape our sense of reality. Wittgensteinian analysis, although it is not explicitly concerned with social and political power the way that Foucault was, deals with power in terms of the relation of language to being, for if we can attempt to actualize only what we can think, and if we can only think what language enables us to think, our worlds are circumscribed by our linguistic practices. And, visa versa, when we change our modes of description and communication, we change our (interpretation of) reality, and sometimes we even change the world; witness, for example, the impact upon the natural world of the mathematical languages that have made possible the creation of technologies such as bulldozers and hydroelectric dams. Indeed, all seven postmodern approaches to knowledge open into questions of positionality, authority, legitimacy, ownership, and other dimensions of power.

If we return now to the Aristotelian formulation of ethics with which this section began—the formulation, that is, that posits correct *action* as the central concern of ethics, we grasp the relevance of the postmodern inquiry into knowledge and power, for certainly actions correlate somehow with the play of knowledge and power in any given frame. In the following passage by Foucault (1994), these relations are drawn together in what is very nearly an emblematic expression of the postmodern problem. Here, again in fashion consistent with the Aristotelian paradigm, Foucault effectively places ethics within the framework of political philosophy:

> What I mean is this: in a society such as ours, but basically in any society . . . (w)e are subjected to the production of truth

through power and we cannot exercise power except through the production of truth. This is the case for every society, but I believe that in ours the relationship between power, truth, and right is organized in a specific fashion. If I were to characterize not its mechanism itself but its intensity and constancy, I would say that we are forced to produce the truth of power that our society demands, of which it has least need, in order to function: we *must* speak the truth; we are constrained or condemned to confess or to discover the truth. Power never ceases its interrogation, its inquisition, its registration of truth: it institutionalizes, professionalizes, and rewards its pursuit. In the last analysis, we must produce truth as we must produce wealth. . . . (Foucault, 1994, p. 214)

Foucault's passage dramatizes the enmeshment of notions of rightness and truth within linguistic or discursive practices, all of which stand in a kind of cybernetic relationship to power. According to Foucault, our knowing and speaking practices are so caught up with the structures of political power that they consciously and/or unconsciously support these structures. Power, then, once established, tends constantly in the direction of hegemony, or overarching and absolute power, a thralldome which admits no difference or dissent. In such a world, how does one know when one's efforts at knowing or at doing the right thing are free, and when they are produced by the movements of power? In a chilling challenge to traditional assumptions about conscience and ethical personhood, Foucault (1994) writes:

> Power is employed and exercised through a net-like organization. And not only do individuals circulate between its threads; they are always in the position of simultaneously undergoing and exercising this power. They are not only its inert or consenting target; they are also always the elements of its articulation. . . . The individual, that is, is not the vis-à-vis of power; it is, I believe, one of its main effects. (Foucault, 1994, p. 214)

By virtually denying agency to individuals—or at least the kind of autonomous agency we would equate with traditional notions of free will—Foucault comes very close to sweeping ethics away altogether; for of what use is it to talk about correct action if individuals are incapable of doing anything but submitting to, transmitting, and perpetuating power? For, even as scientists utilize epistemological practices which secretly or not so secretly reflect the power inherent in society and its discourses, so are individuals effectively coerced into behaving in the ways they do.

In fact, however, these attempts, or overstatements, by Foucault follow from his apparent interest in provoking persons to seriously consider the actual sources of their behaviors and to carefully analyze the workings of power in their own consciousness, their own social relations, and the cultures in which they participate. Although Foucault seems to represent power as a fully reified, almost mythological entity against which resistance would seem futile, it is resistance which Foucault thoroughly valorizes and which he seeks to foment in his readers. Indeed, in Foucault, we have at once a pure continuation and a profound reversal of the Nietzschean encomium to power. For, while both share the view that dominant culture is consuming, self-aggrandizing, and interested only in its own hegemony, and while both explore the extent to which social power relations are recapitulated in the deep psychology of individuals and groups, Foucault rejects Nietzsche's exhortations to strive for power, instead positioning the hypothetical subject in the role of the vassal who, becoming cognizant of the powers that engulf him or her, *must* rebel against them. Indeed, Foucault's notion of the ideal subject would seem to be a person who struggles constantly for ethical clarity in the midst of social relations defined always by power; yet the difference between his worldview and that of more romantic political theorists is that such clarity is nigh impossible, though always to be striven for. Indeed, in his own personal fascination with sadomasochistic subcultures, Foucault at once hoped to expose the naked machinations of power and to find, rather like Rousseau, the postmodern "noble savages" who could, by dint of their refusal to succumb to conventional sociosexual norms, remake society. Interestingly, Foucault admitted that he could not predict how such a person would think or feel, for he himself had been too infected by the powers he abhorred and with which he was obsessed. Moreover, unlike Nietzsche, who argued that once we honestly admit our love of power, we can begin our authentic existences, Foucault is in a much more ambivalent relationship to power, especially official power. In the Foucaultian version of ethics, then, the subject is largely confined to the seemingly endless work of investigating his own practices, interrogating the cultures that surround him, and discovering the limitations upon his authentic freedom. Is it an ethics that extends in the direction of creative action? Perhaps of a sort. It is an ethics that, like Nietzsche's, sets life within an agonistic framework, and so concerns itself primarily with how it is that we might fight and struggle, resist and dominate, control and cut free.

SPIRIT

I have so far focused on the line of thought leading from Nietzsche to Foucault for several reasons. One reason is that this evolution allows us a perspective from which to consider an important historical shift in the focus of ethical philosophy. Second, the Nietzsche–Foucault tradition is the root and trunk of poststructuralism, probably the most widely known and influential form of postmodernism, and so warrants close examination. But third and most importantly, Nietzsche's and Foucault's works alert us to the enormous importance of what might be called the *spirit* of postmodernism, for as our discussion has so far shown, the modes of analysis which are the basic substance of postmodernism are something apart from the attitudes and intentions with which they are plied. I would like now to treat this third area in detail.

But what is spirit? Putting aside for a moment any attempt at a formal definition of this word, we find its meaning in the ways that, in our personal experience, all ethical philosophies or "points of view" seem to be animated by a particular energy, concern, or purpose, and so have a distinctive quality, somehow related to what they exist for, what they are positively and negatively oriented to, and how they make meaning and form of their experience. Indeed, spirit might best be described as the fundamental relational stance of an idea or ideology to the world or to the lives of those who subscribe to it. This relational stance encompasses both purposive and responsive qualities, each category of which sustains—and explains—the other. Often, though not always fairly, we impute a spirit to persons we know, fitting the vast variety of behaviors they display under the rubric of a broad, yet definable ethos. Thus, if a person has established a basic relationship to life which is hopeful, joyful, and largely uncomplaining, we mark this quality in the person and give it central position in our regard for him or her. If we perceive a person as abrupt, impatient, and apt to criticize, we will do the same, but of course, with a different attitudinal slant of our own. Likewise, we can ascertain, though usually working from a very personal interpretative framework, when the spirit of a conversation is torpid or bright, or when the spirit of an author we have read is upbeat or downcast. And although spirit is not an officially recognized part of the vocabulary of clinical psychology, it is a word that would substitute nicely for much that psychologists say as well as explain much of the differences in the ways psychologists work.

This folk level analysis of spirit is good enough for most settings, but to meet the demands of more formal discourse, as in philosophy or psychology, it helps to seek a more formal interpretative approach. One such approach, quite compatible with postmodernist thought, comes to us from literary theory via intellectual history. This model, first articulated by Northrop Frye (1957) in his *Anatomy of Criticism* in order to facilitate a structuralist study of literary narratives, was converted by the intellectual historian, Hayden White, in his 1973/1990 text, *Metahistory*, into a poststructuralist device for conceptualizing the broad ethicospiritual differences between texts devoted to the explication of historical events and processes. This model differentiates four modes of emplotment, or ways of telling a story: romance, tragedy, comedy, and satire. I will quickly summarize these and then move on to the discussion of the one most relevant to postmodernism, which is satire, as well as its parent trope, irony, and its more mirthful sibling, parody.

According to White, the romance is fundamentally "a drama of the triumph of good over evil, of virtue over vice, of light over darkness, and of the ultimate transcendence of man over the world in which he was imprisoned by the Fall'' (White, 1973/1990, p. 9). The romantic spirit, then, is one which seeks the idealistic, positive transformation of the world into a place befitting what is presumed ''best'' in us all. The pure romance, moreover, perceives such victory as both natural to humanity and eminently achievable; it could almost be said that, in the pure romance, transcendence is a *given* that merely ripens into fulfillment over the course of the story. On the other hand, ''Comedy and Tragedy represent *qualifications* of the Romantic apprehension of the world'' (White, 1973/1990, p. 10), qualifications due to their respective interest in ''taking seriously the forces which oppose the human effort at redemption . . .'' (White, 1973/1990, p. 10). ''Comedy and Tragedy take conflict seriously, even if the former eventuates in a vision of the ultimate *reconciliation* of opposed forces and the latter in a *revelation* of the nature of the forces opposing man'' (White, 1973/1990, p. 10). In other words, both comedy and tragedy challenge the pure romantic anticipation of success in the attempt to achieve ''the best of all possible worlds.'' Comedy works by first establishing a problem which, although often absurd, threatens to overtake the generally well-meaning, but inherently flawed characters of the story, and then, at the story's climax, when an absolute cataclysm seems inevitable, suddenly and deftly resolves the problem. Tragedy, on the other hand, validates always the possibility and the desirability of redemption, but often does this through the sacrifice or defeat of its hero, whose loss is expected to whet, not extinguish, the idealism of the audience. Finally, ''The archetypal theme of Satire is the precise opposite of the Romantic drama of redemption; it is, in fact, a drama of redemption, a drama dominated by the apprehension that man is ultimately a captive of the world rather than its master. . .'' (White, 1973/1990, p. 9).

According to White, satire is one facet of the larger ethicospiritual category of irony, which he identifies with the ''rhetorical figure of *aporia* (literally ''doubt'')'' (White, 1973/1990, p. 36). Thus, works written in the ironic spirit emanate from a difficulty with or refusal to believe in the comparatively naive worldview of romanticism, even in its qualified forms (i.e., comedy and tragedy). Irony does not believe, it questions. Moreover, it does more than reject religious and nonrational belief, such as the belief in God or personal salvation, but it rejects what has become commonsensical or "realistic" belief, such as that practiced and encouraged by the sciences. Indeed, irony, in its purest forms, rejects everything foundational, tending to unravel all possible truth claims, even its own. The most ironic works are those which cast doubt even upon their own assertions, promulgating a questioning attitude not just toward a particular subject but toward the very attempt to make meaning, no matter the ideology, methodology, or language utilized. In this sense, ironic works are both self-reflexive and dialectical; they are suspended perpetually between the poles of affirmation and critique, with no single claim standing as uncontested or final. Moreover, irony is, as Bakhtin (1975/1981) says, always "double-voiced" in that it stands in an uneasy tension with its own assertions, engaged in a kind of conflicted conversation, with each voice challenging the other.

As I will show later, this double-voicedness may involve voices of very different qualities and attitudes. Indeed, one may as well create an ironic dialogue out of two voices which disagree good-naturedly and hopefully as out of voices which sardonically refute each other. As a starting place for appreciating the constructive potential of irony, let us look at irony from the perspective of individual psychology, exploring how it is that irony may enable persons to function well in personal and social worlds.

From a psychological perspective, where and how is irony useful? First of all, some capacity for irony is virtually a *sine qua non* of healthy relationship to others, for it permits us at once to allow for the existence of many diverse and yet equally valid points of view. The person who does not take him- or herself too seriously, but can view their wants nondogmatically is much more likely to give and receive pleasure, and to act ethically, than the person who cannot be a bit self-detached. Second, irony allows us to minimize the otherwise too daunting seriousness of many circumstances that would otherwise overwhelm us. The irony practiced by emergency psychologists or soldiers in the field illustrates this point nicely; without the sometimes brazen capacity to greet terrible threats with an incongruous insouciance, persons in stressful circumstances might simply decompensate. Furthermore, in somewhat less severe, but certainly stressful circumstances—for example, during a time of uncertainty or life transition—irony can allow us to hold a number of different propositions about what "should be" for a time without committing ourselves to any of them. Third, irony is more than a little useful in preparing persons to question that which is given; it can function as a ground of resistance to established orders and as a way of finding relief from oppression. To ironize is to call into question, to doubt, to refuse to accept another's aura of power or to acknowledge the validity of a culture's demands. Thus, a person in an ironic mode may be less submissive, more apt to challenge "orders," and less likely, in Kafka's phrase, to "stare at the powers." Engaging in dialectical rapport with things-as-they-are, the person in an ironical mode may well produce a decentering of authority, and thus a transformation in the quality of life. Fourth, irony can be a powerful source of creativity, as is evidenced by postmodern art and architecture, which often creates a kind of ironical laughter by juxtaposing unlike elements in the same frame or by eliminating the boundaries by which ideologies, groups of persons, aesthetic tendencies, or discourses are typically kept separate and distinct from one another. When this laughter is intelligent, achieving not simply mockery, but the illumination of a problem of some human significance, it is of tremendous value. For by puncturing illusions, irony can instill a laughter of relief and self-possession, rather like that which comes—at the emperor's expense and yet in the emperor's best interest—at the end of the famous parable of the Emperor's New Clothes. From a pragmatic psychological perspective, then, we might define irony as a state of detachment or self-sequestering, cognitively erected in order to help us cope with stressful, provocative, or ambiguous circumstances. As a chosen intellectual posture, however, irony is best defined as a kind of active disbelief; it is a rationally selected skepticism employed in order to achieve the purpose of clearer sight and more discerning action.

Yet we are right to ask always, in what or in whose service is this disbelief functioning? What is its purpose? If it has none—if it is not active disbelief, conscious and volitional inquiry—then it is likely only a residual of and a mode of perpetuating the disappointment or wounding of the self in its sense of reality. For, although irony may both yield and support a very functional and ethically conscious social existence, it may also be the product—and the producer—of very negative experiences. Indeed, problem with irony taken to an extreme or lived too completely is that it may lead to a disintegration not just of our idea of the world, but of our sense of reality. The recognition of an internal and an external plurality of being is not in and of itself the problem. The problem lies in going one more step, which is to equate this multiplicity with an ontological theory that posits being as ephemeral fiction. Indeed, it seems that the value, pro or con, of irony hinges on our capacity for sustaining a life-positive, value-seeking skepticism without making the mistake of deriving from skeptical practice an ontological theory that views persons and life as fictions. This is the "misreading" of lived life, of felt experience, that can only lead to participation in practices that are destructive of self and others. In fact, such a reduction of the human being to the level of a fiction is on par with the logic of devaluation that permitted psychologists and psychiatrists to join in the barbarity of the Nazi death camps. Used rightly, irony can lead in the direction of the widening of the sphere of the real and a heightening of our capacities of appreciation for the myriad and diverse qualities of each particular human life. But used without affirmation of the beingness of other people and things, irony can eradicate its own basic dialecticism and be swallowed up in the nondialogue of one voice solipsistically speaking to itself.

THE SPIRIT(S) OF POSTMODERNISM

Having offered these few comments on irony, I hope it is possible now to see how irony, like the other ethicospiritual positions identified by Frye and White, can be subdivided into more precise formal and informal categories. This is especially important to our effort here, as postmodernism should be considered an ironic school of philosophy. Moreover, it is useful to be aware of the fact that these four positions rarely if ever appear in monolithic and uncompromised form; instead, a predominantly tragic work might be peppered with comic moments, or a generally ironic work may validate romantic leanings. Nonetheless, the value of the Frye-White model to any discussion of text, thought, ideology, or psychological practice is striking, for it provides a language for that substanceless yet so palpable quality I have referred to as spirit. Moreover, this language is quite familiar to most of us, even if we have not before used it as a device for philosophical or psychological analysis.

In my opinion, current discussions of postmodernism in psychology and elsewhere can be more or less positioned between two fundamental kinds of irony, similar in their basic truth claims, but far different from one another in terms of their attitude, or spirit, and thus in terms of their ethical responsiveness. The first of these ethicospiritual positions—the *satiric* position—is best captured in the works of Nietzsche and Foucault, and also expressed in the writings of Lyotard (1984), Gergen (1991, 1995), Paglia (1990), Derrida (1972, 1973, 1981), and others. The second might be called the *parodic* position, its attitudes best captured in the works of Mikhail Bakhtin, a Russian literary critic whose works first appeared in the 1930s. The parodic position was then subsequently carried forward in the work of Shotter (1987, 1992, 1993, 1995), Lacan (1968, 1981), Billig (1994), Edwards and Potter (1992), and others. Both positions are rooted in an ironic double-voicedness, acknowledging a multiplicity of points of view on all matters, viewing each perspective as upheld by particular parties for particular reasons. In the satiric position, this polyglot structure of reality induces perpetual struggle and conflict, for each party is presumed to act only self-interestedly. In the parodic position, each party is credited with the capacity to see the validity of both its own *and* the others' positions, finding in this spectacle of divergent views grounds for self-transcendence, mutual appreciation, humor, constructive dialogue, and creative compromise.

As had already been suggested, because satiric postmodernism is rooted in a vision of conflict and struggle from which there can be neither escape nor transcendence, it leads into an ethics primarily concerned with power. Nietzsche, for his part, urges a rejection of all ethics derived from sentimental "higher" aspirations (all of which he saw as the clever inventions of "priestly types" interested in their own gain) and a plunging into the competitive fray. Perhaps because it is unavoidable and necessary, and thus a major feature of reality, conflict becomes, for Nietzsche, a beautiful, valuable thing; and to engage willingly and consciously in conflict *for its own sake,* after the fashion of the ancient Greeks, becomes, for Nietzsche, the heart of a new ethos. Indeed, for Nietzsche, to turn away from the conflictual world in the hopes of personal salvation is the root of unethical behavior, both in terms of personal comportment and epistemological practice. Foucault's works carry forward this worldview, amplifying the degree to which issues of behavior (of either individuals or states) are locked in a mutually causative relationship to issues of epistemological practice, with power being the product of their interactions.

Because satiric postmodernism is suspicious, confrontational, hypervigilant (if not paranoid), and pessimistic, it runs counter to conventional ethics, which, in a Judeo-Christian and rational–scientific culture, we tend to associate with some kind of romantic idealism or romantic pragmatism (e.g., building a better computer is a contribution to humanity). The satiric position easily disappears from our ethical map and enters into forbidden realms of thought and imagination; for this reason it has generated a considerable amount of criticism, some of it quite salient, some of it hysterical. As several recent works in psychology and elsewhere bear witness, it is this kind of postmodernism that is associated with apocalyptic notions such as "the end of culture" or the "defeat of humanism." Satiric postmodernism has also, especially in Nietzsche, crossed into the fictionalization of reality which I warned against above.

But in the positive sense, satiric postmodernism has, more than any other philosophical school in this century, yielded conceptual tools for sociopolitical analysis and critique, each of which may be used for good purpose. Indeed, if we are interested in the relationship between power (or lack of it) and psychological well-being, we will find the satiric perspective invaluable (Rodis & Strehorn, 1997). It is most of all the satirical postmoderns who have taught us how to read existing political and social conditions and to comprehend the ways that they may oppress and repress, enslave and deny. And by providing us with this interpretative technology, they have to an important degree challenged us to use it. Is psychology as blithely ignorant now about the ethical implications of its ways of approaching research or clinical practice as it was a generation ago? I think not. Developments such as the American Psychological Association's recent adoption of norms of culturally appropriate practice would not, I think, have been possible without challenges both from within and without psychology encouraged directly or indirectly by the satiric critique of power. Of even wider impact, however, are the schools within psychology that have moved in the direction of social constructionist interpretations of individual development, psychotherapy, and cognition.

It is important, then, in approaching an ethicospiritual evaluation of satiric postmodernism that we appreciate the degree to which its predominant atmosphere of pessimism may conceal and/or inspire idealism focused upon "doing good," or at least upon resisting evil, thus contributing to the ethicalization of that which it influences.

In contrast to the satiric perspective, Mikhail Bakhtin (1975/1981, 1965/1984a, 1929/1984b), who wrote on Dostoyevsky, Rabelais, and the theory of the novel, originated a *parodic postmodernism* that is notable, among other things, for its cheerfulness. This postmodernism, laughing and musical, affirmative of human differences, and absolutely centered in a spirit of *tolerance*, evolved out of the apprehension of each moment of human experience (both intrapsychic and interpsychic) as "heteroglossic" (many-voiced) and "dialogic" (engaged in mutually transformative conversation). Bakhtin originated a "new" literary criticism, as well as a new model of psychological analysis in the 1930s, by challenging what he called the "monological" assumptions of "official" Western art, politics, and psychological approaches to personality and cognition, proposing instead a "dialogical" perspective, rooted in the notion that multiplicity not uniformity, conversation not dissertation, and the "carnivalistic" dissolution and reformation of power relations, vision, and feeling are the hallmarks of the healthy society and the healthy individual consciousness. Bakhtin's irony lies foremost in (1) his representation of life as a continuous jostling of diverse persons and ideologies, no one of which can succeed in fully dominating or coopting the others, and (2) his valorization of parodic literatures, political forms, social rituals, and psychological strategies as the very real antidotes to the problems of power.

In Bakhtin's view, no person, no group, no text—indeed, not even a single word—is homogeneous or monolithic. Instead, each is formed out of and so contains within it a myriad of diverse moments, meanings, and contexts. Thus, individual consciousness is, in fact, very like an entire society of voices engaged in more or less incessant conversation of ever shifting forms and shades. Participating in this heteroglossia are the voices of the body (e.g., hunger, pain, pleasure), the internalized voices of those who have influenced our development (e.g., mother, father, teachers, siblings, friends, etc.), the voices of our past circumstances and past selves, and also various discourses or socially inscribed ways of making meaning (e.g., the discourse of the church, of politics, of romantic courtship, etc.). For Bakhtin, because no human "space" is occupied by a single voice, the task of the psychologist—like that of the artist—is to understand how these voices stand in relation to one another. That is, psychologists must ask questions such as: What voices are at play in the person(s) I am now encountering? What is the form, spirit, and history of their dialogue? How do they negotiate their differences? What effect is their interplay having upon the person(s)? To what extent is the person(s) aware of them and able to control, modulate, and harness their potentialities?

But of all these voices, the ones with which Bakhtin was most interested were those which, self-consciously or not, used parody, or ridiculing mimicry, to decenter power and open new spaces for play and imagination. For Bakhtin, parody, in mixing laughing criticism into its representation of the powerful other (be it person, institution, or discourse), transgressed, and thus made more flexible, the social codes that would otherwise ossify to the detriment of art and individuals, especially those who are without power. Parody is, in Bakhtin's treatment, a vital form of sociopolitical and ethical critique that is all the same nonviolent. It transmits its influences in such a way that laughter, not slaughter, is the result. Thus, parody functions for Bakhtin as a mode for social and psychological transformation congruent with his peaceable, tolerant attitudes and his pronounced preference for many-voiced, dialectical forms in art and relational existence.

In describing the use of parodic forms—and the eruption of parodic laughter—in ancient Greece, Bakhtin (1975/1981) wrote:

> Parodic-travestying literature introduces the permanent corrective of laughter, of a critique on the one-sided seriousness of the lofty direct word, the corrective of reality that is always richer, more fundamental, and most importantly too contradictory and heteroglot to be fit into a high and straightforward genre. The high genres are monotonic, while the "fourth drama" and genres akin to it retain the ancient binary tone of the word. Ancient parody was free of any nihilistic denial. It was not, after all, the heroes who were parodied, nor the Trojan War and its participants; what was parodied was only its epic heroization; not Hercules and his exploits but their tragic heroization. The genre itself, the style, the language are all put in cheerfully irreverent quotation marks, and they are perceived against a backdrop of a contradictory reality that cannot be confined within their narrow frames. The direct and serious word was revealed, in all its limitations and insufficiency, only after it had become the laughing image of that word—but it was by no means discredited in the process. Thus it did not bother the Greeks to think that Homer himself wrote a parody of Homeric style. (Bakhtin, 1975/1981, pp. 56–57).

This is an enormously rich and dense passage, but its basic message is clear: the parodic mentality simultaneously recognizes multiplicity and ends conflict by including all parties (or perspectives) in a laughing discovery, through jokes and drama, of the ways that each is present in the other. The result is the liberation from a confining and untrue "one-sidedness" (Bakhtin called such one-sidedness "monotonic" or "monological") and the entrance into a cheerfully dialogic consciousness. Moreover, this is a consciousness which preserves romantic and idealized discourses; "the direct and serious word" is not mocked or discredited, but only balanced by alternative points of view. Thus, the parodic becomes a kind of grand hotel in which all mentalities, parties, and philosophies are welcome, but where none is accorded dominance; quite to the contrary, it is the impulse toward dominance that provokes the "corrective laughter" of others.

This "dialogic imagination" engenders cheerfulness exactly because it opens the way to seeing both self and other in far broader, intimate, unbounded, and relational terms than were previously available to those fields involved in the study of human behavior. Bakhtin's postmodernism is stimulated by the movement toward—not away from—human beings in their myriad and particular circumstances; it is a wading into the superabundance of human possibilities. Bakhtin's epistemological practices open into a joyful listening very different in spirit from those preferred by traditional science, which aim "to get things right," to derive final answers, or to settle all disputes, often by parsing complex problems into tiny pieces, which then no longer reflect the lived experiences of persons. In celebrating parody, whose history is identified with marginalized folk cultures, Bakhtin brings to light and values the life practices and modes of knowledge of persons living beyond the (narrow) pale of the logicocentric ethos. Thus, it is fair to say about Bakhtin (1929/1984b) what he had to say about Dostoyevsky: "His entire material unfolds before him as a series of human orientations. His path leads not from idea to idea, but from orientation to orientation. To think, for him, means to question and to listen, to try out orientations, to combine some and expose others" (Bakhtin, 1929/1984b, p. 95).

CONCLUSION

My purpose in this chapter has been to provide an ethicospiritual perspective on postmodernism, thus encouraging the view that postmodernism is neither to be succumbed to nor altogether rejected, but to be conscientiously put to work in the interests of persons. Focusing on irony as the overarching spirit of postmodernism, I have tried also to distinguish between different approaches to and uses of irony, everywhere tying my evaluation of any ironic stance or practice to its degree of congruence with the goal of affirming human beings as precious and important. Accordingly I have argued that, when taken so far as to promote the view that human beings are fictions, irony ceases to be the key to the kingdom of intellectual boundlessness and becomes instead as much a conceptual and spiritual *cul de sac* as any logicocentric scientific practice. Indeed, it seems to me that postmodernism, in having reminded us of the arbitrariness of our beliefs, has also put in our hands a great creative power equaled only by our ethical responsibility. Such a world as postmodernism describes does not negate the possibility of faithful action, but informs us that we may operate more on the basis of faith than ever we knew. Indeed, postmodernism suggests that perhaps the most radical faith of all is that which takes this evanescent world in which we live as profoundly real, and thus worthy of exploration, liberation, and care. Perhaps, then, what postmodernism can lead to is not a fictionalization of the world, but to a grounded psychological existentialism. What do I mean? I mean an existentialism grounded in the multimodal attention to all aspects of beingness, even the most microscopic and scarcely noted. Such an existentialism is less about probing emptiness and more about affirming what we feel, who we are, and how we come into creative being.

In all of these efforts, my aim has been to endorse neither a wholesale embrace nor a wholesale rejection of postmodernism by psychology, but rather a discerning utilization of postmodern concepts and techniques consistent with the formation of an ethically astute and intellectually vital discipline. Postmodernism has simultaneously opened two possibilities for psychology, both of which can be constructively harnessed, yet both of which have sparked a distinct sense of crisis: (1) the possibility of a new era of self-scrutiny and self-construction, following from postmodernism's critique of science and its allegations of arbitrariness and/or power motives in psychology's construction of knowledge, and (2) the possibility of a new era of other-orientedness, following from postmodernism's argument for the validity of the various ways of knowing, feeling, speaking, and living practiced by *all* persons and cultures, including those which have been long ignored, exploited, or trivialized.

It is my hope that these two possibilities may come to stand in supportive relationship of one another, for psychology has the best chance of finding a valid epistemic foundation to the degree that it remains ethically and spiritually concerned with its living subject, which is the human being as a person.

REFERENCES

Allen, K., & Baber, K. (1992). Ethical and epistemological tensions in applying a postmodern perspective to feminist research. *Psychology of Women Quarterly, 16,* 1–15.

Aristotle (1991). *The art of rhetoric.* Harmondsworth, U.K.: Penguin Books.

Bakhtin, M. (1981). *The dialogic imagination.* Austin, TX: University of Texas Press. (Original work published 1975).

Bakhtin, M. (1984a). *Rabelais and his world.* Bloomington, IN: Indiana University Press. (Original work published 1965).

Bakhtin, M. (1984b). *Problems of Dostoyevsky's poetics.* Minneapolis: University of Minnesota Press. (Original work published 1929).

Baudrillard, J. (1988). *America.* London: Verso.

Bernstein, R. (1992). *The new constellation: The ethical-political horizons of modernity/postmodernity.* Cambridge, MA: MIT Press.

Best, S., & Kellner, D. (1991). *Postmodern theory: Critical interrogations.* New York: Guilford Press.

Billig, M. (1994). Sod Baudrillard! Or ideology critique in Disney World. In H. W. Simons & M. Billig (Eds.), *After postmodernism* (pp. 150–171). Thousand Oaks, CA: Sage.

Davenport, E. (1985). Scientific method as literary criticism. *Et cetera, 42,* 338–350.
Denner, B. (1995). Stalked by the postmodern beast. *American Psychologist, 50,* 390–391.
Derrida, J. (1972). Structure, sign, and play in the discourse of the human sciences. In R. A. Macksey & E. Donato (Eds.), *The structuralist controversy: The languages of criticism and the sciences of man.* Baltimore, MD: Johns Hopkins University Press.
Derrida, J. (1973). *Speech and phenomena.* Evanston, IL: Northwestern University Press.
Derrida, J. (1981). *Dissemination.* Chicago, IL: University of Chicago Press.
Edwards, D., & Potter, J. (1992). *Discursive psychology.* Newbury Park, CA: Sage.
Fenn, R., & Capps, D. (Eds.). (1992). *The endangered self.* Princeton, NJ: Princeton Theological Seminary.
Foucault, M. (1978). *Madness and civilization.* New York: Vintage.
Foucault, M. (1979). *Discipline and punish.* New York: Vintage Books.
Foucault, M. (1990). *The history of sexuality: Vol. 1. An introduction.* New York: Vintage Books.
Foucault, M. (1994). Two lectures. In N. Dirks, G. Eley, & S. Ortner (Eds.), *Culture/power/history.* Princeton, NJ: Princeton University Press.
Frye, N. (1957). *The anatomy of criticism: Four essays.* Princeton, NJ: Princeton University Press.
Gergen, K. J. (1991). *The saturated self: Dilemmas of identity in contemporary life.* New York: Basic Books.
Gergen, K. J. (1995). Postmodern psychology: Resonance and reflection. *American Psychologist, 50,* 394.
Held, B. (1995). *Back to reality: A critique of postmodern theory in psychotherapy.* New York: Norton.
Hoesterey, I. (1991). *Zeitgeist in Babel: The postmodernist controversy.* Bloomington: Indiana University Press.
Kvale, S. (Ed.). (1992). *Psychology and postmodernism.* London: Sage.
Lacan, J. (1968). *The language of the self: The function of language in psychoanalysis.* (A. Wilden, trans.) Baltimore, MD: Johns Hopkins University Press.
Lacan, J. (1981). *The four fundamental concepts of psycho-analysis.* London: Norton.
Lifton, R. (1993). *The protean self: Human resilience in an age of fragmentation.* New York: Basic Books.
Lyotard, J. F. (1984). *The postmodern condition: A report on knowledge.* Minneapolis: University of Minneapolis Press.

Nietzsche, F. (1969). *On the geneaology of morals and Ecce Homo* (W. Kaufmann, Ed.). New York: Vintage Books. (Original work published 1887).

Nietzsche, F. (1988). *The antichrist.* Costa Mes, CA: Noontide Press. (Original work published 1888).

Norris, C. (1990). *What's wrong with postmodernism?: Critical theory and the ends of philosophy.* Baltimore, MD: Johns Hopkins University Press.

Paglia, C. (1990). *Sexual personae.* New York: Vintage Books.

Prilleltensky, I. (1997). Values, assumptions, and practices. *American Psychologist, 52,* 517–535.

Prilleltensky, I., & Welsh-Bowers, R. (1993). Psychology and the moral imperative. *Theoretical and Philosophical Psychology, 13,* 90–102.

Ricouer, P. (1992). *The conflict of interpretations.* Evanston, IL: Northwestern University Press.

Rodis, P., & Strehorn, K. (1997). Ethical issues for psychology in the postmodern era: Feminist psychology and multicultural therapy. *Journal of Theoretical and Philosophical Psychology, 17,* 201–219.

Shotter, J. (1987). The rhetoric of theory in psychology. In W. J. Baker, M. E. Hyland, & H. Van Rappar (Eds.), *Current issues in theoretical psychology* (pp. 283–296). Amsterdam, Netherlands: North-Holland.

Shotter, J. (1992). Bakhtin and Billig: Monological versus dialogical practices. *American Behavioral Scientist, 36,* 8–21.

Shotter, J. (1993). Bakhtin and Vygotsky: Internalization as a boundary phenomenon. *New Ideas in Psychology, 11,* 379–390.

Shotter, J. (1995). In conversation: Joint action, shared intentionality, and ethics. *Theory and Psychology, 5,* 49–73.

White, H. (1990). *Metahistory.* Baltimore, MD: Johns Hopkins University Press. (Original work published 1973).

4.

Critical Consciousness and Its Ontogeny in the Life Span

Elena Mustakova-Possardt

It is not for him to pride himself who loveth his own country, but rather for him who loveth the whole world. The earth is but one country, and mankind its citizens.
Baha'u'llah

Critical consciousness is our ability to bring moral understanding to the social, cultural, and political realities and allegiances of our lives. It reflects our readiness to establish morally responsible relationships with those realities, leading to positive social change. Without critical consciousness, we are trapped in racial, ethnic, and class hostilities, in religious and sectarian antagonism, in competing special-interest groups and ideologies. With critical consciousness, we recognize our common humanity and our common responsibility to the future of our world and our planet; with it, we develop a sense of agency which can transform our world.

At present, when our global interconnectedness and interdependence are becoming increasingly evident, it seems anachronistic to continue to conceive of adult development strictly in terms of progressive individual fulfillment without exploring the role of the developing adult in transforming existing social realities. The field of adult development at the turn of the 21st century needs to elaborate the links between personal fulfillment and social transformation, and to describe the evolution of a kind of global human consciousness which can unite humanity and facilitate the establishment of a peaceful society.

Critical consciousness (CC), the integrative psychological construct I define in this chapter, begins to do that. It bridges the gap between our understanding of personality in structural–developmental terms, and the understanding of socialization offered by critical social theory and postmodern thought. The study of CC examines the dynamics of the formation of different kinds of social consciousness, and the ways in which they operate on social reality. This provides an interdisciplinary framework for the understanding of citizenship, combining ideas on moral and social values, community, social responsibility, and moral commitment.

Understanding the genesis of human social consciousness and its critical capacity requires, I assume, integrating neo-Piagetian work on the organic development of structures of thought with Vygotskian concepts of the influence of sociocultural mediation on the formation of higher mental processes.[1]

DEFINITION AND CONCEPTUAL SOURCES OF THE CONSTRUCT OF CC

Critical consciousness (CC) is a social awareness of interconnectedness, which evolves through an intuitive and progressively more conscious quest for truth and justice, both internally and in one's social environment. This quest dominates over self-interest, and moves the individual into moral

[1] I have borrowed from a number of neo-Piagetian models (Commons & Rodriguez, 1990; Cook-Greuter, 1990; Kegan, 1982; Wade, 1996; Weinstein & Alschuler, 1985) in order to evolve a composite structural developmental component of CC. The Vygotskian sociocultural approach (Colby & Damon, 1992; Cole & Scribner, 1974; Wertsch, 1985), and specifically the concepts of sign mediation, induction, internalization, and developmental transformation of goals, have allowed me to examine the motivational sources of CC.

agency, while the understanding of truth, justice, and agency is continuously developmentally reconstructed.

This definition of the construct of CC is essentially interdisciplinary, the outcome of exploring the points of convergence among developmental, moral, and transpersonal psychology, philosophy and religion,[2] Freirean pedagogy (Freire, 1973; Shor & Freire, 1987), critical theory (Bronner & Kellner, 1989), and postmodern thought (Foucault, 1984), as well as research on social activism (Bellah, 1985; Bembow, 1994; Colby & Damon, 1992; Wuthnow, 1991).

The concept of CC originates in Freire's (1973) work on consciousness raising and empowerment in different oppressive contexts. Freire helped illiterate, fatalistic Brazilian peasants, who tend to take their social reality as absolute, to come out of silence and internalized oppression and begin to entertain questions about their condition. This means no longer swimming like fish in water in one's social reality, but becoming aware of its objective characteristics, and experiencing oneself as capable of knowing and understanding them. As the individual becomes empowered in this way, she begins to engage in intentional, responsible, and creative relationships with social reality; she also begins to discover ways to change it. Freire's formulation of CC begins with the premise that "one can only know to the extent that one 'problematizes' the natural, cultural and historical reality in which s/he is immersed," which Freire understands as distinct from the technocrat's "problem-solving" stance (p. ix). The process of problematizing implies a progressive gaining of sociohistorical perspective and awareness of personal role.

Freire's work has shown that CC means unleashing the human potential for creativity and agency with regards to overtly oppressed and paralyzed people (be it illiterate peasants, or people in the former East European communist countries or other military dictatorships). Critical theorists

[2] Some of the main sources, beyond the developmental literature described in note 1, have been Abdullah (1995), Baha'u'llah (1985), Bushrui, Ayman, and Laszlo (1993), Capra (1983), Csikszentmihalyi (1993), Hoffman (1983, 1989, 1991), Kohlberg (1984), Jung (1933), Maslow (1959), and Wade (1996).

(Bronner & Kellner, 1989) have shown how this concept applies to liberal Western societies, and to the covert oppression operating there. Marcuse's (1989a, 1989b, 1989c, 1989d) and Fromm's (1989) analyses of socialization show that, in liberal Western societies, people's capacity for critical social understanding and creative personal and moral agency is obstructed and dulled. In the place of the fatalism which Freire (1973) encountered, Marcuse and Fromm identify a centrality of instrumental, pragmatic concerns, fear, compartmentalization, neutrality, alienation, insufficiency of ego strength to resist social pressures, and an overall inability to see through the veils of material affluence and ideologies.

Clearly, in most parts of the world, people tend to become so embedded in their social reality that they experience it as absolute, and entertain only very limited questions regarding the social systems and ideologies that sustain them. As a result, social injustice, antagonism, and confusion are reproduced; people are disempowered, and live in fear.

Freire identifies as an important quality of consciousness the power to perceive and respond to suggestions and questions arising in one's context, rather than dismissing or compartmentalizing them as "the way things are." Although he describes CC in terms of essentially social–cognitive developmental aspects of evolving rationality and critical analysis of reality, he actually understands CC as a whole-person phenomenon. Central to it is experiencing connectedness, and seeking collective dialogue in constructing an understanding of one's world and one's agency in it.

The above fundamental characteristics of CC, elaborated by Freire and the critical theorists, are further developed in my definition of the construct of CC on the basis of several premises:

1. Social consciousness cannot be reduced to either thought or behavior. In studying CC, I focus on understanding and fostering a certain experience of social life which is wholesome, interconnected, and allows the individual to fulfill her creative potential. Such consciousness is manifested in desirable social behaviors such as social responsibility and moral commitment.

2. The lives of outstanding individuals such as Gandhi (1927/1983), or the people studied by Colby and Damon (1992), and Bembow (1994), exhibit a consciousness so much more expansive, all-encompassing of the human condition, morally and socially responsible, and able to effect significant social change, that the question arises whether it represents some altered state, qualitatively different from the consciousness operating in ordinary people. So far, developmental psychology has explored this phenomenon only in terms of higher stages of consciousness and self-development (Alexander & Langer, 1990; Miller & Cook-Greuter, 1994). However, ontological and humanistic approaches to the study of values (Maslow, 1959) suggest that the centrality and strengthening presence of universal moral values (e.g., unselfish love, service, humility, justice, truthfulness, integrity, etc.) in an ordinary person's life may have a transformative effect on ordinary levels of consciousness.

3. I assume a significant connection between what Freire (1973) describes as the ability to question seemingly absolute sociocultural reality, the ability to release the human potential for creative agency, and those universal moral values which not only foster inner wholeness and union of emotional, sensory, and rational faculties but also result in inner freedom and empowerment (Maslow, 1959). In other words, I treat CC not as an altered state associated with higher developmental levels, but as a moral consciousness, a lifelong developmental pathway toward mature individualism, characterized by fully articulated links with others and with society, and dedication to the common good (Colby & Damon, 1992). This pathway is characterized by a striving toward integrity, an effort to consistently align oneself with a larger meaning in life, as well as by a struggle to overcome and redefine cultural heritage, cultural myths, values and standard behaviors. Ordinary people who exhibit CC manifest personal characteristics such as moral certainty, moral courage, openness to redefining, and a snowball lifelong growth (Colby & Damon, 1992). In this sense, this pathway illustrates a more optimal fulfillment of the human potential at every point in the lifespan.

RESEARCH METHODS

The scope of my study required an open, evolving methodology.[3] The study fell into two parts. In the first part, I used three secondary sources of life histories of CC individuals.[4] Gandhi's (1927/1983) autobiography, Colby and Damon's (1992) case studies of moral exemplars, and Bembow's (1994) phenomenological case studies of social activists. Gandhi's autobiography was analyzed in the most detail, and then I sought parallels with the findings of Colby and Damon, and Bembow. I found a significant convergence in content themes, and was able to identify the two main components of CC, moral motivation and structural development, and subdimensions in each.

In the second part, I carried out 20 in-depth interviews with American midlifers as part of a national study on social responsibility (Colby & Damon, 1994),[5] and 8 cross-cultural interviews with Bulgarian midlifers (Mustakova-Possardt, 1995) selected on the basis of availability, using the same interview format, translated into Bulgarian.[6]

---

[3] I relied on a deductive-inductive "bootstrapping" approach (Loevinger, 1976), combined with an effort to build grounded theory (Strauss & Corbin, 1990) relying on qualitative primary and secondary empirical data.

[4] My research criteria for people who I consider exhibit CC were that these people should: (a) question the set of social relations in the larger social environment in which they find themselves; (b) feel compelled to make active efforts to redefine their relationship with those social conditions in congruence with their understanding; (c) seek an alternative vision of how things should be on grounds of explicit concerns with issues of justice and equity.

[5] The U.S. sample was part of Colby and Damon's (1994) on-going study of Midlife Social Responsibility, supported by the MacArthur Foundation Research Program on Successful Midlife Development (MIDMAC). Colby and Damon's study relies on a national sample of 100 people, roughly half men and half women, residing in or around five urban areas throughout the country, namely Atlanta, Chicago, Boston, San Francisco, and Phoenix, Arizona. My interviews represented the Boston subsample of the Social Responsibility study. That sample consisted of 20 midlifers, 7 women and 13 men, aged 35 to 60. Colby and Damon have claimed demographic representatives of their sample, on the grounds that their national sample was statistically selected by MIDUS. MIDUS is a national survey study of 600 Americans in midlife, statistically selected by the current MacArthur Foundation Research Program on Successful Midlife Development (MIDMAC). From that representative sample of 6000, MIDUS selected a national sample of 100 for the Social Responsibility branch of the study on Midlife, and passed it on to Drs. Colby and Damon.

[6] The Bulgarian sample of eight was selected separately, through a study on "Social Responsibility and Critical Consciousness in Bulgarian Midlifers," supported by the 1995 Henry A. Murray Dissertation Award (Mustakova-Possardt, 1995). This sample cannot claim representativeness. I selected the participants in an effort to have them represent as diverse sectors of Bulgarian social life as possible. Four people were from the capital

The interview has six parts. In the first part, participants were invited to construct the story of their lives, and divide it into several main chapters. They were then asked to focus on the main themes, events, and relationships, which in their estimation contributed to the formation of the person they became. They were invited to explicate the logical links connecting the chapters, and to describe critical events and significant people in their lives. This overview sheds some light on the family and other circumstances which contributed to the way these individuals prioritize their experience in their social world.

The second part revisits in greater detail each of the main areas of social responsibility, namely: work, family, volunteering and donations, and political involvement, and explores the ways in which individuals prioritize their commitments and sense of responsibility, their motivation, and the personal meaning they make of their choices.

The third part focuses explicitly on the participants' moral reasoning and moral sense of self. A fourth investigates their sense of community involvement, and the place of community in relation to the sense of self. Part 5 emphasizes the participants' religion and/or personal philosophy. The last part inquires into interviewees' motivation for participating in the study.

In analyzing both the primary and the secondary data, I applied the same three types of analytic procedures: (a) qualitative coding techniques for conceptualizing the data, i.e., thematic analysis (Strauss & Corbin, 1990); (b) a more quantifiable informal developmental assessment; (c) biographical analysis.[7]

---

of Sofia, and four from a small country town. There were four men and four women. In spite of my efforts, the Bulgarian sample ended up being biased along the education criteria, with a high average length of education.

[7] The thematic analysis involved several levels of coding, open, axial, and selective (Strauss & Corbin, 1990), which allow building grounded theory regarding interrelated conditions in the formation and operation of CC.

The structural–developmental analysis relied on four neo-Piagetian theoretical frameworks, which I found most pertinent to the salient structural developmental aspects of CC. Those aspects are: (a) reasoning about causality; (b) understanding of one's social experience; (c) ways in which the self relates to social experience; and (5) moral reasoning. To address them, I relied on my understanding of adult development theory, and

On the basis of Freire's definition of CC and adult development theory, I hypothesized a structural developmental threshold for CC as an adult phenomenon: formal operational grasp of causality, the ability to identify abstract patterns in one's social environment, a differentiated sense of self, conventional moral reasoning with a Social System and Conscience orientation.

The biographical analysis (with Gandhi and others) revealed thematic overlaps with the cross-cultural biographic accounts obtained from the research participants. From an analysis of both, I was looking to shed some light on the origins of the individuals' motivation in childhood experience, family background, and significant models. I relied on my general clinical understanding to generate plausible interpretations. My understanding is informed by Vygotskian (Wertsch, 1985) theory of socialization, discourse mediation, and internalization in the formation of individual social consciousness, as well as by models of moral induction and self-attribution (Hoffman, 1989), and the developmental transformation of goals (Colby & Damon, 1992).

ONTOGENY OF CC: CONCEPTUAL UNDERSTANDING AND WAYS OF BEING

The CC pathway reveals the continuously evolving dynamic outcome of the synergy between moral motivation and structural development, its two main components. The interaction between moral motivation and structural development produces three levels of social consciousness in the life span, pre-CC, Transitional CC, and CC. At each level, the person negotiates a substantially different range of tasks, concerns, and limitations.

This paper discusses primarily the role of moral motivation in the formation of CC, and briefly describes each developmental level of CC, illustrating it with a case vignette. A more

informally applied (a) Commons and Rodriguez's (1990) general stage theory; (b) Weinstein and Alschuler's (1985) model of the development of self-knowledge; (c) Kegan's (1982) subject/object model of the evolving self (Lahey, Souvaine, Kegan, Goodman, & Felix, 1988); and (d) Kohlberg's (1984) theory of the evolution of moral reasoning.

extensive discussion of the structural developmental component will be the subject of another publication.

Moral Motivation

What is moral motivation, and how can we operationalize its definition? The 28 life stories I heard helped me conceptualize motivation as a continuum between predominantly moral and predominantly expediency concerns. Expediency is an orientation to pragmatic ends, defined by self-interest, through a choice of the most convenient means, with peripheral or no regard for moral implications.

Moral motivation appears to evolve in the life span along four motivational dimensions: (1) identity; (2) motives to negotiate external and internal authority, personal responsibility, and agency; (3) motives shaping relationships with others and one's environment; and (4) motives related to the understanding of the meaning and purpose of life (see Table 4.1). In the case of moral motivation, these dimensions can be described as follows:

1. Moral identity (anchored in universal moral values) and moral character predominate over a sense of identity derived from various social configurations such as class, race, gender, ethnic or other group membership. Identity rooted in moral models and concepts, however simply understood, is the source of a moral imperative, i.e., an inner need to do the morally right thing, which is stronger than self-interest, and strengthens and expands in the course of life.

2. External moral authority in significant others is questioned, as the individual constructs her understanding of authentic moral authority. With the growing critical discernment of and receptiveness to authentic moral authority, it is progressively internalized as personal moral responsibility. This process is accompanied by the emerging sense of internal moral authority and the tendency to reconstruct continuously internalized personal moral responsibility. A sense of moral agency develops, which prevails over the tendency to experience oneself as the victim of circumstances.

3. Experiencing oneself in relationships, and empathic concerns with others, with good and bad, with being loyal and not hurting, gradually expand beyond interpersonal relationships, into larger social concerns with justice and equity.

4. The tendency to ask and value questions regarding the meaning of life, and the lifelong search for authentic meaning, develop in an explicitly or implicitly spiritual environment, with faith in the wisdom of life, and acceptance of the responsibility it imposes. The search for truth provides a larger frame of reference from which to reflect on self and experience, and spurs intense self-reflection and critical examination of reality, expanding toward principled, philosophical, historical, and global vision.

Moral motivational dimensions are more or less preponderant in ordinary people, and are not an absolute state. Only in the lives of outstanding moral leaders and exemplars (Colby & Damon, 1992; Gandhi, 1927/1983) do we see them relatively unmitigated by expediency. In most people I interviewed (Mustakova-Possardt, 1996), these dimensions represent a continuum, with a general tendency toward either the moral end, as described above, or the expediency end. Table 4.1, below, represents the continuum between moral and expediency motivation.

Where moral motivation (the desire to do what is understood to be good and right, and the tendency to conceive of self-interest in moral terms) dominates over narrowly conceived self-interest, it becomes a powerful incentive for personal growth and development. The development of moral motivation varies somewhat in every life story I studied. For example, each moral exemplar describes a different environment that fostered preoccupation with one or another of the four moral dimensions. For Gandhi (1927/1983), as well as in the case of an individual named Paul (cf. Bembow, 1994), the starting point was an intuitive moral sense which grew into a strong sense of moral identity grounded in moral values, and an intense search for truth and meaning (dimensions 1 and 4). For Virginia Durr (Colby & Damon, 1992), a strong empathic concern with relationships and justice, combined with a strong character, helped extricate her from the prejudices of her own

TABLE 4.1
Continuum between Moral and Expediency Motivation

Dimensions	Expediency Motivation	Moral Motivation
1. Identity	Identity predominantly rooted in social conventions (social identity) and lack of moral imperative	Identity predominantly rooted in moral values (moral identity) and moral imperative
2. Authority, Responsibility and Agency	Limited personal authority and responsibility; lack of agency (fear, helplessness, and skepticism in the face of external authority)	Personal moral authority and critical discernment of external authority; expanding sense of moral responsibility; moral agency
3. Relationships	Lack of empathy, alienation, impermeability; lack of concern with justice and not hurting	Empathy, relatedness, permeability; concern with justice and not hurting
4. Meaning of life	Self-referential frames of reference and limited goals	Larger frames of reference as vantage point for critical discernment and self-reflection; life purpose greater than self

upbringing and become a champion for human rights (dimensions 1 and 3). In contrast, Freire focuses on authority, responsibility, agency and social consciousness (dimensions 2 and 3). Among the individuals I interviewed, those who exhibited some level of CC also showed different trajectories, depending on which dimensions became dominant and in what configuration. For example, Jim, an African-American railroad worker and grassroots activist, relates the powerful impact two figures of authentic moral authority (his mother and grandmother), had on his childhood awareness, as well as the centrality of his early relationships. The dimensions of authority-responsibility-agency and relationships appear to be the guiding motivational sources of his adult consciousness.

In every instance of CC, however, all four moral motivational dimensions are present to some degree. The accounts of CC individuals suggest the presence of an undifferentiated moral inclination in childhood which I call intuitive moral sense, or the "better impulses of the heart." They describe early environments which consistently redefined self-interest in moral terms, thus perhaps strengthening the intuitive moral sense.

For example, Paul (Bembow, 1994) recalls stealing a dime from his mother at the age of 7. Although "she was into paddling," she sat down and cried, and talked about the importance of being truthful and consistent (Mustakova-Possardt, 1996). The same manifestly moral and spiritual family environment counteracted young Gandhi's (1927/1983) egocentric self-centered power struggles (Wade, 1996). In Gandhi's single experience of stealing, he was so tormented over time with the burden of his act, that he ended up confessing to his father, expecting corporal punishment. Instead, his father cried, and the memory of that silent encounter did not leave Gandhi throughout his life.

As children, CC people increasingly defined themselves by their moral inclinations, developing closer links between the separate conceptual systems of self and morality (Damon & Hart, 1988). The potential for moral motivation was counterpoised in varying degrees with immediate self-interest, the individual balance in adulthood apparently reflecting the web of interrelated influences of personal history and cultural context. The overall outcome, however, is what Colby and Damon (1992) and Damon and Hart (1988) describe as the progressive formation of a sense of self around a moral center, the bringing together of moral and personal goals, and the gradual expansion of the range of concerns and the extensiveness of engagements.

Levels of Critical Consciousness

In my view, the full range of human social consciousness is a continuum between CC and non-CC along the dimensions of structural development and motivation.

In the period of pre-CC, the four dimensions of moral motivation are formed, and the structural–developmental threshold, discussed earlier, is achieved. Ideally, the period of pre-CC begins in early childhood and reaches into young adulthood. However, if the structural–developmental threshold is not fully achieved, but moral motivation forms, the individual is likely to continue to operate with pre-CC into biological adulthood. If the overall personal history and social environment of the individual foster predominantly expediency motivation, the person seems to embark on a non-CC pathway of adult development. In this case, it is possible that circumstances later in life may stimulate the formation of the moral motivational dimensions and allow the person to grow into the CC pathway. Such circumstances might include meeting people who have a strong impact on one's life, finding oneself in a new and stimulating cultural environment, joining political movements, embarking on a spiritual path, peak experiences, near-death experiences, or any other dramatic event that causes a profound inner reevaluation and transformation.

The three levels of CC, pre-CC, transitional CC, and CC, differ in both motivation and structures of thought; hence, the overall synergistic outcome is a consciousness with significantly different capacities at each level. However, people at each level report a positive, fulfilling experience of social life, and have defined constructive ways to exercise moral agency in their environment. The language in which they describe their lives is earnest, lacking casualness or neutral instrumentality, and often reveals a sense of awe with life.

The possibilities of adult pre-CC are compellingly illustrated by Lin. She is a Chinese American, who came to the United States from Taiwan in her 20s as the wife of a Chinese-American businessman. A humble, quiet, and shy woman in her 50s, she told the simple life story of a devoted mother of two sons, and a woman who had learned to understand and work successfully within a foreign culture, both respecting and appreciating it, and intuitively maintaining a distinct path of her own. Her story included no striking accomplishments or significant activism outside family and work. Yet, as she described the way she made meaning of her place in the world, and the motives that guided most of her choices, I felt like I was in the presence of a sensitive, responsible, and wise human being who did not take surrounding reality for granted, but maintained a critical moral dialogue with it, while striving to act with integrity.

Lin has difficulty understanding social patterns, and political issues confound her. As the example below shows, her intuitive moral sense helps her begin to grasp the moral issues involved in a particular social reality, but as she attempts critical analysis, she has a hard time developing that line of reasoning into a clear causal pattern. Hence, Lin expresses a very limited sense of agency, in spite of which she does not shut off the world that confounds her, but remains engaged in a caring relationship with it, and is responsive to the questions and concerns which arise out of her social context:

> Sometimes war in the world seems to me is created by promoting economic development. In my mind, if you don't use those weapons, a lot of companies will become useless. I was thinking, so many innocent people die, children and all different things happen to them. I just feel sad when there is a war in any country, Sarajevo, Bosnia. I wish there's no war.

Lin's epistemology reveals an interpersonal self (Kegan, 1982) who reasons about social realities in mostly concrete operational terms, does not yet exhibit the abstract operational ability to conceive of a neutral other (Commons & Rodriguez, 1990), and cannot make sense of social reality beyond the most global and dualistic (Perry, 1968) person-to-person patterns:

> I'm very confused about politicians, life. All I wish is peace for the world. But, I don't know. Something happen everywhere, I feel sad about those things. So many children get killed. Even in China we were talking about war, and the people in other country were mean, but Chinese people were pretty cruel too. So that's why I don't understand those things, politics. I think there's always good people, bad people, and one bad person could change a good cause into a bad cause.

Questions about what represents authentic external moral authority—both in public life, and in her personal life—dominate the whole interview with Lin. She also struggles with efforts to define her personal moral authority. In spite of her social–cognitive limitations, she embraces no easy answers, and struggles with poise to bring together conformist values (Wade, 1996), and deeper spiritual values. Lin's evolving sense of social responsibility is best expressed around her choices at work. In her quiet way, she has the power to affect others as a model of moral agency in concrete situations, as the example below shows:

> I'm almost the oldest in the office. Sometimes I stay a little bit longer to make sure all the machines and printers are turned off. Sometimes everybody flies out at five o'clock, with lights on and computers on and network computer and the CD-ROM—and that can be very expensive. So, I want to try to save energy for the office. Be sure the windows are closed, kind of like a mother, housekeeper in there. I try to do a little bit extra. In our office, there are many researchers and mostly very young. And everybody complains about refrigerator not being clean. They'll put a sign like "Please take care of your own things. Your mother's not here." I do things quietly; if I see something spilled or sticky, I just wipe it; it's 30 seconds. Some people will take time to write a note to yell at somebody else. With the same time you can do something constructive without complaining. I'm much older. I feel, if you do a little bit something for other people, clean up a little bit, it doesn't really matter. Nobody have to know. I take care of all the plants in my office. I just take 5 minutes every week, cause I like to have some greenery. I feel if every person can do a little bit for other people, then nobody has to complain or scold others.

The above example illustrates how the basic spiritual values that Lin has internalized (i.e., humility, service, not complaining or blaming), allow her to function adequately and be an agent for positive change, in spite of her difficulty grasping social realities beyond the interpersonal level (Kegan, 1982). The most important principle that guides Lin in all her interpersonal decisions regarding family, work, and the larger world is reflected in the following:

> I think the principle of life is not to hurt other people. Verbally and physically. No matter what reason. And I think it's important not to criticize people behind their back if you want to

settle something. That's important for me. You don't have to please other people all the time, just not to hurt them.

Lin experiences herself as a happy human being who has found meaning in life, and is able to share it with others within her relatively small and protected social world.

Transitional CC marks a breakthrough from pre-CC in that the birth of formal operational thought allows a consistent critical examination of reality from the point of view of Conventional Social System and Conscience orientation (Kohlberg, 1984). At this stage a fully individuated sense of self develops: people are now able to make decisions about choice and agency in the larger world. They are also able to identify increasingly differentiated patterns of interconnections in their social experience, and feel empowered enough to pose questions about perceived contradictions, and enter into dialogue with their social world. Guided by prominent concerns with moral and social responsibility, they initiate interactions with their social environment. These interactions often take the form of positive social work within the exiting system.

People with transitional CC exhibit growing critical discernment, moral introspection, and moral agency, within an ever-expanding social radius of meaningful relationships. They grapple with stereotypes and seek legal ways to address specific forms of social injustice. However, they are still embedded in their sociocultural reality, lack systemic understanding, and operate within conventional sociocultural frameworks, struggling to reconstruct different aspects of the system without being able to encompass the whole. The outcome is a distinctive, yet limited, moral agency for positive social change, partial empowerment, and an ongoing struggle with the contradictory pulls and interpersonal pressure of ideologies. I will illustrate this briefly with the case of Eliot.

Eliot is a Bulgarian dentist and a typical representative of the Bulgarian intelligentsia and its choices under communism. Grounded in a patriarchal family culture, dominated by the authority of strong male figures, he followed the example of his father and grandfather. He used both his education, and later his profession, as a vehicle for resisting political and social pressures, and establishing personal freedom. Each member of his extended family had to deal with some form of social injustice, oppression, or persecution, because of the ideological distrust of communism for professional, educated people. Each stood with courage and dignity, preserved his values and beliefs, and worked hard to survive. In this family, rich in examples of how character is built, accompanied by a high personal moral standard, Eliot exhibits a strong identification with the moral conventions of his family and social class. His life seems dominated by questions about what constitutes his personal moral and social responsibility. Here is how he negotiates these questions with regard to his professional choices:

> In 1992, I decided I had to break away from government medical service and start private practice. I was the first person in the town of Sliven who left a government job, and many colleagues couldn't understand. Today, 5 years later, there are only 5 of us dentists solely in private practice, and 60 who hold both government jobs and private practice. Personally I cannot justify the decision to combine the two. Morally speaking, this is a prerequisite for corruption. Most of my colleagues practice transferring patients they get through their government jobs into their private practice by convincing them that the service they need cannot be done in the government clinic. In addition, they steal materials from the government clinics. I do not want people talking behind my back. I want my clients to come to me because they want my service. . . . Also, if I have to serve 30 people today in the government clinic, I cannot do it up to the standard I want. I don't believe one should work that way.

Eliot's professional life is a story of taking on greater and greater challenges against big odds: insufficiency of current professional information, inadequate material conditions, and the absence of laws which support and foster private practice. He wants to be an innovator in his field, and to change the low public standard which has come to be the unfortunate outcome of socialist free medical service and low paid medical professional work.

Eliot has been politically active since the fall of the communist regime, continuously negotiating a tension between the inclination to protect his well-ordered personal life, and the pull of his moral commitments to public service. In taking on significantly more complex public tasks than Lin, Eliot finds himself more challenged to negotiate between his still apparent self-interest and his sense of moral and social responsibility. He participated in the first antigovernment demonstrations, with substantial risks for his personal and family safety. He offered his organizational competence in the first democratic elections and took on responsible tasks. When recommunization began, he was disillusioned. He commands great personal respect in his town, and was invited to run for mayor. He declined this opportunity to become the enlightened leader that he has the potential to be, feeling that would be too much of a claim on him. Yet, he continues to seek increasingly involved ways to contribute to the social transition under way in Bulgaria. His case illustrates the still incomplete integration of self and morality, characteristic of transitional CC, and its ensuing tensions.

Limitations of space do not allow me to do justice to the complexities of this level of CC, and to the compelling internal struggle I saw in people like Eliot. Such individuals grapple with their incomplete decentering, stereotypical thinking, and internal contradictions, and their intense striving after integrity and consistency. Overall, the tension seems to be negotiated in the direction of less ambivalent and compartmentalized agency, and growing generativity within the larger social world.

The advent of critical consciousness proper is marked by the individual's emerging ability to dereify—and not take as absolute—her entire sociocultural framework. The appearance of this ability is aided by the advent of systemic thinking (Commons & Rodriguez, 1990). Coupled with a progressively more integrated sense of self and morality, systematic thinking allows people to shed more fully their stereotypes and prejudices, and become radical innovators and increasingly empowered moral agents for large-scale social change. People with CC evolve a principled and political vision, which may undergo philosophical and global expansion. Social, moral, and spiritual commitments become increasingly integrated. This level represents the formation of CC proper, i.e., a social consciousness progressively disembedded from its immediate social milieu, engaged in an expanding critical moral dialogue with its sociohistorical world. This is a period marked by the gradual integration of moral motivational dimensions and emerging paradigmatic understanding into an activated depth dimension of existence (Marcuse, 1989b). With it, we see the advent of integrated and interconnected personhood, which shows no compartmentalization of public and private concerns, and a consistent moral agency across domains. The CC pathway culminates in the creation of what Freire (1973) describes as "emancipated subjects"—people who are able to "perceive epochal themes" and "act upon the reality within which these themes are generated" (p. 5).

An example of this level of CC is Jim, the African-American railroad worker mentioned earlier. Jim exhibits empowered and integrated moral agency across all the domains of his life. A liberated, expansive spirit, whose human potential is progressively released, and whose life integrates a wealth of different threads and levels of meaning, Jim, just like Bembow's (1994) activists, talks about being on a path of lifelong growth. He is engaged in meaningful relationships with life on every level. The whole conversation with him was suffused with self-reflection, as he is in a continuous dialogue with himself concerning the purpose of his life.

Jim understands the systemic predicament of black men around him, including his father, but speaks of the ability of a human being to transcend circumstances, and not be defined by them.

> My father was a very productive person up until his mid-20s, and then he began to drink alcohol. He was an alcoholic for a long time. Most of his friends went through the same kind of process, and they're a group of bitter black men. On one level, they had very good lives, and on another level, they probably never reached their potential, and a lot of that had to do with opportunity, basic education. . . . I think that my father was—I can't call him a victim of this system; I think he's a product of it, 'cause I believe you have some control in your destiny, and

> he proved that in his last 20 years of his life. He cleaned up his act.

His own life story is an almost uninterrupted chain of painful encounters with racism and crushing social obstacles which he confronts with spirit and dignity. It is not possible, in this account, to do justice to the courage and positive outlook with which Jim negotiated racism in his educational experiences, in the Air Force, and then in the workplace. He comes strengthened from each encounter—showing little bitterness and sense of victimization, but rather a deepening compassion and an expanding understanding of the human predicament. Jim's vision of social change comes from an understanding of the conditions of ordinary people, and an appreciation of the role of social networks and interconnectedness. He exhibits little separation between moral, personal, and professional life, and no compartmentalization of concerns. His life is a perfect example of what he believes. His home and heart are always open to people. In the crime-ridden and poverty-stricken community in which he lives, he is "kind of like a resource type person": "I'm always the one to get called upon, round the clock." He provides financial and physical help, counsels people, gets men into detox programs, helps them find jobs, connects them to support programs or the right people, etc. His habitual morality makes an appropriate and timely response to someone in trouble a most natural thing. In the workplace, we see him help other black men build their lives and combat racism, without becoming victims overwhelmed by anger; he also evolves a progressively more principled understanding of social justice, transcending the limited point of view of the grievances and interests of his racial group.

> It's not just black people. We've addressed the issue of women, which has been handled, actually, a lot better than the issue of black males. We've addressed the issue that there are other people involved, Asian or other. We can't afford to fight for just black people anymore. We all have to open up the workplace. It has to be an institutional policy, and they can't hide behind all these other subissues.

The example below illustrates Jim's evolving systemic understanding of the interconnectedness of different spheres of life, which moves him into an ever-broadening range of activism:

> I'm a politically involved person. I think that if you breathe air on this planet, at some point, yes, you have to be politically involved. Everything in your life, at some point, has a political impact, whether it be the amount of times they pick up trash on your street, or whether it be the fact that you have a job, and your neighbor doesn't. I think that politics is interwoven into the fabric of life. A lot of people don't want to open their eyes and see this.

Jim's history of volunteer work seems so closely knit into his life that it is hard to separate the two. His life seems characterized by continuously expanding circles of empathy, as he struggles to find deeper meaning in the human experience, and evolves an increasingly complex spiritual life philosophy.

> I love the human race. I think that we're destined to better ourselves at some point. . . . If you read the Bible carefully and listen to what people are saying, the whole human experience can't be for what we're experiencing now. It just doesn't make sense. . . . There has to be a kind of coming together.

CONCLUSION

The Critical Consciousness (CC) pathway illustrates the potential of human consciousness when it evolves around essentially self-transcending universal moral values, such as kindness, generosity, courage, serenity, love, unselfishness, service, goodness, inclusion of broader loyalties together with smaller ones, unity and harmony, and the ultimate unity of truth, beauty, and goodness (Maslow, 1959). The centrality of moral motivation, which gradually evolves into spiritual integration, appears to be a powerful developmental factor requiring broader psychological understanding.

This work suggests that we may be underestimating the human potential for self-transcendence early in life and its capacity to interact with structural development. There seems to be no reason why the study of transcendence should be relegated to the far reaches of adult development (cf. Miller & Cook-Greuter, 1994). Although the full developmental capability for it does not evolve before postconventional thought, we seem to have ample evidence of both the possibility for, and the power of, transcendent frames of reference earlier in life. Further research is needed to explore the phenomenon of the activation of the depth dimension of human experience (Marcuse, 1989b), and the distinctive energy it seems to release into the life span.

These questions pose a significant challenge to the general discomfort rigorous academic researchers have with issues of spirituality. However, I believe that questions about optimal human development can no longer be answered, or even constructively explored without an epistemological shift past scientific compartmentalization and myths of "objectivity" (Aull, 1988). There is a need to place the understanding of optimal adult social and personal development in a broader psychological context—one that unites the discoveries of science with the insights of religion in understanding the nature and essential characteristics of human consciousness. As we explore the kind of global human consciousness which can unite us in the transition to a global peaceful society (Bushrui et al., 1993), it becomes increasingly obvious that the overall examination requires a deeper understanding of human nature itself (Universal House of Justice, 1995).

REFERENCES

Abdullah, S. (1995). Feeding our hunger for the sacred. *Noetic Sciences Review, Winter,* 18–23.

Alexander, C., & Langer, E. (1990). *Higher stages of human development: Perspectives on adult growth.* New York: Oxford University Press.

Aull, B. (1988). The faith of science and the method of religion. *Journal of Baha'i Studies, 1,* 11–23.

Baha'u'llah. (1985). *The hidden words.* Kuala Lumpur, Malaysia: Baha'i Publishing Trust.

Bellah, R. (1985). *Habits of the heart: Individualism and commitment in American life.* Los Angeles: University of California Press.

Bembow, J. (1994). *Coming to know: A phenomenological study of individuals actively committed to radical social change.* Doctoral dissertation, University of Massachusetts at Amherst.

Bronner, E., & Kellner, D. M. (1989). *Critical theory and society: A reader.* New York: Routledge.

Bushrui, S., Ayman, I., & Laszlo, E. (1993). *Transition to a global society.* New York: Oneworld Publications.

Capra, F. (1983). *The turning point: Science, society, and the rising culture.* London: Fontana.

Colby, A., & Damon, W. (1992). *Some do care.* New York: Macmillan.

Colby, A., & Damon, W. (1994). *Social responsibility at midlife: Research plan for 1994–95.* Unpublished manuscript.

Cole, M., & Scribner, S. (1974). *Culture and thought.* New York: Wiley.

Commons, M., & Rodriguez, J. A. (1990). Equal access without "establishing" religion: The necessity for assessing social perspective-taking skills and institutional atmosphere. *Developmental Review, 10,* 323–340.

Cook-Greuter, S. (1990). Maps for living: Ego-development stages from symbiosis to conscious universal embeddedness. In M. C. Commons, L. Kohlberg, C. Armon, F. Richards, T. Grotzev, & J. Sinnott, (Eds.), *Adult development: Models and methods in the study of adolescent and adult thought* (Vol. 2, pp. 79–104). New York: Praeger.

Csikszentmihalyi, M. (1993). *The evolving self: A psychology for the third millennium.* New York: HarperCollins.

Damon, W., & Hart, D. (1988). *Self-understanding in childhood and adolescence.* New York: Cambridge University Press.

Foucault, M. (1984). What is Enlightenment? In P. Rabinow (Ed.), *The Foucault reader* (pp. 32–50). New York: Pantheon.

Freire, P. (1973). *Education for critical consciousness.* New York: Continuum.

Fromm, E. (1989). Politics and psychoanalysis. In S. Bronner & D. Kellner (Eds.), *Critical theory and society: A reader.* New York: Routledge.

Gandhi, M. K. (1983). *An autobiography or the story of my experiments with truth.* Lebanon, TN: Greenleaf Books. (Original work published 1927).

Hoffman, M. L. (1983). Affective and cognitive processes in moral internalization. In E. T. Higgins, D. N. Ruble, & W. W. Hartup (Eds.), *Social cognition and social development: A sociocultural perspective.* Cambridge, U.K.: Cambridge University Press.

Hoffman, M. L. (1989). Empathy and prosocial activism. In N. Eisenberg, J. Reykowski, & E. Staub (Eds.), *Social and moral values* (pp. 65–85). Hillsdale, NJ: Erlbaum.

Hoffman, M. L. (1991). Commentary. *Journal of Human Development, 34,* 105–110.

Jung, C. G. (1933). *Modern man in search of a soul.* New York: Harcourt, Brace & World.

Kegan, R. (1982). *The evolving self.* Cambridge, MA: Harvard University Press.

Kohlberg, L. (1984). *The psychology of moral development: Essays on moral development* (Vol. 2). San Francisco: Harper & Row.

Lahey, L., Souvaine, E., Kegan, R., Goodman, R., & Felix, S. (1988). *A guide to the subject-object interview: Its administration and interpretation.* Cambridge, MA: The Subject-Object Workshop.

Loevinger, J. (1976). *Ego development.* San Francisco: Jossey-Bass.

Marcuse, H. (1989a). From ontology to technology: Fundamental tendencies of industrial society. In S. Bronner & D. Kellner (Eds.), *Critical theory and society: A reader* (pp. 119–127). New York: Routledge.

Marcuse, H. (1989b). Liberation from the affluent society. In S. Bronner, D. Kellner (Eds.), *Critical theory and society: A reader* (pp. 276–287). New York: Routledge.

Marcuse, H. (1989c). The obsolescence of the Freudian concept of man. In S. Bronner & D. Kellner (Eds.), *Critical theory and society: A reader* (pp. 233–276). New York: Routledge.

Marcuse, H. (1989d). Philosophy and critical theory. In S. Bronner & D. Kellner (Eds.), *Critical theory and society: A reader* (pp. 58–74). New York: Routledge.

Maslow, A. (Ed.). (1959). *New knowledge in human values.* New York: Harper & Brothers.

Miller, M., & Cook-Greuter, S. (Eds.). (1994). *Transcendence and mature thought in adulthood: The further reaches of adult development.* Lanham, MD: Rowman & Littlefield.

Mustakova-Possardt, E. (1995). *Critical consciousness and social responsibility among Bulgarian midlifers: Research proposal for the Henry A. Murray Dissertation Award.* Unpublished manuscript.

Mustakova-Possardt, E. (1996). *Ontogeny of critical consciousness.* Doctoral dissertation, University of Massachusetts at Amherst.

Perry, W. G., Jr. (1968). *Forms of intellectual and ethical development in the college years.* New York: Holt, Rinehart & Winston.

Shor, I., & Freire, P. (1987). *A pedagogy for liberation: Dialogues on transforming education.* South Hadley, MA: Bergin & Garvey.

Strauss, A., & Corbin, J. (1990). *Basics of qualitative research.* Newbury Park, CA: Sage.

Universal House of Justice, The. (1995). *The prosperity of humankind.* Haifa, Israel: Baha'i World Center.

Wade, J. (1996). *Changes of mind: A holonomic theory of the evolution of consciousness.* Albany: State University of New York Press.

Weinstein, G., & Alschuler, A. (1985). Educating and counseling for self-knowledge development. *Journal of Counseling and Development, 64,* 19–25.

Wertsch, J. V. (1985). *Vygotsky and the social formation of the mind.* Cambridge, MA: Harvard University Press.

Wuthnow, R. (1991). *Acts of compassion.* Princeton, NJ: Princeton University Press.

PART II

Interrelationship, Intimacy, and Involvement

5.

Relationship and Connection in Women's Identity from College to Midlife

Ruthellen Josselson

When I first began to study identity formation in women back in 1972, I wanted to "find" identity in women in the same terms that Erikson described male identity. I began my 1972 interview by asking, "If there were someone who you wanted to know you, what sorts of things would you tell them about yourself?" I hoped with this question to invite each young woman to explore what aspects of herself she held to be essential to her sense of who she was. I was surprised and chagrined when so many of them offered such responses as, "I'd tell them about my family and my friends," or "I'd tell them about the people who matter to me." This wasn't "real" identity, I thought. Given my schooling in the existing theory of the times, I had expected them to tell me about their occupational aspirations or their ideological positions, the things Erikson said are central to identity. But what all these young women seemed to want to talk about was the people in their lives and,

---

This chapter is condensed and adapted from R. Josselson (1996). *Revising herself: The story of women's identity from college to midlife.* New York: Oxford University Press. A full description of the sample and methodology appears there.

at the time, I still thought this was somehow inferior or dependent or quintessentially female in a shameful way.

In addition, I found, as others (Schenkel & Marcia, 1972) were finding, that issues of religious commitment as well as decisions about sexual behavior were more predictive of "overall" identity status in women than were decisions in regard to occupation and political ideology. Clearly, then, matters of connection to others and to spiritual concerns were weighty matters of identity for women.

This pattern continued. I have interviewed this group of 30 randomly selected college-educated women, at 10-year intervals, from college to midlife. At each interview, as I asked what changes there had been in the last 10 years, most began with what had happened to and with the people in their lives—new intimacies, losses, or illnesses of people they loved, births of children or changes in their needs, or conflicts in relationships with those dear to them. Several women were also prone to begin with changes in their religious commitments—conversions or newfound spiritual expression.

In the intervening 20 years, both I myself and psychology as a field have come a long way in our understanding of women. Psychoanalyst Jean Baker Miller, proposing a new psychology of women (Miller, 1984, 1987, 1988), grounds her thought in the observation that for women, a sense of personhood is rooted in motivation "to make and enhance relatedness to others." And these are precisely the terms my participants have used to define themselves in their ever-changing and complex interplay with others. Identity in women is fundamentally relational. We have come to grasp that, because they are mothered by someone of the same sex, girls grow up feeling more continuous with and less separate from others than boys do (Chodorow, 1978). And we have also come to recognize women's relational embeddedness as a strength that has been deprecated in patriarchal society. I now go back to those early interviews and hear them differently. I hear young women trying to locate themselves with others, to realize themselves in interconnection and to create a "self-in-relation" as Jean Baker Miller has described the course of women's selfhood. As they grew, their locating of self shifted over the years, growing richer and more complex. Their investment in others is never supplanted by occupation or ideology. Instead, work and belief are themselves constructed in relational terms. In a fundamental way, identity is expressed by joining others and taking a unique place within that community. The French existential philosopher Gabriel Marcel viewed identity as "being with," a state for which we have little language. But this is at odds with a culture that tends to locate identity in individuality and lone achievement. (See Gergen [1990] who maintains that "relationships make possible the concept of self. . . . We appear to stand alone, but we are manifestations of relatedness" [p. 170].)

In our highly individualistic age, speaking about connections with others often implies self-abasement, self-denial, or self-abrogation. It is difficult in the vocabulary of the modern age to laud self-definition in the context of relationship. In seeking meaningful engagement with others, women do not seek to depend or submit, but rather to form ever more articulated and multifaceted interconnections which allow for self-expression in a responsive exchange where both self and other are contained, recognized, empowered, valued and enriched.[1] Love becomes a way of delineating the self. In the web of interconnection, a woman locates and expresses herself, knowing who she is in part through those for whom she "is." The yearning for connection is central, maintained through the activities of care and response (Blustein & Noumair, 1996; Gilligan, 1982, 1984; Josselson, 1992).

Identity in women is an ongoing process of balancing and rebalancing needs of the self and investment in the needs of others, an intersection which is so interwoven that it is often foolhardy to ask, "Are you doing this for yourself or are you doing this for others?" The two are often inseparable. Psychological growth in connection involves finding more interesting and challenging ways of being with others, knowing them better (and simultaneously knowing oneself better), discovering more

---

[1] This understanding has formed the core of the work of many women writers (of literature) who have given voice to female experience. Some recent work in the social sciences, however, has also begun to explore the ways in which relational identity configures a woman's life (see Paul [1994]).

precise and meaningful forms of feeling known and validated as oneself, increasing moments of mutuality and bonds of trust, maintaining connection over time and distance, and grappling with the dilemmas of caring for another. Loyalty and fidelity to others become cornerstones of identity.

For this generation of women, however, constituting themselves in relationships has been more an act of creativity than it has ever been for women before. Able to support themselves economically, allowed to "be a woman" in many different ways, these women had the freedom to locate themselves in a wide range of relationships in which their own needs and wishes could be powerful shaping forces. They have given intense thought to possibility, to choice, and to revision. Resisting forces which might subordinate them, these women have sought and worked for relationships of mutuality and empowerment.[2] But such generalizations about women's identity only serve to outline the mold into which identity is shaped. The substance lies in the particular connections women make, in the struggles and gratifications of highly specific relationships. It is to explication of these realms that I turn in the rest of this chapter.

WOMEN AND PARTNERS

The most significant revolution that the generation of women born in 1950 and after[3] have effected in their lives has been the change in their expectation and experience of marriage.

---

[2] For an exploration of the processes of mutuality and empowerment, see the work of members of the Stone Center at Wellesley College, including Jean Baker Miller, Janet Surrey (1987) and Judith Jordan (1986).

[3] The 30 women I have followed for 22 years were initially recruited randomly from the rosters of four colleges and universities in three states. They were contacted by letter and invited to participate in a study of women's development. These 30 represent half of the women in the initial sample. Many participants were lost to me when they changed their names and moved to other places between the ages of 21 and 33. Two also died during this time. All but two of the 32 women who took part in the follow-up at age 33 participated again at age 43. I believe the 30 who remain to be representative of college-educated women in this cohort, but there are certainly other patterns and experiences which are not represented. In this paper, I take the liberty of generalizing in places from my sample of women to the larger generation of which they are a part.

For their mothers, marriage was an economic necessity, a socially demanded life structure for financial survival when independent means of support were largely denied women. Their mothers grew up with the notion that their husbands would be providers while they would have charge of the family. Husbands, then, were valued for their success in provision and were cherished to the extent that they abstained from upsetting and hurtful behaviors such as abusiveness, gambling, infidelity and so on. "He's a good husband," their mothers might have said. "He doesn't run around, he's good to the children, and he comes home at night." But the daughters, the women of this study, witnessed their mothers' subservience and emotional isolation. They saw their fathers as largely absent or, when they were physically present, as relatively silent in the home. Many viewed their fathers as gruff and critical, as men who came home to be physically cared for but emotionally left in peace. Some women saw this pattern of dominance and control in reverse: a demanding, emotionally blackmailing, often depressed mother who kept her husband constantly fearful of her rages and in her thrall. Regardless of which parent was in the ascendant, these women observed between their parents an economic and power arrangement from which flowed the complex dynamics of dependency, which always contain both exploitation and retribution. They may also have observed some affection, but few witnessed between their parents an emotionally engaging relationship of active resonant love. And they vowed to do better for themselves.

In their own marriages, the women I studied were determined to have friendships. They sought men who seemed supportive, interested in them as people, and capable of mutual interchange. Both their own proclivities and the economic necessities of the 1970s led them to share the provider role which set a framework for their equalitarian designs for their marriage. I was struck by how many of the midlife women I interviewed described their husbands as their best friends, people they could count on to talk about their feelings and reactions in life, people they could trust for rock-solid support of their endeavors. "I think we've been incredibly well-suited, been unbelievably lucky," Clara said.

> He's always been there and supportive and loving. I know he thinks I'm wonderful and beautiful. I know he cares enormously about the children. He's a wonderful companion, intellectually, emotionally. My emotions are very on the surface—I cry very easily—he's always been very indulgent. I feel so grateful to have this relationship which is so wonderful, this best friend that I live with, who I can talk to about anything.

Clara is perhaps one of the most happily married, but her experience is not atypical.

Economically capable of supporting themselves, the women I studied valued their husbands as people with whom they shared interests and the ongoing saga of their emotional lives. They betrothed themselves to people with whom they could intertwine themselves but still remain—and be valued as—separate and unique individuals. These were women who shared an educational and occupational history with the men they married. Less segregated by social distance and differentiation of roles than any previous generation, they did not inhabit a different social universe from their husbands. Emily relies on her husband to read her legal opinions. Grace, also a judge, is married to a lawyer and their intellectual sharing is important to both of them, despite trouble between them in other aspects of their lives. And Marlene, as a nurse-midwife, looks forward to swapping patient stories with her physician husband. Although being in the same field can also raise difficulties, a woman's independent professional identity means that couples share rather than divide experiences in the public and private realms of life.

My participants also report relying on their partners for support and encouragement in other aspects of their identities. Betty recognizes that her life-style is made possible by her husband's financial resources, and Andrea acknowledges that she might never have made it to or through medical school without Arnold's reassuring presence. Clara speaks of her husband as always having been the one to push her to greater accomplishment. Their partners provide a secure base from which they explore their competence in the outside world.

Beyond support, partners delimit the personal qualities these women can express easily and what they have to stretch for, thus providing the backdrop for the expression of identity. Andrea, for example, fought her first husband's dependency and inertia by asserting her independence and wish for freedom and adventure. In those days, she described herself as an intrepid explorer, headstrong and reaching for the world. With a more spontaneous and extraverted second husband, Andrea finds herself the one who pulls for more togetherness in the relationship, who asks that they stay home for once. Now she begins to think of herself as someone who loves the pleasures of home and hearth. In part, she has changed, to be sure. But in part, I think she experiences herself differently when her husband contains and expresses different parts of herself. Betty, a very able and resourceful woman, struggles to feel competent next to her gifted, successful husband who, in the early days of their relationship, she had felt she needed to guide. Maria works to maintain her respect for her less ambitious and now-disabled husband and not to allow her own competence to disable him further. Thus, the aspects of herself that come to the fore are in part determined by the qualities expressed by a woman's partner.

Although the women I interviewed tried to select partners with particular personality traits, for most of them, there were surprises. Partners had their own growth and histories which, for better or worse, influenced the course of these women's lives. Being bonded in intimate relationship has meant having to try to change what was malleable and to accept what was not. Natalie wishes her husband "was more social and had more interests," but adapts. Regina had wanted more equality in regard to child care and domestic tasks, but recognizes that for her husband to succeed in his career, he needs more time and fewer demands. She remembers the awful period when he was unemployed and doesn't want to risk inviting such misfortune again. Their relationship is not as she would have had it, but she makes the accommodations she feels are necessary. Integration of identity has meant not only putting the shards of themselves together but also interconnecting their identity with the needs and foibles of someone else. And most participants emphasize that, over the years, they and their partners have come to understand each other more and more.

All but two of the women in my study are in long-term committed relationships. Their husbands (or partners) become a part of them, but they are not subsumed into their husbands' or partners' identities. Their lives are knit together, interwoven in such a way that to think about themselves and who they are in their lives calls immediately to mind an image of their life partner. They experience themselves as moving in tandem with them, together in being and in greeting the future. They carry their husbands or partners "in mind" while having the conviction that their husbands or partners are reciprocally keeping them "in mind." They do not give themselves up to an other but more precisely, they add an other to themselves.

Bonding and commitment ensue from opening themselves to another person, softening their own edges to allow a continuous flow between them. Identity in this relationship requires adapting to the needs and interests of their partner while feeling their own contours complemented by their partners. Many regarded their husbands as stabilizers who checked their own emotionality; others saw their husbands as expressing more of the feelings in the relationship, while they took charge of practicality and reason. Parts of a whole self are bartered, each partner often carrying aspects of the other. One's own self is thereby lodged, in part, in one's mate. The challenge of relationship remains one of balancing self and mutual interests. And this, of course, is an ongoing process of continual renegotiation, adjustments and readjustments in a context of loyalty and mutual devotion.

Where this harmony had been sundered irreparably, these women have gone through the process of disconnection and divorce, and a few among them contemplate that they may yet divorce in midlife. One third of those who were married a first time had divorced and remarried, most of them finding in a second try the mutuality they had missed in the first. Five out of these 30 women continue to live in disappointing or unsatisfactory marriages, valuing the security of companionship, the stability of family, or the comfort of not having to face life alone. They agonize about how much they can compromise—how much they can mute their need for intimacy in the service of maintaining attachments. Like Debbie, they wonder what direction really serves their growth: "If I leave, is that giving up? If I stay, am I giving up? I just don't know."

A woman's ongoing experience of the meaning of her marriage becomes a central aspect of her location of herself in the world—not in terms of her social role as "Mrs. Someone" but as a person trying to understand herself in relation to another.

Children

For the 16 mothers in my sample, their children form a central design in their weaving of identity. Motherhood is such a powerful framework for identity that the having or not having of children is the single most salient distinction among the adult women I have studied. All of the mothers, regardless of their occupational success or commitment, said that their children were the most important aspect of their lives, their self-realization, and their sense of who they are.[4] Aside from severe trauma and life-threatening illness, becoming a mother seems to be the most potent identity-transforming event in a woman's life.

All of the women who became mothers reported undergoing a shocking and unexpected metamorphosis on the arrival of their first child. They felt both an intense emotional pull, more profound than they ever had imagined, toward their child, and more physical exhaustion and loss of moment-to-moment freedom than they had anticipated (see Kaplan [1992]; Oberman and Josselson [1996]). All in all, becoming a mother was cataclysmic, not just a change in role or an addition of duties, but a transformation of desire and emotional organization. All of these women needed time to rearrange themselves and to rework their prior sense of identity with their motherhood now an integral part.

---

[4] Mothers stress the central importance of their children, but they also stress the importance of their mates. Children, during the active mothering years, seem to "feel" more important than husbands, I think, because mothering engages both their competence and their connection and forms an active, insistent part of their lives. Husbands, by contrast, have centrality in being part of the framework rather than the foreground. But I don't think these women ever ask themselves which is more important. Both are utterly defining but in different ways.

Motherhood initiated these women into a new range of emotional expression, unexplored reservoirs of love and care, as well as uncontrollable phases of rage and frustration. They awakened to new experiences of themselves in relationship, now charged with the care of a cherished and dependent being. "I felt things I never knew I could feel," many of them said. Childraising was far from an experience only of caretaking and responsibility. Many discovered in themselves lost springs of playfulness or abandon. And the task of sorting through these feelings, putting them in the perspective of their past and current lives, was a major developmental task. Women got to know themselves differently as mothers, finding wells of capability they never knew they had as well as confronting their limitations in new and painful ways. "I never knew the word *guilt* until I had children and had to deal with what I could or couldn't be for them," Donna said.

The experience of being a mother occurred at two levels. On the one hand, there was the sense of responsibility and care, the often wearying and frustrating routines of looking after children. On the other was the larger sense of relationship, the meaningfulness of connection.[5] The women I interviewed emphasized both of these aspects and their own struggle to bring these two sides of their experience into relation. Here is Jennifer at age 33, with three small children, articulately describing what mothering has meant to her:

> Can I say that motherhood has enriched and diminished me? Sometimes I wonder who I am anymore—then, after 8 hours of sleep or a few hours away from the kids, I feel whole again. Three little ones are a handful. I don't read many books anymore. Our sex life is less often—but great when we have enough energy for each other or when the baby isn't fussing at 10 P.M. . . .

[5] Mary Boulton (1983), in her study of the experience of motherhood, points out the difference between the experience of looking after children and the sense of meaning and significance of having them. The latter emerges on reflection, not so much in the immediate response to interactions of caretaking which may be frustrating and difficult. Similarly, in their cross-cultural study of motherhood, Minturn and Lambert (1964) point out that "few tasks are as harassing as caring for small children and the increased responsibility of other duties is compensated for by the respite from child care" (p. 91). This may in part explain why mothers who work outside the home may have more joy in motherhood than those who do not.

> Constant demands, interruptions, needs of little ones. Nighttime waking. Unpredictability. Illness. Trips to the pediatrician. Sibling rivalry—though this is improving. I feel like I'm running on reserve too often. I need my sleep as never before. I need time for my morning shower and hair washing, just to feel alert and together enough to manage through the day!

Despite the tedium, intrusion, and routine, what has been most meaningful in Jennifer's life—what she has been most proud of—has been her effort "to raise secure, happy, and self-directed kids." Her experience is echoed by all of the other mothers—the paradox inherent in the often hateful daily tasks which are the very fabric of the soul-filling love for their children.

All of these women defined their mothering in contradistinction to the mothering they had themselves experienced. All hoped not to repeat what they felt had been their own mothers' mistakes, but all had to struggle with the negative part of their mothers which they increasingly came to recognize was also a part of themselves. Most spoke with pride about how successful they felt they were in doing things differently. Most saw themselves as more accepting of feelings, more determined to maintain open communication, less critical, and less harshly punitive than their own mothers had been. These women grew up in a psychologically attuned age and all felt themselves to be more sensitive to the implications of their interactions with their children than their own mothers had been.

The identity aspect of motherhood, then, is not the now deprecated sense of being "just a mother," but an effort to become a particular sort of mother with carefully etched values and goals: a good mother, a loving mother, a mother who can offer unconditional love, a mother who tells her children every day that she loves them. Several of the women I have followed are mothers of children with special needs and meeting those particular challenges has formed a cornerstone of their identities. Motherhood is as specific in its role requirements as the highest level professional job, and each woman sets these standards, which form an important new segment of her own identity, when she designs herself as a mother.

A woman's template of the mother she would like to be springs from deeply internal sources rather than social definitions. Certainly, women turn to their contemporary culture for guidelines about what good mothering means; they read the parenting manuals, talk to their pediatricians, and share dilemmas with friends who have children of the same age. But they don't simply appropriate some socially defined role called "mother." The women I studied found motherhood a creative enterprise, a way to give voice to desire, to their wish to experience themselves in a certain way in connection with their offspring. This meant very often struggling with the distance between their ideals of themselves as mothers and their observation of how they found themselves to be in reality. Many worried over their occasional loss of control in which they yelled at their children or slapped them or reacted in an impatient or unkind way. For Harriet, a central focus of her struggle with herself at age 43 was to find a way to stop yelling at her 5-year-old daughter. Each day she wrestled for more patience, chastised herself, analyzed the roots of her anger. She desperately yearned to bring her behavior in line with her image of the mother she wished to be. To a greater or lesser extent, each woman who became a mother spoke of a similar quest. In this struggle, they learn about themselves, about their malleability, about what is core and basic. Having children sharpened their awareness of their own complexity, bringing them knowledge of loving parts of themselves that they had never expressed as well as parts of themselves that they wished were otherwise.

The process of raising children also brought women to the edge of their own flexibility. Mothering evolves constantly as children grow and their needs change. The experience of self as mother, the identity piece of this relationship, was similarly transmuted. Identity as "mother of a toddler" feels very different from identity as "mother of an adolescent." Identity in connection with a child, then, is highly nuanced (although as a culture and in our psychological theories, we have lumped all the phenomena of motherhood together in an undifferentiated mass). These women understand that having become a mother is indelible. One can never again not be a mother. The experience of being the mother that she is of her particular children has its own developmental history which washes over and through everything else that forms a woman's identity.

WOMEN WITHOUT CHILDREN

Having heard all this about the centrality of motherhood in the identities of women who have children, I might have expected women without children to recount tales of loss and absence. But although nearly half of the women I interviewed did not have children, I found little regret among them.

Carolyn Heilbrun observes that "marriage without children at its center, understood as a system of mutual support has largely been beyond the imaginative reach of either biographers or living women" (1988, p. 77). Among my participants are several women who are living this plot, in Heilbrun's terms, although the larger culture remains reluctant to recognize its viability.

Most of the women without children nevertheless sought links to the next generation. Andrea, Emily, and Brenda all were intensely involved with their nieces and nephews, inviting them for extended visits, caring for them, concerning themselves with their well-being. Gwen, a teacher, experienced hundreds of students over the years as surrogate children and made a point of maintaining contact with many of them. These women found opportunities to enjoy the special kind of relationship one can only have with a child. But, in terms of identity, this clearly carried very different weight than for the mothers. These were important and valued relationships, but without the inescapable responsibility or the depth of intense suffusing love and conflict that the mothers reported.

CONTINUING TO BE A DAUGHTER

Being a daughter to their parents remains a highly important identity component even at midlife. Here is another region of experience where the reality of women's lives is not represented well in psychological theory or cultural assumptions. As psychologists, we tend to depict relationships with parents as involving a struggle for independence at adolescence and then necessitating care of aging parents in midlife. But between these marker events there is a long period of adult interaction which the women I interviewed counted as significant in their identity.

All but three of the participants in my study still have at least one living parent. Only a few are caring for ill parents. Throughout their ascent from adolescence to midlife, most of these women have remained connected to healthy and active parents who continue to be important forces in their lives.

Throughout her life, Betty had little emotional communication with her father. But one of her most cherished memories of the past 10 years was a trip she planned to take him to his ancestral home in Russia.

> It was a wonderful experience. I can't say enough about it. To grow up with this Iron Curtain image all your life as a child—this unknown—you just don't know anything at all about where your grandparents came from and what their life was like. . . . And to take my father back was just awesome for me. We both cried a lot.

In taking her father to Russia, Betty experienced a closeness to him that she never had before. And she found a connection with her roots that changed her sense of her own history.

Similarly, Andrea spoke movingly of having taken her mother to the small town in France where she was born. Andrea was grateful to have shared that with her mother, to have had this time of closeness before her mother's sudden death.

When I asked women at age 43 to tell me about what had been the most significant changes for them in the past 10 years, many, like Betty, emphasized episodes of their continuing connection to their parents. In their late 30s and early 40s, many strove to realize themselves and solidify their identity through a modified role in their families of origin, gaining acceptance as independent adults. With pleasure, Millie noted that her parents regarded her and took her for granted as "a middle-aged lady," a triumph for her after having been "the weird one'' from late adolescence through her 20s. For many of these women, an important piece of the "Who am I?" question remained rooted in the answer to "Who am I in relation to my parents?"

As they stood more firmly on their own legs and their path led further and further away from childhood and from home, most experienced an intense need to share the self they created with their parents. But, as was true in adolescence, this was not easy. It often involved struggling for communication across a wide chasm. Regina described this poignantly:

> Whenever I'm with them, I always go through a period of sadness and a desire to withdraw from them because of my disappointment at the lack of emotional intimacy. When we are together, time is spent organizing meals, keeping track of the kids, talking about shopping trips and decorating, but they don't share my life where I feel I really live, and I don't share theirs either. . . . My parents always said, "Whatever you want you can do," but in terms of actually engaging with any of us around life choices, the importance of career or relationships or issues of balancing or making choices, I never remember a single conversation about any of those issues. In terms of religion, my parents have been involved in church for years, but they've never discussed what that means to them. Or I try to talk to my mother about my feelings of disappointment for my son because of the issues he will have to face, and my mother says, "He's doing just fine" and changes the subject. So I feel I've sort of flung my way away from a vacuum in many respects and tried to find ways of engaging with people on a different level and making choices in the absence of specific encouragement and support. [They offer] support in terms of giving a loan if we needed it or helping with moves. But I've had to do life decisions on my own. Yet I'm also aware that they will always be there for me—to provide what they perceive as support. So that's been an issue of tension for me in recent years—trying to reconceptualize my relationship with my family and how that feels.

It rankles Regina that she cannot bring herself to tell her parents that her children were born through artificial insemination because her husband is sterile. Her close friends know, her in-laws know, but to tell her own parents would mean to break through a long-term silence which she does not understand. Still, she was by her mother's side through her mother's recent surgery, spends holidays and birthdays with them, and dutifully calls each week to report on events.

This fundamental orientation to take care of the familial bond—and to keep wrestling with its limits and inevitable disappointments—plays itself out in different ways for different women depending on the unique family circumstances before them. Some women had invited their widowed mothers to live with or near them, which meant having to work out an adult relationship at close quarters. For Theresa and Sandra, the invitation to their mothers to live with them was itself a product of their identification with their ethnic background, a sense of "this is what you do in my culture." In their cases, managing issues of psychological distance and boundaries became a paramount challenge—how to be a "good daughter" and still maintain some autonomy and freedom to live their own lives.

For all the women I interviewed, disruptions in family well-being claim their attention and call them to the pursuit of repair. If someone in their family is sick or worried, they interrupt their other pursuits to agonize about an appropriate response. These women define themselves in part through their efforts to be generative toward their parents, to "be there" for them, to offer them relationship and comfort. They want, for the most part, to see themselves as "good daughters," and they anguish very often over what this entails.

Brenda, for example, strains to find a way to be helpful to her parents who had a hard time recently.

> My father is a strange fellow. I guess that's where I got my being very private from. He doesn't really talk, even to my mother. The roles have changed. Whereas he was always the provider, when they ran into some financial problems, I helped them out, so I think that's kind of. . . . He's very proud and I think it hurt him that he had to come for help. Now he talks to me even less.

Some women are beginning to confront the aging of their parents and preparing themselves to be caretakers. Natalie says,

> I see them getting older. My mother's focus is on what she had for lunch or a golf game, and it's so boring to sit and listen to her. They're failing now and I can see them going downhill. It's very hard. They took good care of me so I will take good care of them. My brother has a family and I don't. I can see that since I'm a girl, there will be more responsibility on me.

Being a daughter-in-law has been another important aspect of identity for many women. Some mention closeness to mothers-in-law which compensates for affection they lack from their mothers. Many are caught up in the family conflicts of their spouses and spend much time and emotional energy negotiating through family battles on their spouse's side. Donna contends with the ongoing tension between her husband and his parents, with whom he works, and the problems of explaining to her children why "grandma and grandpa aren't talking to us" even though they live next door. Betty and Maria are involved in caring for aging in-laws, and others anticipate this prospect in the future. They, too, see care of parents as falling to the girls—this, too, is an element of their identities.

MY MOTHER, MYSELF

For all of these women, relationship to their mothers continues as a central axis of identity definition—even into midlife. Their experience recalls Virginia Woolf's insightful axiom, "We think back through our mothers if we are women." One's mother hovers like an ever-present doppelganger in a corner of one's mind, a ghost in the wings of the stage as a woman enacts her life. A woman's sense of herself is highlighted in counterpoint to her awareness of her mother's choices or style. "I am this way *like* my mother" or "My mother was this way, but *I*. . ." are two primary and pervasive forms of identity experience. (These phrases recurred in just about every interview, at all ages, without my ever having to mention or allude to their mothers.) The sense of "a life as my mother" seems to have been the earliest template for the little girl's imaginings of her future. All else that occurs is revision.

The depth and complexity of this bond surpasses all other connections a woman may have.[6] Women are always, in one way or another, coming to terms with their mothers, with their love for them and their disappointment in them, their admiration and their contempt, with their wish to surpass and their guilt about doing so, their longing for mother's approval and their wish to disavow their need for it.

Many of the women in my study, especially in their 20s, saw themselves as embodying and living out their mothers' unrealized yearnings for worldly involvement and accomplishment, while at the same time recognizing that in the plan for their own lives they were rejecting their mothers' manifest traditional values. They felt that their own occupational success was in some way "for" their mothers but also in opposition to all that their mothers stood for. Most felt their mothers to be most intensely involved in their adult lives through shared concern about family members, particularly their children. Few women mentioned that their mothers were very interested in their work lives. (But these are women whose mothers, for the most part, had little investment in the world beyond their families.)

The more persistent and haunting identifications with their mothers tend to be with their ways of managing emotions and interacting with others. Growing up, these women were exquisitely attuned to their mothers' fearfulness, their flashpoints of anger, their ways of asserting their power with others, their givingness and self-sacrifice. As adults, they compare themselves to their mothers in terms of their courage to take risks, in their forthrightness with feelings, in what they ask for and tolerate from their partners, in how they manage a household, in how much they lose their temper and yell at their children, in taste, in personal habits. Women remain in lifelong internal conversation with their mothers about all of these matters, sometimes only unconsciously, but with conscious manifestations fueling the process of discovering oneself in the context of this ever present bond.

[6] Emily Hancock (1989) also found that transforming the tie to their mothers was the critical factor in women's maturity. See Chodorow (1978) for a theoretical analysis of the mother-daughter bond.

A woman's internal relationship with her mother, rooted in her early experience with her, is also central to her self-esteem. So many of the women I spoke to told me of never having felt "good enough" in their mothers' eyes and of their lifelong struggle to approve of themselves nevertheless. For some, this was the source of a sometimes compulsive need to achieve, often taking the form of a drive for perfection which they only later understood to derive from their mothers' expectations of them. Nancy, for example, came to the realization in midlife that she was repeating with her husband the need to earn approval from a critical person. It was a silent triumph of her adulthood when "I could tell myself I don't have to work all weekend to make the house look spiffy. You know, who cares?"

Beyond this inner conversation, women remain in ongoing outward affiliation with their mothers. At age 33, half of my participants listed their mother as the person they felt closest or second closest to among all the people in their lives. By the time they reached age 43, mother had been surpassed in importance by their spouse and sometimes their children on the list of "people you feel closest to," but she still appeared most often in second or third position. The "separation" from mothers propounded by psychological theory is a highly relative matter for most women who, in reality, stay intensely connected.[7] Several have mothers who, with age, have become increasingly disturbed psychologically; such problems have drawn them into worry and care but has not, in most instances, quelled their need to coax their mothers into continuing to be emotionally available to them.

While some women report feeling estranged or emotionally distant from their fathers, all continue to engage fervently, even in the wake of conflict, with their mothers. A woman remains tempted to bring new self-awareness or subtle changes in perception or choice to her mother for validation. Women, even in midlife, remain absorbed in the project of correcting their mothers' perceptions of them, attempting to bring the

---

[7] Alexandra Kaplan and Rona Klein (1985) discuss the intense connection late adolescent college women retain with their mothers. Despite conflict, most college women continue to regard their mothers as their "best friends."

relationship with their mothers in line with who they have become (see Apter [1990] for a deeply perceptive analysis of the mother–daughter relationship in adolescence and beyond). The earliest self emerges in the encompassing shell of a mother's embrace, and so it continues forever after. The intricacy of a woman's connection to her mother is so profound and far-reaching that I have come to the conclusion that one can learn more about who a woman "is" by knowing about her relationship to her mother than knowing any other single aspect of her life. Whatever a woman is, in a deep psychological stratum of her being, either pays homage to or disavows her mother.

FATHERS

Few women maintain emotionally intense relationships with fathers that approach their level of involvement with their mothers. Most have warm and affectionate relationships with their fathers, but few list their father as someone they feel "very close" to or describe him as someone with whom they make efforts to share themselves deeply. Some women, particularly those who are in troubled relationships with their mothers, mention valued, loving connections to their fathers whose company they enjoy, whose support they cherish. These women are more likely than the others to have clearly articulated relationships with their fathers, ones not mediated by the overshadowing presence of their mothers. Clara, who has largely given up on having a good relationship with her "difficult" mother, cherishes her father for the love and closeness he has always offered her and tries to repay him with her concern and involvement in his interests. Overall among these women, however, relationships with fathers tend to be simpler bonds, much less wrenching and tumultuous, much less emotionally piercing than connections to mothers.

Fathers seemed to have had a more important role in these women's identities in their adolescence. For many, fathers were the authorities in the home, the makers of the rules. Their adolescent struggle was to negotiate their independence from his control or to maintain his good opinion while making their own choices. Once this battle was past, the involvement with fathers seemed to diminish. Throughout their 20s and 30s, their fathers' influence dims and fathers start to be subsumed into their mothers as part of "my parents."

Many women at midlife report that they have begun to establish a relationship "as adults" with their fathers, venturing to have real conversations or to share parts of themselves with their fathers which they never had before. For some women, growing into their 40s has brought them to a place where they can try to know their fathers as people rather than as distant and mysterious authorities. Betty, for example, regards the trip she took with her father—and crying together with him—as an indelibly important moment in her life.

SIBLINGS

None of the women I interviewed has created in her adult life anything resembling the extended family groups in which many of them grew up. For many of my participants, the family life of their childhoods encompassed aunts, uncles, cousins, and grandparents, all living close together. Many had three or more siblings. "Family" for them was a kind of community tribe of belongingness which they experienced, in most cases, both as loving and confining.

By contrast, most of the women I interviewed live far from most or all of their siblings, and although they may try to maintain kinship connection through visits and shared vacations, none offer a "family compound" to their own children. This change has meant having to recast themselves in different terms of belongingness, rooting connections to others in different phrasing.

The greater openness of society and the availability of choice has meant that sibling groups have often taken quite different paths. Those whose adult identity is very different from what they grew up with feel themselves often at a great distance from their siblings. Regina, a professor, is the only one of the children of her family to have gone to college. "I don't think the members of my family process life the way I do," she says, "especially my sister who tends to be flighty and exuberant, and I doubt she has the same questions and concerns that I do. I have an older brother who still lives with my parents and he keeps very much to himself." But once her children were born, she found more to share with her sister who had herself raised four children.

Maria's brother has had massive financial problems and Maria worries that her parents' continuing to bail him out will leave them financially stranded in the future. There are always crises with him. Sometimes she feels that she is the only one who can talk to him and she struggles with how to be of use. For many women, shared worry about a sibling becomes a focus of continuing family connection.

A few have brothers and sisters who they feel are enough like them to have a deep interconnection based on mutuality—Laura's sister, for example, has been her best friend all her life. Some of the women I interviewed have developed real friendship with their brothers and sisters as adults and maintain bonded and meaningful, though usually infrequent, ties. Clara grew intensely close to her younger brother after his daughter's death—an event which pulled all the siblings into closer touch. Natalie feels close to her brother, feels she can really talk to him or could turn to him if she had a problem, but he is preoccupied with his own family and seems to have little time for her.

Most of the women I interviewed, however, more or less mechanically and more or less affectionately, go through the motions of attachment with siblings whose lives have been patterned quite differently from their own. But they continue to rely on their siblings to "be there" (and they expect themselves to "be there" in return) in case of crisis or need.

FRIENDSHIP

Friends are a source from which identity possibilities spring, and they provide an audience for the woman who wants to "try on" different ways of being. Friendship has most impact on identity when women are in the process of defining or revising themselves. Friends help women explore themselves and envision who they might be. (Women may be who they "are" with men, but they "try out" who they might be with other women.) Friends are charged with being a sounding board and helping to painstakingly examine all the nuances of a problem or decision. And friends are there to compare and contrast the self: How are you? How am I? Women often sharpen their boundaries against the experiences of their friends and may come to regard themselves in a new way. Within the bonds of friendship, women may achieve insight into themselves and muster courage to make changes. It was through a deeply intimate conversation with an old friend that Alice came to rethink her childhood and to grasp the dysfunctional nature of her family. Similarly, Andrea came to the decision to divorce her first husband after vicariously going through the divorce process with a friend.

But once launched on a path, women have less need of and less time for friendship. Enveloped in the tasks and primary relationships of their lives, women rely on friends more for companionship and recreation, and this is, in general, low on the list of priorities.

In college, friends seemed to constitute "the world." Locating themselves as funny, brave, wild, shy, open, snobbish, prudish or honest—all this took place in the community of friendship. It was through friends that these women discovered who else was "out there" which, in turn, made it possible to know better who was "in here." Enjoying and enlarging themselves through the association with different types of people, people of different backgrounds and ways of thinking, finding themselves in those they could feel similar to, and distinguishing their own uniqueness in contrast to those whom they could disparage or reject—these were the surfaces against which women honed and polished their identity. But this process began to taper off after college and into adulthood. By the time they were in midlife, women tended to seek constancy and validation rather than stimulation and challenge, and therefore tended to maintain stable, close long-term friendships rather than to welcome new connections. Where friends represented possibility for change and growth in the college years, in midlife, they were asked more to provide support and companionship.

In the realm of friendship, many of these women were also pioneers. Many spoke of having grown up in homes where her mother's friends were her sisters or sisters-in-law. Having real friendships from outside of the family was a novel—and sometimes radical—idea within the subcultures they came from. Theresa, for example, takes pride in having a wide circle of relationships, so much in contrast to the fear of strangers that dominated her family. Brenda, who counts her cousins among her closest friends, thinks of herself as having "branched out a little over my mother's age group where her friends are her sisters."

As women grow, they become more exacting in their requirements of friendship and more clearly delineate superficial friends from emotionally intimate, enduring ones. Although many say they have many acquaintances, most regard only two or three people as "friends." As Regina put it, "I place a much greater emphasis on emotional intimacy than I did in previous years. In adolescence and early adulthood, I had a much wider circle of friends than I do now. Yet the relationships I do develop tend to be enduring, meaningful ones." Some have maintained long-term friendships, from college or before, with people who they feel they have known and have known them for a long time. They are therefore witnesses to each other's growth. These friends, although they often live far from one another, pick up the relationship as soon as they meet again and usually share fully with each other, keeping track of what they have become, what they have learned about life. In addition, these are friends my participants feel they could call upon for help in a crisis, that they, like family members, would "be there." Other women develop friendships out of a common work situation, where daily struggles can be shared and explored. Still other women feel that they have retreated from friendship, some out of disappointment and a sense of betrayal from friends, some out of lack of time, some because intimacy with sisters or sisters-in-law takes the place of closeness to friends. There is no common pattern, except that all of the women I have interviewed say that friendship has been very important to them and that friendships are harder to develop as one grows older (see O'Connor [1992] for a complete review of friendship among women). As women become more centered in family life, they often reflect nostalgically on time spent with friends, wishing they could make space for it but, with a sigh, let it lapse into the realm of what is postponed for later. "Maybe as my children grow up I'll have more time to foster deeper friendships. I feel like I see friends as I'm flying from one thing to another," said Millie. Some women make a serious effort to keep these connections alive, planning regular get-togethers with friends from distant states or scheduled lunches with those nearby. But this requires effort and is seldom the spontaneous togetherness they had known in earlier days. Harriet had recently organized a "pajama party" for several of her close friends from work. "It was fun, but I miss having a best friend," Harriet said.

For Clara, crisis in friendship led to a rethinking of her values and identity, of how she wanted to live her life. The past few years had been overshadowed by living through the dying of her closest friend and trying to be consoling to her friend's 8-year-old daughter. And this worry and involvement occurred just as Clara was beginning to work in the rare books collection of the Yale Library, and was trying to balance her increased professional investment with the needs of her two young children. Clara took her friend to her chemotherapy, visited her, brought her meals, and was with her most of the week before she died. "It just seemed like the sort of thing you'd do for a good friend," Clara said.

> One of the things that troubles me about the way the world has evolved is that women have so little time anymore to give to their friends and I have these moments of having nostalgia for the 50s when women had time. I can't even think of anyone to put down as an emergency backup person on my children's school cards. I was lucky at the time to have a job that was flexible. I'm a fiercely loyal person and it's very hard for me not to be there if my friends need me.

Clara has decided that she does not want to allow her work and family commitments to preclude being the kind of friend she wants to be.

Women who are without partners are more likely to turn to friends for companionship, and this often involves complex cycles in relationships with long-term friends. Gwen charts her life parallel to the life course of her closest friend, Edna. Raised on a farm, she looked to Edna, who was raised in the city, to expose her to "cultural things." "It was a very important part of my life," Gwen said of her friendship with Edna:

> But we have had a very cyclical relationship. When I got married and she wasn't, we kind of strayed and then when we both were married, we came back together. Then she got divorced and we kind of separated, didn't have things in common, then when I was divorced we did a lot together. But now that I'm engaged I don't see her as much.

Women in a period of actively redefining their identity are most likely to turn to friends for input, feedback, response and support. Marlene, when her first marriage was in tatters, full of dread and uncertainty about her future, turned to a group of women in a women's collective who supported her in mapping a plan for herself. Donna, now in the process of trying to anchor herself, is similarly looking to other women to help her reorganize, to show her a way. She speaks of her search for the "wise woman" who could guide her toward her "feminine energy" and help her learn to nurture herself. Having renewed her attention to who she is, in quest of who she would like to be, she relies on friends for:

> Seeing how I interact, seeing the effects of things I might say to people, and really wondering why somebody said something and trying to receive what has been said, and feeling it enough to respond and find a response, really trying to understand a lot about a person's intentions and their true actions, . . . finding a space to express myself.

Donna felt drawn toward women who seemed to know how "to take care of themselves." From them, she hoped to learn how to take care of her own needs. She appreciated her new close friendships with women for the opportunity to explore "the differences in the way women have actualized who they are" and to "deeply look at things from all perspectives." Donna was turning to friendship, much as people did in adolescence, to help define herself.

INTERNAL REVISION

The most profound revisions of identity for the women I have studied are internal. They involve making meaning and thinking about the self in new ways, fundamental transformations in experiencing life. Women describe these moments of change as "awakenings," knowing in a new way what they have in some ways known all along.

As Donna reflected on the unfolding of her life from age 43, dividing her life into chapters, she noted, "from chapter to chapter, there is an increasing consciousness." This seemed to me true of all the women I interviewed. Going through the process of thinking aloud about their lives, most women found themselves lacking the words to tell me about the deepest sense of their revision, but all spoke in one way or another about "increasing consciousness."

Clara, struggling for words, said, "[These experiences] have opened a window into what other people feel. All these experiences just make you understand so much more." Understanding so much more, opening up more, having more confidence are the ineffable revisions these women tried to describe to me. The memorable turnings of their lives are ones that allowed them to look upon the world with expanding vision and to know better their own connection to it—in short, an expansion of meaning making, a growth, perhaps, in wisdom. This involved learning about the compromises and inevitabilities of life. For some, new awareness centered on coming to terms with disappointments in the work world, recognizing that one could not do all one wished or that work itself was often dull or unrewarding, or seeing possibilities of effectiveness that they hadn't known were there. For others, a shift in or loss of an important relationship was a catalyst to revisit their idea of themselves. Sometimes gaining a new relationship, as in motherhood, was the force that turned the kaleidoscope.

Increased psychological awareness led them to regard more seriously the importance of their own emotional needs. Having learned very often in childhood that feelings were to be put aside, controlled, or ignored, or having learned that pleasing others took precedence over consideration of one's own desires, many women came to greater appreciation of the parts of themselves contained in emotional response. They grew to embrace their anger as well as their tenderness, their guilt, their sadness, their pain, and their joy. As Andrea tried to summarize the essence of her sense of revision, "I have grown to be more aware of myself and my feelings than ever before."

For other women, the increase in consciousness was woven into their understanding of relationships. Many spoke of their quest to know better what love is, their effort to know if the intense feeling they had for their husbands, for example, was "really love" as it seems to be depicted by the culture. Some were aware of passionate longings that went unfulfilled, desire which they let themselves know about but kept from acting on in order not to dislodge or jeopardize other commitments they treasured. Others spoke of growing into a greater understanding of motherhood, both its rewards and its limitations, all they discovered they could feel and the perfection they could not embody.

Most of these women felt that as they aged, they could understand better their own life course. Many had to get distant in years from their childhood in order to be able to see how it had shaped them. For some, this understanding involved becoming critical of their childhood parents and seeing themselves as mistreated or oppressed in some way. Even the more disorganized and less certain women spoke of greater understanding of their early lives and their mission to make a self that is not crippled by whatever the noxious conditions were. The image of the "inner child" was appealing to some as a way of reclaiming what felt authentic and unsullied, bringing forward an innocence that had not bent to their family's harmful influence.

On the other hand, insight also involved new understanding and forgiveness of their families of origin. Many of the women I spoke to mentioned that they were now at an age where they could remember their mother at the same age. Suddenly, their own mothers began to make a new sense to them. They began to see their mothers as women in their own right rather than idealized embodied spirits of perfection or as vilified images of imperfection. They seemed to conceptualize in a new way the essential humanity and private subjectivity of their own mothers—"a woman just like me."

As growth unfolds and life progresses, the most far-reaching modifications and revisions are in the way a woman positions herself in regard to others. But these revisions exist in a felt sense of the self, an orientation to one's place in one's world and they are inordinately difficult to put into words. We seem best able to describe relationships when they are in conflict, when someone is angry or feels wronged and mistreated. It seems to be nearly impossible to describe the course of learning about relationships and developing satisfactory ones without sounding pious. This is in part because we have so little vocabulary for relationships and the words we do possess have all taken on sentimental greeting-card associations.

Changes in orientation to relationship and the location of the self within relationships are even harder to articulate. These revisions involve a gain of knowledge about how people are together, an increase of complex awareness, an appreciation of the nearly unfathomable variability in the ways we humans orient ourselves with each other. Women spoke to me of this in terms of "keeping it all in balance," or "taking account of myself *and* others." What these women were undertaking was redoing their connections with an effort to keep both self and other in focus.

This revision is ongoing. In midlife, these women are each day refining this understanding, moving backwards and forwards, now churlishly demanding their own way, now resentfully doing what others want, but more and more articulating the self with others, struggling to maintain empathy, respect, and authenticity.

OUTWARD INVESTMENTS

Beyond the self and its relations with others lies the realm of purpose and dedication to something larger, something beyond immediate concerns. Those women who had found purpose to their lives in allegiance to some cause or goal seemed to be among the most vital and engaged of all the participants in this study. Millie, for example, in her sense of religious calling or Fern's dedication to helping the underprivileged exemplified women consecrating themselves to some larger meaning system. But this kind of investment was rare.

While nearly all of the women I interviewed stress the importance of moral *values* (beliefs), few have engaged in moral *purpose* (action) that reflects concern for the larger social good. For those few, such commitment evolved out of their awareness of needs beyond the self, sometimes deriving from religious conviction, sometimes arising out of work tasks. And it seemed not to take shape until some time in their late 30s, after the occupation of tending to the self and others close at hand had waned a bit. Some were aware of the stirring of these wishes but pled lack of time. Alice, for example, wants to devote herself to environmental causes but the demands of her teaching and her family keep her from taking on more. Perhaps this larger ethicality and breadth of vision still awaits many of these women who have yet to discover, like Millie, that "you truly find yourself by giving yourself away."

SPIRITUALITY

For many, the quest to better understand themselves and their place in the world contained a spiritual dimension as well. Spirituality is another form of identity that is grounded in connection, a sense of embeddedness, larger and more ethereal perhaps, but a tie to some force larger than the self. The movement from childhood's concrete forms of religiosity to adult spirituality is a profound process of renewed understanding of oneself in relation to others and to finding meaning for one's life.

Half of the women I interviewed define themselves in an important spiritual way. For some, religious conviction feels like an unbroken line since childhood; others left off their belief in or practice of their religion of childhood only to take up some strong religious commitment later. Fern and Millie, both Catholics, regard all their actions as emanating from some higher power. They feel "called" to be what they are. For Fern, this has been an unbroken faith since childhood, but its quality has changed as she grew from adolescence into midlife:

> I have become more prayerful or deeper, the quality of it has changed. I don't know how people manage to exist without some form of faith. . . . I wonder how they are a complete person without it. At least I am too vulnerable not to have something to fall back on. As an individual, I can fall back on George or the kids or friends, but there are things about myself that I need to fall back on, something that is larger than them.

Millie had left the Church and any form of religious commitment for 15 years after college, then found herself "called" back to work for the Church and to resume her faith.

Edie, following a series of personal crises after college, found her need "for a richer and more meaningful spiritual life" met by an Eastern religious group. At age 33, she described her religious commitment as a way of life involving daily meditation, vegetarianism, chastity, and following the commandments and advice of the spiritual leader. As she grew into midlife, however, this commitment became less rigid as a system for controlling her behavior and more a sense of a "path," a means of "recognizing God and striving for truth and honesty in living."

For other women, spirituality was an additional form of connection in their lives rather than a force in organizing themselves. Regina, for example, says:

> I am a very spiritual person. I think about those issues on a daily basis—the meaning of death, of life, and relating to God spiritually. I think of my religious experience as a deepening of my relationship with God. Religious practice is a way of opening channels within my self to broader spiritual experiences and broader connections with other people rather than rules that I have to subscribe to.

But these expressions of deep religious commitment or spiritual reflection occur in a minority of the interviews. Some women take up religious commitment as a form of community, joining with others in shared ritual, maintaining tradition, feeling an increased sense of belonging. Some define their spirituality in individualistic terms, working out their relationship to nature, to ethics, to higher forces in existential and universal terms, thereby articulating their identity as a person in the larger scheme of things. Spirituality serves as ideology, a moral force which grounds them and helps them define what is "good." For many of these women, this is an even more consuming quest than occupational self-definition.

Many of the more pragmatic women who had defined their identity paths in late adolescence, had thrown off their childhood religion and found self-expression and meaning in their work and their relationships. They sought for the good in this world. In *Middlemarch,* George Eliot explores the growth of identity in her characters through the unfolding of their spiritual development. She says, "By desiring what is perfectly good, even when we don't quite know what it is and cannot do what we would, we are part of the divine power against evil . . ." (p. 393). This seems to give voice to what many women tried to tell me about their own effort to find themselves in relation to their desire for the good—in their desire to be good wives, good mothers, good friends, good people. The search to know what good is and the quest for the personal means to implement it, often in what Eliot later terms "unhistoric acts," this is what is central to a woman's identity.

REFERENCES

Apter, T. (1990). *Altered loves.* New York: St. Martin's Press.

Blustein, D. L., & Noumair, D. A. (1996). Self and identity in career development: Implications for theory and practice. *J. Counseling and Development, 74,* 433–441.

Boulton, M. G. (1983). *On being a mother.* London: Tavistock.

Chodorow, N. (1978). *The reproduction of mothering.* Berkeley: University of California Press.

Eliot, G. (1972). *Middlemarch.* London: Folio Society. (Original work published 1871)

Gergen, M. (1990). Finished at forty: Women's development within the patriarchy. *Psychology of Women's Quarterly, 14,* 471–493.

Gilligan, C. (1982). *In a different voice.* Cambridge, MA: Harvard University Press.

Gilligan, C. (1984). The conquistador and the dark continent: Reflections on the psychology of love. *Daedalus, 113,* 75–95.

Hancock, E. (1989). *The girl within.* New York: Fawcett Columbine.

Heilbrun, C. G. (1988). *Writing a woman's life.* New York: Ballantine.

Jordan, J. (1986). The meaning of mutuality. *Work in Progress.* Wellesley, MA: The Stone Center.

Josselson, R. (1992). *The space between us: Exploring the dimensions of human relationship.* San Francisco: Jossey-Bass.

Kaplan, A., & Klein, R. (1985). The relational self in late adolescent women. *Work in Progress.* Wellesley, MA: Stone Center Working Paper Series.

Kaplan, M. M. (1992). *Mothers' images of motherhood.* London: Routledge.

Miller, J. B. (1984). The development of women's sense of self. *Work in Progress.* Wellesley, MA: Stone Center Working Paper Series.

Miller, J. B. (1987). What do we mean by relationships? *Work in Progress.* Wellesley, MA: Stone Center Working Paper Series.

Miller, J. B. (1988). Connections, disconnections and violations. *Work in Progress.* Wellesley, MA: Stone Center Working Paper Series.

Minturn, L., & Lambert, L. W. (1964). *Mothers of six cultures: Antecedents of child-rearing.* New York: Wiley.

Oberman, Y., & Josselson, R. (1996). Matrix of tensions: A model of mothering. *Psychology of Women Quarterly, 20,* 341–360.

O'Connor, P. (1992). *Friendships between women: A critical review.* New York: Guilford.

Paul, E. L. (1994). The complexities of a young adult woman's relational world: Challenges, demand and benefits. In C. E. Franz & A. J. Stewart (Eds.), *Women creating lives: Identities, resilience and resistance.* Boulder, CO: Westview Press.

Schenkel, S., & Marcia, J. E. (1972). Attitudes toward pre-marital intercourse in determining ego identity status in college women. *Journal of Personality, 3,* 472–482.

Surrey, J. (1987). Relationship and empowerment. *Work in Progress.* Wellesley, MA: Stone Center Working Paper Series.

6.

Loving with Integrity: A Feminist Spirituality of Wholeness

Jennifer L. Rike

Violence and the terror it breeds headline our news reports daily in America. Social services in cities from coast to coast are overwhelmed by the numbers of victims; our criminal justice system is overwhelmed with the number of prosecutions it must handle; our prisons are overwhelmed with the number of prisoners they must warehouse. Communities demand that government officials find solutions. State and federal governments respond by scrambling to enact stricter gun control laws to inhibit the most egregious outbreaks of violence, and to beef up police forces. Slowly, the realization is sinking in of the enormity of the problem and the total incapacity of such external solutions to resolve it. Violence, as the original sin of postmodern Western society (Suchocki, 1994), is the fount of most other sins: It is both effect and cause of other acts of violence, as well as many other problems—addictions, depressions, and a large proportion of the accidents and illnesses plaguing us. Violence perpetuates itself through a dreadful and devastating cycle in which victims become perpetrators who create more victims who perpetrate.

Clearly, there is no easy solution to this abysmal state of affairs, and yet there are resources within the Judeo-Christian traditions on love for developing one. Too often the Christian has construed such Biblical passages as "if anyone strikes you on the right cheek, turn the other also; and if anyone wants to sue you and take your coat, give your cloak as well" (Matt. 5:39–40) to enjoin total nonresistance to violence. But such an interpretation ignores the original context of Jesus' sayings, as well as the truth about total self-sacrifice. For instance, a strike on the right cheek would have to be administered with the left hand, but in the Jewish society of Jesus' time only unclean tasks are performed with the left. Such a blow would be a back-handed slap—not a physical attack but an attempt to insult and humiliate. To respond by turning the left cheek is to resist by making it logistically impossible to back-hand again with the left or the right (Wink, 1992, pp. 103–106). Jesus called his followers not to total nonresistance but to creative nonviolent resistance to violence.

The issue is not, should we resist violence with more violence or should we be pacifist? It is, rather, how can we resist violence nonviolently and creatively, in a way which will stop its dreadful cycle and heal victim-perpetrators from its debilitating after-effects? I believe that Christian love, when properly conceived and put into practice, can do just that. Unfortunately, the healing dynamics of Christian love have been misconstrued and submerged through centuries of controversy, but the prospect of retrieving them and reappropriating them in light of more adequate understandings of human development and relationality has reemerged. Since it is obviously impossible to realize this task of retrieval and reconstruction within the confines of a single chapter, I propose here to develop only the chief criteria and fundamental dynamics of the Christian concept of love in terms of care.

To rush into the fray proclaiming that the solution to violence lies simply in surrendering oneself to the Christian call to love is guaranteed to provoke the justified outrage of virtually any victim. For the chief paradox of religion is that religion has been used to promote violence as much as to resist it, and the Christian traditions on love are hardly exempt from this. Feminist theologians, including myself, have recognized that the healing dynamic of love has often been subverted by the traditional concepts of Christian *agape* and *caritas*, and we have attempted alternative solutions before (Farley, 1977; Harrison, 1986; Rike, 1996a). Unfortunately, prior attempts to formulate how Christian love, properly understood and practiced, can stop violence have failed to recognize that the foundational criterion of any conception and praxis of love must be integrity. To properly conceive the solution to violence, one must understand that violence splits a person's psyche, and destroys one's ability either to act with integrity or to promote that ability in others. To be unable to act with integrity is, in effect, to be incapable of loving. Love is essentially the power which enables a victim-perpetrator of violence to reconnect that which has been split apart, and to transform that which was once split into something new and good in the process.

In 1960, Valerie Saiving (1979; Plaskow, 1980) criticized Anders Nygren's and Reinhold Niebuhr's emphasis upon the self-sacrificial character of Christian *agape,* charging that it disclosed an androcentric bias devastating to women. Her seminal work signaled the beginning of the feminist theological movement, and inspired countless works investigating the harm androcentric spiritualities and theologies can effect in women. Today, the feminist movement is divided into many camps, and yet feminists are united by their commitment to promoting the well-being or wholeness of women. They believe that the institutions of Western society are organized according to a gender–sex system which thoroughly penetrates the symbolic and institutional contexts in which identity develops, and that this system creates and reinforces various modes of violence toward women. My ultimate goal is to explore the dynamics of these modes of violence against women in order to discover the way to eliminate them. In this I seek to promote the wholeness of women as well as of men. That eliminating violence against women will promote the wholeness of both genders is key to my argument, and distinguishes my project from the rest.

Today, many feminist academics are engaged less with the issues of violence than with the difficult enterprise of determining what difference being a woman might make. They tend to split into two camps—the cultural feminists who think it is possible to determine some essential feminine nature, and the poststructuralist feminists who insist that all gender differences are simply social constructions. I propose instead to leave questions of root causes and essences aside, and to follow Linda Alcoff's positionalist alternative. Alcoff suggests that we explore the differences that the "complex of habits, dispositions, associations, and perceptions" being engendered female makes (Alcoff, 1988, p. 424). This methodology makes possible the tasks of elaborating the differences gender has made for Western theologians engaged in reinterpreting the Christian traditions on love, and of exploring the ways these traditions might be perpetrating further violence upon women.

My immediate goal in taking on these tasks is to explore the psychodynamics of the cycle of violence in order to discover a way to stop it and to enable its victim-perpetrators to heal. In particular, it is to elaborate the dynamics of splitting and healing somehow anterior to or independent of gender difference—dynamics women and men share and yet tend to manifest differently. I am motivated by the thoroughly feminist desire to promote the wholeness of women, but unlike many other feminists, I believe that stopping violence against women requires exploring its dynamics not only within men but within women themselves. Both men and women participate in the cycle of violence, and both must resist it and heal from it for either to achieve the wholeness we all yearn for (Rike, 1996b).

INTEGRITY IN PHILOSOPHICAL, PSYCHODYNAMIC, AND FEMINIST PERSPECTIVE

The concepts love and integrity are central to the Biblical traditions, but their interconnections are rarely recognized or explored. Considering that the concept of love is commonly used to sum up the Christian gospel, while the metaphor for faithful action in the Hebrew Scriptures is "walking with integrity with/before God" and its variants (Gen. 17:1; Deut. 28:9; 18-19; 1 Kings 2:2-4, 3:6, 8-23, 25; Ps. 26, 84:11, 101:2; Prov. 10:9, 14:2, 19:1, 20:7, 28:6), this is odd indeed. On those rare occasions when the relationship between Christian love and integrity is actually explored, the tendency to oppose them to one another predominates: to act with integrity is to act consistently in accordance with a set of rules or principles in order to maintain one's own moral rectitude; in contrast, to love is to sacrifice oneself for the other without concern for either rules or one's own state of moral rectitude (Stendahl, 1976, pp. 52–67).

This tendency to oppose integrity to love is fundamentally misguided. Philosophers and theologians alike have forgotten the deepest meaning of the term *integrity,* a meaning suggested by its etymology. The word *integrity* comes from the Latin *integritas,* meaning wholeness, soundness, which (like integral and integrative) comes from *integer,* untouched, whole, entire. To have integrity is to possess the mode of unity or wholeness proper to one's nature.[1] It is relatively easy to recognize whether a piece of fruit or an animal is whole because their natures are usually defined chiefly in terms of their physical presence, and so their state of wholeness is readily discernible. But it is quite problematic for human beings because one has to factor in freedom. A person may be lacking an eye or a limb but still be deemed whole because of the dynamic of receptivity and responsivity to all dimensions of himself and others that he exhibits, while a person may be in superb physical shape and yet be so inappropriate in responding to himself and others as to be deemed quite lacking in wholeness, fragmented. Conceiving the human mode of wholeness properly is essential to understanding the true meaning of both integrity and love, and to this task we now turn.

Recently moral philosophers seem to have forgotten about the connection between acting with integrity and the distinctively human mode of wholeness. They commonly understand integrity rather narrowly, in terms of the moral integrity which requires that one maintain one's commitment to act in accordance with certain moral rules and principles or to act in ways which promote certain values and goals, even under unpleasant or adverse conditions (Halfon, 1989, pp. 4–17). But they fail

[1] *Wholeness* is an analogical term: it has many, interrelated meanings. In fact, it is a variation on one of a small class of inherently analogical terms found in every known sphere of discourse—the transcendental terms. Minimally speaking, the term *wholeness* expresses *oneness,* the concrete unity or completeness of an entity. To have integrity is to be unified and whole in the manner appropriate to the entity under consideration.

to consider how such moral integrity bears an essential relation to the fully personal integrity which results from continually striving to become whole. Maintaining one's commitments will certainly tend to unify one's life into a continuous whole in which one's activities are ordered by these values and goals, but not necessarily.[2] For instance, if one were to live according to the principle that lying is recommended if it promotes one's material gain, one might have integrity in a narrowly circumscribed sense but fall far short of having the kind of character usually associated with integrity. Lying consistently would manifest itself in disjunctions between what one says one will do or has done, and what one does or in fact has done. The net effect of lying would be to cause turmoil and interruptions in one's life—many caused by outraged friends and business associates! At the very least, we expect a person of integrity to be honest, even at a price. Hence, maintaining just any set of commitments will not necessarily bring us the more fully human integrity which characterizes the fulfillment of the human mode of being. Which commitments reflect the more fully human integrity which we seek?

In fact, purely philosophical accounts of integrity frequently struggle with the issue of norms, others simply ignore it. Most accounts acknowledge that integrity is not just one moral virtue among others, but a supereminent virtue which implies the presence of certain others, such as courage, compassion, kindness, truthfulness, and justice, rather than cowardice, hardness of heart, and indifference to the truth. Integrity rules over the expression of these other virtues (McFall, 1987, pp. 9–11). Some accounts suggest that it includes a willingness to go far beyond what is usually expected in order to maintain one's commitments, in spite of the suffering it may cause to oneself (Halfon, 1989, pp. 41–43). Moreover, it is generally recognized that certain emotions, such as compassion, pride,

[2] I say, "tend to unify" because certainly events out of one's own control might easily shatter the most carefully constructed, morally serious life. And yet it is possible to maintain one's moral integrity in spite of devastating circumstances, for even though moral integrity is primarily a matter of effecting a coherence between one's inner intentions, values, and goals, on the one hand, and one's external acts, on the other, there is usually a way to express one's true intentions even when one's full range of freedom is taken away.

and indignation, suggest the presence of integrity, while others, such as guilt, shame, remorse, and envy, suggest its lack (Halfon, 1989, pp. 116–117).

And yet, to my knowledge, no recent philosophical account has been able to explain why some norms rather others are implied by true integrity. By "true integrity" I mean the integrity which demands maintaining not just any set of commitments but commitments essential to promoting the good; that is, those rules and principles which promote our humanity. In other words, some commitments are somehow "truer" than others because they are grounded in a deeper sense of what it is to be human. That deeper sense includes believing that it is truer to our humanity to nurture and protect new life than to destroy it, and to be loyal to others rather than betray them when the going gets tough. More specifically, such commitments promote a fully human mode of integrity, the integrity which results from acting out of a fully reflective consciousness of all that one knows, feels, and is.

By enjoining a fully personal mode of integrity, I am not suggesting that one needs to have all of the cylinders in one's engine running simultaneously, so to speak: one need not always act as a good spouse or parent or scholar or teacher all of the time; one need not express all of one's emotions, or all of one's aesthetic, moral, and spiritual sensibilities at once. In fact, insofar as one's time and energy remain limited—indeed, insofar as one's being can only be located in one place and one's action is limited to performing one or two things at a time—this is impossible. But to strive toward personal integrity—for who can claim to have ever perfectly achieved it?—one does need to cultivate awareness of all of these roles and dimensions of oneself (Carter, 1996, pp. 52–65), and to harmonize and integrate them into an ordered whole. Certain roles complement one another; others conflict and cannot be maintained with integrity by the same person. Certain moral principles and ideals promote the ability to achieve such harmony and integration of one's life into a differentiated whole. Truth-telling, the courage and fortitude to maintain commitments even when it is inconvenient or downright dangerous, and patience are among these, although these principles and ideals are subservient to the task of promoting wholeness in oneself and in others. For instance, telling the truth no matter what the consequences may serve to protect one's own sense of moral superiority but could wreak havoc on certain others implicated by one's disclosures. While someone who lives out of a narrowly moral conception of integrity might insist on telling the truth in such a situation, no one with fully personal integrity would. From my perspective, the courageous pursuit of wholeness for oneself and the promotion of wholeness in others is the innermost dynamic of the self-transcending power of Christian love.

If acting with moral integrity brings such rewards, why is it that so many must struggle so hard to act morally, while fully personal integrity remains elusive for them? One perspective, proposed by the German Jesuit philosopher-theologian Karl Rahner, among others, focuses upon the hazards of human contingency and temporality. Rahner argued that we always "spirit in world," in the sense that our spiritual freedom can only find expression in space and time, through the expressions of incarnate spirit in concrete and limited historical acts, and that as a result our forces tend to be dissipated by countless limited acts that fail to achieve our goals. Because we are finite and historical, we do not realize all of our possibilities at once but must freely develop them over time. This development is not predetermined, like that of a plant growing, but fraught with the contingencies of human freedom. As a result, contingency and temporality render us susceptible to being denied the opportunity to fulfill ourselves, and this brings frustration, suffering, and pain (Rahner, 1977, pp. 229–235). But frustration and suffering are not just the result of contingency and temporality but of sin. In effect, they are the result of our fall into violence. It is time for theologians to learn from psychoanalytic theorists how violence splits the human psyche and destroys its ability to act with integrity, so that they might better understand how they might respond to violence in a way which brings healing and peace to all.

The Integrative Processes of Human Identity Formation

Purely philosophical accounts of integrity as well as traditional Christian doctrines of love encounter a variety of intellectual and existential problems because they ignore the significance of the integrative processes of human identity formation—specifically, of what promotes the integration of the human psyche into a differentiated dynamic unity and what undermines it. Needless to say, these processes are enormously complex but for my purposes it suffices to begin by saying that love promotes the integration of the human psyche, while various modes of violence undermine a person's ability to act with integrity. How? Put simply, violence and abuse cause psychic splitting, and such splitting thwarts an individual's ability to act with integrity.

Splitting can occur in a variety of forms, depending upon a variety of factors—the nature, mode, and degree of abuse or violence sustained, the age of the victim, the particular content and context of the experience, and so on. Splitting is an extreme exercise of the psyche's ability to dissociate in healthy, controlled ways, such as putting reality aside to meditate, to become immersed in a movie, music, or a daydream, or to do two things at once, like drive while talking. The ability to dissociate functions to protect the self from being overwhelmed by the pain of some singular trauma. But when the trauma is severe and repeated, particularly at an early age when the child's psychic structures have not yet formed, the splitting which originally served as a healthy defense against the harshness of reality becomes a relatively permanent structure of the psyche which prevents it from responding appropriately and productively to reality.

The term *splitting* is commonly distinguished from repression, and yet repression might also justifiably be called splitting because it participates in the same defensive dynamic: forcibly separating off some psychic contents and blocking them from full consciousness (Akhtar, 1992). *Repression* is the term usually associated with forcing psychic contents (ideas, impulses, memories, "objects" representing persons) into the unconscious where they remain dynamic and continue to influence conscious choices and behavior. In other words, models of repression posit a horizontal split between consciousness and the realm of unconsciousness, usually conceived as lying somehow below consciousness. *Splitting* is a term usually associated with the forcible dissociation of essentially incompatible psychic beliefs and attitudes about the self and others which are held either consciously or unconsciously. In essence, then, repression is the forcible dissociation of psychic contents horizontally; splitting does the same thing both horizontally and vertically. For these processes are frequently intertwined, as when one introjects (represses) an object and this introjection causes a split in the unconscious. They distinguish a psyche that is fragmented rather than a dynamic, integrated whole. Needless to say, there are many competing theories about the dynamics of psychic splitting. A simplified account, one adequate to our purpose of conceptualizing what heals it, can be drawn from the work of Kohut (1971), Alice Miller (1994), Winnicott (1960), and Fairbairn (1952).

A child has healthy narcissistic needs for empathic understanding, respect, admiration, and support. When parents either do not or cannot meet these needs, when they harshly ignore or reject them rather than responding to them empathically, in ways which encourage the child to learn to meet them for himself as his development allows, the child will learn to split off and repress them and to respond to the parent's unhealthy narcissistic needs instead of his own. The price the child pays for the parents' lack of development is extraordinarily high. Instead of using his or her natural needs, talents, interests, and desires as sources of energy and guides through life, he will split them off and repress them, becoming depressed and lethargic as a result. Moreover, the feelings of hurt and rage at being abandoned and used will be scuttled away because they are thoroughly unacceptable—either to the little child who needs the parents for survival, or to the parents who refuse to recognize their abusive ways. In fact, the child will hate the parents for their countless refusals to care, but repress this hatred deep within because it threatens the bond to the parent—at least until something or someone in his adult environment provokes its release and then the person will attack with the explosiveness of fury too long repressed.

In this way, splitting occurs: these children will develop a false self to present to their parents and the world, repress their hatred, and become ineffective in developing their true selves, those identities expressing their innermost selves. Unless they are led to remember and recognize how the love and support they needed as children was denied them, even as adults they will repeatedly look for it and erupt into rage when it is refused. Moreover, they will remain split: they will present their false selves to the world hoping that this will buy them love, and allow their true selves to remain underground and undeveloped (A. Miller, 1990, pp. 79–91; 1994, pp. 55–86; Winnicott, 1960).

Alternatively, a child who struggles in error with neglectful or abusive parents would rather make himself bad than admit that he has bad objects (bad parents) as models. By splitting his parents into good and bad parts and then introjecting the bad parts into the self, he creates the illusion of security in his conviction that his real objects/parents are actually good and loving. The good dimensions of his parents are internalized as a superego in relation to which he is bad. At a later time, certain conditions will, then, permit or provoke the release of these bad internalized objects. When this occurs, the person will start seeing bad objects everywhere in the world; in effect, the world becomes peopled with demons. This is the psychological mechanism behind paranoia: the paranoic projects persecutors out of the self and into the world. This projection mechanism undergirds the scapegoat mechanism by which such child-adults blame others for the violence they hold within themselves. The splits in these persons' psyches manifest themselves in their split worldviews: when things are going well, they are bad and the world is good; when things are going badly, the world is bad and they are good. Moreover, they find themselves unable to perceive or handle ambiguity in their objects appropriately: they will respond to someone warmly when that person is gratifying them, but with cold hostility when the same person is frustrating them (Fairbairn, 1952).

From a psychodynamic perspective, healing requires that these child-adults be empowered to accomplish two tasks—those of reintegration and of establishing appropriate boundaries. First, they must be empowered to remember and recognize the neglect and abuse they experienced as children. This can only happen in a safe holding environment in which empathic understanding and support grant them the courage to face even the shadow side of themselves (Kohut, 1971, 1984, pp. 172–191; Jordan, Surrey, & Kaplan, 1991; Surrey, 1991). In other words, to heal they must face their splits. They must jettison the truly unacceptable parts of themselves and build on those potentially creative parts of themselves that have been repressed and neglected. Only then will they be able to reintegrate past and present to come up with something new as they nurture their true selves into expression. Only then will they be able to act with integrity to promote wholeness in themselves and in others.

This process of acting with integrity requires that these child-adults accomplish a second task: they must take responsibility for themselves, and to do this, they must establish and maintain appropriately empathic and flexible boundaries between themselves and others, boundaries which demarcate the limits of their responsibility (Jordan, 1991). The parental failure to respond to a child's true needs—a failure which can range from emotional neglect and exploitation to physical and sexual abuse—involves a failure to maintain proper boundaries with their children in order to manipulate them to serve the parents' own needs. Such parents are intrusive when they want their own needs met, but distant when the child needs something from them, creating the terror of possible abandonment in the child. Moreover, such parenting will create a child who has little or no sense of his own needs and his boundaries, and who will tend to become enmeshed in others as needy as himself. Victims of such parenting will have no idea where they end and another person begins, and will invest themselves totally in identifying and acting to meet the needs of others—the classic scenario for codependency. Only when the enmeshed learn to affirm their own boundaries by affirming their own needs, desires, and consequent limitations, only when they demand that their partners take responsibility for their own needs and desires instead of making others do it for them, will healing occur.

Now these two tasks—reintegration and establishing appropriate boundaries—set up three criteria for any conception of love capable of curing violence, and return us to our original issues. Do the traditional doctrines of Christian love meet these criteria or do they promote splitting and more violence? If the traditional doctrines fall short of meeting this criterion, how might we reconstruct them so that the Christian understanding of love might truly cure violence?

The first criterion is relatively uncontroversial: such love will be patient, forgiving, and kind; it will enable a person to face his violent past, both as a victim and as a perpetrator; such love is warm and empathic and supportive no matter how terrible the atrocities considered. Few would contest Paul's claim that true love is patient, forgiving, and kind (1 Cor. 13), although some might struggle with how these attributes relate to the judgment of God.

The second criterion is seldom rendered explicit in the traditional doctrines of love, and yet, I shall argue, it is implicitly pervasive: for this conception of love must help the victim reintegrate the multidimensional self into a dynamic whole whose parts work in harmony with one another. It must empower the person to reintegrate repressed, split off, and projected parts of the self which are desirable, jettison the parts that are not desirable, and create something genuinely new and good. True love "builds up," as Paul so aptly put it (1 Cor. 8:1). Love is understood to be the power of integration and reintegration in the nearly universal charge that Christians be self-sacrificial, that they give up the self (or certain dimensions of it) in order to find it. Yet, as we shall soon discuss in greater detail, the tendency within the Christian traditions to reduce open self-transcendence to self-emptying self-sacrifice renders this model potentially dangerous when it comes to curing violence.

Third, this conception of love must help the person establish and maintain appropriate boundaries. It must empower the person to affirm the self in relation to the other in a way which calls each to greater responsibility for him- or herself.

As we shall soon discuss, the traditional emphasis on self-sacrifice has undermined the ability of agents to recognize the need to establish and maintain appropriate boundaries.

All told, these three dynamics of the love which heals from violence might true promote the ability to the victim-perpetrator to act with integrity if they were formulated as dimensions of a coherent concept that is based in a truer understanding of what it is to be human. Before we turn to the Christian traditions to see whether and how they meet these criteria, let us consider feminist critiques of traditional views of humanity and integrity.

Feminist Perspectives

Feminists have long recognized that patriarchy in Western civilization has promoted splitting in the sexes in ways which undermine the ability of each to act with integrity: Little boys are discouraged from being emotional, dependent, or interdependent, soft, gentle, and yielding; as a result, they learn to suppress such traits in themselves and project them onto little girls. Little girls, in turn, are encouraged to realize these traits to a fault, and discouraged from being masculine—rational, autonomous, hard, tough, aggressive. In many ways both men and women have been forced to conform to standards that distort and deny integral parts of themselves. But there is an additional spin on this splitting, which I like to call the vampire connection.

Feminist psychoanalysts such as Nancy Chodorow (1978; 1989, pp. 23–65, 99–113) have recognized that the splitting which characterizes the personalities of victims turned perpetrators is itself a function of the patriarchal family structures and the gender-specific ways in which children separate from their mothers and resolve the oedipal crisis. Since it is women who mother, girls experience less pressure than boys to differentiate from their mothers in order to develop their identities as women; as a result, their fundamental identity consists in being in empathic connection with others. Girls and women learn to be acutely aware of and responsive to the needs of others. Boys, on the other hand, learn to identify themselves as masculine in the absence of caretaking fathers by spurning this connection to mother: they learn to understand masculinity negatively, in terms of that which is not feminine, not mother. This leads them to understand their masculinity in terms which repress their need to sustain empathic connections with others. Moreover, during the oedipal period, little boys begin to fear castration in retaliation for their wanting their mothers. Thus together, the denial of empathic connection and the fear of castration produce within boys a need to separate themselves off from others and block empathic connections to them, connections which would render them vulnerable to being affected by others. As a result, Chodorow argues, women experience themselves to be fully themselves in empathic relationships and struggle extensively with differentiation, while men experience themselves as fully themselves when separated from others and asserting themselves autonomously, and they struggle extensively with opening themselves to empathic connections. These gender-specific child-rearing patterns, then, encourage men and women to split in a particular way: women struggle to meet the emotional needs of men for empathic understanding and support, becoming enmeshed with them as a result, while men split off and repress their own ability to be empathic and require women to be so for them.

Catherine Keller has drawn from Chodorow to develop a feminist critique of the heroic ideal which she argues is intrinsically masculine or androcentric: the ideal of a self who realizes himself by severing all relations with others except with those who allow him to siphon off their energy to feed his own needs. Her formulation highlights how the gender specific ways in which we split render women particularly vulnerable to the vampire connection, although men also succumb to it: the self demonically asserts itself by sucking off the vital energies of anyone foolish enough to offer herself up for the sacrifice, hoping for new life but succumbing instead to a slow death by drain. Thus gender analysis clarifies why the vast majority of vampires in Western mythology and popular culture have been male, and illuminates certain differences between male and female vampires. Typically, male vampires remain fundamentally detached while sucking the life out of another (usually, though not always, a woman), while female vampires remain intensely enmeshed while enacting for male vampires those characteristics which they have repressed and split off (Auerbach, 1995, pp. 17–18, 29–51, 87, 97, 101, 185). Hence, male vampirism is the mythic expression of the dysfunctional mode of relating so common to men terrified of the vulnerability entailed by genuine relationships—remaining detached in one way, while deeply attached in another; female vampirism is the mythic expression of women's propensity to become too enmeshed in others, male or female.

Anyone who has read Anne Rice's *Interview with the Vampire* (1986) (or has seen the film) will grasp the meaning of this metaphor with special clarity. In it, the vampire Lestat wants to keep another vampire he created, Louis, as his companion—not in spite of Louis' refusal to give up his guilt and regret over having to kill, but because of it. In other words, Lestat splits off his emotions and makes Louis carry them—an extreme expression of the typically masculine, grandiose mode of narcissism which drains off the nurturing understanding and support of others but refuses to recognize and respond to either his own or another's emotions (A. Miller, 1994, pp. 58–60). When Louis, in a remarkably healthy move, refuses to continue carrying Lestat's guilt and grief for him and so abandons him, Lestat succumbs to a dreadful, deathlike existence and only regains his former powers when Louis reappears. This linking of detachment from others (through repression and denial) with enmeshment with them is one mode of many possible distortions of the healthy boundaries essential to fully personal integrity. Healthy boundaries separate self from other enough to enable one to recognize, experience, and take responsibility for one's own emotions (precisely what Lestat refused to do), while allowing enough empathic connection to recognize and respond to another's emotions when appropriate without taking them over.

Clearly feminist thinkers would do well to consider what the true dynamics of a fully human integrity might mean for transforming gender-specific patterns of parenting. Unfortunately, those few who have thought about integrity have worked with woefully inadequate conceptions of it, probably for two reasons. Cultural feminists, by raising up the so-called "feminine" expertise at being empathic, tend to idealize it in a way which ignores the need for firm boundaries. (Most psychotherapists, however, would argue that empathy is a capacity of being fully human, not being specifically feminine.) Others simply do not grasp the role of boundaries in the integrative and reintegrative processes of identity formation. For instance, Keller begins with a male model of wholeness as a phallic monad—an ego with hard, virtually impermeable boundaries—and tries to transform it in light of women's heightened capacity for empathy. She rightly grasps that empathy is a strength that enables women to feel themselves as all human beings truly are—connected to everything else—and it empowers them to differentiate both internally and externally. Given the truly relational character of human creativity, properly empathic relationality does not drain; when empathy is mutual, it empowers (Doehring, 1995; Surrey, 1991). But because she does not grasp the true dynamics of the integrative and reintegrative processes of identity formation and the role of boundaries in those processes, her attempt to develop a conception of the "integrity of the multiple" or "connective integrity," fails (Keller, 1986, pp. 181–202). Her explication of integrity contains no structural safeguards against encouraging women to split by denying their own needs, and to succumb to the death by drain of the vampire connection. In fact, the net effect of her discussion does quite the opposite by encouraging women to supererogate, thus compensating for their own lack of genuine empathic connections characteristic of patriarchal society.

In other words, Keller's attempt to develop a model of the proper relationality of love drowns both human finitude and the freedom of self-transcendence in the infinite sea of empathic connections. She seems to think that the only alternative to the static integrity of the encapsulated ego is to substitute superpermeable boundaries for hard and rigid ones. But to have and assert boundaries is not evil in itself but an essential ingredient to self-differentiation, and this differentiation is essential to healthy relationships. Such firm but permeable boundaries are, in fact, preconditions of becoming momentarily empathic without merging with the other. In fact, Keller's own rejection of "soluble selfhood," the model of selfhood in which one self dissolves her identity in another's, recognizes how such merging can be devastating to women—and to men, for that matter (1986, pp. 7–18). To have empathy in a way that is healing for the other is to have the ability to feel what another feels without merging with them, without confusing one's own identity and responsibilities with the other's identity and responsibilities. To have empathy in a healing way requires the ability to move between a sense of the inward experience of the other and a sense of the true alterity of the other in a dialectic which never loses the tension of its polarity. To maintain this dialectic requires never hardening oneself against the experience of the other nor merging one's own experience into that of the other (Jordan, 1991). Feminists have long recognized how such hardening can lead to destructive power over the other, but they have often failed to recognize how overempathic merging can itself become an overpowering of the other, because it refuses to respect the boundaries of the other—in effect, to recognize the other *as* other—and disperses the other's ability to take initiative.

The problem that women in particular, and many narcissistic personalities in general, have with enmeshment highlights the core problematic of reformulating the Christian doctrine of love to focus its potential to cure violence. The very openness to God in faith and love which makes it possible for persons to engage in the self-transcendence intrinsic to the integrating and reintegrating process of identity formation has too often been understood to require a dissolution of healthy boundaries. This is the double bind of the Christian doctrine of love: to reintegrate one has to be open, but to be *too* open is to succumb to the death by drain of the vampire connection. Unfortunately, neither traditional nor radically feminist thinkers have found a way out of this conundrum, but I shall soon suggest guidelines for avoiding this when I develop the model of love as care as an alternative to the *agape* and *caritas* traditions.

Too often feminist critiques of the Christian doctrine of love have pointed out how *agape* and *caritas* have been disempowering; too seldom have they noticed that their proposed alternatives lead to enmeshment and not to the affirmation of boundaries so essential to acting with integrity.

THE SPLITTING EFFECTS OF AGAPE AND CARITAS

Agape: The Splitting of Unremitting Sacrifice

The history of *agape* is too long and complex to analyze here, but it suffices for our purposes to explore a view that has dominated 20th century discussions, that of Anders Nygren. In his view, two kinds of love do battle with one another: *eros,* the acquisitive love which seeks its own good, and *agape,* the self-sacrificial love which seeks only the good of the other. Given Nygren's radical doctrine of sin, no human desire remains untainted by selfishness. The human love of *eros* and the divine love of *agape* are totally inimical to one another, and Augustine's putative attempt to mix the two in conceptualizing *caritas* in analogous to trying to mix oil and water—they always separate. As a result of his understanding humanity as inexorably selfish and acquisitive, Nygren has no model of human agency to inform how the divine *agape* empowers human beings to love. He is reduced to using the metaphor of funnel or channel: humanity is simply a funnel through which God channels the divine love to the neighbor (1982, p. 735). This is hardly an adequate solution for those struggling to know what their Christian faith would have them do for the neighbor.

Women have been alerted to the dangers of understanding love as unremitting self-sacrifice since Valerie Saiving's revolutionary exposé of Nygren's views as androcentric in her article, "The Human Situation: A Feminist View" (Goldstein, 1960). Saiving argues that the gender-specific differences in the ways children differentiate from their mothers and experience the development of their identities set men and women up to develop different character structures; these different character structures, in turn, render men and women susceptible to different kinds of sin. Male psychosexual development tends to produce not just assertive, but aggressive and ruthlessly competitive character structures, and these overactive character structures render men prone to the sins of pride and selfish manipulation of others.[3] Saiving then proposes that pure self-sacrifice might indeed be the proper antidote to such male forms of sin but not to female forms. Since female psychosexual development tends to produce relatively passive character structures, and these passive character structures make women prone to the sins of a lack of development of self—triviality, distractibility, lack of an organizing center or standards for behavior—then self-sacrifice is not antidote but poison for most women. Indeed, we might add, insofar as society encourages women to sacrifices themselves to their roles as wives and mothers, the classic doctrine of *agape* not only reinforces their passivity, it encourages them to develop false selves while repressing their true ones, and so to become pathologically narcissistic. Such conditioning radically undermines women's ability to develop selves capable of any genuinely creative sacrifice, of sacrifice that is not just self-immolation but that builds up the woman herself and others. There is a sacrificial dynamic operative in all true love, but authentic sacrifice is chosen to promote the greater wholeness of oneself and others, not their annihilation through exploitation.

What Saiving, Jean Baker Miller (1976), and other feminists have failed to notice is that pathologically narcissistic personalities are not only fragmented, they are filled with hate from a thousand rejections and repressions of their own healthy narcissistic needs. We all know about the passive–aggressive personality, the person who smiles innocuously one moment, but stabs the objects of his or her repressed hostility in the back the next. The splitting of unremitting self-sacrifice

[3] This is not to deny that women can also be aggressive and ruthlessly competitive, while men can be passive and self-denying. The exceptions disclose the importance of the individual's family environment for resisting the pressures of the way the prevailing patriarchal ideology reinforces the tendencies of psychosexual development. But Saiving's reasoning does go a long way to explain many of the gender differences which characterize patriarchy.

cannot be resolved simply by throwing in a little self-affirmation and self-love. The hatred and the false selves must be let go—sacrificed, if you will—in order that the true self might blossom forth. And this flowering results from a self-love which nourishes the unique self by maintaining both its responsibilities to itself and appropriately empathic boundaries with others.

Caritas: The Splitting of Polarities and Hierarchies

Now to be fair, most Protestant theologians before and since Nygren have recognized the need for some mode of justified self-love, and have struggled to conceptualize how self-love can be an integral dimension of Christian love (Lindberg, 1965; Outka, 1972, pp. 55–74, 221–229, 285–291).[4] Unfortunately, orthodox Protestant theologians have tended to neglect developing adequate models of selfhood. If we are saved solely through faith in Christ crucified, they argue, we need not develop models of being and knowing to help us exercise our natural powers more adequately. In fact, for those schooled in Lutheran theology of the cross, developing such models always smacks of trying to justify oneself apart from faith in Christ. This has prevented them from grasping how human agents can mediate divine grace or love to others, not simply through remaining open to empowerment from beyond but through the self-conscious and disciplined exercise of intellect and will.

The Roman Catholic tradition on *caritas* has fared better, for it appreciates the need to understand Christian knowing and loving in continuity with human needs, desires, and actions. Augustine understood love to be both human desire and more: love was the movement of the soul, the directed energy of mind, heart and will. His view included an affective component: love seeks after and clings to that which it enjoys. The

[4] Personally, I believe that Paul Tillich has come closest to grasping the integral relationship between self- and other-love, probably because his extentialist appropriation of neo-Thomist metaphysics enabled him to understand faith to be self-affirmation in the face of the threat of various modes of nonbeing—meaninglessness, guilt, death (1952, pp. 32–57, 156–177; 1957, pp. 99–125). Such self-affirmation is not possible without self-love.

character of a person is revealed by the object toward which her will is directed. Augustine's neo-Platonic, hierarchical worldview enabled him to develop the notion of an order of love, a hierarchy of values or goods in which the lower values are, or at least should be, subordinate to the higher ones. If the will is directed upwards, toward its proper object, God, it is fundamentally good, that is, it is *caritas* or true Christian love. But if it is directed downwards, toward such lower goods as food, sex, and material things which bring transitory, worldly pleasures, it is evil, that is, *cupiditas.* Within this hierarchy, Augustine argued that we should use temporal, earthly goods to express our love of God, who alone is rightly enjoyed (Augustine, 1958; Burnaby, 1938, pp. 113–140; Teselle, 1970, pp. 202–203). Unfortunately, this hierarchy of goods tends to denigrate mundane embodied existence. In particular, Augustine's conviction that rationality should always control and order the other faculties reflected his deep distrust of the lower affections, particularly sexual passion, because of their ability to distract human minds and spirits from seeking their highest goal, the vision of God.

Augustine struggled mightily throughout his life to discern the proper way to relate to the body and other temporal goods, and his views on the matter did fluctuate. Moreover, he recognized that while one mode of self-love is selfish and reflects a disordered love, another is natural and fitting, while a third is to be commended because it is the necessary after-effect of proper love of God. Nygren thoroughly distorted Augustine's vision when he reduced all eros or self-love to acquisitiveness (Burnaby, 1938, pp. 117–118). But the overall impact of Augustine's fundamentally hierarchical and dualistic vision in its various permutations upon the history of Christianity has continued to be devastating to women, for his denigration of embodiment has especially implicated them. Because women are so intimately involved in the messy process of bearing and caring for children, they have been placed at the lower end of the hierarchy, and at the subordinate pole of the dualisms of spirit-body, mind-matter (Ortner, 1974; Ruether, 1983, pp. 72–114). The hierarchical visions and dualistic polarities of Roman Catholicism have done much to devalue women and sexuality by perpetrating more splitting between objects truly meriting man's love and objects that merely tempt man away from his true home and salvation in God. Women, sexuality, the affective dimensions of selfhood are understood as threats to man's solitary search for fulfillment. Needless to say, this false oppositionalism between mind and body, spirit and matter has done much to harm both men and women. It has particularly encouraged men to relate to their bodies and to women in domineering ways, as simply instruments for their own pleasure and aggrandizement.

Both traditions on love are fatally flawed, but both do have their strengths. The Protestant emphasis upon the unremitting self-sacrifice of *agapic* love has encouraged splitting into true and false selves, and contributed to creating pathologically narcissistic personalities. Moreover, the tendency of some of its theologians to relegate the spiritual relationship to God to an interior realm where one stands alone before God, and to deny the significance of the external, worldly realm to that relationship has also worked to oppress women (Rike, 1982). But Protestantism has also affirmed the equality of men and women as well as the inherent goodness of sexuality and the married state. As a result, it has encouraged the leveling of hierarchies which separate persons from one another and from God. At least some of its traditions have encouraged embracing and transforming created existence. The predominantly hierarchical and dualistic visions of Roman Catholicism have encouraged splitting the spiritual away from the embodied; consequently, they have contributed to the devaluation of sexuality, embodiment, and all of the related functions of birthing and caregiving with which women are so closely associated. And yet few among us (except neo-pagans such as Camille Paglia) would deny that the ordering of our lives and our loves according to their value for us is absolutely essential to human fulfillment. Few would deny that in addictions, our desires become glued (to use a favorite Augustinian metaphor) to our illicit loves in a way that disorders our lives, and only openness to a power from beyond will set it free. Still, I believe that both traditional models of Christian love should be jettisoned, first, because they are so prone to encouraging psychic splitting, and second, because they are expressions of antiquated anthropologies. A new model, based on independently developed principles, is required to cure violence.

FEMINIST CHRISTIAN LOVE AS CARE

Both the *agape* and the *caritas* traditions are based on an individualistic model of humanity, according to which persons must separate themselves off from others and act autonomously to find fulfillment or salvation. From this perspective, to give to the other is always to take from the self (Rike, 1996a, pp. 248–252). Some feminist theologians and philosophers, however, have attempted to reformulate love in terms of care on the basis of a relational model of humanity; that is, one that understands human beings to be constituted, not through separating from others, but in and through relationships with one another. From a relational perspective, to give to the other is always to give to the self through the other. And yet, many feminists (particularly cultural feminists) emphasize the power of empathy to create connections without adequately recognizing that empathy is only effective when appropriate boundaries between self and other remain. As a result, they end up in the same quandary as the androcentric views—perpetually worried that by giving to the other they will succumb to death by drain by the vampire connection.

A prime example of this is Nell Noddings' model of caring which she developed explicitly on the basis of insights gained by Carol Gilligan and others into human relationality. Noddings (1984) ridicules the use of rules and principles in ethics because she understands them to be just another evasive tactic of those who wish to deny their interdependence with others, and the full range of their responsibility to them. Such rule-driven morality, she believes, promotes separation and detachment from the other, and suppresses the sensibility which calls forth genuine caring. Yet Noddings' own delineation of the dynamics of caring in terms of engrossment and motivational displacement opens the "one-caring" up to endless exploitation by the "one cared-for"—something Noddings herself recognizes and struggles with. In her view, engrossment is the empathic state of mind and emotions we enter into when we are concerned about another, and open ourselves to perceiving their genuine needs. Such engrossment causes a motivational shift—the one-caring becomes motivated by the needs of the one cared-for, and acts to fulfill them (1984, pp. 17–20, 30–34, 40, 60–61). In motivational displacement, the needs of the one cared-for become essentially the needs of the one-caring (1984, pp. 16–34, 69–70). But is this not a good definition of the kind of enmeshment which ignores boundaries between self and other? By identifying the needs of the other as one's own, one effectively denies that there are boundaries between oneself and the other. Although such a state of motivational displacement might serve to keep someone in dire straits going until they can care for themselves, making it a principle of human interaction effectively takes away the other's responsibility for his or her own self.

Empathic understanding of another coupled with taking on the needs of the other as one's own, in themselves, will only build the other up into wholeness if they are exercised in ways which self-consciously attempt to promote the ability of the other to act with integrity, and so to take responsibility for him- or herself. The one-caring cannot take the pain of the one cared for away; the one-caring can only be empathically present to the other to help the other work through his or her own pain. To pretend otherwise is to undermine the integrity of both the one-caring and the one cared-for. For to act with integrity is to act out of a self-consciousness of all dimensions of oneself, and to promote the development of such integrity in both self and other requires that one call the other to act out of a similar self-consciousness.

The promotion of such integrity requires being empathic in a way which enables one to let down boundaries briefly, enough to understand and experience what the other is thinking and feeling. But true empathy will continue to recognize and respect the other as other, not self, and encourage the other to recognize, accept, and respect what he or she is thinking or feeling. Such empathic caring then must also be forgiving and kind. Any harsh or negative judgment of the other's more or less repressed feelings of resentment, jealousy, or hatred will simply encourage the other to shore up defenses against them. And as long as one defends the self against them, one will continue to deny, project, and act out on them. Finally, from an explicitly theological perspective, only a merciful forgiveness—secure that all are embraced and accepted by a love from beyond—can help another let down such defenses. Such caring will find itself empowered from beyond itself in its openness to and patient forgiveness of the other. This self-transcendent openness will, in turn, empower the other to open up the self by letting down defenses and denials of its repressions and projections. In other words, it will motivate and empower the other to recognize its state of brokenness, and to reintegrate the good and creative parts of the self back into the self and nurture them into fullness, while rejecting and letting go of the destructive ones. Such loving with integrity responds to those caught up in the dreadful cycle of violence in a way which enables them to stop the cycle and to work their ways back toward wholeness.

In summary, loving with integrity requires the courage to be open to the truth, and this requires commitment to surrendering oneself to the integrative and reintegrative processes of developing one's identity. Loving with integrity frequently requires agapic self-sacrifice, for only then can the old be transformed into a new and better whole. It requires the disciplined and humbling reordering and reintegration of loves to enhance the achievement of the greater good, for only then can the splintering disorganization of the broken and addicted life work its way through to a coherent wholeness. But these are built upon the relationality of care, for only such caring can build up self and other into a new network of mutually empathic and creatively self-sustaining relationships. Only in this way can men and women alike become whole.

REFERENCES

Akhtar, S. (1992). *Broken structures: Severe personality disorders and their treatment.* Northvale, NJ: Jason Aronson.

Alcoff, L. (1988). Cultural feminism versus post-structuralism: The identity crisis in feminist theory. *Signs: Journal of Women in Culture and Society, 13,* 405–436.

Auerbach, N. (1995). *Our vampires: Ourselves.* Chicago: University of Chicago Press.

Augustine of Hippo. (1958). *On Christian doctrine,* Book 1 (Trans., D.W. Robertson, Jr.). Indianapolis: Bobbs-Merrill.

Burnaby, J. (1938). *Amor dei: A study of the religion of St. Augustine.* Norwich, U.K.: Canterbury Press.

Carter, S. L. (1996). (*integrity*). New York: Basic Books.

Chodorow, N. (1978). *The reproduction of mothering: Psychoanalysis and the sociology of gender.* Berkeley: University of California Press.

Chodorow, N. (1989). *Feminism and psychoanalytic theory.* New Haven: Yale University Press.

Doehring, C. (1995). *Taking care: Monitoring power dynamics and relational boundaries in pastoral care and counseling.* Nashville, TN: Abingdon Press.

Fairbairn, W. R. D. (1952). The repression and the return of bad objects (with special reference to the "war neuroses"). In *An object relations theory of the personality.* New York: Basic Books. (Original work published 1943)

Farley, M. (1977). New patterns of relationship: Beginnings of a moral revolution. In W. Burkhardt (Ed.), *Woman: New dimensions* (pp. 51–70). New York: Paulist Press.

Gilligan, C. (1982). *In a different voice: Psychological theory and women's development.* Cambridge, MA: Harvard University Press.

Goldstein, V. S. (1960). The human situation: A feminist view. *Journal of Religion, 40,* 100–112.

Halfon, M. S. (1989). *Integrity: A philosophical inquiry.* Philadelphia: Temple University Press.

Harrison, B. W. (1986). The power of anger in the work of love: Christian ethics for women and other strangers. In C. S. Robb (Ed.), *Making the connections: Essays in feminist social ethics* (pp. 3–21). Boston: Beacon Press.

Jordan, J. V. (1991). Empathy and self boundaries. In J. V. Jordan, A. G. Kaplan, J. B. Miller, I. P. Stiver, & J. L. Surrey (Eds.), *Women's growth in connection. Writings from the Stone Center* (pp. 67–80). New York: Guilford Press.

Jordan, J. V., Surrey, J. L., & Kaplan, A. G. (1991). Women and empathy: Implications for psychological development and psychotherapy. In J. V. Jordon, A. G. Kaplan, J. B. Miller, I. P. Stiver, & J. L. Surrey (Eds.), *Woman's growth in connection. Writings from the Stone Center* (pp. 27–50). New York: Guilford Press.

Keller, C. (1986). *From a broken web: Separation, sexism and self.* Boston: Beacon Press.

Kohut, H. (1971). *The analysis of the self.* New York: International Universities Press.

Kohut, H. (1984). *How does analysis cure?* (Ed. A. Goldberg). Chicago: University of Chicago Press.

Lindberg, C. H. (1965). *Luther's concept of love. A critique of Anders Nygren's interpretation of Martin Luther.* Unpublished doctoral dissertation, School of Religion in the Graduate College of the University of Iowa.

McFall, L. (1987, October). Integrity. *Ethics, 98,* 5–20.

Miller, A. (1990). *For your own good. Hidden cruelty in child-rearing and the roots of violence* (Trans. H. & H. Hannum). New York: Noonday Press.

Miller, A. (1994). *The drama of the gifted child. The search for the true self* (Trans. R. Ward). New York: Basic Books.

Miller, J. B. (1976). *Toward a new psychology of women.* Boston: Beacon Press.

Noddings, N. (1984). *Caring: A feminine approach to ethics and moral education.* Berkeley: University of California Press.

Nygren, A. (1982). *Agape and eros* (Trans. P. S. Watson). Chicago: University of Chicago Press.

Ortner, S. (1974). Is female to male as nature is to culture? In M. Z. Rosaldo & L. Lamphere (Eds.), *Women, culture and society* (pp. 67–87). Stanford, CA: Stanford University Press.

Outka, G. (1972). *Agape. An ethical analysis.* New Haven: Yale University Press.

Plaskow, J. (1980). *Sex, sin and grace: Women's experience and the theologies of Reinhold Niebuhr and Paul Tillich.* Lanham, NY: University Press of America.

Rahner, K. (1977). Unity-love-mystery. In *Theological investigations, 8: Further theology of the spiritual life II* (Trans. D. Bourke) (pp. 229–247). New York: Seabury Press.

Rice, A. (1986). *Interview with a vampire.* New York: Ballantine.

Rike, J. L. (1982, June). Faith under trial: Ethical and Christian duty in the thought of Soren Kierkegaard. *Tijdschrift voor filosofie, 44,* 266–297.

Rike, J. L. (1996a). The lion and the unicorn: Feminist perspectives on Christian love as care. In E. Stuart & A. Thatcher (Eds.), *Christian perspectives on sexuality and gender* (pp. 247–262). Grand Rapids, MI: William B. Eerdmans.

Rike, J. L. (1996b). The cycle of violence and feminist constructions of selfhood. *Contagion: Journal of Violence, Mimesis and Culture, 3*, 21–42.

Ruether, R. R. (1983). *Sexism and god-talk.* Boston: Beacon Press.

Saiving, V. (1979). The human situation: A feminine view. In C. Christ & J. Plaskow (Eds.), *Womanspirit rising: A feminist reader in religion* (pp. 25–42). San Francisco: Harper & Row. (Original work published 1960)

Stendahl, K. (1976). *Paul among Jews and gentiles and other essays.* Philadelphia: Fortress Press.

Suchocki, M. H. (1994). *The fall to violence: Original sin in relational theology.* New York: Continuum.

Surrey, J. (1991). Relationship and empowerment. In J. V. Jordan, A. G. Kaplan, J. B. Miller, I. P. Stiver, & J. L. Surrey (Eds.), *Women's growth in connection. Writings from the Stone Center* (pp. 162–180). London: Guilford Press.

Teselle, E. (1970). *Augustine: The theologian.* London: Burns & Oates.

Tillich, P. (1952). *The courage to be.* New Haven: Yale University Press.

Tillich, P. (1957). *The dynamics of faith.* New York: Harper & Row.

Wink, W. (1992). Neither passivity nor violence: Jesus' third way (Matt. 5:38–42). In W. M. Swartley (Ed.), *The love of enemy and nonretaliation in the New Testament* (pp. 102–125). Louisville, KY: Westminster/John Knox Press.

Winnicott, D. W. (1960). Ego distortion in terms of true or false. In *The maturational processes and the facilitating environment* (pp. 140–152). New York: International Universities Press.

7.

Cognitive Aspects of Unitative States: Spiritual Self-Realization, Intimacy, and Knowing the Unknowable

Jan Sinnott

Just as mysticism is not a rejection of science but a transcendence of it, science is not a rejection of mysticism but a precursor of it.
(Herb Koplowitz, 1978, p. 3)

This chapter is a theoretical consideration of the ways in which the human mind might cognitively process mystical experiences and their behavioral aftermaths in both individual and interpersonal contexts. I will focus mainly on *cognitive* questions in this chapter, although these cognitive questions overlap with emotional and interpersonal factors.

In this chapter, ideas based on my Postformal Theory[1] and the years of study related to it (e.g., Rogers, Sinnott, & Van Dusen, 1991; Sinnott, 1984, 1998b; Yan, 1995; Yan & Arlin, 1995) are used to address the creative ways that humans might reflect on and cognitively represent these unitative and mystical experiences, *and* use them to aid their intra- and interpersonal

[1] The terms *Postformal Thought* and *Postformal Complex Thought* are capitalized when they refer to my own theory, i.e., Sinnott's theory of postformal thinking.

development. Here I plan to stretch the limits of Postformal Thought in a speculative new way. Problems in living which might result from difficulties with the cognitive representation of spiritual, unitative experiences are also discussed. I use concepts from my Postformal Theory to suggest ways to resolve such problems.

Postformal Theory (Sinnott, 1981, 1984, 1989a, 1989b, 1991a, 1991b, 1993, 1994a, 1994b, 1996a, 1996b, 1997, 1998a, 1998b) states that Postformal Thought is the logic that develops in adulthood through interpersonal experiences. It is the logic that organizes contradictory "scientific" logics by allowing the knower to be aware that he or she is necessarily a cocreator of reality and meaning. Postformal Thought as I define it will be explained in greater detail below.

The major subdivisions of this chapter address three major issues related to adult development: the postformal cognition of the spiritual or unitative experience; the postformal creative process of creating a complex spiritual self; and, finally, the nature of a postformal/spiritual understanding of intimate relationships *after* mystical experiences.

POSTFORMAL COGNITION OF THE UNITATIVE EXPERIENCE

When it comes to understanding the *cognition* of complex spiritual experiences, mystical experiences, and unitative states (terms which I will use somewhat interchangeably in this present chapter to refer to the nonpathological, experienced state of joyful, loving oneness with God and the universe), cognitive life span developmental psychologists are faced with a dilemma. We intend to study how humans "know" whatever "reality" is occurring around them, how that knowing changes over a lifetime, and what it implies for behavior. We hope to study these questions in as rich and realistic and humanistic a way as possible, avoiding the reductionism which is a serious risk in traditional scientific inquiry. *Mysticism* poses a unique dilemma for us. How do we as psychologists, whose vocation is to study the whole spectrum of human behavior and experience, describe that which essentially goes *beyond* human knowing but is nevertheless known by humans? And what has this timeless experience, mysticism, to do with life span human development, which is a phenomenon locked into linear time?

Over the past few years we life span developmentalists have been faced with another new challenge to our theories, that of the "new physics" (that is, relativity theory and quantum physics). The new physics demands a paradigm shift in the understanding of "objective" reality, in that new physics defines objective large-scale physical reality as incorporating paradoxical logical contradictions and necessarily subjective choices about the nature of that physical reality (e.g., Wolf, 1981; Zukav, 1979). At the same time these developments were unfolding, we were faced with the task of accounting for the *positive* intellectual development that we saw in some adults as they aged, positive development in spite of losses in such things as nerve conductance velocity, memory, etc. Earlier research on aging had focused heavily and almost exclusively on the negative changes that come with later years. Now we were collecting data that indicated numerous positive ones. It seemed to be astounding and radical in certain circles to even suggest that experience and development might make at least some people wiser and permit them to function at higher levels.

Responding to these challenges led me to create a theory of *Post*formal Complex Thought (e.g., Sinnott, 1981, 1984, 1994b, 1996b, 1998b). In my theory, Postformal Thought is the last step in logical development during the life span, and goes beyond Piaget's traditional stages of logical development (i.e., sensorimotor operations, preoperations, concrete operations, and formal operations). Knowers sometimes find themselves working with multiple contradictory formal logical systems. Postformal Thought helps to organize these logically conflicting formal operational systems and demands. This logical superorganization is done within a specific context at a specific time. At that point Postformal Thought allows a choice of one formal logical reality (namely, one formal system), a choice that is adaptive for that time and context. That choice is then incorporated into ongoing thought and behavior, made "real," through subsequent living done within its framework (Sinnott, 1996a).

Postformal Thought as I define it develops especially through the logical contradictions about "reality" encountered during social interactions, when one person's formal operational logical "truth" about the interaction contradicts that of another person or contradicts the shared truth of the culture. At that point of conflicting logics, a necessarily somewhat subjective (albeit passionate) choice is made of which reality to consider "real" in this case. The knower decides the rules of the game as part of playing the game, and goes on to *live* the reality selected, therefore cocreating reality, so to speak.

This Postformal Thought could describe the form of the way that an Einstein could know the strange logical reality of the new physics (as described above). It could also describe the way individuals know on a deeply adaptive level the coconstructed realities of their relationships with one another and the coconstructed realities of a culture. For example, when I begin teaching a college class, the class and I begin to structure the reality of our class relationship by mutually deciding the reality of our relationship, behaving based on that decision, and mutually creating our class relationship in the days that follow. One student may see me as a surrogate parent and act within the formal logic appropriate to that vision, to which I might respond by being parental. Another student may logically construct me as a buddy and act within that logical frame, to which I might respond by thinking and acting in the buddy logical frame, or by thinking and being more parental (to compensate). The result over the time of a semester will be a relationship with this class that is created based on the logics we have chosen.

Postformal Logical Thought seems to develop later in life, after a certain amount of intellectual and interpersonal experience, according to my earlier research. For example, only after experiencing intimate relationships with their shared, mutually constructed logics about the reality of intimate life together, can a person be experienced enough to know that, "If I think of you as an untrustworthy partner, then treat you that way, you are likely to become an untrustworthy partner."

One of the most interesting aspects of postformal thinking is the way in which it interlaces with the demands of life periods we customarily call middle age and old age. For example, a thinker in middle age needs to consciously synthesize and balance work and family demands, not just choose one or the other of the logical structures of family *or* work. Likewise, an aging individual needs to *integrate* the formal logic of identity that says "I am partly my body" with the formal logic of identity that says "I am not entirely defined by my body."

Another interesting aspect of postformal thinking is the way it can help describe and clarify familiar life-stage conflict themes such as those articulated by Erikson (1950), e.g., intimacy, generativity, and integrity. For example, a thinker hoping to be generative or reach integrity, in Erikson's terms, needs to be able to handle the logics of self versus others and the logics of the many possible interpretations of the meaning of his or her life. Postformal thinking seemed to describe how individuals expand and make sense of the creations called their identities and their lives.

After the challenges of new physics paradigms and positive development in aging led me to construct my theory of Postformal Thought, I began to discover how useful a tool it was for describing many kinds of complex thought in adult life settings. For example, I gradually came to realize that this Postformal Self-Referential Thought helped describe what went on in the minds of mature and older adults who were addressing the issue of their own death or the issues raised by deeply mystical experiences and near-death experiences. The choice of some of these older individuals to "disidentify" with their bodies and their ordinary mentation reminded me of meditation states and states of unitative ecstasy described by some persons in nonresearch related spiritual groups in which I have participated over the last 20 years. The choosing of realities (by some of these mature respondents) was akin to that of spiritual seekers who consciously move among different realities or different constructions of reality and are aware of their part in that process. The descriptions (personal reports) of complex reality that these mature persons were giving me, especially by those older persons facing imminent death, were very much like the descriptions of reality and of reality choice offered by the Roman Catholic mystics with whom I am familiar. Thus it appears that similar wise intellectual processes seemed to be serving both kinds of knowers (Sinnott, 1993, 1994a, 1994b, 1996a, 1997).

Based on this thinking and on related experiments I now offer several ideas about the relation between Postformal Complex Thought and four aspects of adult development and their relationship to spirituality. The four developmental topics which interweave through these ideas are: aging, identity, intimate relationships, and living in balance. First, I propose that spirituality and mysticism, when they become conscious experiences, become known by individuals who can access reality and represent it through the use of postformal thinking operations. Second, we can use the Postformal model to see how individuals come to understand their freedom to enter mystical states and to choose to join the "flow of love" in unitative states, particularly as life comes to its earthly end. For example, to know that one selects the formal logic through which to view one's world in normal or altered states, but then is free to choose again and is not "stuck" in a state, facilitates visits to spiritual nonordinary realities. We can then help individuals who may be having difficulty with these nonordinary experiences and individuals preparing for death. Third, I propose that we can promote the development of postformal thinking in maturity, and, in turn, facilitate a person's ability to be spiritually minded and to live in balance, integrating mind, emotions, body, and spirit into the dance of living. For example, we can do this by challenging younger adults with the give-and-take of others' logics, others with whom they want to have relationships. Sometimes this even happens, as mentioned above, in the free-wheeling dialogues of college classrooms. Fourth, I see that we might do research on the cognition of spiritual experiences using my model of Postformal Thought.

Postformal Thought as a Necessary Skill

Postformal Thought is a necessary cognitive skill for representing deep, mature, spiritual development. It can be found in the thinking of spiritually wise individuals, saints, and mystics. It is the form logic takes in these mature thinkers and it develops through the thinkers' relationships with others, God, and the universe. For example, when I understand "evil" with a different logic than I think a friend or God does, I am motivated to reconcile those two logics about evil with some overarching logic in order to maintain the relationship with the friend or with God. Postformal skills potentially include the understanding of the union of mind and emotion, as well as a modified and expanded concept of self, plus a relative comfort with the certainty of personal death.

Postformal Thought as I define it could allow the mature spiritual thinker to know that he or she is operating by two or more mutually contradictory but simultaneous logics while that thinker is experiencing higher awareness. For example, Postformal Thought could allow awareness of unconditional love for an abusive colleague within one logic to coexist with awareness that defensive and limit-setting behavior and emotional responses are present and appropriate within the other logic. Creating a consciousness, bridging awareness, setting limits in a state of unconditional love, might be the result of the postformal awareness on a good day, or it might be a conscious choice that one or the other reality will be allowed to "win" on another day. Postformal Thought, in this situation, could leave the knower[2] comfortable with such knowledge and with any behavior that is nested simultaneously in both spiritual and practical logics. The spiritual seeker who (as the saying goes) experiences all persons as Buddha, all places as Nirvana, and all sounds as Mantra is either totally out of touch with ordinary reality without a reality to replace it, or much *more* able to orchestrate the multiple ordinary and nonordinary states of consciousness by virtue of improved cognitive abilities. What if the built-in human possibilities include a cognitive possibility of transcending the prison of our own cognition to enjoy a god's eye view of it?

[2] The "knower" is the person who is having the cognitive experience and creating the representations.

Points of Interface and Related Research Possibilities

There are four potential points of interface between the domains of cognition and spirituality, points from which it would be relatively easy to start our studies. These four are: the *form* of this logic; the *developmental process* to attain this thought; the connection between this sort of thought, its underlying logic, and *emotion* and *will*; and the multiperson, *cooperative cognition element.*

With respect to the form of this logic, the scientist can examine the information processing and the cognitive style of any thinker, including the thinker in a unitative state. The scientist can elaborate on the logical processes being used by that thinker (as Piaget elaborated on the processes of infants and scientists) whether that thinker is Blake or an adolescent, St. Teresa or an Alzheimer disease patient, Buckminster Fuller or an unknown gifted musician. Just as Sinetar (1986) used questionnaires and methods from organizational psychology to study the process of becoming self actualized (Maslow, 1968), cognitive developmental psychologists can examine the memory, problem solving, and the logic of the healthy, spiritually questing person. Tart (1983) explored the cognitive processes of those in many states of consciousness; we can explore the logic of mystics and spiritually questing persons in many settings.

Second, the *developmental process* by which a person arrives at multireality logic skills is also ripe for study. Of course Wilber's (1995) work is well known.[3] Pearce (1973) has described developmental stages in which the first pass through the stage leads to *intra*psychic growth while the second pass through the same stage leads to *transpersonal* psychological growth. That second pass through the stage is expected, according to Pearce, in the middle and later years of adult life. But not every adult achieves this growth.

Spiritual yearnings often accompany generativity and integrity for many persons, who sometimes, then, make comments that sound like the comments of the wise ones, mystics,

[3] Ken Wilber is well known for his multidisciplinary syntheses which are extremely comprehensive and creative analyses of factors in a spiritual model of development.

and saints. The person conscious of his or her generativity and integrity sees the self in the local everyday reality as well as in the more extensive reality of community, an entire life story, and/or transcendence. So does the mystic straddle multiple realities. Underhill (1911/1961) has written that the mystic lives in a world unknown to most others where he or she sees through the veil of imperfection to view creation with God's eyes. The mystic is lifted out of the self to a higher self in order to see everything and everyone as lovable. There is a sense of choice about whether one spends a certain hour or day in a place of limited (ordinary) understanding or in a place of the larger understanding. The shaman walks in the upper and lower worlds, as animal spirit and human spirit simultaneously. The fictionalized Don Genero (Castaneda, 1971) can choose to see in a unitative way, with the eyes of the sorcerer, or see in the more ordinary way; he can violate physical laws or obey them. Spiritual seekers who are mystics say that they share in all of being while being one part of it. To sustain and understand these experiences requires the ability to coordinate multiple contradictory formal logical systems and to be able to choose (in a self-referential way) one logical system to commit to at a given moment. This sounds like Postformal Thought.

A third way to approach the cognitive study of spiritual development is to tap the methods that incorporate *emotion and will* (or intention) into cognition. Emotional elements in processes such as problem solving are difficult to study, but some developmentalists and cognitive scientists (e.g., Bastick, 1982; Isen & Shalker, 1982; Labouvie-Vief, 1987; Rogers et al., 1991; Sinnott, 1989a, 1989b) have taken steps to incorporate these factors. Since spiritual experience is often felt to be an *emotional* knowing that *does* demand the use of intention and will, being able to incorporate such elements into studies is important. Emotional reactions and intuition might be one way to enlarge problem space, which is defined, in artificial intelligence terms, as the number of elements one considers or uses while solving a problem. This enlargement of problem space permits an enlarged worldview, which, in turn, facilitates the development of Postformal Thought or spiritual thought.

The fourth set of studies also may be difficult, but possible. Studies of *cooperative cognition* (or multiperson cognition) are fairly rare in standard cognitive experimental settings with controlled variables. Such controls are not very practical in real life organizational or educational settings. Cooperative cognition studies are recommended by a number of authors (e.g., Meacham & Emont, 1989), and sometimes done (e.g., Laughlin, 1965; Laughlin & Bitz, 1975; Rogers et al., 1991; Sinnott, 1991a, 1991b). Studying multiperson cognition and the behavior and philosophy related to it would help us understand spirituality in two ways. First, we could understand how any shared belief system challenges or facilitates cognitive or emotional or interpersonal growth. Second, unitative states are, in certain ways, shared cognitive states. We can study *how* they come to be shared and the behavior and philosophy related to that experience of shared cognition.

So, these four areas (process, development, emotion and will, multiperson cognition) offer a promise of research utility in our study of the cognitive aspects of spirituality.

Balance between Mind, Emotions, Body, Spirit, and Others

I propose that access to Postformal Thought permits the individual to balance, to orchestrate, the physical and mental elements of the self with the element of spirituality. "Self" seems composed of a sort of collection of selves that we need to coordinate. We struggle to balance the often competing needs of our bodies, our minds, our emotions, and our spirits, each of which seems to "know" (in its own way) a separate and very logical reality about what it is experiencing.

For example, the body self may be very interested in having sex with an attractive person that body self met this past summer, while the emotional self may feel love toward a long-term partner and guilt about even being aware of this attraction, much less acting on it. Meanwhile the intellectual self may be thinking through the meaning of this attraction and how much the individual should say about it to his or her partner while being honest about trouble in the long-term relationship. The spiritual self, in this example, may have an intuitive sense that the individual needs to learn something, somehow, about the nature of universal love (what? how?) by means of interaction with this new person.

In this example, each aspect of the self may offer a different "vote" about reality and therefore about the intra- and interpersonal behavior which should occur here. Some of the behavioral votes may contradict each other. In fact, the human condition is as interesting as it is because these balancing dilemmas are so frequent. Yet some behavior must be chosen actively or passively by the human who wishes to survive. Denial of any aspect of our complex human agendas, refusing to honor that aspect's needs, leads to trouble down the road in the form of mental or physical or emotional or spiritual illness. It is only when we can work out a balance among the needs of aspects of the self that we can make choices that maximize our ability to fulfill the needs of all aspects of the self.

Using our spiritual challenges and spiritual awareness as a chosen logic that overarches the several often contradictory logical system demands of body logic, mind logic, and emotional logic, can hardly be expected to occur if the postformal cognitive system has not yet developed. While the body and mind and emotional system can to some degree "run on automatic" or instinct, spirit cannot be added to a coordinated consciousness and mature balance honoring *all* of these without the operations of postformal thinking. This is true because Postformal Thought would seem to provide the conscious balance including spirit tools to make it possible to *creatively* reach this sophisticated, transpersonal balance for ourselves, or to reach it through awakening in an intimate relationship with a partner (Welwood, 1996).

COCREATING THE MYSTICAL "SELF"

Regulation of Stimulation Overload

At each stage of life the organism is confronted with multiple demands which must be met to sustain life. The spiritual or mystical person at first experiences even more demands to regulate the logic of spirituality with the other logics that exist. For example, not only does the spiritually oriented person see an abusive colleague as a threat to his or her local ego-defined self, but *also* sees that colleague as an instrument for personal higher learning *and* as the potential recipient of unconditional love. A situation of overload exists when the knower cannot effectively process the amount of information that presents itself. At first this is also true (perhaps especially true) for information about the reality of spirit. The self who processes is in danger of being fragmented. Reality seems to hold much more contradiction! Things are not what they previously seemed to be! Postformal Thought is a powerful tool for reducing overload adaptively. Reality's contradictions can be bridged. Things are both what they seemed to be, and even more, but strangely more coherent than ever before!

Of course there are *mal*adaptive and *non*creative ways to reduce overload. For example, overloaded adults may limit their cognitive stimulation by limiting their experience to those situations where *only one formal logical system,* or only concrete operational logic, needs to be considered. Or, they simply might reject the spiritual dimension. The adult also might reduce overload by *developing a rigid identity* that permits only certain messages to be received. For example, I might declare that I'm simply "not a spiritual person." Finally, the adult can reduce overload by *focusing on only selected goals or interests.* For example, I might declare that I can't act on my yearnings for a life in the spirit because my first priority is to earn a living.

In contrast, here are some possible creative, adaptive, solutions to overload and "self" preservation that make use of postformal cognition. First the adult might reduce overload by understanding the *many* possible logical structures (e.g., spiritual and practical) that can underlie an experience. This is an adaptive strategy that can only come from experience and familiarity with many types of logical systems and possession of Postformal Thought which holds all logics as possible simultaneously, including a mystical or a spiritual logic. Second, the adult might reduce stimulus overload by making a *more efficient total integration,* using a complex self (described below) as a *complex* filter. A complex filter allows the more inclusive perception of the experience "in," enabling it to be considered. The mystical or unitative experience helps build such a "complex self" filter. Developing the integrative skill is an adaptive solution to overload. It makes use of complex theorizing that is based on experience. No content or complexity is lost when more efficient total integration is used. The mapping surface (i.e., the metaphoric two-dimensional surface on which reality can be represented) is so large and the topography (i.e., the "hills and valleys" of this three-dimensional "map") so varied that most messages fit in somewhere, through use of Postformal Thought. In the storage closet of the mind, when "overload clutter" finally has an interpretive place, it is no longer really "overload." Defined in relation to the fuller self and a bigger picture of reality, it then can all have a meaningful place.

Creating the Self

Creativity literature usually does not address one of the most difficult creative acts of all, that of creating the sense of who I am, the sense of myself. Spiritual writers and clinical psychologists seem to enjoy this existential topic more. This act of creation may be the most complex and far-reaching creative experience any adult can perform, and it takes a lifetime. Integrity, Erikson (1950) wrote, is the culmination of that creation in the challenge of the final stage of life.

While life in any era demands that the individual create a coherent self, the postmodern industrial world demands that we be conscious of our act of self-creation. We knowingly create a sense of self, partly by responding consciously to the demands of the many people who constitute our constituencies and who want us to "be" in a certain way, and partly unconsciously in our yearning to be understood (Gergen, 1991; Kohut, 1977). For the person with a significant spiritual life which includes a mystical component, the task of creating a coherent life includes incorporation of this spiritual component. This is a difficult task. While we are less trapped by confining roles in postmodern society, and therefore can incorporate our mystical side into daily roles, we are also free to feel very unusual, alone, or confused about any atypical sides of our "self." In Western industrial society, the mystical self is atypical. This is one reason many individuals make use of a spiritual guide.

In light of our discussion in this chapter, what are some characteristics of such a spiritual guide or of a transpersonal therapist? First the guide must be accepting of the spiritual side of the self. Second, the guide needs to think postformally to avoid unskilled recommendations that could lead to the loss of a part of the self rather than to a synthesis across the many parts of the self. Third, the guide must be able to distinguish psychopathology and the need to do basic psychological homework from the need for integration of the spiritual self into the created self.

INTIMATE RELATIONSHIPS WITH OTHERS AND THE UNIVERSE

The mystic is in love with the universe and may be in intimate relationships with other specific human partners, friends, and family as well. The theory of complex Postformal Thought can help us understand some of what occurs with these close, loving relations. First, postformal thinking ability seems to have an effect on the dynamics of adult intimate relationships, as described in the following sections. Second, as discussed above, it helps regulate information overload and the creation of a coherent self in spite of multiple close relationships. This regulation may be needed even more than usual by the mystic who may be caught up in the oceanic feelings of being in love with the universe and all creation. Finally, it serves as a bridge to an understanding of and an empathy for the *non*mystic who may be less than sympathetic toward the mystic's actions or reality. Therefore it may be worthwhile to examine postformal cognition as a potential mechanism to help individuals survive the human relational impact of a complex spiritual life. Naturally, in discussing this aspect we will start with what we know about Postformal Thought and its interface with more ordinary intimate relations such as those found in couples.

Interplay of Postformal Thought, Mysticism, and Other Elements in Intimate Behavior

The adaptive value of Postformal Thought is that it can help bridge logical realities so that partners in a relationship can reorder logically conflicting relational realities in more complex ways. For example, with Postformal Thought I can understand the logic of my partner's and my being *both* strong and needy at the same time, rather than labeling one of us as "strong"/"good" and the other as "needy"/"bad." This ability is also useful where one participant in the relationship is the universe. I might be able to think of myself as both an individual *and* a manifestation of universal love without the less useful responses of fearing engulfment or giving myself up to escape personal responsibility. This skill can let each knower handle more information, live in a state of multiple realities that logically conflict, and become committed enough to a chosen reality to go forward and act, thereby reifying the chosen (potential) reality.

In any intimate relationship individuals attempt to join together to have one life, to some degree. As the Apache wedding blessing says, "Now there is one life before you . . . (so) . . . enter into the time of your togetherness." For a couple, three "individuals" begin to exist: partner 1, partner 2, and the relationship which begins to take on a life of its own. For a family, of course, there are even more "individuals" present, as family therapist Virginia Satir (1967) noted when she worked with not only the real humans in her office but also with the remembered aspects of other absent relatives with whom the real humans psychologically interact. To have one life together, to whatever extent they wish to have it together, the logics of the individuals must be bridged effectively. Those logics might be *about* any number of things, some of which do not sound especially "logical," including concepts, roles, perceptions, physical presence, emotions, spiritual experiences, and shared history. The mystic, being "intimate" with all of creation, has, in effect, relations with members of a huge "family" to which all of these relational rules apply.

Effects of the Individual's Postformal Skills on Intimate Relationships

In some cases the individual has access to a cognitive bridge across realities, but not a postformal one. After all, realities *are* bridged, though poorly, if one person in a relationship dominates another and that one's reality becomes the other's, too. But this domination does not require a synthesis of logics since one logic is simply discarded. An analogy in the spiritual domain is the experience of having the mystical reality overwhelm the physical or ordinary one.

Alternatively, the bridge across relational realities may be a postformal one. The incompatible logical realities of the relationship then might be orchestrated more easily and orchestrated at a higher cognitive level to permit a more complex logic of the relationship to emerge. Differences between us now might be a welcome possibility when seen as the basis of a learning challenge for both of us, for now we are each other's therapist and teacher, too. Postformal thinkers can adapt to the challenges of intimate relationships better than those without Postformal Thought because no one's logic needs to be discarded for the relationship to go on. For the postformal couple, power and control are not the same level of threat looming on the relational horizon as they are for the individuals without Postformal Thought who must worry about cognitive survival in their relationships. Those worried about cognitive survival may worry, for example, that if their ideas are not shared by a partner, they are wrong and should be given up. In formal logical clashes someone must be "wrong" and be "convinced" for psychological peace to return. Shared history for the postformal intimates reflects the synthesis of cognitive lives, that is, the joint building of a joint knowledge of reality, rather than alternating dominance of one reality over another. Each logical difference or disagreement ends up being another piece of evidence that the relationship remains a win-win situation for individuals within it. This enhances the relationship's value and tends to stabilize it even further.

In the situation where one individual in the relationship is the *only* postformal one, we see a different opportunity and challenge. Several resolutions are possible each time an interpersonal logical conflict occurs. Perhaps the less cognitively skilled individual will use this chance to grow cognitively, with predictable benefits. Alternatively, the increasingly aggravated postformal individual might let emotions overtake him or her and will temporarily resolve the situation by regressing cognitively and acting out against or withdrawing from others in the situation. Perhaps the more cognitively skilled individual will decide to wait and hope that the other(s) will come around to a more skilled view of the situation, in time.

Postformal Thought, Distress, and Healing in Intimate Relationships (Including Mystical Ones)

You may have gathered from the discussion above that acknowledging the role of Postformal Thought in intimate ongoing relationships might lead to some new ways of conceptualizing couple and family distress and some new approaches to healing distressed relationships. Postformal Thought may be an additional tool for keeping relationships from running into serious trouble when the inevitable difficult times occur. But it may be the source of discord, too. Sometimes this occurs when an "alternative" relationship with God or the universe enters the relational system.

Looking at the bad news first, attaining this more complex cognitive level might lead to trouble and discord in a relationship. Imagine the case of a couple, neither of whom was Postformal when they first became a couple. Time and the events of life passed, and one (but only one) member of the couple developed the ability to think Postformally, and about spiritual aspects of life, too. This led to their each seeing the world and their life together from very different vantage points on many occasions, living different cognitive lives within the boundaries of their life together. For a couple that desires a deep level of closeness, this becomes a challenging situation; they no longer "speak the same language." Of course differences of opinion, differences in ways of seeing the reality of the world, happen for every couple, to some degree, at one time or another in their relationship. Their task as a couple is to grow through the difficulty and build a stronger union. However, in the case of a difference in the ability to understand at a postformal level, the couple has begun a time of profound and far-reaching differences in worldviews. The very nature of their usual realities is different much of the time; one sees it as concrete and existing "out there," while the other sees it as coconstructed and cocreated through commitment to its reality. Even more challenging, one of the partners (the Postformal one) can visit the reality of the other (the non-Postformal one), but the other cannot yet visit back. So when one develops but the other does not, discord in worldviews may provide a temporary challenge (or a permanent one). On a spiritual level, this unfortunate circumstance can lead to one partner seeing the world through a mystic's (postformal) vision while the other does not.

The Other Side of the Coin: Effects of Intimate and Mystical Relationship Factors on Development of Postformal Thought

The factors in ongoing intimate relationships which we have been discussing, mainly emotional defense mechanisms, shared relationship history, and shared cultural reality, potentially can *influence* the development and use of Postformal Thought, not just be influenced by it. For example, if an individual is emotionally damaged and is responding to all situations out of need, that person is less likely to take a risk in a relational situation and let go of his or her own cognitive verities long enough to be willing to make a bridge to someone else's realities, or to the larger reality of universal Love. Maslow (1968) discussed the need for safety and its chilling effect on growth. The help of a therapist or guide may be useful at that time.

But love is a powerful factor, especially when it is universal Love. When the reality of one person in a relationship clashes with another's view, the intensity of the bond is what motivates them to seek a resolution. This is a push toward development of Postformal Thought, or perfection of it, since lower level logics will leave the conflict unresolved. The bond between an individual and the universe often allows him or her to develop a deeper "understanding" of life or relationship "on faith," and then gradually grow into that more complex cognition. The love allows the less skilled person to hold the door open for multiple realities to be considered, long enough to have the experiences which permit cognitive growth.

The spiritual relationship with the universe can effectively spur the growth of complex cognition by creating a safe environment for viewing the bigger picture of reality. The person is more willing to turn on the floodlights and to know the expanded reality at all of the levels of logics. In this way the intimate relationship of the spiritual person with the universe can bring about cognitive and emotional healing and growth in that person. The truth can then set them free.

CONCLUSION

This chapter applies my Postformal Theory to help us understand some cognitive aspects of mystical and spiritual experiences and some spiritual aspects of cognition. The chapter should be considered an introduction to an expanded, speculative dialogue about these topics. The study of cognition that includes knowing the unknowable is not beyond the range of scientific inquiry. Far from being antithetical to the logics of either science or religion, this sort of study bridges them. Undertaking it may be our responsibility, both in our roles as scientists studying the *full* spectrum of the human condition, and in our roles as thinking mystics.

REFERENCES

Bastick, T. (1982). *Intuition: How we think and act.* New York: Wiley.

Castaneda, C. (1971). *A separate reality.* New York: Washington Square Press.

Erikson, E. (1950). *Childhood and society.* New York: W. W. Norton.

Gergen, K. (1991). *The saturated self.* New York: Basic Books.

Isen, A., & Shalker, T. (1982). Effects of feeling state on evaluation of positive, neutral, and negative stimuli: When you "accentuate the positive" do you "eliminate the negative"? *Social Psychology Quarterly, 45,* 58–63.

Kohut, H. (1977). *The restoration of the self.* New York: International Universities Press.

Koplowitz, H. (1978). Unitary operational thinking. *Brain/Mind Bulletin,* October, 3.

Labouvie-Vief, G. (1987). *Speaking about feelings: Symbolization and self regulation through the lifespan.* Paper presented at the Third Beyond Formal Operations Conference at Harvard, Cambridge, MA.

Laughlin, P. R. (1965). Selection strategies in concept attainment as a function of number of persons and stimulus display. *Journal of Experimental Psychology, 70,* 323–327.

Laughlin, P., & Bitz, D. (1975). Individual vs. dyadic performance on a disjunctive task as a function of individual ability level. *Journal of Personality and Social Psychology, 31,* 487–496.

Maslow, A. H. (1968). *Toward a psychology of being.* New York: Van Nostrand Reinhold.

Meacham, J., & Emont, N. (1989). The interpersonal basis of everyday problem solving. In J. D. Sinnott & J. Cavanaugh (Eds.), *Bridging paradigms: Positive development in adulthood and positive aging* (pp. 7–23). New York: Praeger.

Pearce, J. (1973). *The crack in the cosmic egg.* New York: Pocket Books.

Rogers, D., Sinnott, J., & Van Dusen, L. (1991, July). *Marital adjustment and social cognitive performance in everyday logical problem solving.* Paper presented at the 6th Adult Development Conference, Boston, MA.

Satir, V. (Ed.) (1967). *Conjoint family therapy.* Palo Alto, CA: Science and Behavior Books.

Sinetar, M. (1986). *Ordinary people as monks and mystics.* Mahwah, NJ: Paulist Press.

Sinnott, J. D. (1981). The theory of relativity: A metatheory for development? *Human Development, 24,* 293–311.

Sinnott, J. D. (1984). Postformal reasoning: The relativistic stage. In M. Commons, F. Richards, & C. Armon (Eds.), *Beyond formal operations: Late adolescent and adult development* (pp. 298–325). New York: Praeger.

Sinnott, J. D. (Ed.). (1989a). *Everyday problem solving: Theory and applications.* New York: Praeger.

Sinnott, J. D. (1989b). Lifespan relativistic postformal thought. In M. Commons, J. Sinnott, F. Richards, & C. Armon (Eds.), *Beyond formal operations: Late adolescent and adult development* (pp. 239–278). New York: Praeger.

Sinnott, J. D. (1991a). *Conscious adult development: Complex thought and solving our intragroup conflicts.* Invited presentation, Sixth Adult Development Conference, Suffolk University, Boston.

Sinnott, J. D. (1991b). What do we do to help John? A case study of everyday problem solving in a family making decisions about an acutely psychotic member. In J. D. Sinnott & J. Cavanaugh (Eds.), *Bridging paradigms: Positive development in adulthood and cognitive aging* (pp. 203–220). New York: Praeger.

Sinnott, J. D. (1993). The use of complex thought and resolving intragroup conflicts: A means to conscious adult development in the workplace. In J. Demick and P. Miller (Eds.), *Adult development in the workplace* (pp. 155–175). Hillsdale, NJ: Erlbaum.

Sinnott, J. D. (1994a). Development and yearning: Cognitive aspects of spiritual development. *Journal of Adult Development, 1,* 91–99.

Sinnott, J. D. (1994b). *Interdisciplinary handbook of adult lifespan learning.* Westport, CT: Greenwood.

Sinnott, J. D. (1996a). Postformal thought and mysticism: How might the mind know the unknowable? *Aging and Spirituality: Newsletter of American Sociological Association Forum on Religion, Spirituality and Aging, 8,* 7–8.

Sinnott, J. D. (1996b). The developmental approach: Postformal thought as adaptive intelligence. In F. Blanchard-Fields & T. Hess (Eds.), *Perspectives on cognitive change in adulthood and aging* (pp. 358–383). New York: McGraw-Hill.

Sinnott, J. D. (1997). *Knowing the unknowable: Some approaches to the study of the cognition of spiritual experience.* Paper presented at the Second Annual Roundtable on Religious Research: A Further Exploration of Religious and Spiritual Dimensions, Columbia, MD.

Sinnott, J. D. (1998a). Creativity and postformal thought. In C. Adams-Price (Ed.), *Creativity and aging: Theoretical and empirical approaches* (pp. 43–72). New York: Springer.

Sinnott, J. D. (1998b). *The development of logic in adulthood: Postformal thought and its applications.* New York: Plenum.

Tart, C. (1983). *States of consciousness.* El Cerrito, CA: Psychological Processes.

Underhill, E. (1961). *Mysticism.* New York: Dutton. (Original work published 1911)

Welwood, J. (1996). *Love and awakening: Discovering the sacred path of intimate relationship.* New York: HarperCollins.

Wilber, K. (1995). *Sex, ecology, and spirituality: The spirit of evolution.* Boston: Shambhala Press.

Wolf, F. A. (1981). *Taking the quantum leap.* New York: Harper & Row.

Yan, B. (1995). *Nonabsolute/relativistic (N/R) thinking: A possible unifying commonality underlying models of postformal reasoning.* Unpublished Ph.D. dissertation, University of British Columbia, Vancouver.

Yan, B., & Arlin, P. K. (1995). Nonabsolute/relativistic thinking: A common factor underlying models of postformal reasoning? *Journal of Adult Development, 2,* 223–240.

Zukav, G. (1979). *The dancing wu li masters: An overview of the new physics.* New York: Bantam.

8.

Fifth-Order Consciousness and Early Greek Christianity

Leslie P. Fairfield

Bosnia and Rwanda remind us that the end of the Cold War has not led automatically to peace on earth. And the bombs of Oklahoma City and Atlanta underscore for Americans the reality that they inhabit the same dangerous world, where security from violence cannot be assumed as a guaranteed human right. The fragility of peace in the 1990s recalls to us what we ought to have remembered, namely that our habits of tolerance and respect for diversity need to be cultivated intentionally, if they are to be achieved at all. Human beings do not grow into compassionate and respectful adults without active encouragement. But how do we educate for civility? What conditions produce human beings who are capable of tolerance and respect? How can we grow beyond the emotions of the blood-feud, and the intellectual anger of ideological warfare?

ROBERT KEGAN'S MODEL

Robert Kegan's (1994) *In Over Our Heads* offers a model of human development which helps us understand the stages by which human beings may grow into compassionate and respectful adults. In successive stages, as Kegan views human maturation, we are able to think objectively about, and to choose intentionally, certain ideas and behaviors which had hitherto been unconscious in us. For instance, many modern teenagers absorb the values of their peer group unconsciously, whereas later, say in their 20s, they may be able to reflect critically on those values and adopt a worldview voluntarily and intentionally. Of particular interest regarding toleration and respect are Kegan's fourth and fifth stages, or orders of consciousness. Kegan argues that in modern Western societies, people may be capable of a "fourth-order consciousness" in their 20s, though he admits that the phenomenon is rare at that or any age. In fourth-order consciousness we are able to articulate a worldview with clarity, which we have chosen reflectively and which we affirm thoughtfully as true. In mature fourth-order consciousness, moreover, we can concede that other worldviews have at least a formal right to voice and vote. At the same time, we do not suppose that "the stranger" has anything very important to tell us, or indeed that we share anything important in common. Fourth-order consciousness assumes that the basic building block of reality is the self-sufficient, autonomous individual. So any relationship which I acknowledge with another represents a voluntary choice on my part, not a preexistent obligation to which I am accountable, or a web which supports me (Kegan, 1994, pp. 271–304).

Now as Kegan observes, fourth-order consciousness would represent an enormous increase in human civility if large numbers of people practiced it in Sarajevo or Portadown or Los Angeles. Most of us in the Western world are still struggling to organize our lives into those habits and attitudes which fourth-order consciousness represents at its most mature (Kegan, 1994, p. 317). But this fourth stage does have limits. While it can produce a formal or procedural tolerance for diversity, it cannot foster true interrelationality. Since in fourth-order consciousness I still experience myself as an isolated, self-sufficient monad, I'm not motivated to recognize or to cultivate a relationality or an interdependence which is other than elective, or to which I am accountable. If blood enemies are to meet and be reconciled, and own their true interdependence, the 21st century needs a quality of human maturity that goes beyond even the already scarce fourth order of consciousness.

Kegan in fact argues the possibility of a subsequent order of knowing and feeling, in which autonomous fourth order individualism gives way to a capacity for true meeting—a stage which transcends the explosive fragmentation of typical late modern societies (Kegan, 1994, pp. 307–352). Kegan argues that in this further stage of adulthood, in fifth-order consciousness, we recognize that our self-contained, ideological ("fourth-order") selves are in fact incomplete, and that their pretensions to autonomy and wholeness are unreflective. In fifth-order consciousness I recognize that much of what I previously repudiated, and viewed as alien in the stranger, is actually part of my own self as well. I can concede that those hated features of the stranger are actually unrecognized features of my own attitudes and behavior. If I am a Protestant Unionist in Northern Ireland, I recognize painfully in my own heart the feckless irresponsibility which I caricature and hate in my Bogside Roman Catholic neighbors. If I am a Bosnian Serb, I reluctantly acknowledge in my own character the aggressive, militaristic land-hunger which terrifies me in the Muslim next door. Fifth-order consciousness entails pulling in my projections and conceding that the hated stranger occupies a place at the table of my own internal town meeting. So instead of splitting off those parts of myself which I deprecate (often with considerable justification) and projecting them onto others, declaring war on the "bad guys out there," I own that I am more internally complex than I have hitherto been willing to concede. And I accept responsibility for dealing with my own internal "militant Irishman" or "aggressive mullah," not blaming on other people the parts of myself which I intensely dislike.

When I pull in my projections and recognize my own internal enemies, I am in a clearer-eyed position to assess other people more realistically, and to identify those features of common humanity which we do in fact hold in common. Hence I can concede to the stranger not only a formal or procedural right to be heard, but a wholehearted welcome, as to one with whom I share a great deal. True empathy begins to be possible at this time, as we grow beyond the self-constructed autonomy of fourth-order consciousness. As the Jungian analyst Edward Whitmont put it (1969): "true relatedness requires the awareness of shadow, animus and anima in order that they may not distort our view of the "other" through their projection; hence the possibility of relatedness belongs essentially to the second half of life" (p. 281). At this point relationships are available for reflection, as I accept the limitations of my erstwhile split-off and illusory fourth-order independence.

Another benefit of growth into fifth-order consciousness is that I can acknowledge that I am profoundly constituted by my relationships. It's not the case that I *am* my relationships, as a teenager in Kegan's third stage is unconsciously embedded in that network. Rather, in the fifth stage I can assess thoughtfully the degree to which I owe all that I am (my biological existence, my formation as a person, my daily survival) to others, and receive it all as a gift. Likewise I can recognize that social interaction reveals to me not only who other people are, but who I am as well. Even an introverted grandfather may admit that the first grandchild elicits from him a capacity for doting which astonishes the entire family. So fifth-order consciousness allows me to contemplate reflectively not only the parties in a relationship (my grandson and myself) but also the degree to which the relationship actually constitutes both of us. There's no grandfather without a grandchild. I can begin to experience consciously, therefore, not only a range of emotions and behavior which are novel to me, but also a web of relationships which construct and define me anew.

A final benefit of fifth-order consciousness is that I am newly accessible to open-ended learning. True meeting with others enables me to appreciate the infinite variability of human nature in others. With my clear-boundaried fourth-order self now permeable—not discarded but transcended—I can experience a "second naiveté" in which I discover surprises in a universe which I once considered to be closed and entirely predictable.

THE IMPORTANCE OF STORIES

Even a tiny group of human beings in fifth-order consciousness would be a catalyst for healing in Belfast or Sarajevo or Bujumbura, however severely any of these instances may push the envelope of realistic hope. But what does it take to produce grown-ups in this stage of consciousness and behavior? What kind of curriculum does growth into fifth-order human maturity require? What kind of ideological rationale would support this achievement? What kind of environment can nurture it?

In fourth-order consciousness we are not so apt to admit the need for mentoring. At that stage we are inclined to assume that in order to grow, we need only be liberated from illegitimate constraints to our self-fulfillment—whereupon we will spontaneously turn into autonomous, critical, and independent adults, models of fully mature human beings. All it takes is the removal of roadblocks. So from the fourth-order perspective, the ideal curriculum would look like Harvard, Oxford, or the Sorbonne with minimal personal supervision, and an entirely elective curriculum. But the failure of modern Western education to produce durably civilized societies calls into question the libertarian optimism of fourth-order consciousness. Is freedom *from* all that's required to produce citizens with reliable habits of mutual respect? Chastened realism in the 1990s suggests that fourth-order character doesn't happen automatically when tyranny and oppression collapse. Even fourth-order maturity requires intentional cultivation, and a willingness to embrace freedom *for* the pursuit of virtues like respect and toleration. And if hard work necessarily precedes the harvest of fourth-order consciousness, how much more must the subtle and sophisticated fifth-order require the right curriculum and an intentional investment of personal effort?

One hopeful sign suggests an increasing possibility of educating for fifth-order consciousness in the late modern West, namely a renewed appreciation for the way in which stories shape human character. As Stanley Hauerwas (1981) and many others have observed, stories give human communities their identity and sense of purpose, and offer a rationale which may encourage individuals to subsume their private self-interest to the requirements of the common good. Likewise stories tell of heroes, whose "big" lives offer templates by which "little" people (the rest of us) may shape their behavior in the direction of virtue. In many ways, this renewed appreciation of stories and their importance represents a rejection of Enlightenment attitudes. As Hans Frei (1974) and others have pointed out, modernity came to identify the scientific method as the only legitimate way to establish truth. Stories lacked the precision and the empirical verifiability which scientific propositions represented. Hence stories came to be relegated to the private sphere of life, valued for their capacity to entertain us and to stimulate inner self-reflection, but no longer reckoned to be vehicles of "hard" truth. The latter was abstract, universal, mathematical, and scientific. Stories were concrete, particular, literary, and personal. If the emergence of autonomous, critical, and analytical human maturity (i.e., fourth-order consciousness) required only an absence of restraint, then stories played no necessary role in shaping human character. Character needed to be liberated and revealed, but not shaped.

Of course, the modern West has in fact told two stories about reality, despite its methodological repudiation of story as the means by which truth is established. Both of these modern stories contain action-corollaries to guide human behavior, and both predictably commend fourth-order consciousness, individual autonomy, and liberation from constraint as their principal values. The "Enlightenment Story" (the first one to emerge) has been the "myth of origins" that explains and justifies the public dimension of life in the modern West. Implicit in the values of modernity (Baumer, 1977, pp. 26–78, 140–217, 302–366; Tarnas, 1991, pp. 248–365) the Enlightenment Story went something like this.

> After the Big Bang, the universe has evolved according to patterns which we can observe scientifically today. We know, too, that the universe is all there is. It's a closed system. Nothing exists other than what the scientific method can observe, quantify, and verify.
>
> Life appeared on earth through the random interaction of the necessary components and conditions. Human life in

> particular is the product of a long, unplanned series of genetic mutations, interacting with specific environments, and evolving through natural selection. Now in the late 20th century we are able to understand this process, and we have the power to shape our genes, and to create a biotechnical Good Society. In the pursuit of this future, we are accountable to no authority save ourselves for the choices we make. The intellectually fittest make the choices.
>
> Therefore (action corollary) we should assume that every human being has the potential for contributing to the progress of the human race, especially through scientific research. We should call upon our governments to guarantee to each individual his or her life, liberty and property, so that each one may enjoy the necessary preconditions for fulfilling their potential. No person should inhibit another in the free exercise of intelligence, provided that each one respects the ground rules which protect the corresponding rights of others. The ground rules in the open marketplace of life are laws which are specified by human legislation, and they do not represent any absolute moral order, other than the one formal principle of individual rights.

This powerful and effective Story assumed the critical, detached, scientific mind as the goal of human maturation. It posited fourth-order consciousness as both normative and inevitable, absent any illegitimate restrictions on individual development. And by the mid-20th century this Story came to appear self-evident to most inhabitants of modernity, so self-evident as to seem less a story than an objective description of How Things Are.

The Enlightenment Story defined reality in the public spheres of government, the marketplace and education in the modern West. But the private dimension of life developed a correlative Story, not gainsaying the assertions of the Enlightenment narrative, but adding a dimension of spirituality which the public Story omitted. This Romantic Story gained strength and plausibility throughout the 19th century, and today (in its own dimension of life) it enjoys as much persuasiveness as its Enlightenment correlative (Baumer, 1977, pp. 268–301 and Tarnas, 1991, pp. 366–394). The Romantic Story goes like this.

> Everything in the Enlightenment Story is correct, with one exception. At the heart of the universe there has always been a "spirit," not susceptible to empirical verification but nonetheless real. This "spirit" is neither personal nor conscious, but is metaphorically like an underground river of soul, or perhaps like the DNA code of the universe. At last with the evolution of human consciousness, this underground river has burst above the surface. We now have the capacity to connect consciously with our source, and we can do so by looking inward and finding it in the depths of our psyches. As we do so, we experience peace and healing from the wounds which we receive in the admittedly competitive public marketplace of modern life.
>
> Therefore (action corollary) we should recognize that "spirit" lies deep within each one of us. We should experience and express as fully as we can the creativity of this inner "spirit." We should especially value those moments of intense, heightened consciousness when we feel at one with the universe. We should acknowledge and value the infinite variety of ways in which "spirit" actualizes and expresses itself in human personality. No person should inhibit another in the free expression of human creativity, provided that each one respects the ground rules which protect the creativity of others. As in the case of the public sphere, these ground rules are human conventions, reflecting no moral order in the universe, other than the one formal principle of individual autonomy.

In contrast to the analytical, utilitarian individualism encouraged by the Enlightenment Story, the Romantic narrative commends a different range of behaviors, namely expressive creativity and the quest for affective experience. But the Romantic adult is still the autonomous individual in this Story, and the liberated artist is the goal of human development. Apart from relationship with the impersonal ground of one's being, relationality is no more central than in the Enlightenment saga. Connectedness with other human beings, other than on an elective ("exploring my personal relationships") basis, does not appear in the outline of human maturity which the Romantic Story describes.

One other significant feature of both modern Stories is the picture of the universe which they articulate. In either case, ultimate reality equals the universe, and the cosmos is all there is. However varied and diverse that cosmos may be, it is nonetheless a single whole, characterized by consistent laws operating throughout its expanse. This is a "monistic" worldview: there is no supranature, no transcendent dimension, nothing other than the cosmos. The latter has no relationship to anything else. Just as the ideal human being is autonomous and complete, so is the universe. The individualism of modernity's anthropology is reflected by the monism of its cosmology. Nothing in either the Enlightenment or the Romantic Story suggests to us that relationality is central to our existence.

Each of these stories retains its plausibility today. The Enlightenment saga which had its genesis in the age of Newton's *Principia Mathematica* (1686/1934) still finds eloquent exponents in the late 20th century, despite multiple traumas of world wars and ecological decay. It's not hard to be moved by Carl Sagan's peroration (1980) at the end of *Cosmos,* his famous PBS television series.

> For we are the local embodiment of a Cosmos grown to self-awareness. We have begun to contemplate our origins: starstuff pondering the stars; organized assemblages of ten billion billion billion atoms considering the evolution of atoms; tracing the long journey by which here at least, consciousness arose. Our loyalties are to the species and the planet. We speak for each. Our obligation to survive is owed not just to ourselves but also to that Cosmos, ancient and vast, from which we spring. (p. 286)

We have our roots in inanimate "starstuff," but we're fully conscious now, and ready to use our expertise to organize the future of the planet.

Interestingly, a number of Sagan's contemporaries in late 20th century physics have given the correlative Romantic Story a boost. Contemporary awareness of systems and holism has stimulated writers like Fritjof Capra (1983) to think of human consciousness as participating in a universal mind which is the spiritual dimension of the cosmos.

> In the stratified order of nature, individual minds are embedded in the larger minds of social and ecological systems, and these

> are integrated into the planetary mental system—the mind of Gaia—which in turn must participate in some kind of universal or cosmic mind. The conceptual framework of the new systems approach is in no way restricted by associating this cosmic mind with the traditional idea of God. In the words of Jantsch, "God is not the creator, but the mind of the universe." In this view the deity is, of course, neither male nor female, nor manifest in any personal form, but represents nothing less than the self-organizing dynamics of the entire cosmos. (p. 292)

The Jungian tradition also takes cues from modern physics and tells the Romantic Story in its clearest late 20th century form. As Edward Whitmont (1982) writes, there is a mind or a soul within the universe, and it is constantly growing "upwards" into self-consciousness.

> The new Aquarian world view, ushered in by twentieth-century physics, no longer thinks in terms of discrete objects; rather it conceives of a continuous flux of process, vibrational fields, quantum pulses of an indefinable, nonmaterial substratum. This is a universal consciousness, perhaps, yet prior to what we call consciousness. Prior to energy and matter, it results in both. It is a self-directed flow that gives form. The dynamics of our world, in the view of the modern myth, do not flow from a maker or director outside of it, who manipulates it like an object. The world is inner or self-directed, an immanence groping for self-realization in the three dimensions of space, and in the fourth dimension of time as well. Consciousness and conscience now discover self-direction. (p. 221)

The inner soul of the universe has come to consciousness in us, and presumably is reaching forward to fuller self-expression in the future.

Both the Enlightenment and the Romantic Stories express confidence in the benign and dependable character of this cosmic process. However, neither of these accounts (for all their emphasis on holism) provide a reliable grounding for fifth-order consciousness or for interdependence. There's the impersonal universal mind, and the individual mind, but no necessary interrelationship between persons in these myths. We hear of the "one" and the energy-field of the "One," but nothing about Buber's (1923/1970, pp. 53, 63) "I and Thou" as central to reality. Personal interdependence between human beings needs to be grounded in a Story which features more than an ego and an energy field.

In any case, modern confidence in the benign reliability of historical process has worn thin in the late 20th century. In the last two decades postmodernism has challenged the two creation myths of modernity. As Anderson, Gergen, and others have pointed out (Anderson, 1990; Gergen, 1991) postmodernism argues that there are no grand Stories, no metanarratives, no *grands récits.* The postmodern world has no overarching coherent narrative. Things happen, and we see discrete events, but there's no point, and no beginning or middle or end. Postmodernists make a crucial inference from one feature of the Enlightenment and Romantic Stories, namely that there is no personal narrator in either of them. In the former saga, chance and time drive the evolutionary escalator. In the latter saga, the engine of history is an impersonal force, Hegel's Idea or Wordsworth's Spirit of Nature in their various modern costumes. Both versions of modernity tell a Story without an author. So postmodernists draw a conclusion which modernity preferred not to contemplate: no Author, no Story. But postmodernism is negative, and offers no action corollary other than resignation and despair. Neither does deconstructive postmodernism offer any escape from the lonely individualism of the modern world.

Kegan (1994, pp. 324–334) wonders whether there may be a reconstructive postmodernism, offering a way forward. He posits fifth-order consciousness which acknowledges a relationality, a connection which holds separate individuals together. But what kind of Story would support this fifth-order consciousness? Is there an available account of reality which would justify this interdependence of individual persons, and ground it in the heart of the cosmos?

IRENAEUS OF LYONS: CREATION AND HUMAN DESTINY

One possibility worth considering is the early Greek Christian tradition, where there are some resources which the West has not fully explored. One of the earliest story-tellers in the Greek Christian tradition was a teacher named Irenaeus, whose version of the Christian narrative placed interdependence at the center of reality. Irenaeus was born in western Asia Minor, and grew up to be a leader in the Greek-speaking Christian communities there. He emigrated to the Rhone Valley in southern France, however, when members of his fellowship moved there in search of employment. When the leader of the Christian congregation in Lyons died in a persecution around 180 A.D., Irenaeus replaced him as bishop. Over the next 20 years, until he too died as a martyr, Irenaeus focused his efforts on teaching the Christian community in Lyons, and reminding them of the Story for which they were risking their lives (Frend, 1984, pp. 244–250).

Irenaeus' version of the Christian Story drew some important inferences from the biblical account. Irenaeus understood the universe to owe its origin to the creative act of a deity who exists eternally in three "Persons," or participants in a divine relationship. The Christian scriptures had named these Persons "Father," "Son" and "Holy Spirit," but had not defined their relationship in detail. Irenaeus stood near the beginning of a long tradition of reflection, extending over several centuries, in which Christian thinkers would explore the nature and significance of the "Trinity" (as this threefold personal deity came to be called). Irenaeus' telling of the Christian Story (early in the process) made particular applications of the Trinitarian idea vis-à-vis the creation of the universe, and the goal of human development.

Irenaeus argued that the personal interdependence within the Trinity found expression in the way in which creation occurred. Father, Son, and Holy Spirit produced the universe cooperatively and out of nothing, giving it both being and an independent identity apart from themselves. The Father was the source and origin of the universe's existence. Irenaeus (1952, p. 50) went on to say that the Son " 'establishes,' that is, works bodily and consolidates being, while the Spirit disposes and shapes the various 'powers. . . .' " The Son's role was to be the intermediary between the ineffable depths of the Father, and the universe to which the Son communicates existence. And the Spirit was and is the presence of God within the universe, nurturing and shaping the created order. So the universe was the product of a cooperative and interdependent activity. Likewise, the Trinity was not an exclusive or a closed relationship. As Irenaeus developed the Christian Story, he emphasized the openness of the Trinity to the creation. Father, Son, and Holy Spirit brought the cosmos into being with a view to welcoming that new reality into the divine relationality which already existed (Gunton, 1993, pp. 158–160; Moltmann, 1985, pp. 242–243).

God's openness to the universe was especially clear in the creation of human beings. Here Irenaeus' teaching was unique, and was significantly ignored in the later Latin tradition in the West. God-in-Three-Persons created human beings, said Irenaeus, making them specifically in the image of the Son, who would later manifest perfect humanity in time and space as Jesus of Nazareth. But human beings were not created fully mature from the start. Adam and Eve, the paradigmatic couple, came into being with the *potential* to grow up into the capacity for relationship which the Son epitomized. As Irenaeus (1952) put it,

> So, having made the man lord of the earth and everything in it, he made him in secret lord also of the servants in it. They, however, were in their full development, while the lord, that is, the man, was a little one; for he was a child and had need to grow so as to come to his full perfection. (p. 55)

The purpose and destiny of human beings was to learn and to grow in relationship, so that they might take their place in due course as members (not as gods, but in their humanity) in the family of the Trinity. Irenaeus' understanding of human nature was dynamic. Lifelong growth was the curriculum for human life. And God's plan for human beings was a Story with a beginning, a middle, and an intended happy ending.

Something obviously went wrong with the plan, and Irenaeus (1952, pp. 57–58) acknowledged that the Story got complicated. As one feature of their authentic personhood, human beings had free choice. They enjoyed the option of sticking to the curriculum and growing up into relationality, or not. As Irenaeus retold the story of Genesis, Evil tempted the human race to short-circuit their long course of instruction, and to "be as gods" instantly (in other words, to take over the university and seize the administration building). So Adam and Eve, the prototypical human beings, rejected their relationship with the Trinity, and elected to take charge of their own education. Tragically, they did not foresee that their rebellion would cut them off from the source of their being, as well as from the relationality which was their goal in life. So they began to free-fall, not only into personal animosity one to another (viz. Genesis 3:16) but down into physical disintegration and death.

Irenaeus' account of their rescue is a classic version of the Christian Story. He tells (Gunton, 1993, pp. 80–81; Richardson, 1970, pp. 385–391) how the Son came "down" (as it were) to where human beings were free-falling into nothingness. He took on human nature as Jesus of Nazareth, and bound himself solidly to the human condition. But at every point in life at which fallen humans relentlessly choose egotism over relationship, Jesus stayed connected to God the Father, through the Holy Spirit, and to other human beings. Therefore not even death (the ultimate disconnection) could separate him from Life, and he rose up by the Spirit's power back to the Father, carrying with him all those human beings who cling to him for rescue. A modern follower of Irenaeus, the British scholar C. S. Lewis, paraphrased (Lewis, 1970) the Story at this point:

> . . . one has the picture of a diver, stripping off garment after garment, making himself naked, then flashing for a moment in the air, and then down through the green, and warm, and sunlit water into the pitch black, cold, freezing water, down into the mud and slime, then up again, his lungs almost bursting, back again to the green and warm and sunlit water, and then at last out into the sunshine, holding in his hand the dripping thing he went down to get. This thing is human nature. (p. 82)

As Irenaeus understood it, the purpose of this rescue operation was to put human beings back on the long path of instruction which they had foolishly abandoned. Now they were to grow up once again toward mature personhood, and ultimately be capable of that interdependence which was the chief quality of the heavenly Family. That common life would be so luminous that Irenaeus did not hesitate to call it Glory.

Several features of Irenaeus' Story are worth remarking, as representing a rationale for fifth-order consciousness today. First of all, Irenaeus' account of creation describes a universe in which individual human beings have the space to be themselves, and therefore the ability to choose relationship. (Here Irenaeus' account falls in line with many other versions of the Christian Story, but his rendition is especially lucid.) In Irenaeus' tale, the divine Trinity created a cosmos which was separate and distinct, and which possessed a measure of independence. Father, Son, and Spirit intended the universe for relationship with themselves, and they continued to uphold, guide, and sustain the cosmos. But they gave it space to be itself, they did not minutely determine every event, and in particular, they gave human beings the freedom of choice to join the divine program, or not. Creation was not simply an emanation out of the divine essence, with no freedom to do otherwise than express necessary Being. Nor was the universe a vast impersonal machine, with human beings as tiny cogs, slaves to the blind forces driving the whole. There was distance between the Trinity and creation, in Irenaeus' account, and running-room for humans within the cosmos. As Irenaeus received and developed the Christian Story, its worldview was explicitly "theist" and not "monist" (Gilkey, 1985, pp. 41–80). In contrast to the Enlightenment and Romantic Stories, the Christian narrative describes a God who is intrinsically relational, who is different from the cosmos, and who is nevertheless most intimately present to the universe. If we are to identify interdependence as the significant mark of human maturity, it would be an advantage to understand human life as occurring in this universe created by interdependence, but with sufficient space to allow us both our own individual particularity, as well as the opportunity to grow up into mutual reciprocity.

Another significant feature of Irenaeus' version of the creation story is the fact of divine authorship. Again in contrast to the Enlightenment and Romantic Stories, the Christian account specifically acknowledged intention and purpose behind the universe. Neither blind chance nor the unfolding of an impersonal "spirit" characterize history, but rather a dramatist-cum-director who can weave a story out of the actors' own outrageous ad-libbing. So Irenaeus' universe is a place where individual life-stories make sense, there being an overall Story with a beginning, a middle, and an end, within which particular stories can find their meaning. History is going somewhere. It is neither a cycle in which humans are trapped, nor a coldly random postmodern theater of the absurd. In Irenaeus' worldview (Gunton, 1993, p. 120), human lives have the option of reflecting a coherent narrative structure. In that universe, a developmental model of human growth (with a beginning, a middle and an end) could make a lot of sense.

Finally, Irenaeus makes character development central to his Story (in a way that later Western versions do not). Growth toward interdependence is the chief purpose of human existence, as Irenaeus understands the divine plan. God wants people to become mature adults, in the sense that they come to have ego structures which are stable, yet permeable enough to allow connectedness with others. Irenaeus' developmental vision of human life found little support in the Latin, Western tradition, where the medieval theologians preferred to think of Adam and Eve as statically perfect before their fall, rather than as kindergartners in the school of relationship. Irenaeus' version is the more useful one, in terms of supporting a vision of human maturity which leads to fifth-order consciousness.

THE CAPPADOCIAN FATHERS: ULTIMATE REALITY AS RELATIONAL

Two centuries after Irenaeus wrote, a group of theologians in Asia Minor made some important additions to the Christian understanding of the Trinity, that interrelational Author of the

Christian Story. Their contribution further grounds interdependence in the heart of reality, and supports a developmental model of human life which posits fifth-order consciousness as its goal. These three theologians in the late 4th century were known as the "Cappadocian Fathers," from their place of origin in what is now east-central Turkey. Basil of Caesarea, his brother Gregory of Nyssa, and their mutual friend Gregory of Nazianzus all lived in this region at a time when Greco-Roman ideological challenges to Christianity were forcing theologians to think through precisely what their inherited biblical tradition meant (Frend, 1984, pp. 630–634). The Cappadocian Fathers' contributions were mostly lost to the West after the latter collapsed into barbarism in the 5th century, though they continued to shape the Greek strand of Christianity which survived in the eastern Mediterranean. In the late 20th century, the Cappadocians' teaching on the nature of ultimate reality could be a valuable resource to recover.

In the 4th century Christians were struggling to differentiate their Story from the different versions of the Greco-Roman worldview, and the idea of the Trinity lay at the heart of this conflict. The Cappadocian Fathers needed to think more deeply about the nature of ultimate reality than Irenaeus had done, in order to respond to the legitimate criticisms of thinkers outside the Christian faith. Like Irenaeus, the Cappadocian Fathers were conscious of hints in the New Testament that there existed a differentiation within the God of Israel whom they continued to worship. There had been casual, almost throwaway lines in the letters of Paul of Tarsus in the New Testament, for instance, which seemed at the very least to nuance the cry of Israel that "The Lord thy God is One Lord." For example, Paul concluded his second letter to the Christian community at Corinth by saying (II Corinthians 13:14),

> The grace of the Lord Jesus Christ and the love of God and the fellowship of the Holy Spirit be with you all.

Since the essence of the ancient Hebrew faith had been ethical monotheism, and since the belief in one God radically differentiated both Judaism and its Christian offspring from Greco-Roman polytheism, it was very important for Christian thinkers to explain how and why the Apostle Paul had not been talking about three different gods here. In the Greek-speaking eastern Mediterranean, Christians were still debating this issue vigorously in the late 4th century, some 300 years after the New Testament documents first began to circulate.

The Cappadocian Fathers offered some answers to this question, developing their inherited tradition's understanding of the heart of reality as a "Trinity" of three "Persons." Gregory of Nazianzus is the clearest of his colleagues on the subject. Gregory makes several points. First of all, as Irenaeus had argued earlier, he explains that the one God who created the universe exists eternally in three distinct modes of being-in-relationship.

> To us there is one God, for the Godhead is one, and all that proceeds from him is referred to one, though we believe in three Persons. For one is not more and another less God; nor is one before and another after; nor are they divided in will or parted in power; nor can you find here any of the qualities of divisible things; but the Godhead is to speak concisely, undivided in separate Persons; and there is a mingling of lights, as it were of three suns joined to each other. When, then, we look at the Godhead, or the first cause of the monarchia, that which we conceive is one; but when we look at the Persons in whom the Godhead dwells, and at those who timelessly and with equal glory have their being from the first cause, there are three whom we worship. (Hardy, 1954, p. 202)

Whenever human beings use finite language to try to speak of transcendent realities, we necessarily speak in analogies, and so does Gregory here. For example, when he uses the word *person* he is not thinking of the word as we would use it of a human being, for whom (amongst other differences) the physical body is a crucial element of personhood. The Greek word which Gregory uses here is *hypostasis* (literally "substance") which he adapted in order to denote the distinct, individual modes of being whom Christians worshipped as Father, Son, and Holy Spirit. Western theologians used the Latin word *persona* (or "mask," also analogically) from which we obviously derive our word *person.* The key idea which Gregory emphasizes is that the heart of the universe is personal: more than personal, surely, suprapersonal or transpersonal, but not less than personal. The heart of the universe is not a blind force or a random process. Human personhood is grounded in the very core of Being.

The second important point which Gregory makes is that what defines the three Persons is relationality. Father, Son, and Holy Spirit are what they are by virtue of what they are to one another. Gregory says (Hardy, 1954) for instance that:

> Father is not a name either of an essence or an action. . . . But it is the name of the relation in which the Father stands to the Son, and the Son to the Father. For as with us these names make known a genuine and intimate relation, so in the case before us too they denote an identity of nature between him that is begotten and him that begets. (p. 191)

The three Persons who compose the heart of reality have their individual existence by virtue of their relationships with one another (for the same is true of the Spirit as is the case with the Father and the Son). They are not differentiated in being, or substance, or power or any other way save in their differing modes of relationship. The three exist as a fellowship of Persons and not otherwise. So interrelationality is at the very heart of existence. If this is the case, then (Gunton, 1993, p. 191) human relationships are more than an option which individuals may voluntarily elect. They are grounded in the deepest level of reality, to which we are accountable.

The Cappadocian Fathers all emphasized the cooperative and mutual relatedness of the three Persons, this reciprocal interweaving which later thinkers in the Greek tradition came to call *perichoresis.* Etymologically composed of *peri-* ("around," as in "perimeter") and *choros* ("dancing"), the word *perichoresis* describes analogically the three Persons at the heart of reality, dancing around each other in a stately, grave, and luminous minuet. Gregory of Nyssa (Hardy, 1954) rings the changes on this idea of *perichoresis.*

> We do not learn that the Father does something on his own, in which the Son does not cooperate. Or again, that the Son acts

> on his own without the Spirit. Rather does every operation which extends from God to creation . . . have its origin in the Father, proceed through the Son, and reach its completion in the Holy Spirit. . . . Thus the holy Trinity brings to effect every operation in a similar way. It is not by separate action according to the number of the Persons; but there is one motion and disposition of good will which proceeds from the Father, through the Son, to the Spirit. (pp. 261–262)

The idea of *perichoresis* includes cooperative movement, creativity within order, and mutual respect amongst Persons of equal dignity but different relationship. By contrast (Gunton, 1993, pp. 149–154) the Western, Latin tradition tended, not to deny the particularity of the three Persons, but to stress their unity as well as their unanimity. Western theology offered a more static understanding of God, with consequences which we shall consider below.

The Cappadocians' understanding of the Trinity offers a rationale for encouraging growth toward a fifth-order consciousness. First of all, it guards the important gains of fourth-order knowing. The proposition that ultimate reality is personal supports the beliefs that conscious and reflective selves are real, legitimate and worth fostering. To say that personhood is at the heart of reality (however supra- or transpersonal that reality must be) is to say that individual human consciousness is not a freak. Discrete, self-conscious fourth-order personalities are not inexplicable accidents of natural selection, with no survival value and no evolutionary justification. Nor is individual consciousness an illusory nightmare from which we should aspire to awaken. The individuality of each Person of the Trinity argues that the individuality of fourth-order consciousness is legitimate. Individual particularity is based in ultimate reality, and it is therefore a valid midrange goal for human maturation.

But the idea of *perichoresis* describes a reality which transcends the personal boundaries and the autonomy of fourth-order selves. The idea of the divine dance suggests that interdependence is deeper than autonomy. In the Trinity the relationships constitute the Persons, who do not exist otherwise than by their relationships. *Perichoresis* neither confuses the Persons nor effaces them. In their interdependence, their unique identities are secure. If this mutual reciprocity of fully articulated individuals is at the heart of the universe (Gunton, 1993, pp. 163–173), then fifth-order interdependence is both a plausible and a necessary goal of human maturation.

Finally, the idea of a perichoretic Trinity addresses the twin societal pitfalls of late modernity, namely solipsism and collectivism. Solipsism ("I alone am real") is the perennial temptation of human beings who live within a Story which posits autonomy as the apogee of personal growth. In the public life of the modern world, utilitarian individualism always threatens to reduce the world to the status of a tool which I own, and which I use to build the castle of my independence. As Martin Buber (1923/1970, pp. 53–64) shows, "I-Thou" relationships are very fragile in the Enlightenment world, and the temptation is always strong to reduce everyone else to an "it" which I exploit. Likewise in the private dimension of modernity, the expressive individualism of Romanticism constantly entices me to "taste" other people, in a succession of "meaningful relationships." Again the other becomes an "it." At its extreme, the Romantic absolutism of individual consciousness ("perception is reality") slips down the slope into cognitive solipsism. As Shirley MacLaine put it (1987),

> I could legitimately say that I created the Statue of Liberty, chocolate chip cookies, the Beatles, terrorism and the Vietnam War. I couldn't really say for sure whether anyone else in the world had actually experienced those things separately from me because these people existed as individuals only in my dream. (p. 174)

But the idea of the Trinity argues that other people exist. I am not alone; the other Person is a "Thou" and not an "it." Respectful relationship between us is obligatory and not elective. In the Christian universe, the capacity for interdependence is at the heart of human maturity (Gunton, 1993, p. 172).

As for collectivism, the absorption of the individual into 20th century mass movements, the idea of the Trinity safeguards the dignity of the individual. When excessive 20th century individualism runs to anarchy, and then to the collectivism of the left or the right as the only solution, the idea of the Trinity maintains that mutually respectful association between individuals is the true goal of society. Human beings are not made to be swallowed in the one. Monism ("everything is one") justifies collectivism. The trinitarian worldview is collectivism's deadly enemy. Once again, the implications of this idea for fifth-order interdependence are worth considering.

AUGUSTINE AND THE WESTERN TRADITION

As we noted above, the Latin tradition of theology in Western Europe developed the Christian Story in certain ways which stood in contrast with the emphases of Irenaeus and the Cappadocians. This Western tradition owed its direction to one thinker more than any other, the great North African theologian Augustine of Hippo (354–430 A.D.). Writing while the Roman Empire was collapsing in the West, Augustine established the guidelines for Latin theology for over a thousand years to come. Fertile as his thought was in many ways, Augustine's teaching on the nature of God and of humanity moved in a direction which downplayed interdependence and the other qualities of fifth-order consciousness as the goals of human maturity.

First of all, Augustine's doctrine of God stressed the unity of the three Persons, whereas the Cappadocians had sought to balance unity and diversity in their idea of *perichoresis.* Gregory of Nazianzus and his colleagues had begun with the Father, Son, and Holy Spirit as distinct modes of being, and then had tried to describe how they were one. Gunton (1993, pp. 53–54, 120–121, 190–191), Kelly (1960, pp. 272–273), Moltmann (1985, p. 235), and others show how Augustine began with the unity of the three, and put less emphasis on their differentiation. Thus Augustine underscored the three Persons' oneness in substance, their joint possession of all the qualities which characterized each one, and the total unity of their will, especially as directed toward the created universe. While Irenaeus had described the Son and the Spirit as the "two hands of

God'' in creation, each with distinctive functions, Augustine argued that all the external activities of the Trinity were wholly unanimous. This line of thought was certainly consistent with Judeo-Christian monotheism, and helped protect the Latin tradition from any temptation to fall into the polytheism of the barbarian West. But it did lack the subtle interplay between unity and individuality which had strengthened the Cappadocians' doctrine of God.

As Augustine's emphasis on the divine unity did not place relationality so clearly at the heart of the universe, so also his teaching on human nature lacked the emphasis on sociality which we noticed in the Greek Fathers. As the deepest nature of God is to be one, so Augustine held that to be human is to be independent and self-contained. Augustine explicitly identified normative human nature (''the image of God'' in humanity) as the individual soul. As Moltmann (1985) put it, ''The human being corresponds to the single Being of the triune God, not to the threefold nature of God's inner essence'' (p. 235). Furthermore, the human soul is characterized especially by reason, not by relationality. Reason is the gift of God which distinguishes human beings from the animals, and therefore reason is at the core of human identity. It is true (as Augustine argued) that reason has an inner, threefold structure that mirrors the divine Trinity. Kelly (1960, pp. 276–279) and Moltmann (1985, p. 237) describe Augustine's argument that as a rational human being, I reflect the Trinity in that I exist, I know that I exist, and I love that existence and the fact that I know it. But this trinitarian image is wholly intrapsychic. I don't need to be in relationship with any other human being in order to be the image of God. I simply need to become conscious of my own unique individuality. In the later Western tradition, as Gunton (1993) puts it, all too often we conclude that, ''to 'realize' or to 'fulfill' ourselves, to 'do our own thing' is to be human, not to find our being in reciprocal relatedness with our neighbor'' (p. 65). For Augustine, then, fourth-order knowing would fulfill human nature and represent our highest developmental goal.

In point of fact Augustine also held that human beings had originally possessed this fourth-order consciousness at creation. It was our pristine state, not an achievement toward which we originally had to work. In contrast to Irenaeus' idea of Adam and Eve as children in Eden, sent to school by God to learn relationality, Augustine and his successors assumed that the first humans were created as independent and completely rational adults. When we rebelled against God, we lost our rational poise and competence, and our freedom of choice. We became liable to involuntary behavior over which our reason had no control. But now through faith in Christ, we can recover our rational maturity. There is not much developmental consciousness in this Western story of human life. One consequence of this tradition was a difficulty in imagining how it is possible to be both a Christian and a sinner simultaneously. If Adam was fully mature, and Christ restores me to Adam's original condition, how is it that I continue to be a fallible, weak, and struggling incompetent? One early solution in the Latin West was, as Kelly points out (1960, p. 177), to conclude that in fact Christ has reconstructed me only partially, and that I am responsible for cleaning up the rest of my life, under my own power. This notion led to a good deal of anxious workaholism in the Middle Ages, and to the dividing of Christendom in the Reformation. The Western Christian tradition might have been wiser, had it followed Irenaeus' insight that the essence of being human is to be a learner, and that when Christ rescues us, he restores us not to perfection but to kindergarten.

For all its strengths in other ways, Augustine's understanding of human nature lacked the emphases on growth and on interdependence which characterized the early Greek tradition. Furthermore, there was an explicit gender-hierarchy in the North African theologian's model as well. If Adam by himself represented human nature in its entirety, he didn't need Eve to be completely human. And although Eve shared human nature with her husband, said Augustine, she was made in *his* image and to be his helper. She participated only indirectly in the divine image, through him. Augustine justified this hierarchy by reference to the superiority of the rational soul over the body. Just as the rational soul must command and direct the physical body, so also the man (the rational partner) must hold the "weaker vessel" in protective custody. As Moltmann (1985) puts it, for Augustine the image of God "is then on the one hand a pure analogy of domination, and on the other, as we have seen, a patriarchal analogy to God the Father'' (p. 240). So the Western version of the Christian Story tells how individual men lost their rational superiority and then got it back. This was a theological tradition which was unlikely to encourage relationality between women and men as partners, or to support human maturation beyond the individualism of fourth-order consciousness.

KARL BARTH: RELATIONALITY AS TRUE HUMANITY

Fortunately a number of 20th century Christian thinkers have recovered the themes of relationality and growth toward interdependence which Augustine and his successors missed. They have reopened the questions, What is it to be human? And what is normative human maturity, toward which we should be growing?

The biblical Story had offered a cryptic definition of humanity in the midst of the creation narrative, saying in Genesis 1:27 that ''God created man in his own image, in the image of God he created him; male and female he created them.'' It wasn't immediately obvious what ''in his own image'' meant. Was the divine image some interior quality like reason, as Augustine and the Western tradition tended to suppose? Or was it an interpersonal quality of relatedness, as Gregory of Nazianzus suggested (Moltmann, 1985, p. 235)? In the past century, a number of German theologians have picked up the hints dropped by the Greek Fathers, and have begun to explore the idea that the true essence of humanity is a capacity for relationship. Juergen Moltmann (1985, pp. 215–243) is one thinker who has followed this line of thought. But above all the monumental work of Karl Barth, spanning many decades in the mid-20th century, has capitalized on the insights of the Greek Fathers in his treatment of ''the image of God,'' the *imago Dei*. Barth makes three important points.

First of all Barth argues that the primary image of God in time and space, and therefore the model for ideal human development, is Jesus Christ. Barth says that in the New Testament, in Paul's letter to the Colossians (1:17), the apostle refers to Jesus as "the image of the invisible God." Likewise John's Gospel (1:1 ff.) speaks of Jesus as the "Word," the definitive expression of God's nature in time and space. By looking at Jesus of Nazareth, we can begin to understand who God is. And if Jesus was the prototypical "image of God," then other human beings in the "image of God" must have been patterned after him. Now Barth (1958a, III/1, pp. 205, 321–324; 1958b, III/2, pp. 296–300) goes on to point out that in the Bible Jesus appears as the center of a community. He is always seen with others, especially with his friends and students. Jesus calls himself the "bridegroom" (one of his favorite metaphors) and that title necessarily implies a bride. That bride is the Christian community. Says Barth (1958a, III/1), "Christians are also present in all that Jesus Christ is, and therefore in the fact that He is the image of God" (p. 205). Elsewhere in the New Testament other authors develop the idea that Jesus is always to be thought of in conjunction with the Church. The Letter to the Ephesians (5:32) argues that Christ and the Christian community are figuratively represented in every marriage—which mystery "is a profound one, and I am saying that it refers to Christ and the Church." Since the heart of the transcendent God is an eternal interweaving of three Persons in the *perichoresis,* the expression of that mystery in time and space is appropriately a relationship, specifically that between Christ and the "Bride." And if Christ is also the normative model after which human beings are created, then humanity too must be relational. Human beings must exist after the pattern of Christ and the Christian community in fellowship.

And Barth's second point is precisely this, that the "image of God" in humankind is the sexual relationship-in-differentiation between man and woman. The "image of God," normative humanity, is not some individual or private quality, or some characteristic which one human being can embody exhaustively. Rather, says Barth (1958a, III/1), to be fully human we must be in relationship with at least one other who is alike but different, with whom we stand in this sexual conjunction-in-differentiation (p. 186). Barth (1958a, III/1) expresses his astonishment that the implications of Genesis 1:27 in this regard should have eluded the Western Christian tradition for so many centuries.

> It is not astonishing that again and again expositors have ignored the definitive explanation given by the text itself, and instead of reflecting on it pursued all kinds of arbitrarily invented interpretations of the *imago dei*?—the more so when we remember that there is a detailed repetition of the biblical explanation in Genesis 5:1, "in the day that God created man, in the likeness of God made he him; male and female created he them." Could anything be more obvious than to conclude from this clear indication that the image and likeness of the being created by God signifies existence in confrontation, i.e., in this confrontation, in the juxtaposition and conjunction of man and woman which is that of male and female. (p. 195)

For its embodiment true humanity requires more than the solitary individual. The image of the relational Trinity, figured forth normatively in time and space by Christ and the Bride, requires a man and a woman together in mutual interdependence.

Now Barth offers some clarifications at this point. For example, he argues (1958a, III/1, pp. 185–186, 195) that we cannot infer from the Genesis narrative that God is sexual. We cannot argue "upward" (as it were) from human sexuality to a male or female god or goddess. Biological sexuality is a feature of the created universe, and not a characteristic of the transcendent dimension of the Trinity. Barth argues that God chose this phenomenon within the universe, namely sexual differentiation, to express a reality which is far beyond this polarity, yet at which the latter hints in a distant way. The only analogy intended by the Genesis metaphor is therefore between human sexual conjunction-in-differentiation and the relationality of the Persons of the Trinity. It is an "analogy of relationship" and not an "analogy of being."

Barth also specifies that marriage is not the only expression of the image of God in human nature. Marriage does indeed embody that image. But all relationships between women and men have the capacity to express the differentiation-in-unity which distantly mirrors the life of the Trinity. Barth (1961, III/4) insists that:

> [T]he sphere of male and female is wider than that of marriage, embracing the whole complex of relations at the centre of which marriage is possible. And the divine command concerns this whole complex which is not simply coincident with marriage, though the criteria of the latter apply in it and the whole sphere stands in the light of the reality and problem of marriage. . . . They are also man and woman . . . when they are unmarried and have not yet attained this special concrete form of the sexual encounter, when they are widowed or divorced and no longer realise it, especially when for some reason they can never realise it at all. (p. 140)

Full human maturity therefore entails learning how to achieve that same respectful mutuality vis-à-vis the opposite sex which (in a manner far exceeding human imagination) the life of the eternal Trinity celebrates. Therefore while Barth (1961, III/4, pp. 168 ff.) anticipates that women and men will each display different qualities in their mature interdependence (qualities which he wisely refuses to enumerate or specify) he rules out any hierarchy or subordination. There are differences of relationship and role in the divine *perichoresis,* but no essential hierarchy of being or value. Thus the mature woman and the adult man each face the other with poise and confidence, but with no sense of inferiority or superiority on either side. Their meeting is not a contest for dominance, but a graceful dance which reflects from afar the life of the Trinity.

Barth is hardly unaware that practically all encounters between women and men fall tragically short of this ideal. He rehearses the Christian Story as it describes the collapse of human relations into domination and subordination, and traces the way in which the Story anticipates the healing of this conflict. Adam and Eve, the archetypal humans, chose to reject the curriculum in which God had placed them, which would have gradually raised them toward mature interdependence. After driving the rebellious pair from the school, God predicts how Eve's rejection of her education will render her vulnerable to entanglement in an abusive relationship with her henceforth domineering husband. "Your desire," God says, "shall be for your husband and he shall rule over you" (Genesis 3:16). So the mysterious rebellion of humankind entailed not only a free-fall down into death, but a fracturing of relationships between women and men as part of the social disintegration which accompanies the collapse.

But Barth's third point is that (as we saw in Irenaeus' narrative) the Hero came to the rescue. All those who cling to Jesus for help have the option of beginning the curriculum again, as he brings them up again out of relational fragmentation. Now Barth argues (1958a, III/1, pp. 310–329; 1958b, III/2, p. 301) that Christ's rescue mission is a *fait accompli.* The reconciliation of women and men, the possibility of growing up into mature interdependence, is not a pious fantasy. It actually happened in 1st century Palestine. Barth says (1958b, III/2) that:

> We must first remember the general truth that when the New Testament speaks of Jesus Christ and his community it really speaks of the goal . . . of all earthly things. Jesus Christ and His community is not an additional promise given to men. The existence and history of Israel in covenant with Yahweh was a promise. The reality of Jesus Christ and his community . . . concludes this process. It is the complete fulfillment of the promise. It is the goal and end of all the ways of God. (p. 301)

The historical presence of Jesus and his community in 1st century Palestine means that the power to reconcile polarity has already appeared in time and space. In principle, everything necessary to heal human fragmentation is now accessible. All that remains is for God to manifest the consequences of that marriage between the Hero and the community which he came to rescue.

We live, however, in the meantime between the *fait accompli* and the realization of its consequences. The human free-fall into disintegration appears to be accelerating. Women and men persist in rejecting the curriculum, and mutual interdependence as the goal of human maturation seems to recede farther and farther into improbability. Yet the biblical Story peers into the future and grasps the vision of a cosmic restoration, in which the marriage of Christ and the Bride will be revealed and all its consequences fully established. The Book of Revelation (21:2–4) describes the marriage feast of Christ and the Bride:

> And I saw the holy city, new Jerusalem, coming down out of heaven from God, prepared as a bride adorned for her husband; and I heard a loud voice from the throne saying, "Behold, the dwelling of God is with men. He shall dwell with them, and they shall be his people, and God himself will be with them; he will wipe away every tear from their eyes, and death shall be no more. . . ."

In the Christian Story, the marriage feast of Christ and the Bride is a magnet drawing time toward its healing. This image of archetypal masculine and feminine in respectful mutuality offers an environment in which all the little stories of women and men may find a place, and where their aspiration to fifth-order interdependence finds support and justification.

As Barth recapitulates the biblical Story, therefore, he draws upon the Greek Fathers for themes which stress relationality as the heart of reality, and interdependence as the goal of human maturation. Stories are important, as we have seen. They shape our identities and teach us our goals. They nurture our sense of what is possible, and what human beings may become. And so we should choose our stories carefully. What stage of human maturity do they imply, as the goal of human development? In particular, are the Enlightenment and the Romantic Stories adequate accounts of reality? Is the fourth-order consciousness which they encourage actually a fully sufficient goal for human development? What kind of Story would nourish our aspiration to transcend the individualism of this fourth order, and aim at a fifth-order mutual interdependence as the purpose of human maturation? We might well recall the tradition of Greek Christianity, then and now, as we wrestle with these issues.

REFERENCES

Anderson, W. T. (1990). *Reality isn't what it used to be.* New York: HarperCollins.

Barth, K. (1958a). *Church dogmatics III/1.* Edinburgh: T. & T. Clark.
Barth, K. (1958b). *Church dogmatics III/2.* Edinburgh: T. & T. Clark.
Barth, K. (1961). *Church dogmatics III/4.* Edinburgh: T. & T. Clark.
Baumer, F. L. (1977). *Modern European thought.* New York: Macmillan.
Buber, M. (1970). *I and thou.* New York: Charles Scribner's Sons. (Original work published 1923)
Capra, F. (1983). *The turning point.* New York: Bantam Books.
Frei, H. F. (1974). *The eclipse of biblical narrative.* New Haven, CT: Yale University Press.
Frend, W. H. C. (1984). *The rise of Christianity.* Philadelphia: Fortress Press.
Gergen, K. J. (1991). *The saturated self.* New York: Basic Books.
Gilkey, L. (1985). *Maker of heaven and earth.* Lanham, MD: University Press of America.
Gunton, C. (1993). *The one, the three and the many.* Cambridge, U.K.: Cambridge University Press.
Hardy, E. R. (Ed.). (1954). *Christology of the later fathers.* Philadelphia: Westminster Press.
Hauerwas, S. (1981). *A community of character.* Notre Dame, IN: University of Notre Dame Press.
Irenaeus. (1952). *Proof of the apostolic preaching.* New York: Newman Press.
Kegan, R. (1994). *In over our heads.* Cambridge, MA: Harvard University Press.
Kelly, J. N. D. (1960). *Early Christian doctrines* (2nd ed.) New York: Harper and Row.
Lewis, C. S. (1970). *God in the dock.* Grand Rapids, MI: William B. Eerdmans.
MacLaine, S. (1987). *It's all in the playing.* New York: Bantam Books.
Moltmann, J. (1985). *God in creation.* San Francisco: Harper & Row.
Newton, I. (1934). *Principia mathematica.* (A Motte & Rev. F. Cajori, Trans.). Berkeley: University of California Press. (Original work published 1686)
Richardson, C. C. (Ed.). (1970). *Early Christian fathers.* New York: Macmillan.
Sagan, C. (1980). *Cosmos.* New York: Ballantine Books.
Tarnas, R. (1991). *The passion of the Western mind.* New York: Harmony Books.
Whitmont, E. C. (1969). *The symbolic quest.* Princeton, NJ: Princeton University Press.
Whitmont, E. C. (1982). *Return of the goddess.* New York: Crossroad Books.

9.

On Constructing an Engaged Life

Jackson Kytle

Human motivation is not a tidy, small topic. Staying motivated in the face of distraction, fatigue, and stress is a personal challenge for individuals who are making lives for themselves. This is why, perhaps, self-help books are popular even though what is offered up many be formulaic. More generally, helping other people become motivated is a critical assignment for social institutions like schools and the family. Teachers and counselors have special roles as specialists in motivation. Modern critics of education such as Sizer (1984) say, however, that students emerge from these social institutions with uneven skills, little understanding of themselves as learners, and life purposes that are unfocused.

We know much less than we should about this central human concern. Indeed, human motivation is one of psychology's "black boxes"—we think we know some of the inputs and guess at the outputs, but the mediating dynamics inside are obscure. Indeed, the difficulty of studying motivation as a hypothetical

This chapter is a report made to the Society for Research in Adult Development at its Boston meeting, 1996, based on a book in progress on motivation and educational reform. I am grateful for the comments of reviewers and my colleagues from Antioch, Goddard, and Norwich University/Vermont College—Al Erdynast, Jim Malarkey, Mel Miller, Verbena Pastor, Andy Schmookler, Ann Stanton, and Eric Zencey. Joan Clack and Ethan Kytle helped me prepare the manuscript.

construct has led some theorists to focus on involving behaviors, setting aside internal states and the phenomenology of the experience of involvement (Astin, 1985). I will also argue that we know less than we should about the variety of states of consciousness in daily life ranging from boredom to partial engagement to the most focused, intense concentration. How do changes in attention span and mood affect psychological engagement? How are the purposes that motivate people selected and sustained? And most important, and elusive, of all, what are the essential pieces needed to construct an engaged life, one packed with diverse peak experiences, high achievement, and service to others? These questions are important for society, for education, and for the well-being of individuals who must define their personal existence in a fast-changing world of problematic choices.

The term *engagement* has a certain face validity when applied to focused human activity, but it suffers from multiple definitions, such as making a commitment to marry, a commitment to a course of action or belief, and even the rules of engagement that regulate war. Still, most definitions imply some form or degree of deep personal commitment rooted in the original French word, *engagement,* an intense commitment to a political or religious cause (Kemp, 1973).[1] For our purposes, engagement is defined as a hypothetical psychological state of motivation characterized by sustained, purposive attention, and accompanied by elevated mood.

I have been thinking and reading about motivation and engagement for several years, trying to understand the general domain while looking for ideas with which to improve schools and colleges as human institutions intended to motivate and inspire. My interest began in 1968 when as a graduate student in social psychology at Columbia, I saw how the social protests of the day engaged students, giving a sense of power and purpose in life, if only for the moment. These powerful psychological experiences were, for me and many others, in sharp contrast

[1] Consider all the variations: (a) to employ or hire; (b) to employ busily or occupy; (c) to hold fast, as in a person's attention; (d) to bind by contract; (e) to arrange beforehand; (f) to interlock two pieces of a mechanism; (g) to come into battle, as in rules of engagement; (h) to take part; (i) to pledge oneself as in marriage. *Oxford Modern English Dictionary,* 1993.

to the lonely student experience of a large urban institution. Thus, this paper is both a progress report and personal invitation to the reader to think about human motivation, in general, and the project of constructing an engaged life, in particular, both personally and as an intellectual topic.

THE BEST USE OF A LIFE

What is the best use of a life? To what purposes or beliefs do we commit, and how do we sustain this commitment in a busy, modern world? Consider how the late Canadian classical pianist and composer, Glenn Gould, used his life. Gould was best known, perhaps, for his crystalline interpretations of Bach. He is also known for the lengths to which he went to prepare for a performance (playing from a shortened stool so that he could watch his hands on the keys, and soaking his hands in warm water before a concert). Gould gave great importance to achieving focused attention in his concerts and recordings, perhaps to the point of obsession, at least as judged by the rest of us whose drive for perfection is less intense.

The radical methods he chose for focusing attention did not stop with minor performance rituals, which many artists cultivate. When he was at the peak of his performing career, Gould changed his entire work and living schedule. He abruptly stopped public performances, choosing to live and work out of his apartment in Toronto where he had built a recording studio. He also changed his work day to be awake most of the night, sleeping during the day. Except for phone calls to friends, which he enjoyed, Gould consciously chose to limit the distractions of modern times, what he called "the terror of daily living" (Cott, 1984).

Few of us go to such lengths to be creative or productive, of course, but all face Gould's challenge: How to make the best use of a life? Artists are closer to this daily struggle for purpose and meaning than most, perhaps, because artists do not have the comfort-structure of an office routine, and the clear signposts of a career to assure them of progress. Every day, the artist must build a temporary structure to live in, so to speak, when the rest of us, at least those with jobs and careers, have a work routine that pulls us along. For people who go to a steady job, the daily drill does not need conscious mediation as one day blurs into the next. The momentum of a structured daily existence tends to lull us into small, momentary concerns. Many people manage to be self-reflective, of course, but the pull is away from being awake-in-the-world (Greene, 1988).

As social critics like Gergen (1991) have observed, modern society is busy and noisy, making true reflection and the construction of an intentional life difficult. The distracting noise of mundane affairs is the "terror" that Gould feared. In addition to the distractions of daily life, we are also caught up in a tangle of unexamined, more-or-less accepted assumptions about human behavior and motivation, the nature of reality, and the nature of society and social change. Thus, existentialist philosopher Maxine Greene (1988) worries about "the routine" in life, and warns us about falling asleep in a world defined by the routine (that is, the given world that is just accepted, uncritically). And she asks for acts of imagination by which to challenge hidden assumptions, to break free and become awake in the world. I would add that the choices need not be dramatic, because an engaged life will be built of many small acts of courage, as one of my students put it, decisions to do something different, to not stand in line, to challenge convention.

Gould's example of how he used his life raises two topics that will be the focus of my paper: first, the psychological characteristics of different levels of engagement with emphasis upon changes in attention and mood, and second, the critical importance of the human values that make certain choices and purposes better than others.

THE PSYCHOLOGICAL CHARACTERISTICS OF PEAK EXPERIENCE

Although William James (1902/1958) raised many of the issues at the turn of the century in *The Varieties of Religious Experience,*

Abraham Maslow (1968) in the late 1960s was the first to build a body of research about peak experience as a psychological state (and the self-actualized personality, a related character trait). He sought a humanistic psychology and a positive theory of existence in contrast to two intellectual traditions of his day: first, the mechanistic behaviorism that dominated psychology, and second, what he considered to be the negative existentialism of Sartre and European intellectual circles.[2] He wrote about human potential and peak experience, and how profoundly motivating such moments are, but did not address intermediate range experience, or more importantly, the dynamics by which people try to focus attention to build engaged moments. One can read Maslow as if peak experiences are "all or nothing."

Maslow (1968) asked several hundred subjects to describe attributes of their most powerful experiences. He identified the attributes of such states: wholeness, an integrating experience, suspension of critical judgment, clear perception, loss of ego centeredness, perception of beauty and goodness, sense of awe, a felt sense of being active and responsible, a feeling of being physically bigger, taller, and stronger, feelings of gratitude and disorientation in time and space after the peak experience, feeling intelligent, perceptive, witty, strong, graceful, effortless, self-confident, expressive, and creative (1968, pp. 103–114). Maslow argued that peak experiences, whether from creative or religious experiences (such as James wrote about), are, in fact, acute identity experiences where people are at the peak of their powers, feeling "more intelligent, more perceptive, wittier, stronger, or more graceful than at other times" (1968, p. 105). Such moments, Maslow argued, express the highest potential of the species, a human capacity to which everyone has a right. Peak experiences are not a special advantage of educated elites (even though most of his subjects were, in fact, elites).

---

[2] Maslow moderated his view of existentialism in at least one place. While criticizing its unscientific perspective and excessive gloom, he said "the existentialists may supply psychology with the underlying philosophy which it now lacks. Logical positivism has been a failure, especially for clinical and personality psychologists" (1968, p. 10).

Maslow also described the self-actualized personality based on his research on peak experience. The self-actualizing personality uses "Being-values" to orient to life, and he extends the attributes of peak experience cited above to enduring attributes of character: wholeness, perfection, completion, justice, aliveness, simplicity, beauty, uniqueness, effortlessness, playfulness, and the like (1968, p. 83). While Maslow was not explicit about how this ideal character was formed, his insistent humanism influenced a generation of psychologists and teachers.

Like Maslow a generation earlier, contemporary psychologist Mihaly Csikszentmihalyi (1991, 1993) is interested in optimal human experience, and he and his colleagues have published a body of imaginative research on the theory of flow, "the process of total involvement with life." Csikszentmihalyi studies the moments when a person is stretched to the limits in the pursuit of a challenge, such as rock climbing or performing music. Concentration is total, the psychological process is all important, and the psychological characteristics of such moments of flow are comparable to those of Maslow's peak experience: intense concentration, loss of self-consciousness, loss of time consciousness, and a certain effortlessness to the entire experience.

In addition to flow defined as a psychological state, Csikszentmihalyi extends his theory by positing an autotelic personality. Maslow wrote about the self-actualizing personality, whereas Csikszentmihalyi's notion of the autotelic personality is less about goals than about the psychological process as *an end in itself.* Autotelic refers to "a self-contained activity, one that is done not with the expectation of some future benefit, but simply because *the doing itself is the reward*" (1991, p. 67; emphasis added). Csikszentmihalyi wants to help people "reclaim their experience" by learning to better control their consciousness, behavior and environments. He defines flow as the control of consciousness, "the ability to focus attention at will, to be oblivious to distraction, to concentrate for as long as it takes to achieve a goal, and not longer" (1991, p. 31). While goals are important insofar as they motivate people, Csikszentmihalyi focuses on the quality of the involvement.

Like Maslow, Csikszentmihalyi interviewed people who had had flow experiences. He used a method called Experience Sampling wherein hundreds of subjects in many cultures and occupations were equipped with electronic pagers that were activated eight times a day at random intervals. The study participants were asked to write down what they were feeling or thinking when paged, and the record for each person provided a transcript of their lives and moments of flow.[3]

Ellen Langer and her associates developed an imaginative series of social psychological experiments over more than 10 years on the topic of mindfulness and the cognitive dynamics of attention. In choosing experimental methods to test her ideas, Langer's (1989) work goes beyond the interview methods of Maslow or sampling methods of Csikszentmihalyi. One dramatic line of experiments demonstrated that increased mindfulness led to increased longevity among the elderly in nursing homes.

Langer argued that people will sometimes persevere with the wrong solution to a problem, trying over and over to make it work. Preset or prior cognitive commitments like stereotypes limit the ability of people to make better choices. A mindful approach to a problem, according to Langer, will be flexible—people will create *new categories* while working, continue to be open to new information, and be aware of multiple perspectives. Thus, Langer suggests that cognitive reappraisal will help people reframe the situation they are in, perhaps seeing new possibilities not obvious before, such as might happen during successful psychotherapy.

Mindfulness or paying attention can be developed, if not taught. Not unlike John Dewey (1938/1963), one suggestion from Langer's research is to focus on the process, not the product or result. If the process involves choices the person can make, Langer argues that students will tend to feel more responsible for what results, and be more mindful in the process. Like Maslow and Csikszentmihalyi before her, Langer finds that

---

[3] The subjective dimensions of peak experience and physiological mechanisms should be explored through formal experiments where greater control is possible over experimental variables. Most studies are based on self-report and surveys.

mindfulness is exhilarating and focused attention is experienced as pleasant. People find "a second wind" when they are able to focus attention (1989, p. 137).

Langer's research suggests that students are more likely to be engaged or mindful in learning situations that elicit personal choice and increase personal responsibility; where the focus is the process of problem solving, not only the results; and where students are taught flexible, mindful approaches to problem solving.

As creative as Langer's experiments are, her theory is incomplete. She does not offer a framework for evaluating the purposes of being mindful. Like Csikszentmihalyi's research, it is, in the end, another theory of human potential that seems to begin and end with the individual.

THE VARIETIES OF ENGAGED EXPERIENCE

Engagement is defined as a motivational state characterized by sustained, purposive attention, and elevated mood. Intense concentration is more likely to stimulate the state, and there are behavioral changes, like increased effort on task, that result. The attentional system, which responds to threat, novelty, complexity and other variables, sets the rhythms of daily life from day dreaming through floating attention to rare peak experiences, and the quality and nature of the changes over a day defines the quality to life, both as it is experienced and with regard to the level of achievement and service to society. *What* humans pay attention to, and *how* they focus attention, are perhaps the most distinguishing characteristics of the species, leading to great contributions in art, philosophy, politics, and medicine (Hobson, 1994). An interesting day or a "fun" day will be marked by periods of sustained attention if one is playing a sport, traveling, or pursuing a hobby. After a few moments, attention is full and the self is totally involved in an activity like tennis or sewing. At other times, one struggles mightily, for example, to stay awake when driving, surely one of the most uncomfortable human experiences. Even on an hourly and daily basis, the range of changes in attention and mood, which underlie the possibility of engagement, is wide.

Engagement is a special case of focused attention, differing in intensity, the nature of the purposes, and duration. That is, I can momentarily attend to a song on the radio, or the cold in the room, but engagement is a *sustained, purposive* activity like sorting out abstract terms while revising a draft of my paper. Consider also a complex activity like tennis where there are many variables that account for effective play, especially the ability to concentrate on winning the point as a rally of six or so shots develops. Attention roams among a number of channels including posture, the pace, spin, and location of the ball, the blurry movement of an opponent, cognitive images of possible shots, and self-exhortations to "stay positive." The brain-mind also perceives sounds from other courts, and may be distracted by watching the play nearby. Perceptually, tennis is a complex situation, which contributes to its appeal.[4]

To play well, one tries to master different ways of paying attention from focusing on small routines, such as the serve, to a general cognitive strategy by which the player somehow monitors a defined set of stimulus channels like posture, moving one's feet, stroke preparation, and game strategy while being alert to new information. Thus, engagement is sustained, purposeful activity in time toward a complex goal rather than a simple addition of individual moments of focused attention. To speculate, it may be that becoming effective at tennis or other complex activities means learning varied attention strategies with which to cope with stimulus-rich situations. The process of involvement or flow is important to the quality of the experience as Csikszentmihalyi argues, but engaged activity as I have defined it is goal directed. In the above example, social tennis has both cooperative and competitive motives within it, and a "good" game will involve both process and goal direction.

---

[4] Engagement is an interactive, complex product of brain–mind–body dynamics such as those involved in neural transmission, central nervous system arousal, the attentional system, and hormonal systems, most of which are still not well understood despite progress in cognitive science in the last two decades.

When thinking about so-called higher or deeper levels of human potential as Maslow did, there is a temptation to focus on and reify the highest levels—the peak experience, its psychological characteristics, causes, and consequences.[5] While such moments are quietly powerful, they are rare. Most of the time we experience intermediate states of attention and mood, the ebb and flow of engagement that define ordinary human experience and give quality to life. As a colleague put it, "My life is one of low peaks, high valleys, and a continual stream of diverse rewards and enthusiasms; this isn't Maslow's ravishing ideal, but it more nearly reflects the life that many of us lead" (Eric Zencey, personal communication, 1996).

Considered next are different levels and types of engagement, which are meant to be suggestive categories based on personal introspection. At the lowest level, there is not an intense focus on any purpose even though we are perceiving, consciously and otherwise, several stimulus channels more or less at the same time. Attention wanders without conscious direction, and the mood people experience, if prolonged, is not especially positive. There may be a feeling of low level agitation, a floating anxiety, as if one has just watched television for five hours straight.

At other times, we find ourselves day-dreaming as when we consciously elaborate upon a fantasy theme while sitting in a boring meeting. Many jobs are not intrinsically rewarding, and we should ask how people adapt to a numbing routine like assembly line work or certain service jobs, e.g., cleaning hotel rooms. That is, service workers have to be engaged enough to not earn the wrath of a supervisor, but they also find ways to covertly work on life problems, or at least break the monotony by day-dreaming about an anticipated vacation.

Most human behaviors, even complex acts, do not require intense concentration. For example, I go for a hike and while walking, I am distracted by a business problem while also getting glimpses of fall foliage. If the terrain becomes steep, the sound of my breathing gradually takes over. The mind roams

[5] Spatial metaphors like "higher" or "deeper" are misleading as are notions that consciousness or the most complex human attributes are best denoted by a body organ like the brain. Instead, we need to think in terms of systems and networks.

and I am not concentrating on any one object, feeling, or idea. Most of the behavior is automatic, and with regard to evolution, this is adaptive—to have to focus on every detail of a hike, one foot after the other, would be exhausting (Dennett, 1996).

We have learned many complex behaviors that can, in effect, run as unconscious subroutines in the background. When a person's behavior appears to be automatic and there is no evidence of active concentration such as walking on a country lane, the surface behavior is controlled by unconscious perceptual sets that come to awareness only if some information is anomalous, presumably, or outside expected ranges. While washing dishes, for example, most people do not think about what they are doing unless the water suddenly burns them, and the person is not engaged by the activity (although by concentrating, one can make these engaged activities, at least for a period).

When concentrating on an activity, general perceptual vigilance is heightened and scanning increases. The person is more alert than before, and reports fresh, vivid images. Mood is enhanced, at least if the stimuli do not produce revulsion or fright, which may have instinctual causes. Paying attention, itself, is not the same thing as engagement, but is one way the mood state can be elicited. For example, it is not much fun to play the piano when I am tired; it feels forced, more like work than play. If I can, however, concentrate for perhaps two pages of a piece on which I am working, I will usually, but not predictably, experience a moderate level flow of the type that Csikszentmihalyi describes. As he reports, it is a pleasant experience, and I notice the difference in mood, which will last for a short time. Such moments are pleasant, but they are not peak experiences in the way that Maslow used the term.

At rare times, however, usually in late morning when my perception seems to be the most clear, I find myself caught up in the moment. I cannot force the feeling—it is not consciously directed. I am surprised by its onset or intensity, and lose any sense of being separate from the music or the instrument. There is no self-consciousness as I listen to myself "be" the rich harmony of the opening bars of Beethoven's Moonlight Sonata.

Playing music is only one arena, and the reader undoubtedly has had similar experiences with teaching, writing, or hobbies, given the wide range of human passions. The right words to express such moments are elusive; as rare as it is, the psychological experience is truly a peak experience, one quite unlike normal daily experience. Compared to most mood–attention states, the sudden onset and intensity seem qualitatively different from other states. When the mood state is intense or prolonged, one may experience feelings of transcendence, of being slightly removed, feeling apart from the normal flow of events and time. If interrupted while in this mood, people report feeling disoriented as, for example, when a jazz musician takes a few minutes to get reoriented after finishing a creative moment. Players speak of being "lost" or "out there."

When there is sustained, full, and purposive concentration, regardless of what the activity is or the reasons for the focusing, a distinctive mood state may result. The psychological experience varies considerably with individuals, and it varies in intensity and duration. But several ideal attributes may be hypothesized. The person is fully attentive without, however, having to force attention. At such moments in a college class, a student's worldview may be suddenly, unexpectedly shaken, or there may occur a feeling of closeness with a theorist, another age, or a distant culture. Because the human organism in this state is alert and mood is elevated, the student will remember the moment and some of the class material without having to memorize.

Hard work will usually have preceded the moment (to master needed technique like musical scales), and work is required after the experience for learning to happen (such as listening to a teacher's critique and trying the piece again at a slower tempo). In this regard, learning requires additional, intentional steps other than having had a powerful experience. Although it usually takes a conscious act to try to become engaged, to commit to an activity like going to the gym or sitting down to practice, engaged experience, once begun, is more play than work. The experience feels natural, not forced or consciously mediated in a Taoist sense.

William James would say that perception is everything. In his classic example, the same event, a pebble bounced off a window pane, can be experienced as ordinary, or intensely important if one imagines it was thrown by a lover. Almost any activity from doodling to rock climbing can become engaging, or boring (and dangerous) depending upon one's purpose and the duration of focus. The nature of the activity is much less important than how we perceive the event and attach meaning to it, sometimes without regard to accuracy or validity. Fallible, fluid human perception is more important in motivation than the nature of the object or activity.

The ability to focus attention is seldom total or enduring. But I would speculate that certain activities, like human interaction or risk situations, appear to elicit higher levels of engagement because of the rich stimulus conditions they present. The examples below span a wide range of activities from sleep to risk behaviors like sky diving and motorcycling. In the case of solitary activities, engagement may be low or moderate, and perhaps even high if one concentrates under the right conditions. Imagine an involving drama on television, a televised hockey game where the score has suddenly become close, or a beautiful musical passage. Reading, in particular, can be highly involving, and yet, it can be mechanical. Meditation and prayer also elicit a range of responses, not always peak experiences. Most proponents of meditation, whether religious or used in sports psychology, point to the discipline that must be learned to practice effective meditation (Kabat-Zinn, 1994).

Interactive situations, which involve other people and the unpredictable and diverse stimulation they introduce, tend to elicit higher levels of engagement, and that is why, in part, we value such activities. (It is likely that smart machines like personal computers increasingly offer this stimulation.) Sexual intimacy, gambling, child's play and other activities that seem to structure novel stimulus conditions elicit engagement. Perhaps some people come to love such moments because they help focus a perpetually wandering attention.

Certain religious experiences are an important type of peak experience. Many peak human experiences throughout history have been interpreted in spiritual terms as visions, or the result of prayer. While they share the core attributes discussed above, additional characteristics have been observed. Maslow (1993) reported a "plateau experience" in religious settings where the engagement has a quiet, reflective quality. The experience is "serene and calm, rather than poignantly emotional, climactic, autonomic response to the miraculous, the awesome . . ." (1993, p. 335). Maslow describes a "serene, cognitive blissfulness" to suggest an involvement in the moment that is more detached, what he terms "witnessing" (p. 336). Maslow also describes "merely-healthy self-actualizers" who do not have many transcendental moments, or as intense ones. Transcenders have more peak experiences, however, and having peak experiences has become a central goal in life. They also use the spiritual language of poets and mystics, and blend the sacred and the profane (1993, p. 273).

William James (1902/1958) also wrote about peak experience and religious conversion experiences. The language is different, that era being more intensely religious than psychological in its values, vocabulary, and symbols, but individuals had peak experiences that they attributed to "God" or the "Holy Spirit." James speculated that the critical component in the conversion experience is the very personal act of surrender to God, of begging for forgiveness and mercy. In terms of psychological dynamics, this surrender to an external, higher authority like a god is comparable to surrendering to a charismatic cult leader like Rev. Jim Jones, a topic to be considered later.

Another type of peak experience seems stimulated by danger, and it may be even more arousing, if not pleasurable, than the experience resulting from the quiet concentration of playing music. This type of engaged attention is not the same as that sometimes experienced in giving a lecture or playing the piano, but it is uniquely potent. There are, for example, over 200 undercover transit police in New York City subways whose job it is to catch pickpockets and muggers (Krauss, 1994). Sometimes, the police are asked to serve as decoys. When asked why they volunteer for dangerous work, the officers talk about the idealism of trying to help others, and also about how this duty can advance a career. But they also talk about the "adrenaline rushes" that accompany catching a criminal in the act.

Physiological arousal becomes a powerful reinforcer of the behavior, especially if it is dangerous or novel.

Burglars, too, have a similar peak experience in gaining access to an apartment, especially if it is occupied, and they can get in and out without being detected. The risk behavior of crimes like burglary is self-reinforcing, thus leading the person to want to have that experience again, in spite of danger. Perhaps the psychological reinforcers contribute to high recidivism—not many activities in normal life offer comparable focused attention and excitement.

Certain high risk activities demand we pay attention, and that is why we are motivated to engage in them. When the activity is dangerous, like driving a BMW motorcycle on a twisting Vermont road, the consequences of not being alert are serious. To understand human motivation and the constructing of an engaged life, we have to understand why people go to such lengths when the behavior seems irrational, if not dangerous. Why do people train for years, spend $60,000 to finance a climb, and travel halfway around the world to risk their lives on Mt. Everest? Despite the possibility of dying, some people take to hobbies like sky diving, hang gliding, and mountain climbing, and become passionate in their defense. Risk behaviors demand we pay attention, or else. Mountain climber Anne Smith writes about her experience running at high altitude while training for a future climb, and she suggests one source of motivation, the nature of the psychological experience:

> Up top with my skin tingling, my head light, my shoes soaked from the thick dew, I felt light, and good, and clean, and strong. These runs became my personal communion; my daily mass. . . . It usually took me about twenty minutes to forget myself, to become the motion, to enter the state where I almost lost consciousness of what I was doing. My mind and body became the rhythm, the breathing, the snow or the rock. I've read about "flow," about entering "the zone," and about endorphin highs. I guess that's what it is, but for me, it's a time when I don't have to be myself for a while, and I can become a part of something else. (Smith, 1996, p. 23)

In summary, Smith's experience points to several issues. Engaged activities like running in preparation for an upcoming climb are experienced as intrinsically pleasurable. People are motivated to take on difficult challenges because of the nature of the psychological experience and the positive changes they undergo. The subtle and complex mechanisms underlying changes in attention and mood as they shape psychological experience are important topics for research. The process of involvement is important, to be sure, but these activities are goal directed, which points directly to the question of choice of purposes. Finally, it seems likely that we learn varied and flexible attention strategies in pursuit of the activities that give meaning to our lives. There are many ways to "pay attention"—ranging from highly focused concentration on a discrete act like finding the right word for a sentence to the diffuse mindfulness experienced by a runner.

GROUP IDENTIFICATION AND PSYCHOLOGICAL ENGAGEMENT

One of the most intriguing facets of psychological engagement occurs in groups, especially the most involving type of groups like cults where diminished self-consciousness is accompanied by increased psychological attachment to the group, a certain we-feelingness. I felt the seductive power of this dynamic when I was a Columbia graduate student during the 1960s. I was involved for a year with an anarchist student group that became increasingly cultlike and demanding of its members, leading my partner and I to leave the group. From that experience as well as a class project a colleague and I did, an observational study of communes in Northern New England, religious and political groups of this type help members feel less self-conscious and uncomfortable as a lone individual. Ambiguity is reduced, one has instant friends and a crowded calendar of meetings, and there is usually a codified meaning system, what Hoffer (1951) called a true belief system.

As self-consciousness is reduced, psychological identification with the group seems to increase. People report feeling they are part of a project larger than self, and they enjoy that sense of belonging to a group. This attribute, alone, is a powerful motivator for people who feel the deep human need to belong, especially those who feel alienated by the pace and anonymity of modern times. The type of attachment varies: a benign group such as a college class in Greek tragedy; a student protest movement on an urban campus; a social movement like the Freedom Riders in the 1960s; or a mass movement like National Socialism in Germany in the 1930s. Different dynamics are involved in mass movements, to be sure, but to a social psychologist, what appears constant is the seductive power of group identification, which can become irrational and self-destructive.

Religious and political cults share internal social psychological dynamics that attract and bind members to the group, create the illusion of invulnerability, enforce value and attitudinal conformity, and make it hard to leave (Janis, 1972). Cults are led by charismatic leaders, who know how to exploit group dynamics to produce feelings of engagement and we-feelingness. Previously alienated people find themselves embedded in a regulated community that offers human contact and a meaning system (there is a large literature on alienation that is worth consulting; see Schacht [1994]). The allure is such that members will give over their inheritances, surrender personal freedoms, and in the most extreme cases, kill themselves as we have seen with People's Temple (914 dead in 1978), Branch Davidians (80 dead in 1993), Solar Temple (74 dead in 1994–1997), and Heaven's Gate (39 dead in 1997). While it can be argued that these were not all voluntary acts of suicide, these chilling examples underscore the seductive power of true belief cults in which potent group dynamics prove so engaging to certain people that they overwhelm individual character structure and deep instincts like self-preservation (for an interesting theoretical approach to how organizations can increase engagement, see Kahn [1990, 1992]).

THE IMPORTANCE OF VALUES REFLECTED IN PURPOSES

If engagement is defined as sustained, purposive attention, we need an ethical framework for evaluating the purposes chosen.

After all, not all purposes are equal. How would we compare Gould's choice of an ascetic life on behalf of his music to a weekend motorcyclist? If a burglar has a peak experience while robbing a house, on what grounds can we compare it to the focused, psychological experience that a police officer will have going into that house to arrest the burglar?[6] The same ethical question about choice of purpose can be put to soldiers who commit barbaric acts, to white collar criminals, and indeed, to all who face the mundane, undramatic choices about how to use time and energy in constructing a personal existence.

Although many religions have tried to do so, it may never be possible to develop a universal ethics with which to evaluate human choices and behavior in all societies for all time. But advancing a tentative argument as to why certain life choices are better than others, based on existentialist philosophy, seems preferable to sidestepping a difficult area. We need social philosophers like Nietzsche (1878/1986), Maxine Greene (1967, 1973, 1978, 1988), Sartre (1956/1994), and Albert Camus (1948/1972) to ask why such questions are worth studying, and to embed psychological–technical insights about psychological states and traits, valuable as this knowledge is, in a larger perspective, one asking about truth, meaning, and justice, the deep dilemmas of the human condition, all balanced by skepticism for reductionist theory and method. Indeed, the value of developing an explicit ethic of human development seems all the more important in the present era. The critical theory movement, which was stimulated by the Vietnam War and social dislocations of the 1960s, raised important critiques with regard to the pernicious effects of racism, sexism, and social class on human and community development (Diggins, 1992). But these relentless critiques also served, perhaps, to reduce individual responsibility in the face of what have come to be overpowering social determinism and group identity, contributing to a certain victim mentality. In contrast, existentialist philosophy focuses, first and foremost, on personal freedom to make

[6] This may seem like an odd example, but several conversations I have had with experienced police officers support the point that one of the reinforcers for deviant behavior is the intense psychological experience that illegal acts stimulate.

choices, even under dire circumstances, and the absolute responsibility to construct an authentic existence by making conscious choices in a problematic world of poor choices (Friedman, 1964; Guignon & Pereboom, 1995; Sartre, 1956/1994).

Sartre sets a high, almost impossible, standard of absolute individual freedom, which argues that radical change is always impossible in the direction a life is taking (1956/1994). One can change a job, or apply to college, or try to make a new friend. Every day brings the possibility of evaluating one's life anew and then changing direction. Such steps are difficult, perhaps, but they are always possible. Equally important, Sartre couples the ideal of freedom to the ideal of individual responsibility, namely, that people are responsible for their existential choices, or lack thereof.

The existentialist argument for becoming an active subject in constructing one's life, rather than a half-awake, passive object buffeted by external forces, assumes that there is no higher purpose, order, or God that defines human existence externally. In this regard, the famous existentialist credo "God is dead" is not to be taken literally. Rather, Nietzsche argued that humankind can no longer use the *idea* of God, an afterlife, or formal religion to justify human choices. Therefore, individuals who are almost always alone in the world make choices of how to use the one short life given to them, and the active choice of purposes in life, alone, creates meaning in a finite, problematic existence.

While this has been a limited discussion, the outline of the existentialist argument provides one plausible ethic of human development. There is an imperative to use one's short existence fully, to make that self-development project intentional, and to work hard at it. Another imperative found in many of the world's religions and secular ethical systems is that a well-used life should be constructed in service to others and the community, not just accumulating possessions (Wachtel, 1983).

Therefore, constructing an engaged life requires that we understand both the quality of the purposes chosen and the process used to pursue them. In that regard, Maslow and Czikszentmihalyi make questionable assumptions about human nature and society. Maslow was critical of European existentialism, which he thought too pessimistic. But this view led him away from deep dilemmas in the human condition. Csikszentmihalyi's emphasis upon flow as a process, although an important contribution, leaves his theory somewhat sterile because the noble purposes that guide so much human behavior are left out. It is questionable that individual happiness is, or should be, the central motive in human experience. He later (1993) expanded his theory to assume entropy as the natural state to which consciousness will return, if not ordered by human actions and thought. By extension, human culture provides a shield from the chaos of the world. But even with this elaboration, his theory does not contain an explicit framework with which to evaluate human purposes other than to say that flow experiences are positive and advance character development.

In contrast, the existentialist perspective asks us to acknowledge a difficult, if not grim, worldview that emphasizes personal choice, personal responsibility, and authenticity in a problematic world, one in which the possibility of lasting happiness is remote. While Csikszentmihalyi's assumption that human behavior is motivated by a search for happiness is plausible, human beings are motivated by many needs. Following Maslow (1968), let us assume a hierarchy of motives where at the highest level, human beings learn to become meaning-making, self-sacrificing creatures who are motivated to serve others and the community, often to their detriment. The focus is making daily ethical choices about how to construct one's existence. Dr. Rieux's somber choice in Camus's *The Plague* is to serve the community, to fight the plague decimating his community, and Camus seems to say, to struggle against the dulled consciousness of a modern community (1948/1972). Given the existential choice of surrender or service, so to speak, Camus uses the character of Rieux and his service to patients to argue that a meaningful existence comes not from pleasure or other escapes, but from facing a difficult reality, doing what one can to make a difference.

CONCLUSION

As my reading project has unfolded, I have begun to look at my own behavior and that of others differently, and the metaphor that comes to mind when I think about how human attention works is that we are like sand sharks that keep moving endlessly, one experience after the other, with varying intentionality and concentration. Certain activities hold our attention for brief moments and we seem drawn to events that are novel or complex, but we keep moving through time and activities. Many patterns and motivations in human behavior can be explored as expressions of a human need to focus attention, if only for the moment, and this dynamic plays itself out all day long as one moves through different levels of engagement. Thus, if we study the underlying causes, correlates, and consequences of attention and the search for psychological engagement, it helps us understand the richness of lives and the diverse life activities in which people engage—from sewing to rock climbing. In doing so, we also learn that these activities are attractive to people, at times, because they are used to capture a restless attention, and, at other times, because they engage our lives at deeper, existential levels.

As a result of this project, I have become less interested in peak experiences in favor of middle range dynamics of engagement. Most occupations, in fact, require midrange abilities to monitor simultaneously a number of tasks where the person must be able to focus quickly and accurately on one activity, and then on another. Women with children in the home learn how to handle multiple tasks like working on a house project and answering the phone, while attending to young children who are constantly in motion.[7] For people who have competitive, stressful occupations, a pleasant day on the weekend may be not more competitive stress, as some of my examples suggest, but rather a gentle, meandering attention as one moves

[7] Thanks to Ann Stanton for her observation that the demanding social role of mother and wife brings special demands on the attentional system.

from reading the papers to cooking to reading a novel to gardening.[8]

Placing too much emphasis upon peak experiences also distracts us from the reality that we sometimes have to motivate ourselves to do unpleasant things, to endure stress and danger, and to work hard and attend to stimuli when the brain–mind–body is tired. While it is worthy to explore human potential, social institutions set expectations for people to pay attention when they might not choose to do so on their own. How many times in life, in fact, does one hear the injunction, "Pay attention!" The ability to pay attention, however, seems to be misunderstood in American cultural myths, as if all one needs is will power. What we need is a full understanding of how attention and mood dynamics work in human motivation and everyday life. This project is advanced to enhance such an understanding.

In conclusion, let us return to Gould's challenge about the best use of a life, which is where we began. How Gould used his life may be too extreme for most people. Few among us have his talent, and he lived alone. But his life is remarkable because of the lengths to which he went, first, to focus his attention and creativity as a performer, and second, to minimize the distractions of daily life on his work as his career evolved. We all face the same challenge in modern times—to somehow construct an engaged life, to find a balance of meaningful purposes and involving process, to do so on a daily basis, and to extend that project over a lifetime.

REFERENCES

Astin, A. (1985). *Achieving educational excellence.* San Francisco: Jossey-Bass.

Camus, A. (1972). *The plague.* New York: Vintage Books. (Original work published 1948)

Cott, J. (1984). *Conversations with Glenn Gould.* Boston: Little, Brown.

[8] Thanks to Margaret Blanchard for this observation (personal communication, 1996).

Csikszentmihalyi, M. (1991). *Flow: The psychology of optimal experience.* New York: Harper.

Csikszentmihalyi, M. (1993). *The evolving self.* New York: HarperCollins.

Dennett, D. C. (1996). *Kinds of minds.* New York: Basic Books.

Dewey, J. (1963). *Experience and education.* New York: Macmillan. (Original work published 1938)

Diggins, J. P. (1992). *The rise and fall of the American left.* New York: Norton.

Friedman, M. (1964). *The worlds of existentialism.* Chicago: University of Chicago Press.

Gergen, K. (1991). *The saturated self.* New York: Basic Books.

Greene, M. (Ed.). (1967). *Existential encounters for teachers.* New York: Random House.

Greene, M. (1973). *Teacher as stranger.* Belmont, CA: Wadsworth.

Greene, M. (1978). *Landscapes of learning.* New York: Teachers College Press.

Greene, M. (1988). *The dialectic of freedom.* New York: Teachers College Press.

Guignon, C., & Pereboom, D. (Eds.). (1995). *Existentialism: Basic writings.* Indianapolis: Hackett.

Hobson, J. A. (1994). *The chemistry of conscious states.* Boston: Little, Brown.

Hoffer, E. (1951). *The true believer.* New York: Harper & Row.

James, W. (1958). *The varieties of religious experience.* New York: Modern Library. (Original work published 1902)

Janis, I. L. (1972). *Victims of group think.* Boston: Houghton Mifflin.

Kabat-Zinn, J. (1994). *Wherever you go there you are: Mindfulness meditation in everyday life.* New York: Hyperion.

Kahn, W. A. (1990). The psychological condition of personal engagement and disengagement at work. *Academy of Management Journal, 33,* 692–724.

Kahn, W. A. (1992). To be fully there: Psychological presence at work. *Human Relations, 45,* 321–345.

Kemp, P. (1973). *Pathetique de l'engagement.* Paris: Seuil.

Krauss, C. (1994). Undercover police ride wide range of emotion. *The New York Times,* August 29, B3.

Langer, E. J. (1989). *Mindfulness.* Reading, MA: Addison-Wesley.

Maslow, A. (1968). *Toward a psychology of being* (2nd ed.). New York: Van Nostrand Reinhold.

Maslow, A. (1993). *The farther reaches of human nature.* New York: Penguin Arkana.

Nietzsche, F. (1986). *Human, all too human.* New York: Cambridge University Press. (Original work published 1878)
Oxford Modern English Dictionary (1993). s.v. "Engagements"
Sartre, J. (1994). *Being and nothingness.* New York: Gramercy Books. (Original work published 1956)
Schacht, R. (1994). *The future of alienation.* Urbana: University of Illinois Press.
Sizer, T. (1984). *Horace's compromise.* Boston: Houghton Mifflin.
Smith, A. (1996). Sidebar. In *Patagonia Catalog,* Fall. Reno, NV.
Wachtel, P. L. (1983). *The poverty of affluence.* New York: Free Press.

PART III

The Self in Transformation

10.

On Being at both Center and Circumference: The Role of Personal Discipline and Collective Wisdom in the Recovery of Soul

John J. McKenna

Midway in our life's journey, I went astray
from the straight road and woke to find
myself
alone in a dark wood.
(Dante's Inferno, 1320/1982, p. 28)

In the middle of life's journey, Dante suggests, one may awaken to find oneself lost in the woods, without a clear sense of direction or purpose. Like Dante nearly 700 years ago, people at midlife in our day confront a similar challenge to find meaning and purpose (Chinen, 1992; Gerzon, 1992; Stein, 1983). Recent literature, much of which is addressed to mature adults, discusses this challenge in terms of a recovery of soul and spirit (e.g., Keen, 1994; T. Moore, 1992; Robinson, 1995).

Acknowledgement. This chapter is a substantial revision of a presentation made at the Vermont Psychological Association Conference on Spirituality and Psychotherapy in September, 1995. The author thanks the following for their helpful comments and suggestions on earlier drafts of this chapter. Steven Garger, Kelli Provost, and particularly Melvin Miller and Al West.

Integrating themes from recent literature, I propose that recovery of soul entails a radical rediscovery and reaffirmation of meaning and purpose in life and a reintegration of life energy. Soul recovery is realized through bringing about an alliance of mind, body, and spirit, and of individuals with earth/nature and other members of the human community. In this chapter I describe the work of soul recovery as consisting of two complementary tasks or, to use a metaphor from music or dance, two movements. The first is summed up in the phrase, "know thyself," and is symbolized by "being at the center." Personal spiritual discipline fosters self-knowledge, a "centered life," a life in which mind, body, and spirit are brought into harmony. The second movement, symbolized by "being at the circumference," involves a dialectic between personal experience and knowledge derived from study of collective wisdom traditions. This dialectic is illustrated by examples drawn from the teachings of four wisdom traditions on four poles of human experience: Buddhism on the mind, feminism and goddess spirituality on the body, Native American traditions on the earth, and Judeo-Christian and Islamic traditions on the human community (Spretnak, 1991).

SOUL, SPIRIT, AND SPIRITUALITY

T. Moore (1992) states that "soul is not a thing, but a quality or a dimension of experiencing life and ourselves. It has to do with depth, value, relatedness, heart, and personal substance" (p. 5). Hillman (1975) argues that by soul one should understand "a perspective rather than a substance, a viewpoint toward things rather than a thing itself" (p. x). Both argue against a reification of soul, and contend that soul brings a capacity for experiencing life and the world in a special way, an ability to recognize texture and color, dimension and tone in our experience. Hillman proposes that soul makes it possible that mere events are deepened into experiences which have significance. He suggests that soul acts like a mirror which allows us to reflect and process our experiences, but primarily of interest, soul allows us to conjure possibilities through imagination in fantasy, image, dream, and reflective speculation (p. x). By contrast, the loss or absence of soul is reflected in a paralyzing demoralization, isolation, ennui, and emptiness—a level of disease that runs deeper than isolated patterns of symptoms; without soul, people are alienated from their own experience, from one another, and from the energizing and vitalizing forces of nature (Hillman, 1975; May, 1991; T. Moore, 1992, 1996).

Cousins (1992) proposes that what various traditions call "spirit" refers to "the deepest center of the person. It is here that the person is open to a transcendent dimension; it is here that the person experiences ultimate reality" (p. 128). Dunne (1975) contends that spirit can best be understood as the relationship we have with all that enters into our life.

> If there is something that endures in man, it is the life of spirit that carries on from one relationship to another. . . . The spirit lives in its adventures, in its voyage of discovery, and these adventures never cease. . . . As he voyages out into the unknown he discovers the life of the spirit. (Dunne, 1975, pp. 39–43)

Sam Keen (1994) suggests that spirituality be understood as a "soulful path," a quest or journey to discover our highest and deepest selves, to open ourselves to being moved by a transcendent force that ultimately makes us human, and by virtue of which we are connected "with something beyond the self, something more everlasting than the self" (p. 58). Similarly, Jack Kornfield (1993) describes the spiritual journey as "a path with heart" (p. 11), a path connected to the deepest yearnings of our spirit. He proposes that spiritual practice on this path is directed toward enlightenment, or a "knowing born of love . . . the intimacy that links us to the core of all things" (p. 334). Kabat-Zinn (1994) suggests that "ultimately, spiritual means simply experiencing wholeness and interconnectedness directly, a seeing that individuality and the totality are interwoven, that nothing is separate or extraneous" (pp. 265–266).

Despite differences in emphasis, these definitions or descriptions of spirit and spirituality share common themes: spirit concerns what is deepest and innermost; it gives expression to our profoundest yearnings; it is open to the unknown, the mysterious, the transcendent; and it connects us to our own history and experience, to others and to the universe. By enabling us to establish a relationship with the events, persons, and places that have entered our lives, a life of spirit enlarges our soul.

The idea of holding with reverence and awe a sense of connectedness to one's life experiences, one's personal history, and indeed to all things—not in any abstract form, but rather as this particular life in this time and this universe—is integral to the notion of spirituality. So also is the idea that in doing so we are open to the transcendent, the sacred, the divine. Spirit is thus both a unifying and enlarging force in one's life, a power that brings about intimate connections among aspects of ourselves and of ourselves with others and the universe of being.

Both Hebrew and Christian scriptures tell us that "we are to love the Lord God with all our heart, all our soul, all our mind, and all our strength" (Deuteronomy 6.5; Matthew 22.37; Mark 12.30; Luke 10.27). Ultimately, it would be wrong to make a case for sharp differences among all these terms—heart, soul, mind, strength. Most probably the parallel structure in these texts indicates that these terms refer to something that is shared or held in common more than to different functions of the human spirit. What this saying does suggest is that spirituality somehow involves being in love, and that being in love is ultimately a unifying experience which engages our whole heart, whole soul, and whole mind.

THE PROCESS OF SOUL RECOVERY

Several authors have described the malaise of our age as one of "demoralization," or "dispiritedness," or a diffuse "anxious apprehension" (May, 1953, 1991; T. Moore, 1992). While no one in the culture is exempt from this malaise, recent literature identifies a group that is particularly vulnerable to acting out in self-destructive ways in order to escape from demoralization, and that group is people at midlife (Gerzon, 1992; Robinson, 1995). The central character in John Cheever's novel, *The Swimmer* (cited in Cath, 1980, p. 71), represents one kind of "tragic man" at midlife, one who, in a desperate attempt to ward off the effects of aging and to identify with the grandiose fantasies of adolescent machismo, "needs to swim in everyone's pool, to chase every woman, to drink of every neighbor's resources and to be a part of everyone else's life" (Cath, 1980, p. 71).

Jung (1933) believed that the second half of life entails a reversal of the ideals and values that were cherished in the first half. He concluded that many mistakenly think they can live out the second half of life by following the same program that they adhered to in the first half. The challenge of the second half of life is to realize those aspects of soul that have been neglected, that have gone unacknowledged and unattended in the process of ego development to which much of the first half is devoted. Recent studies of adult development (Gould, 1978; Levinson, 1978; Lidz, 1980) describe midlife as a time for reevaluating our relationship to work, intimacy, gender-based roles, and mortality. The task of later life becomes one of recovering soul and discovering anew one's place in the world (Gerzon, 1992; Robinson, 1995; Stein, 1983).

In this context soul recovery may be seen as a radical reclaiming and reintegration of those parts of our selves and our experience from which we have become separated. The aim of this process is to restore the connections among body, mind, and spirit, and of the individual with the earth and the human community, as well as with the divine or transcendent. It helps to think of the process of soul recovery as a set of complementary movements, of which one involves the practice of a personal spiritual discipline—"being at the center," while the second entails a reflective dialogue with the heritage of major wisdom traditions—"being at the circumference."

The first movement in soul recovery concerns knowing one's self. Apollo's temple bore an inscription, "Know thyself," enjoining self-knowledge on the ancient Greeks. Essentially, this motto was a deterrent to unbridled hubris, an admonition to those entering the temple to remember that they were merely human and "that an unbridgeable gulf separates them from the gods" (Snell, 1953/1982). Self-knowledge entails awareness of one's mortality, one's finiteness, one's contingency. It is intimately associated with middle age for middle age brings home the realization that one shall not achieve all that one has dreamed of, and the opportunity to wrestle with the shadows of unacknowledged ambition, aggression, and longing for intimacy (Gould, 1978; Levinson, 1978). However, accepting the limits to one's life also enables a sweet satisfaction with all that one has experienced (Lidz, 1980).

A unique quality to self-knowledge at midlife results from the confrontation with one's own mortality (Stein, 1983). Little else so powerfully brings about a centering of life as the personal realization of one's mortality (Sheehy, 1995). Such a realization of personal mortality may arise from a traumatic loss, a life-threatening accident, contracting a terminal disease, or from the process of aging itself with its gradual diminishments. Unfortunately, these realizations can be transient, and typically, one rarely attains a firm reference point, a center, without the active practice of some form of personal discipline. A primary outcome of the practice of a personal spiritual discipline such as meditation is a stable standpoint, a center to one's life.

The second aspect of soul recovery involves redefining a sense of purpose and meaning by taking one's bearings within the world that one has come to know as a result of life experience. Recent writers have emphasized how middle age is a time to reevaluate one's life project and relationship to the next generation, and to reassess false assumptions and illusions in the context of one's accumulated knowledge of the world (Datan, 1980; Gould, 1978; Levinson, 1978). In carrying out such a reassessment, one seeks guidance by looking to the horizon defined by the boundaries of human achievement and aspiration. This horizon is delineated by landmarks which are the heritage of the great sacred traditions, since these traditions enshrine the noblest aspirations of humans throughout recorded and prerecorded history (Smith, 1991).

The second movement in the work of soul recovery consists in a dialectic and dialogue with the collective wisdom traditions. The dialogue involves passing over by way of empathic understanding to the wisdom of the great religious traditions and then coming back to oneself with new insight about how this wisdom applies to one's own life (Dunne, 1972). The dialectic is anchored by the concurrent work of centering and fixing one's own standpoint through practice of a personal spiritual discipline. Together these two movements are essential and constitutive activities in developing a life of spirit, and recovering soul.

The product of the first exercise in soul recovery, of coming to know self, we might say, is a lesson in contingency, of possibility, of what might have been, and of what still may be. And the product of the second exercise, of coming to know our place in the world, is a lesson about necessity, of what had to be, what needed to be just as it happened, of what was and of what is (Dunne, 1975). In both of these tasks we are ably assisted by the teachings and writings that are the heritage of sacred traditions. We must know ourselves but we know ourselves only as we stand within the world and as we stand within certain traditions. We know ourselves through the stories we tell ourselves, and our stories are shaped by the world, the people, and the traditions which have nurtured us (Runyan, 1990).

Virgil served as Dante's guide on his journey through hell to the summit of purgatory, there to be supplanted by Beatrice and ultimately by Bernard for the final course through Paradise. One wonders whom a modern Dante would accept for the role of guide on the deeply personal journey toward recovery of soul and discovery of life's meaning. Given that one characteristic of the modern mindset is profound skepticism regarding any voice whose authority derives from extrinsic sources, a modern person is perhaps more likely to listen to one whose authority derives from knowledge rooted in personal experience.

Nonetheless, recent cultural analyses highlight the role of tradition in shaping the story of our experience (Spretnak, 1991; Tarnas, 1991; Wilber, 1996). Tradition makes available the words, images, and plots with which to tell our story (McAdams, 1990; Runyan, 1990). Dante's discovery of the meaning of life and his place in the world was told with words and images drawn from the classical philosophers, poets, artists, and spiritual writers of Christendom's first 1100 years (E. Moore, 1896/1968a, 1899/1968b). A contemporary story of the discovery of life's meaning and purpose must draw upon an even more pluralistic and less unified view of the universe and of history than was available to Dante (Smith, 1991; Spretnak, 1991).

Since soul and spirit cannot be known directly nor adequately defined, they are best grasped in images and stories. Theophane the Monk (1981) tells a story about "The monk whose face was red" because, having died at 50 and gone to judgment, he was ashamed of his lack of "soulful" living, but was granted 7 years grace:

> So I came back to my cave. I went in and I kept going. I went in deeper than I'd ever gone before, in and down, in and down. . . . Finally I began to hear a rumbling sound, like mighty waters. You know what it was? It was the tears of the whole world! I heard the bitter tears of EVERYONE'S fear, hurt, despair, disappointment, rage. Everyone's. And I heard the sweet tears too—you know, when you're loved, when you're safe at last, a loved one restored, those tears of joy. Yes, I heard the death of Christ and his resurrection. I must have been at the heart of the earth, because, while I couldn't hear any words, I heard ALL the tears and therefore experienced total communion. I was separated from my separateness. . . . I finally decided how I would spend my seven years. I would go back to the mouth of the cave and conduct people back and forth to the depths. (p. 27)

PERSONAL SPIRITUAL DISCIPLINE

Any tradition concerned with fostering a soulful life, a life of spirit, a path with heart, incorporates some form of practice, discipline, and soul work. Perhaps most commonly recognized are traditions such as Buddhism or Hinduism which prescribe meditative practices to center the mind, to focus attention, to open the heart and soul to enlightenment and compassion. Both Eastern and Western traditions offer many methods that lead to imaginative, affective, and intellectual quieting and among them one can find an approach to meditation or prayer that suits just about any temperament or intellectual orientation (Goleman, 1988). This section will touch on three practices: *lectio divina,* centering prayer, and mindfulness meditation.

Lectio divina, literally "sacred reading," was prescribed by Benedict of Nursia in his Rule, a fifth century document which sets forth guidelines for monastic life (McGinn, 1994). Western monastic tradition (McGinn, 1994) links the activities of reading *(lectio),* meditation *(meditatio),* and prayer *(oratio)* as preparation for contemplation *(contemplatio).* As the first step in this sequence, *lectio divina* involves reading principally from the scriptures and from commentaries on the scripture by early church writers. These texts, often read publicly, offer continual reminders to the listener to the call to union with God, and to share in the feast of wisdom (Proverbs 8–9).

The aim of *lectio divina* is to nurture the soul; it entails reading meditatively, lingering lovingly over phrases and images which awaken hope, deepen faith, inspire commitment, and evoke attitudes of acceptance, compassion, and forgiveness. A helpful metaphor for the attitude of one engaged in sacred reading is that of a soldier stationed abroad reading letters from home; according to Augustine the scriptures are "letters from home."

Lectio divina is not study, nor does it aim to provide intellectual stimulation and challenge, nor to foster discursive reasoning or problem solving. Rather it is about taming the heart and mind, about cultivating an inner garden of delights, to which one can return throughout the day to draw refreshment, renewed clarity, and commitment to the "path of the heart."

Centering prayer is grounded in centuries of spiritual practice in Western monasticism and religious life. In this tradition, the goal of meditation is not merely to discipline the mind or heart; rather it is to dispose the mind and heart to receive the gifts of contemplative prayer, and ultimately to experience union with God. The contemporary practice of centering prayer grew from an interpretation of the fourteenth century work, *The Cloud of Unknowing* (Anonymous, 1957). According to this classic, by repeating in connection with one's breathing a simple word or phrase, such as "God" or "One," the mind and heart can be focused and disposed to the higher forms of prayer.

As the second step in the sequence noted above, meditation *(meditatio)* keeps the awareness of the divine call present in the mind and heart. Meditation then gives rise to prayer *(oratio)*, which consists in brief, one word utterances that pierce the heavens (Anonymous, 1957). These activities are, however, merely preparation for contemplation *(contemplatio)*, a form of prayer which is beyond unaided efforts, or "infused," that is, the result of grace freely bestowed.

Pennington (1995) and Keating (1986, 1992) discuss the practice of centering prayer in great depth and put the practice in the context of Christian spirituality. They stress how the practice is a response to the gospel call to follow Christ. They also indicate how faithfulness to the practice of centering prayer opens the mind and heart to deeper levels of contemplative prayer. This deeper form of prayer, *contemplatio*, the fourth term in the classic sequence cited above, is the flowering of meditation practice and consists of a lifting up of the gaze of the heart to God, a lovingly attentive resting in God, and being consumed with a burning desire for the vision of God (McGinn, 1994).

Mindfulness meditation draws on the tradition of *vipassana* or insight meditation, the heart of Theraveda Buddhist practices (Dalai Lama, 1965; Goleman, 1988). As with centering prayer, the practice of mindfulness meditation seeks to establish an attentive awareness and openness to the present by means of methods such as paying attention to one's breathing or repetition of a simple phrase or set of phrases. A good example of the latter is the following from Nhat Hanh (1987): "Breathing in, I calm my body. Breathing out, I smile. Dwelling in this present moment, I know this is a wonderful moment" (p. 5).

In mindfulness meditation, as in centering prayer, the aim is not to develop concentration, nor does the approach itself emphasize concentration; rather it fosters awareness of and openness to the inclusiveness of the present moment. Fruits of mindfulness meditation practice include enlightenment, a realization of the profound interconnectedness of all things, transcendence of dualistic thinking, a deep compassion for others, and commitment to peace and reconciliation (Kornfield, 1993; Nhat Hanh, 1976, 1987).

Along with the practice of mindfulness meditation as with the practice of centering prayer, there is commonly a corresponding simplification of one's life, and as ascesis, or restraint of instinctual drives and impulses, through adherence to the practice of the Beatitudes (Matthew 5) in the case of centering prayer, or the Four Noble Truths, in the case of mindfulness meditation. The aim of all of these practices is awakening or deepening consciousness, developing a keener appreciation of the significance of the present moment, and evoking dispositions of surrender, compassion, and commitment. Of course one may use these or any other spiritual practice for different purposes, such as to escape from troubling circumstances, to attempt to achieve control over one's body or thinking, to placate a rigid superego, or to attain some ideal state of consciousness or union with God. Once put in the service of ends other than simply opening our minds and hearts to the guidance of the spirit, they cease to be useful in our spiritual journey. However, faithfulness to the practice ultimately brings the practice under the sway of the spirit rather than the ego. Through its inner dynamism and the fruits that are produced, the practice itself teaches us how this goal may be accomplished.

Several excerpts from a collection of anecdotes about early monks (Waddell, 1962) will illustrate the power of personal discipline in developing a spiritual path. These excerpts tell of the battle that is waged within for purity of heart and singleness of purpose, and about the importance of solitude and faithfulness to soul work.

> Abbot Antony said, "Who sits in solitude and is quiet has escaped from three wars: hearing, speaking, and seeing; yet against one thing shall he continually battle: that is, his own heart." (p. 81)
>
> A certain brother came to the abbot Moses in Skete and said: "Father, give me a saving word." Abbot Moses told the brother: "Go to your cell, and your cell will teach you everything." (p. 83)

> The fathers used to say, "If temptation befall you in the place where you dwell, desert not that place in the time of temptation; for if you do, wherever you go, there shall you find what you have fled." (p. 103)

Although these traditions emphasize the role of personal discipline and solitude, they also recognize the importance of community. As we stated earlier, in Western monasticism, sacred reading was often done in public, and much of prayer was communal as well. In the Buddhist tradition the community is known as a *sangha*, which may be viewed as a support group. Nhat Hahn (1992) reminds us that "a teacher can be important and also the teachings, but friends are the most essential element of the practice. It is difficult or even impossible to practice without a *sangha*" (pp. 102–103).

COLLECTIVE WISDOM TRADITIONS

Collective wisdom traditions serve as guideposts in understanding our place in the world. While a great many traditions might provide guidance, I chose the traditions to be discussed below on the basis of two criteria. A first consideration was that the tradition used images, rituals, and stories in a way that affirms the presence and reality of the divine at the heart of the human experience. In making this choice, I do not deny the value of spiritual practices which belong to the *via negativa,* the way of negation, and which emphasize the transcendence of the divine over the human, and the inadequacy of human experience, imagination, and intellect to represent the divine (Williams, 1961). However, given the prominence long granted such practices, and a desire to acknowledge spiritualities and practices long neglected, it seemed appropriate to focus on those traditions which belong to the *via positiva,* the way of affirmation, which emphasize the connections between human experience and symbolism and the realm of the transcendent (Fox, 1991).

A second consideration in choosing the traditions was their clarity in articulating the role of one or more basic dimensions or "poles" of human experience in the world: mind, body, earth, and community. The collective wisdom traditions represented by Buddhism, Goddess spirituality, Native American spirituality, and the teachings of the Semitic traditions, contain uniquely rich treasures of wisdom with a profound relevance for critical issues of our age (Spretnak, 1991). The teachings of Buddha clarify the nature and origin of suffering as well as its cure through discipline of the mind. The rediscovery of Goddess spirituality has taught us how to honor our own bodies (as well as the earthbody). The practices of Native Americans celebrate our deep connection with the earth and the natural world and our responsibility as stewards of the earth. Lastly, the teachings of the Semitic traditions—Judaism, Christianity, and Islam—speak powerfully about community and social justice. The following sections describe these four traditions in more detail, highlighting principles of each that can help us on our spiritual journey.

BUDDHISM

As Buddha, Gautama taught a path that was very different from the customary Hindu practices of the time. Smith (1991) has noted that Buddhism was and is a religion like no other. It dispensed with authority in the form of brahmins, and taught that *dharma* (truth and reality) could ultimately be known by one's own inner light. Buddhism dispensed with rituals, and with dogma and tradition as the seal of truth. It emphasized personal initiative and effort rather than grace, and it minimized the role of mysticism and the supernatural.

The heart of Buddha's teaching was the Four Noble Truths, a set of propositions that distilled the insight that accompanied his awakening and understanding of *dharma*. These Truths provide answers to basic questions in life: What is the nature of suffering? What is the origin of suffering? What is bliss (the end of suffering)? What is the way to achieve bliss? Buddha specifically linked suffering with birth, sickness, infirmity of age, fear of death, being tied to what one dislikes, and being separated from what one loves. He taught that suffering occurs because we crave fulfillment in selfish ways. Therefore, to end suffering, we must be liberated from selfish craving. The way to bliss is following the Eightfold Path.

The Eightfold Path contains three steps related to moral action (right speech, right action, right livelihood), three related to meditation (right concentration, right mindfulness, right effort), and two concerning wisdom (right understanding, right thought). The Buddha also taught Five Precepts concerning right action: to refrain from killing, stealing, lying, sexual misconduct, and intoxicants.

What is it then about Buddhism, at least the core teaching of Buddhism, that would be attractive to a Westerner traveling the spiritual path? Certainly its antiauthoritarian attributes lend appeal. Beyond this Buddhism holds out the ideal of moderation to people caught up in extremes. It offers a profound analysis of the origin and cure of suffering, the prospect of overcoming isolation and aloneness through compassion for others, and of realization of oneness with reality in the awakened state. Perhaps most relevant, judging from the books, retreats, and workshops now available, are Buddhism's rich lessons on the practice of mindfulness or insight meditation, and how to open the heart to the knowledge and wisdom born of compassion.

Although we have touched only briefly on a few elements of the Buddha's teaching, one can discern the central importance of the Four Noble Truths. They point to the necessity of a moral life, a life of right thinking and right action to overcome the "dislocation" in human life (Smith, 1991). This dislocation in the eyes of Buddha is rooted in the tendency to view suffering and misfortune as merely private afflictions of the individual, an unfortunate turn of the wheel of life. Through compassion one breaks the bonds of self-absorption which keep one tied to the wheel of private fortune and misfortune (Dunne, 1972). Gautama himself was a prototype in that he chose not to stay apart as a forest dweller and enjoy enlightenment in solitude, but returned among his people and shared with them his insight. In so doing he revealed compassion for his people.

> As he sat under the fig tree, [Gautama] saw the failure of the worldling to conquer fortune and the failure of the recluse to conquer himself, and in that failure the failure of all conquest, the failure of taking; but at the same time he saw the possibility of another kind of life, a life of simple giving and receiving, and in this he saw the way to wisdom and bliss. (Dunne, 1972, pp. 222–223)

FEMINISM AND GODDESS SPIRITUALITY: RECLAIMING THE BODY

Though goddess and feminist spirituality traditions are quite diverse, at least three broad streams in these traditions can be identified (Eller, 1993; Plaskow & Christ, 1989). The first involves the renewal of pagan or natural worship and witchcraft (Starhawk, 1979); the second, correctives to patriarchal religion whether within or outside of traditional religious institutions (Daly, 1973); and the third, a metaphor for healing feminine woundedness (Reis, 1995).

Despite the plurality of voices within the traditions of feminist and goddess spirituality, there are common themes: the divine is immanent within each person and within all of nature; all life and nature are sacred and reveal the divine to us; a woman's body and natural cycles are honored; the powers of intuition, the medium of dreams, creativity and spontaneity, and rituals are also honored and cultivated as means of connection with the sacred (Eller, 1993; Stone, 1984).

At the heart of goddess spirituality is the belief that the divine is immanent. Whether the divine is conceived as the source of creativity or as an ultimate mystery, it pervades the cosmos and makes it a sacred whole. The many images of the goddess express her creative power which is the source of ongoing regeneration, as well as of diversity within unity.

Belief in the profound and intimate identity of every woman with the goddess, of a divine power immanent within each woman, is also central to goddess spirituality. Often cited as an expression of this realization is Shange's (1976): "I found god in myself and I loved her/I loved her fiercely." In the literature recording personal conversions to goddess spirituality, this idea is also expressed as a "coming home" or a "coming home to self" (Morton, 1985).

A corollary of the immanence of the goddess in each woman is a profound sense of empowerment. Morton (1985) remarked that "the goddess shattered the image of myself as a dependent person and cleared my brain so I could come into the power that was mine, that was me all along" (p. 167). This empowerment is not modeled on male images of power; rather it entails a deepening of interiority and subjectivity within a matrix of caring and solidarity. Feminist and goddess spirituality traditions commonly stress the personal effort necessary for enriching interiority and critical subjectivity, for example, through journal work. They also emphasize the role of community in consciousness raising groups, collective sharing of stories, and shared rituals (Kidd, 1996).

A third important aspect of goddess spirituality involves a radical shift in outlook toward existence, away from construing existence as a project by which one strives to overcome death—a view which underlies patriarchal culture—to a recognition of the central place of cycles of death and rebirth in the unfolding of the cosmos (Spretnak, 1991). Many contemporary feminists call on women to celebrate their instinctual gifts, to recognize the power associated with these natural instincts, that is, with the life/death/life force or soul, and to appreciate the grace inherent in instinctual power (e.g., Estes, 1992).

Estes describes the work of comprehending the instinctual nature as "a knowing of soul" (1992, p. 9). Integral to this knowing of soul is an acceptance and appreciation of the natural rhythms and cycles of a woman's body, of dreams and intuition as ways of connecting to the sacred dimension of nature, and of the power of story and of ritual in healing deep psychic wounds. In large measure this accomplishment is the fruit of an arduous and often lengthy process of reclaiming the body and intuitive powers from the disdain and disparagement to which they have been subjected by a privileged patriarchy (Griffin, 1978; Reis, 1995).

Kidd (1996) shares the following reflections which occurred after several years of working at grounding herself in images of the feminine deity:

> Opening the Matryoshka doll spoke to me about the need to discover Herself—the Feminine Self, the feminine soul—deep inside and to open her layer by layer. . . . Healing came for me as I integrated images of a strong, powerful, compassionate Feminine Being, one who was creating the universe, creating Herself, birthing new life, and holding everything in being. For me this was the most significant factor in creating a restoration of feminine value, dignity, and power inside—seeing female as *imago dei,* the image of the Divine, revealed now through women. . . . On the altar in my study I hung a lovely mirror sculpted in the shape of a crescent moon. It reminded me to honor the Divine Feminine presence in myself, the wisdom in my soul. (p. 181)

NATIVE AMERICAN SPIRITUALITY

Native American spirituality celebrates the harmony and balance in nature and the fundamental unity of humans with the rest of the earth community. This spirituality is rooted in a profound realization of the interconnectedness of all life with the earth.

The Hopi have a word, *navoty,* which is used to express the concept of being in complete harmony and balance with the laws of the universe. According to Black Elk, a Lakota spiritual teacher, humans will know peace "when they realize their relationship, their oneness, with the universe and all its powers, and when they realize that at the center of the universe dwells *Wakan-Tanka,* and that this center is really everywhere; it is within each of us" (Spretnak, 1991, p. 90).

The following comments of Smohalla, a leader of the Nez Perce peoples of the Great Basin area, demonstrate this sense of unity:

> You ask me to plow the ground. Shall I take a knife and tear my mother's breast? Then when I die she will not take me to her bosom to rest. You ask me to dig for stone. Shall I dig under her skin for bones? And then when I die I cannot enter her body to be born again. You ask me to cut grass and make hay

> and sell it, and be rich like white men. But how dare I cut off my mother's hair. (Astrov, 1992, p. 85)

Native peoples believe that we have a fundamental responsibility to the cosmos to know intimately the profound connectedness that exists among all things and the spiritual force that gives life to all beings. Furthermore, we must live our lives in accord with this knowledge. Among native cultures, knowledge of the rhythm, order, and structure of natural cycles is considered sacred (Spretnak, 1991).

Among the Navajo, women's rites of initiation dramatically enact this belief in a radical connectedness with the natural order. At the same time these rites elevate mundane tasks to the realm of the sacred. Woman is the bearer of the young and the one who raises crops and provides food for the community. "Each time a woman is initiated, the world is saved from chaos, for the fundamental power of creativity is renewed in her being" (Lincoln, 1981, p. 107).

In keeping with these principles of solidarity with the earth and with living things, Hobday (1981) cites several Native American practices which contribute to a sound spirituality, what she describes as "keeping the heart moist and strong" (p. 318). In addition to loving the land, and cherishing silence, other practices include remembering the dead; vision quest; and story telling. Native peoples see death as part of life and keep the dead alive to themselves through memorial feasts and markers which honor the dead. "The dead and the land are intertwined in memory, but also with many signs of public and private reminder" (p. 322). Remembering the dead is one way to ensure continuity of the present with the past.

Vision questing is an adventure of the spirit. It often involves seeking out solitude in a place of wilderness, remote from the distractions of a daily routine, fasting to cleanse the body and to heighten sensory awareness, and prayer to humble the heart. Through vision quest, the seeker may contact the Great Spirit and receive knowledge of life's mysteries and powers of healing.

The tradition of story telling and oral history runs deep among native peoples; these are the essential means of teaching and passing on spiritual values. For the listener, they are also a means of coming to learn and understand the values of the culture. "[The story] is like a wisdom river flowing through the generations, offering refreshment to this one, direction to that one, amusement to another, and an ideal to another" (Hobday, 1981, p. 327).

In the storytelling traditions of native cultures, the trickster holds a special place which reflects the deep respect that native peoples accord the ultimate mysteriousness of nature and reality (Erdoes & Ortiz, 1984). Trickster stories honor playfulness, creativity, and generativity. The trickster represents the ultimate unknowable aspect of the divine power of creation and the mystery of the life/death/life cycle. The trickster is thus intimately associated with the healing and life-renewing powers of the shaman (Chinen, 1993; Kelsey, 1992).

Consistent with their heritage, native artists of British Columbia convey in their works a deep appreciation and respect for the natural environment and a profound sensitivity and love for the great web of life. Their sentiments are reflected in rich graphic symbolism, evident in totems, paintings, masks, sculptures, and jewelry, as well as in storytelling. In Vancouver, at the unveiling of his monumental bronze casting, the Jade Canoe, Bill Reid, an artist of Haida descent, recounted a tale expressing his concern about the future of his people. He cast well-known mythic figures to the Haida peoples as passengers in the canoe—the Bear, the Bear-Mother, the Beaver, the Dogfish Woman, the Chief, the Mouse-Woman, the Raven, the Wolf, the Eagle, and the Frog. These figures and their presence in the canoe convey the joint and uncertain destiny of the human and natural world:

> Here we are . . . not too sure where we are or where we're going, still squabbling and vying for position in the boat, but somehow managing to appear to be heading in some direction. At least the paddles are together, and the man in the middle [the Chief] seems to have some vision of what is to come. . . . There is no doubt what [Raven] looks like in this myth-image. . . . Of course, he is the steersman. So, although the boat appears to be heading in a purposeful direction, it can arrive anywhere the Raven's latest whim dictates . . . Is the tall figure who may or may not be

> the Spirit of Haida Gwaii, leading us, for we are all in the same boat, to a sheltered beach beyond the rim of the world as he seems to be, or is he lost in a dream of his own dreamings? The boat goes on, forever anchored in the same place. (Reid, 1994)

SEMITIC TRADITIONS

While all of the traditions we have considered thus far recognize the importance of community and compassion toward others, the Semitic traditions—Judaism, Christianity, and Islam—give a central place to the concept of a chosen people. All of these traditions find their origin in God's promises to Abraham of a land flowing with milk and honey and a progeny more numerous than the stars. They also celebrate the revelation of God's plan for this people and include mystical traditions which are centered on a personal relationship with God. The Christian scriptures describe the extension of this communion with God to all peoples, and the prospect of a universal reign or family of God.

In line with the profound awareness of God's favor (loving kindness) toward their people, these traditions emphasize building community through waging peace and working for justice in social life. The scriptures of the Semitic traditions prescribe an active opposition to social evils and injustice, and underline the special concern of God for the poor and disadvantaged—the orphaned, the widowed, the homeless or sojourner.

The Hebrew scriptures contain frequent examples of prophets confronting injustice and oppression especially when enacted by those holding positions of power at the palace, the courts, or the temple (for example, Amos 5, 6–24; Hosea, 10, 11–15; Isaiah 1, 21–26; Jeremiah 22, 13–15). In Christian scriptures, Jesus spoke with authority from that tradition when he confronted the hypocrisy of the religious leaders of his time. He condemned the burdens they imposed on the people through ceremonial and ritual observances while neglecting the centrality of God's mercy and loving-kindness (Matthew 23, 1ff.). Responding to charges that his disciples failed to wash their hands as prescribed, Jesus said: "nothing outside a man . . . by going into him can defile him, but the things which come out of a man are what defile him (Mark 7, 15).

To serve one another, to meet the needs of one another, is to celebrate the God immanent in creation and in every person. In Islamic scripture we read: "No one of you is a believer until he desires for his brother that which he desires for himself" (cited in Spretnak, 1991, p. 161). The third pillar of Islam, after acknowledging that Allah alone is God and Muhammad his prophet, and being faithful to daily prayers, is charity.

Several figures of our era stand out as prophetic witnesses to the values which are at the heart of the Abrahamic tradition. Within Judaism, Abraham Joshua Heschel and Elie Wiesel bear witness to God's basic leaning toward humankind, and God's forbearance and understanding of the forgetfulness of the human heart (Friedman, 1987). In the Christian tradition, Thomas Merton and Henri Nouwen articulate forcefully the call to prayerful and courageous pursuit of justice, peace, and compassion (Pennington 1987; Nouwen, 1993).

Among the parables of Matthew's gospel appears what many regard as the paradigmatic statement of standards for membership in the kingdom or family of God. At the final judgment, as the Son of Man separates the sheep from the goats, he says to the sheep on his right:

> Come, O blessed of my father, inherit the kingdom prepared for you from the foundation of the world; for I was hungry and you gave me food, I was thirsty and you gave me drink, I was a stranger and you welcomed me, I was naked and you clothed me, I was sick and you visited me, I was in prison and you came to me. . . . Truly, I say unto you, as you did it to one of the least of these [my brothers and sisters], you did it to me. (Matthew 25, 31–46)

CONCLUSION

We have described a process of recovering soul and bringing spirit into our lives through a complementary set of activities, practice of a personal spiritual discipline, and dialogue with the major wisdom traditions. This remedy for the demoralization which afflicts many today, and for the distress of those coping with midlife crises, is hardly original. For centuries these practices have been the business of members of contemplative communities and religious orders in both Western and Eastern traditions. What may be newly appreciated in today's secular world is the relevance of mindfulness meditation as a method of promoting health, improving recovery from and immunity to illness, and reducing stress (Kabat-Zinn, 1990), along with a heightened ecological sensitivity which is a hallmark of feminist/goddess and Native American wisdom traditions (Spretnak, 1991).

The fruit of perseverance in spiritual practice and dialogue with the wisdom traditions is a deeper connectedness in spirit of mind with body, and of the individual with the earthbody and with the human community. In this work of plotting and weaving connections through the cultivation of interiority and through dialogue with the great wisdom teachings, the spirit is both agent and beneficiary. The work is above all an act of love and its fruit is love.

Heiler's (1959) comparative study of world religions revealed a striking convergence among seven major religions on fundamental elements. Among the shared convictions are the following: that ultimate reality is love, mercy, compassion; that the way of humans to union with the divine involves sacrifice, discipline, and prayer; that as believers seek God so too they must seek their neighbor's well-being, even the well-being of their enemies; and finally, while religious experience is endlessly manifold, the superior way to God is love.

The end of our journey, like that of Dante, culminates in the realization that, while we lack the power to comprehend the divine mystery, we may yet taste something of the power of divine love. Through choosing wisely and exerting our powers of imagination, intelligence, and will in practicing a spiritual discipline and researching the teachings of the wisdom traditions, we will likely conclude, as have fellow travelers on this path before us, that we are unable to fathom how our image someday may blend with the circle of the Light Eternal. However, through the course of our journey, we may have found ourselves at both center and circumference and learned that ultimately we are moved by the Love that moves the Sun and the other stars (Dante, *Paradiso,* 1320/1970, p. 365).

REFERENCES

Anonymous. (1957). *The cloud of unknowing* (I. Progoff, Trans.) New York: Dell.

Astrov, M. (Ed). (1992). *The winged serpent: American Indian prose and poetry.* Boston: Beacon Press.

Cath, S. H. (1980). Suicide in the middle years: Some reflections on the annihilation of self. In W. H. Norman & T. J. Scaramella (Eds.), *Midlife: Developmental and clinical issues* (pp. 53–72). New York: Bruner/Mazel.

Chinen, A. (1992). *Once upon a midlife: Classic stories and mythic tales to illuminate the middle years.* Los Angeles: J. P. Tarcher.

Chinen, A. (1993). *Beyond the hero: Classic stories of men in search of soul.* Los Angeles: J. P. Tarcher.

Cousins, E. (1992). States of consciousness: Charting the mystical path. In F. R. Halligan & J. J. Shea (Eds.), *The fires of desire: Erotic energies and the spiritual quest* (pp. 126–145). New York: Crossroad.

Dalai Lama, The Fourteenth. (1965). *An introduction to Buddhism.* New Delhi, India: Tibet House.

Daly, M. (1973). *Beyond god the father: Toward a philosophy of women's liberation.* Boston: Beacon Press.

Dante Alighieri (1970). *The paradiso.* (J. Ciardi, Trans.). New York: Penguin. (Original work published ca. 1320)

Dante Alighieri (1982). *The inferno.* (J. Ciardi, Trans.). New York: Penguin. (Original work published ca 1320)

Datan, N. (1980). Midas and mid-life crises. In W. H. Norman & T. J. Scaramella (Eds.), *Midlife: Developmental and clinical issues* (pp. 3–19). New York: Bruner/Mazel.

Dunne, J. S. (1972). *The way of all the earth: Experiments in truth and religion.* New York: Macmillan.

Dunne, J. S. (1975). *Time and myth: A meditation on storytelling as an exploration of life and death.* Notre Dame, IN: University of Notre Dame Press.

Eller, C. (1993). *Living in the lap of the goddess: The feminist spirituality movement.* New York: Crossroad.

Erdoes, R., & Ortiz, A. (Eds.). (1984). *American Indian myths and legends.* New York: Pantheon Books.

Estes, C. P. (1992). *Women who run with the wolves: Myths and stories of the wild woman archetype.* New York: Ballantine.

Fox, M. (1991). *Creation spirituality: Liberating gifts for the peoples of the earth.* San Francisco: HarperCollins.

Friedman, M. (1987). *Abraham Joshua Heschel and Elie Wiesel: You are my witnesses.* New York: Farrar, Straus, & Giroux.

Gerzon, M. (1992). *Listening to midlife: Turning your crisis into a quest.* Boston: Shambala.

Goleman, D. (1988). *The meditative mind: The varieties of meditative experience.* Los Angeles: J. P. Tarcher.

Gould, R. L. (1978). *Transformations: Growth and change in adult life.* New York: Simon & Schuster.

Griffin, S. (1978). *Woman and nature: The roaring inside her.* New York: Harper & Row.

Heiler, F. (1959). The history of religions as a preparation for the co-operation of religions. In M. Eliade & J. M. Kitigawa (Eds.), *The history of religions: Essays in methodology* (pp. 132–160). Chicago: University of Chicago Press.

Hillman, J. (1975). *Revisioning psychology.* New York: Harper & Row.

Hobday, M. J. (1981). Seeking a moist heart: Native American ways for helping the spirit. In M. Fox (Ed.), *Western spirituality: Historical roots, ecumenical routes* (pp. 317–329). Santa Fe: Bear & Co.

Jung, C. (1933). *Modern man in search of a soul.* New York: Harcourt Brace.

Kabat-Zinn, J. (1990). *Full catastrophe living: Using the wisdom of your body and mind to face stress, pain, and illness.* New York: Dell.

Kabat-Zinn, J. (1994). *Wherever you go, there you are: Mindfulness meditation in everyday life.* New York: Hyperion.

Keating, T. (1986). *Open mind, open heart: The contemplative dimension of the gospel.* Rockport, MA: Element Books.

Keating, T. (1992). *Invitation to love: The way of Christian contemplation.* Rockport, MA: Element Books.

Keen, S. (1994). *Hymns to an unknown god: Awakening the spirit in everyday life.* New York: Bantam.

Kelsey, M. (1992). *Dreamquest: Native American myth and the recovery of soul.* Rockport, MA: Element.

Kidd, S. M. (1996). *Dance of the dissident daughter: A woman's journey from Christian tradition to the sacred feminine.* San Francisco: HarperCollins.

Kornfield, J. (1993). *A path with heart: A guide through the perils and promises of spiritual life.* New York: Bantam.

Levinson, D. J. (1978). *The seasons of a man's life.* New York: Ballantine Books.

Lidz, T. (1980). The phases of adult life: An overview. In W. H. Norman & T. J. Scaramella (Eds.), *Midlife: Developmental and clinical issues* (pp. 20–37). New York: Bruner/Mazel.

Lincoln, B. (1981). *Emerging from the chrysalis.* Cambridge: Harvard University Press.

May, R. (1953). *Man's search for himself.* New York: Norton.

May, R. (1991). *The cry for myth.* New York: Norton.

McAdams, D. P. (1990). Unity and purpose in human lives: The emergence of identity as a life story. In A. I. Rabin, R. A. Zucker, R. A. Emmons, & S. Frank (Eds.), *Studying persons and lives* (pp. 148–200). New York: Springer.

McGinn, B. (1994). *The growth of mysticism: 500–1200 A.D.* New York: Crossroad.

Moore, E. (1968a). *Studies in Dante, first series: Scripture and classical authors in Dante.* New York: Greenwood Press. (Original work published 1896)

Moore, E. (1968b). *Studies in Dante, second series: Miscellaneous essays.* New York: Greenwood Press. (Original work published 1899)

Moore, T. (1992). *Care of the soul: A guide for cultivating depth and sacredness in everyday living.* New York: HarperCollins.

Moore, T. (1996). *The re-enchantment of everyday life.* New York: HarperCollins.

Morton, N. (1985). *The journey is home.* Boston: Beacon Press.

Nhat Hanh, T. (1976). *The miracle of mindfulness.* Berkeley: Parallax Press.

Nhat Hanh, T. (1987). *Being peace.* Boston: Beacon Press.

Nhat Hanh, T. (1992). *Touching peace: Practicing the art of mindful living.* Berkeley: Parallax Press.

Nouwen, H. (1993). *Life of the beloved: Spiritual living in a secular world.* New York: Crossroad.

Pennington, B. (1987). *Toward an integrated humanity: Thomas Merton's journey.* Kalamazoo, MI: Cistercian.

Pennington, B. (1995). *Call to the center: The gospel's invitation to deeper prayer.* Hyde Park, NY: New City Press.

Plaskow, J., & Christ, C. P. (Eds.). (1989). *Weaving the visions: New patterns in feminist spirituality.* San Francisco: HarperCollins.

Reid, W. (1994). *The spirit of Haida Gwai: The jade canoe.* Vancouver, BC: YVR.

Reis, P. (1995). *Through the goddess: A woman's way of healing.* New York: Continuum.

Robinson, J. C. (1995). *Death of a hero, birth of the soul: Answering the call of midlife.* Sacramento, CA: Tzedakah.

Runyan, W. M. (1990). Individual lives and the structure of personality psychology. In A. I. Rabin, R. A. Zucker, R. A. Emmons, & S. Frank (Eds.), *Studying persons and lives* (pp. 10–40). New York: Springer.

Shange, N. (1976). *For colored girls who have considered suicide/when the rainbow is enuf.* New York: Macmillan.

Sheehy, G. (1995). *New passages: Mapping your life across time.* New York: Random House.

Smith, H. (1991). *The world's religions: Our great wisdom traditions.* San Francisco: Harper.

Snell, B. (1982). *The discovery of mind in Greek philosophy and literature.* New York: Dover. (Originally published 1953)

Spretnak, C. (1991). *States of grace: The recovery of meaning in the postmodern age.* San Francisco: HarperCollins.

Starhawk. (1979). *The spiral dance: A rebirth of the ancient religion of the great Goddess.* San Francisco: Harper & Row.

Stein, M. (1983). *In midlife: A Jungian perspective.* Dallas, TX: Spring.

Stone, M. (1984). *Ancient mirrors of the Western mind: A treasury of goddess and heroine lore from around the world.* Boston: Beacon Press.

Tarnas, R. (1991). *The passion of the Western mind: Understanding the ideas that have shaped our world view.* New York: Ballantine.

Theophane the Monk. (1981). *Tales of a magic monastery.* New York: Crossroad.

Waddell, H. (1962). *The desert fathers.* London: Collins.

Wilber, K. (1996). *A brief history of everything.* Boston: Shambala.

Williams, C. (1961). *The figure of Beatrice: A study in Dante.* New York: Farrar, Straus & Cudahy.

11.

Meditation and the Evolution of Consciousness: Theoretical and Practical Solutions to Midlife Angst

Ronald R. Irwin

THE MIDLIFE CRISIS

As we enter midlife we are confronted with our finitude. At midlife, the issue of mortality affects us with a poignancy unlike that of any earlier period (Levinson, Darrow, Klein, Levinson, & McKee, 1978). While it is commonly thought that adolescents believe they can live forever, by the time we reach midlife we can no longer project our yearnings into an unlimited future. The signs of aging abound: graying hair, wrinkles, bulging paunches, less reliable memories, and slower reaction times. We may have our first operation or serious illness. We note the passage of time at high school reunions and family get-togethers—how our friends and relations have become more "weathered" or "seasoned." While in our youth our parents may have provided us with assurances of solidity and composure, we now watch as they become infirm or die. And while our children provide us with a connection to youth and exuberance, we cannot fail to notice how quickly they grow up.

Our ideals have had sufficient time to be jarred by "the slings and arrows of outrageous fortune." We realize we may never obtain the home of our dreams. Our children do not turn out perfect. We never have enough time to read the books or travel to the countries we have read about. As every New Year's Day passes we realize our resolutions have become empty, banal, or repetitive. We fail to reach the highest level in the company. Nor do we achieve the most proficient knowledge in our field or the highest skill level in our profession. And there is less time to improve on what we have achieved. At work, we are threatened by a younger generation who can pick up new information and new technologies more quickly, working around the clock to meet a deadline we failed to meet.

Whereas in our thirties the life structure seemed to serve us well, in our forties that same structure is felt to limit us as much as it enriches, to neglect as much or more than it includes, and to be more partial than complete. Whereas before the life structure provided a clear figure to the ground of our existence, now the figure only seems to occlude the ground unnecessarily. Too much has been sacrificed to the maintenance of our identity, to the bolstering of our social selves.

Levinson believed that these phenomena, and many others, signal the onset of the individuation process of midlife, initially written about by Carl Jung. The life structure is experienced as arbitrary, partial, and incomplete, and therefore comes to be questioned. Early in life we constructed identities that only included those aspects of our selves that fit in with our project; now the excluded aspects cry out for consideration. The old polarities of early adulthood are rebalanced. We no longer identify exclusively with the good versus the bad, the male versus the female, or the mind versus the body. There is a disillusionment with youthful dreams. Ideals come to be seen as more abstract and inauthentic. A shift occurs from being externally oriented and concerned with making it in the tribe, to becoming oriented to the body, to intuitions, and to archetypal voices. There is an appreciation of mortality and suffering.

Gould (1978) wrote of the unmasking of self-deceptions at midlife. We relax our vigilance and experience "internal" sensations and thoughts more freely, liberated from the shackles of conformity to external prescriptions. The superego no longer has the same hold on us. Kegan (1982, 1994) wrote of the loss of meaning in the transition out of what he called the Institutional balance. In the Institutional Stage we are identified with our self-authoring, our self-control, our self-administration. This is a result of our emergence out of the Interpersonal Stage, embedded as it is in relationships and authorities. As we continue to evolve out of the Institutional Stage, we relax or let go of our identification with self-authoring, self-control, and self-administration. This can free us from internal constraints but it can also open us to what Washburn (1994), in a more psychoanalytic context, calls the *non-egoic core.* In this process, we experience threats to our self-esteem, a loss of control that can entail anxiety, a sense of "not-knowing," a feeling that emotions and relationships are sometimes devouring us. Kegan noted how individuals may feel that they are "beyond good and evil." There is a new willingness to experiment with emotions and sexuality. Relationships may be threatened, careers may be undone, substance abuse may worsen. Or, reacting defensively, individuals may contain themselves in a repressive stuckness that provides security even as it constricts. More positively, the individual may set about making changes: seek out a therapist or begin to read about spiritual teachings.

In Pascual-Leone and Irwin (1994a, 1994b), we explained some of these changes at midlife as due to decline in certain types of mental functioning that begin in our forties, declines which result in a weakening of the cognitive mechanisms responsible for attending and inhibiting (Dempster, 1992). These declines can lead to an openness to internal or psychological contradictions. This openness to internal contradiction can, in part, account for the individuation process described by Jung, Levinson, and others. This perspective on viewing what had been traditionally associated with decline in a new and more positive light is similar to the perspective of Baltes (Baltes, Dittmann-Kohli, & Dixon, 1984) on the trade off between the mechanics and pragmatics of intelligence in aging.

UNDOING THE VERTICAL DOMINANCE OF KNOWING OVER FEELING

Earlier development in childhood and adolescence involves increasing control of emotion and experiencing, whereby the body and affect are vertically regulated from "higher" centres of cognition which encode cultural roles and rules (Labouvie-Vief, 1992, 1994). In adulthood, this structure is challenged as the individual seeks a more balanced and integrated psychological life. With movement out of the institutional balance of Kegan (1982, 1994) or the intrapsychic stage of Labouvie-Vief (Labouvie-Vief, 1990; Labouvie-Vief, DeVoe, & Bulka, 1989; Labouvie-Vief, Hakim-Larson, DeVoe, & Schoeberlein, 1989) cognitive and affective processes become coordinated in a "lateral" or "horizontal" manner, in that affective processes are not subordinated to cognitive processes. The self is therefore more open to intuitive and affective realms.

Labouvie-Vief (1994) has summarized her theory of adult development under the terms *logos* and *mythos*. Childhood and adolescence involve achieving control of the *mythos*, which includes the bodily, the imaginative, the sensuous, the narrative, and the intuitive. These processes come under the control of the *logos*, which includes the rational, the calculated, the abstract, and the logical. Positive development in adulthood is largely about undoing this vertical hierarchy, restructuring the personality such that the cognitive need not always control the affective, nor the rational subordinate the nonrational. Later development balances the cognitive and the affective in a horizontal, more mutual relationship.

While many researchers have viewed adolescent and early adult development positively as leading to greater agency or autonomy, Labouvie-Vief perceives it also as resulting in further alienation from the organismic sources of being. The more individuals align themselves with the abstract identity required of them in society, the more they become estranged from their inner selves. Midlife individuation is about getting behind the mask of civil propriety and opening up to what lies within, acknowledging the shadow side of the personality and experiencing the full spectrum of emotions and bodily desires, without constant censorship or control. Because this change involves a turning away from external sources of reinforcement and gratification, individuals may experience depression as they let go of their former ways of securing happiness.

THE END OF THE EGO

While the phenomena associated with the midlife crisis are interpreted by Pascual-Leone and Irwin (1994a, 1994b) as the processing of internal contradictions and are interpreted by Labouvie-Vief as the lateralizing of the relationship between logos and mythos, I would like to stress how the midlife crisis is a crisis of ego, of the breakdown of ego, and how eventually it can be an evolution into egolessness. The problems presented by the midlife crisis are a problem from the point of view of the old self-structure—the conventional identity. But from the point of view of a transpersonal psychology, the midlife crisis is a harbinger of an evolution into egolessness. And, as the ego lets go of its old satisfactions and its hard-won securities, the individual experiences loss and depression.

Ken Wilber (1986a, 1986b, 1986c, 1991, 1996) describes perhaps the most detailed theory of life-span development in the literature, particularly detailed in the richness with which he describes the higher stages not described in Western psychologies. Of particular relevance to the present discussion of midlife angst is his description of his sixth stage, or as he terms it, the sixth *fulcrum* of development—the *Centauric.* He calls it centauric because it is an integration of mind and body. Wilber holds that mind and body are integrated at this stage because consciousness is now no longer exclusively identified with mind. Consciousness now has a perspective on mind, and can therefore integrate both mind and body in a higher level of consciousness.

While this has a positive effect on well-being in terms of precipitating authenticity or in reorienting the self in a more organismic and "existential" mode, many feelings at this stage are described as frightening, while some are described as melancholic. Wilber (1996) presents this stage in dark and somber shades, because this stage is the preamble to the "dark night of the soul."

> The whole point of the existential level is that you are not yet in the transpersonal, but you are no longer totally anchored in the personal—the whole personal domain has started to lose its flavor, has started to become profoundly meaningless. And so of course there is not much reason to smile. What good is the personal anyway—it's just going to die. Why even inhabit it? (p. 195)

> The world has started to go flat in its appeal. No experience tastes good anymore. Nothing satisfies anymore. Nothing is worth pursuing anymore. Not because one has failed to get these rewards, but precisely because one has achieved them royally, tasted it all, and found it all lacking. (p. 195)

> This is a soul for whom all desires have become thin and pale and anemic. This is a soul who, in facing existence squarely, is thoroughly sick of it. This is a soul for whom the personal has gone totally flat. This is, in other words, a soul on the brink of the transpersonal. (p. 196)

Frightening descriptions of the threshold of the transpersonal are described similarly in Washburn (1994). His theory is more explicitly psychoanalytic. For him, the midlife transvaluation involves a breaking through of the nonegoic core into the ego. Childhood, adolescence, and adulthood have been about bolstering the ego from the nonegoic core by means of both primal repression and primal alienation. Identity is produced in part by casting out the polymorphously perverse sexuality of early childhood and its preoedipal object choices. This repression and alienation break down around midlife and the ego becomes overwhelmed by primal forces not of its own making. The midlife transvaluation ushers in the dark night of the senses and the dark night of the spirit, both of which involve regression in the service of transcendence. While this is an evolution of consciousness toward transcendence, it requires reconnecting to nonegoic potentials that precipitate regressive and infantile affects. And this regression can result in some truly shuddering experiences including engulfment, dread, depression, terror, hypersexuality, loss of control, and many other frightening experiences. Eventually, the integration and regeneration of the spirit ensues, and more ecstatic, peaceful, and blessed states occur, but not before there has been a crisis of often violent proportions.

If the higher reaches of consciousness development are not understood, it is possible that a mental health professional may interpret these experiences as symptoms of depression, or some other pathology such as anxiety or borderline. A psychiatrist or medical doctor may prescribe medication or a clinician may recommend conventional treatment to, perhaps, increase self-esteem. For clients entering the transpersonal stages, such interventions may suppress their development, by alleviating or tranquilizing a pain that is authentically crying out to be experienced in all its existential richness and complexity.

I would like to propose that part of the reason that these phenomena may be misunderstood is because of our culture's identification with the ego and our culture's corresponding fear of egolessness. Kegan's (1994) research on the evolving self indicates that most of our society has not arrived at his Institutional Stage. Part of the fear or lack of comprehension regarding egolessness can be addressed by a theory of consciousness development that posits egolessness as a natural function of the process of higher development. In the next section, I shall sketch a theory of consciousness development that includes both ego and egolessness, the personal and the transpersonal.

THE DEVELOPMENT OF CONSCIOUSNESS

When we examine descriptions and theories regarding development at higher adult stages we see that often this development is described as *spiritual* in nature. Clear examples can be found in the work of the earlier adult developmental theorists: Kohlberg, Erikson, and Jung. Kohlberg and Ryncarz's (1990) speculations regarding a seventh stage of moral judgment had a clearly spiritual content. Erikson's higher stages of psychosocial development—the Generativity and Integrity stages—consisted of an orientation away from ego and a concern more for others than for self (Erikson, Erikson, & Kivnick, 1986). Jung described *individuation* as a transformation of the personality through which previously repressed or unacknowledged aspects of the self emerge into consciousness, bringing up archetypal images which he identified with the central images and motifs of the world's mythological and religious traditions (Campbell, 1979).

Whether we examine moral development or psychosocial development or midlife individuation, the descriptions of higher stages involve characteristics that we can agree are spiritual. It is as if development "naturally" tends toward spiritual development. That is, spirituality is part of normal or optimal development, and not something unusual or even pathological. In fact, because these stages typically occur in the latter years of life, coming after the earlier stages, spirituality may be considered a higher or more evolved aspect of normal development. We may regard developmental psychology as an emerging psychology, revealing something about spirituality from a new perspective, similar to the ways cognitive science is emphasizing insights shared with Eastern traditions (Hayward, 1987; Varela, Thompson, & Rosch, 1991) and psychoanalysis is demonstrating parallels with Zen Buddhism (Fromm, 1960).

How we conceive of the highest stages of development will shape the way we conceive earlier development. Early stages become framed in the light of where they are seen as leading. The concepts deriving from our theories serve as a lens filtering and shaping our observations. In the adult development field, it is commonly accepted that Piaget left out the higher developmental stages, and that this, in turn, shaped the picture of earlier development that he drew (Commons, Richards, & Armon, 1984; Commons, Sinnott, Richards, & Armon, 1989; Commons, Armon, Kohlberg, Richards, Grotzer, & Sinnott, 1990).

Many have criticized the exclusively cognitive and intellectual focus of Piagetian work, and this can in part be explained by the end point to development that Piaget postulated. His project of *genetic epistemology* was intended to analyze the child's development from sensorimotor contact with the physical world to the logical competence of the scientist. *Formal operations,* defined as the highest stage of development in this scheme, is the structural competence necessary to employ scientific reasoning. With this endpoint to development, it was only natural for Piaget to construct measurements and methodologies that articulated his assumptions. But reliance upon this framework left out other aspects of development not contained within what many agree is a predominately cognitive, epistemological and intellectual orientation.

We may regard theories in terms of their *breadth* or their *depth.* On the one hand, regarding the dimension of *breadth,* Piaget neglected aspects of social, interpersonal, and affective development. On the other hand, regarding the dimension of *depth,* later possibilities and transformations in human potential were also neglected.

> How narrowly or unidimensionally one conceives of cognitive processes and their capacity for integrated growth determines not only the breadth and upper boundary of development, but also one's formulations of all lower stages, which are invariably cast as sequential approximations of the final stage. (Alexander, et al., 1990, p. 290)

If one defines higher development as spiritual development, thus adding new and higher stages to one's developmental scheme, then earlier stages of development have to be reformulated. If the general path of development is not solely about the equilibration of logical–mathematical structures, as Piaget said, then what is it about? What is the underlying dimension or process or structure that develops?

One route researchers and theorists have taken is to posit that social development is the central structuring principle (e.g., Kegan, 1982, 1994; Loevinger, 1976; Noam, Powers, Kilkenny, & Beedy, 1990). The self as it is understood from this perspective is an essentially social self. Development is said to consist of internalization, imitation, perspective taking, interpersonal relations, socialization, etc. The social domain is conceptualized as prior to and constitutive of the individual.

Another route, the one I am fashioning here, is to posit that consciousness is the structuring principle (e.g., Alexander et al., 1990; Pascual-Leone & Irwin, 1994a, 1994b; Wilber, 1986a, 1986b, 1986c, 1991). Social development is only a part of such development. The higher stages of development transcend social development. By contrast, if social development is regarded as the causal matrix, we will not have a way of accounting for trans-social development—we will not have a way of including transcendence and freedom in our psychological maps. Furthermore, I believe that a theory of consciousness development is more interactionist than a theory of social development: more interactionist in that it accords a greater role to the person in the person–environment equation. Social development alone is too one-sided in its emphasis on environmental determination (i.e., social constructionism).

I propose to define consciousness as the structuring of *attention* and *awareness.* Infants have attention and their attention is what directs their awareness. Attention is the biologically determined activity of the brain—an active, effortful, and limited resource. Attention is what some cognitive psychologists call working or short-term memory. Awareness is the result. Awareness is what is processed in the environment, what aspects of the world are attended to. But perception also enters into what constitutes awareness. Infants possess both attention and awareness, but do not possess consciousness, as I am defining it. We can speak of consciousness as developing when learning and society mediate the processes that control attention and awareness. Consciousness arises when the learned component, the cognitive structuring, in terms of plans, goals, projects, expectations, anticipations, etc., actively directs attention. One such mediating social structure is ego: the cognitive-affective representation of self.

I shall argue that awareness transcends social mediation in the higher stages of development so that while ego structures remain as part of the mind's repertoire, they do not always direct attention in habitual ways. Because of this, awareness acquires a degree of autonomy from social structures—a space to breathe, as it were—apart from ego. And this can be facilitated by practices involving mindfulness.

According to the theory I am developing here and elsewhere (Irwin, 1996), the ego begins to develop in early childhood as an accommodation to social powers. The ego enables self-control so that the child can insert him- or herself into a predictable social world. The child can control herself and relate herself to others in the social world if she can represent herself as an *object* in relation to other *objects* in the world. The child's ego controls are first based on primitive mechanisms such as guilt and shame, methods of internalizing the sanctions of discipline and punishment, as well as on later mechanisms of self-reward such as ego ideals. In adolescence, as the ego becomes more abstracted and less bound to the interpersonal context, we call a part of that ego *identity*.

Consciousness at higher stages of development goes beyond ego controls, beyond continuous self-monitoring and self-talk, which are required in order that we remain conscientious citizens. Consciousness begins to have a spacious quality, accepting inner realities and depths without the habitual operation of defenses and conditionings. There is an openness to the entire sensorium without mediating concepts which interpret with reference to a centre. This higher consciousness is a letting go that yields to a nonattached acceptance of things as they are. Higher consciousness is found through egolessness.

NARRATIVE THERAPY

Returning to our discussion of midlife angst, people have advocated many different approaches to the treatment of depression and anxiety, and particularly depression and anxiety that might be associated with midlife phenomena: psychoanalytic, cognitive, cognitive–behavioral, medical/pharmacological. However, what all of these approaches seem to have in common is a bolstering of autonomy and personal agency, a sustaining of identity and self-esteem. And, as I shall argue, it is these qualities that make these kinds of psychology unfit to conceptualize the evolution into the transpersonal, because they still hold to the centrality of ego.

A recent cognitive approach that might be championed is narrative psychology. Narrative is relevant when the concern is with self-authoring. Narrative approaches might be advised when there is a breakdown in the individual's confidence in her self-authoring capability. In fact, we might interpret midlife angst to mean a breakdown in self-authoring capacity. Narrative psychology is a particular way of thinking about psychology (Bruner, 1990; Freeman, 1993; Irwin, 1996; Polkinghorne, 1988; Randall, 1995; Sarbin, 1986; Tappan & Packer, 1991) based on a different metaphor for understanding what social scientists do than the metaphors of behaviorism or cognitive science. The metaphor of narrative is that people are the writers or the authors of their lives; their lives as storied possess elements of fiction. Although people are the free authors of their lives, their stories are nevertheless permeated by the canonical texts of their cultures which provide narrative structures and patterns. When we try to make sense of our own actions and those of others, we "emplot" events into sequences that make up stories.

The act of rewriting our lives underscores the awareness of the invented nature of our being. When we rewrite the story, we play, we reinvent, and reinterpret, and it is in this ability that we have our freedom. From a narrative point of view, we possess a temporal nature that exists as much in the future of our imagination and the past of our memories as it does in the present of our actions. We understand ourselves and others by applying structures of meaning in a largely top-down fashion, not by absorbing information bottom-up. By providing story templates, our culture and tradition serve as the major source of the structuring of experience. Therefore, our lives have to be approached as texts of meaning, not as objective behaviors to be measured and quantified.

Narrative psychology is a type of psychology to be filed in our library along with other psychologies: behavioristic, cognitive, humanistic, psychoanalytic, etc. Presumably, if narrative approaches become more mainstream, we shall have a section on narrative in our introductory texts. But I have argued (Irwin, 1996) that narrative approaches are appropriate only to individuals at a certain *stage* of development. And, as I hope to show, in the same way that narrative approaches are not appropriate for children and adolescents who are at conventional stages of development, so too are narrative approaches not appropriate to adults at higher stages of development who are ready to go beyond narrative—that is, to enter the stages of transpersonal development.

The Conscientious Stage of Loevinger, the Institutional Stage of Kegan, and the Formal Reflexive Stage of Wilber can be described as *self-authoring:* the self is said to script its own story rather than live out received scripts. It is at these stages that the capacity for narrative emerges, and not earlier. At the narrative stage, the self stands apart from the conventional roles and rules in which it had been embedded and self-consciously constructs a story more authentic to its existential, cognitive and affective experience. As this self-authoring capacity matures in the Individualistic and Autonomous Stages of Loevinger, the Interindividual Stage of Kegan, or the Existential Stage of Wilber, there is a loosening up of personal worlds, and therefore an attenuation of the perceived solidity of the "real world." The so-called "real world" is now viewed in large measure as a projection of our own interpretative activity, as a fiction. An invented world is a potentially more fluid world, a world more open to the interpenetration of self and other. Although the invented world is more fluid, it is not changeable in a fanciful way, because we do in fact continue to engage ourselves with others by means of commitments which possess duration and identifiable goals. But as the narrative competence matures, our worlds are defined more self-consciously as chosen by us rather than defined as worlds which chose us. If the world is no longer only what exists "out there," stable and apart from us, we can experience it as a part of the self by virtue of our interaction with it. We can see our lives as a dance with the world.

I think that the narrative stage prepares for and precedes the transpersonal stages, but it has characteristics that have to be transcended if consciousness is to evolve. First, the self has to go beyond language. Language is absolutely central to narrative; indeed, most narratively oriented theorists believe that we simply cannot perceive or think without language. But transpersonal development goes beyond language in its ability to exist fully in the immediate now without any reference point, without any determining fixed conceptions. Second, narrative stages are oriented around an "author," a self that constructs and stories events on the basis of its cognitive interpretations and its affective motivations, i.e., it is still egocentric, albeit, at a new and higher level than the egocentrism of the concrete operations stage or the egocentrism of adolescence. The authorial self has to be let go if transpersonal development is to take place.

MEDITATION AND DEVELOPMENT

Rather than narrative, cognitive, psychoanalytic, or even pharmacological approaches, I would like to recommend meditation and spiritual practice as a treatment specifically for midlife angst (although this does not rule out using a combination of meditation and other approaches when the issues being dealt with are complex). Meditation and the spiritual path are based not in a bolstering of self or ego, but in learning to abide in egolessness. Midlife angst is an indication that the structure of ego is breaking down, and that the individual may be prepared for egolessness.

I shall refer to meditation in general, but I should note that my own studies and practice have been with Buddhist *shamatha* and *vipashyana* meditation (Goldstein, 1976; Lerner, 1977; Levine, 1979; Sogyal, 1993; Tart, 1994; Trungpa, 1988a, 1988b, 1992, 1995), as well as *zazen* practice (Buksbazen, 1978; Hoshin, 1994; Suzuki, 1970). Within Buddhism there are various meditation techniques; other spiritual traditions have different techniques (Dass, 1978; Goleman, 1977). But I hope that my comments are general enough in significant ways to apply to those other practices as well.

Meditation brings about significant changes in consciousness, although meditators are not supposed to pursue these changes because pursuing is said to reinforce the grasping qualities of ego (Trungpa, 1988b, 1995). While mindfully aware and open to the flow of change around them, meditators become conscious of the pervasiveness of *anicca,* or impermanence. Practicing a mindful witnessing to what is before their mind without judgment, meditators learn to accept themselves as a part of *Buddha-nature,* to accept themselves as they are and not as they or others think they should be. Such an openness to oneself allows for an openness to the phenomenal world and to others, an openness that is both fearless and tender. The contrivances of ego, with its credentialing and posturing, are *let go of*—not suppressed—but *let go of* with a patient forgiveness for what is essentially a confusion and not an evil. In Buddhism, *samsara*—the world of ego—is regarded not as a sin but as a confusion (Trungpa, 1992).

If meditation facilitates the development of consciousness as herein described, then the success of meditation will depend on the *developmental level* of the meditator, as well as on other things. In the East it is believed that what you experience in the present life is due to your past *karma,* the law of cause and effect. What you are now is a function of actions you have committed in past lives. I would like to suggest that the level of development you have achieved in the present life can be understood as an aspect of your *karma,* although not *karma* from past lives, but *karma* from development in this life. This same *karma* determines when you are ready to benefit from certain practices and when you are ready to achieve certain insights.

Ken Wilber's model was mentioned earlier. It describes the path of karmic development, or the evolution of consciousness, that I am outlining here (Wilbur, 1986a, 1986b, 1986c, 1991, 1996). Wilbur writes about treatment modalities as being specific to a level of development on his continuum, where the continuum is defined in terms of the spectrum of consciousness development, the spectrum being divided into nine fulcrums. Each of the psychological treatments or techniques is effective when it addresses the issue being negotiated at a fulcrum on the continuum or when it addresses fixations along points in the continuum. For example, Wilber shows how psychoanalytic uncovering techniques are best for addressing issues at the third fulcrum and how cognitive rescripting has value at the fourth fulcrum. Meditation is one treatment modality, appropriate only to individuals of a certain developmental level or within a certain range of developmental levels.

If development of consciousness is necessary to spiritual practice, then how may we identify when somebody is authentically ready to take up a spiritual tradition? What psychological prerequisites indicate a readiness for spiritual transformation? Are there stage levels that have to be achieved before an individual is "mature" enough to enter a spiritual path? The brief survey of developmental research covered in the first part of this chapter provides some indications of what the prerequisites of spiritual transformation are.

While stationing a psychometrist at the front doors to meditation centers, ashrams, and temples, assigning prospective seekers of the truth a "spiritual potential" score, seems absurd, nevertheless there is some rationale behind the recommendation. On the one hand, some people may not be ready for the type of spiritual practice required of them in meditation. On the other hand, spiritual practices—whether or not offered in conjunction with psychological interventions—may be precisely the thing that is needed for those at higher developmental levels, although the mental health profession may not recognize this need.

According to Levinson and others who have written about the midlife crisis, the transformations that take place in the second half of life make us more conscious of suffering and mortality. The first noble truth of Buddhism is *dukkha,* that life is suffering. It is said that you can only enter the path of Buddhism when you know this thoroughly—in your bones and in your blood. When we are young we are sheltered from suffering by our parents and by the institutions of our society. When we become adolescents and then young adults we shelter ourselves from suffering with our thoughts and our ideals, avoiding things that are not consistent with our chosen goals and ideals. And this is made easier by the confirmation provided by our young and healthy bodies. But in maturity we know suffering more truthfully and more accurately than before, largely because of the inability of our thoughts, our ideals and our visions to account for things as they really are. Things begin to fall apart. Our thinking about things as they should be has inexorably collided with the reality of things as they are. Acknowledging and accepting our suffering, not defending ourselves from it or escaping from it at every opportunity, is a sign that a person is ready to enter a spiritual path. When we let go of our ego ideals and our defenses, our projections and self-deceptions, we become more aware of our mortal natures. With the acknowledgment of suffering we begin to see who we are, and not only the version of ourselves that we want others to see. And being ready to see ourselves as we are is a precondition for the practice of mindfulness.

Midlife individuation, as described by Labouvie-Vief and Jungian writers, can be seen as leading to the spiritual path. In affirming the rights of mythos against those of logos, in viewing identity as a socially contrived persona, in regarding our adjusted personality as essentially unbalanced and dualistic, the theory of individuation opens the way to the appreciation of egolessness. Midlife individuation can help prepare the way for qualities that are required in meditation: letting go of conventional conceptions, penetrating beneath language to immediate experience, attending to flow and process rather than fixed conceptions, unlearning the habitual mechanisms of control and self-surveillance, etc.

Cook-Greuter (1990, 1994) has studied ego development, focusing on the data she has obtained using Loevinger's Sentence Completion Test. Her Stage 5/6, what she terms the Postautonomous Stage, has characteristics that I see as pinpointing the transition to the transpersonal. Cook-Greuter shows that it is only when the self attains the Postautonomous Stage that it becomes aware of the filtered nature of reality, contingent on language and the perception and thinking that language affords. When such a self longs to break through to a more immediate reality, the self is ready to take up a spiritual path. Using a tactile metaphor, we can describe the self as longing now for a *naked* mode of experiencing. Meditation is a discipline and practice aimed at mindfully keeping one's contact with sensations at the raw, unmediated level, without protective screens or covers. Again, pursuing the tactile metaphor, emphasizing the sense of muscular effort and resistance, the change at the Postautonomous Stage is a shift from desiring greater autonomy and control to wanting to let go of the reins of control altogether. Again, this is what meditation is about: learning a mindfulness which sidesteps the ego's constant need to be in control. Meditation provides the solution to the basic paradox that Cook-Greuter identifies at the Postautonomous Stage—how to use effort to go beyond control.

Meditation addresses the difficulties experienced at the Centauric Stage of Wilber (1996) or the Midlife Transvaluation Stage of Washburn (1994). In order to practice meditation, the individual must be open and undefended, and to be open, it helps if there is a crack in the habitual functioning of the ego, a cleft in the system of meaning making that is the conventional self. But as the ego relinquishes its grip, as the knot of self unravels, many of the less desirable aspects of the nonegoic potential surface. Meditation provides a discipline that cultivates an openness and acceptance of whatever arises and a non-grasping letting go that allows everything—both positive and negative, beautiful and terrifying—to pass in due course. Without a practice such as meditation, an individual might get fixated on different complexes or affects that arise from the nonegoic core.

Meditation attunes the mind to the present moment. Our being exists without our contrivance or our effort in the moment in all its fullness. When we dwell in the past or the future, we are letting the present escape us. In meditation, the past and the future are only thoughts. Narrative approaches, in contrast to meditation, require that we keep to a time-oriented consciousness so that we may have our identity, an identity that holds together the past, present, and future in an active process of constructive consciousness. Stories have beginnings, middles, and ends. From the perspective of narrative, the past as memory and history and the future as goals and projects penetrate our consciousness of the present. While we experience the present we are, at the same time, actively constructing ourselves as storied beings with a past and a future. In narrative theory, it is said that the present moment cannot be experienced purely or nakedly, without the mediation of a time-oriented and linguistic consciousness (Freeman, 1993; Randall,

1995). While on the one hand, this can be seen as part of the richness of the narrative stage, on the other hand, with the emergence into the transpersonal stages, this richness is at the same time a prison house of chatter from which release is sought.

While narrative thinking encloses us in time, it also provides us with an entrance to the path of transpersonal development. At earlier conventional and more interpersonal stages of development we live out our social scripts without being conscious of them. We *are* the scripts. With narrative competence, we become capable of stepping out of, of disembedding from, our socialized frameworks of meaning, able to rewrite and reinvent new scripts or stories more self-consciously and self-reflectively. We become more aware of the constructed nature of our storied being, and therefore more able to see our constructive activity as fiction. It is now possible to see that time itself is a construction we impose upon the flow of the phenomenal world. The possibility dawns that we can step outside of all constructed worlds.

CONCLUSION

Many individuals may be attracted to meditation for the wrong reasons, and these wrong reasons may have something to do with their development. Perhaps some individuals who are just beginning to break with conventional or conformist levels of ego development may be drawn to exotic teachings and practices because these teachings may be seen as providing a solution to problems of identity. Individuals at conventional levels of development may be searching for something to believe in: an ideology or a creed. But, it is different for individuals at higher levels of development. For example, depression may benefit from cognitive–behavioral modification at the *personal* levels of development, but may require an entirely different and more contemplative approach for those entering the *transpersonal* levels of development. The method or treatment should be targeted to the developmental level of the individual.

People may be turning to spiritual teachings and practices when what they really need is some form of therapy: whether a psychoanalytic uncovering technique, or a cognitive–behavioral rescripting method, or perhaps a philosophical examination of identity issues. On the other hand, people may be given psychological treatment when what they really need is some form of spiritual teaching or practice. The literature on adult development I have outlined here can help provide clinicians, teachers of spiritual traditions, and those looking for answers to their very real existential concerns, with a road map of the possible precursors to transpersonal development. With such a road map in hand, people may be better able to make important decisions about what certain phenomena mean with respect to human development and potential.

REFERENCES

Alexander, C. N., Davies, J. L., Dixon, C. A., Dillbeck, M. C., Druker, S. M., Oetzel, R. M., Muehlman, J. M., & Orme-Johnson, D. W. (1990). Growth of higher stages of consciousness: Maharishi's Vedic psychology of human development. In C. N. Alexander & E. J. Langer (Eds.), *Higher stages of human development: Perspectives on adult growth* (pp. 286–341). New York: Oxford University Press.

Baltes, P.B., Dittmann-Kohli, F., & Dixon, R. (1984). New perspectives on the development of intelligence in adulthood: Toward a dual-process conception and a model of selective optimization with compensation. In P. B. Baltes & O. G. Brim, Jr. (Eds.), *Life-span development and behavior* (Vol. 6) (pp. 33–76). New York: Academic Press.

Bruner, J. (1990). *Acts of meaning.* Cambridge, MA: Harvard University Press.

Buksbazen, J. D. (1977). *To forget the self: An illustrated guide to Zen meditation.* Los Angeles, CA: Zen Center of Los Angeles.

Campbell, J. (Ed.). (1979). *The portable Jung.* New York: Penguin.

Commons, M. L., Armon, C., Kohlberg, L., Richards, F. A., Grotzer, T. A., & Sinnott, J. D. (Eds.). (1990). *Adult development: Vol. 2. Models and methods in the study of adolescent and adult thought.* New York: Praeger.

Commons, M. L., Richards, F. A., & Armon, C. (Eds.). (1984). *Beyond formal operations: Late adolescent and adult cognitive development.* New York: Praeger.

Commons, M. L., Sinnott, J. D., Richards, F. A., & Armon, C. (Eds.). (1989). *Adult development: Vol. 1. Comparisons and applications of developmental models.* New York: Praeger.

Cook-Greuter, S. R. (1990). Maps for living: Ego-development stages from symbiosis to conscious universal embeddedness. In M. L. Commons, C. Armon, L. Kohlberg, F. A. Richards, T. A. Grotzer, & J. D. Sinnott (Eds.), *Adult Development: Vol. 2. Models and methods in the study of adolescent and adult thought* (pp. 79–103). New York: Praeger.

Cook-Greuter, S. R. (1994). Rare forms of self-understanding in mature adults. In M. E. Miller & S. R. Cook-Greuter (Eds.), *Transcendence and mature thought in adulthood: The further reaches of adult development* (pp. 119–146). Lanham, MD: Rowman & Littlefield.

Dass, R. (1978). *Journey of awakening: A meditator's guidebook.* New York: Bantam.

Dempster, F. N. (1992). The rise and fall of the inhibitory mechanism: Toward a unified theory of cognitive development and aging. *Developmental Review, 12,* 45–75.

Erikson, E. H., Erikson, J. M., & Kivnick, H. Q. (1986). *Vital involvement in old age.* New York: Norton.

Freeman, M. (1993). *Rewriting the self: History, memory, narrative.* New York: Routledge.

Fromm, E. (1960). Psychoanalysis and Zen Buddhism. In E. Fromm (Ed.), *Zen Buddhism and psychoanalysis* (pp. 77–141). New York: Harper & Row.

Goldstein, J. (1976). *The experience of insight: A natural unfolding.* Santa Cruz, NM: Unity Press.

Goleman, D. (1977). *The varieties of the meditative experience.* New York: Dutton.

Gould, R. (1978). *Transformations: Growth and change in adult life.* New York: Simon & Schuster.

Hayward, J. (1987). *Shifting worlds, changing minds: Where the sciences and Buddhism meet.* Boston: Shambhala.

Hoshin, A. (1994). *The straight path: Zen teachings on the foundations of mindfulness.* Ottawa, ON: Great Matter.

Irwin, R. R. (1996). Narrative competence and constructive developmental theory: A proposal for rewriting the *Bildungsroman* in the postmodern world. *Journal of Adult Development, 3,* 109–125.

Kegan, R. (1982). *The evolving self: Problem and process in human development.* Cambridge, MA: Harvard University Press.

Kegan, R. (1994). *In over our heads: The mental demands of modern life.* Cambridge, MA: Harvard University Press.

Kohlberg, L., & Ryncarz, R. A. (1990). Beyond justice reasoning: Moral development and consideration of a seventh stage. In C. N. Alexander & E. J. Langer (Eds.), *Higher stages of human development: Perspectives on adult growth* (pp. 191–207). New York: Oxford University Press.

Labouvie-Vief, G. (1990). Wisdom as integrated thought: Historical and developmental perspectives. In R. L. Sternberg (Ed.), *Wisdom: Its nature, origins and development* (pp. 52–83). New York: Cambridge University Press.

Labouvie-Vief, G. (1992). A neo-Piagetian perspective on adult cognitive development. In R. J. Sternberg & C. Berg (Eds.), *Intellectual development* (pp. 197–228). New York: Cambridge University Press.

Labouvie-Vief, G. (1994). *Psyche and eros: Mind and gender in the life course.* Cambridge, U.K.: Cambridge University Press.

Labouvie-Vief, G., DeVoe, M., & Bulka, D. (1989). Speaking about feelings: Conceptions of emotion across the life span. *Psychology and Aging, 4,* 425–437.

Labouvie-Vief, G., Hakim-Larson, J., DeVoe, M., & Schoeberlein, S. (1989). Emotions and self regulation: A lifespan view. *Human Development, 32,* 279–299.

Lerner, E. (1977). *Journey of insight meditation: A personal experience of the Buddha's way.* New York: Schocken.

Levine, S. (1979). *A gradual awakening.* Garden City, NY: Anchor Books.

Levinson, D. J., Darrow, C. N., Klein, E. B., Levinson, M. H., & McKee, B. (1978). *The seasons of a man's life.* New York: Ballantine.

Loevinger, J. (1976). *Ego development: Conceptions and theories.* San Francisco: Jossey-Bass.

Noam, G. G., Powers, S. I., Kilkenny, R., & Beedy, J. (1990). The interpersonal self in life-span developmental perspective: Theory, measurement, and longitudinal case analysis. In P. B. Baltes, D. L. Featherman, & R. M. Lerner (Eds.), *Life span development and behavior: Vol. 10.* Hillsdale, NJ: Erlbaum.

Pascual-Leone, J., & Irwin, R. R. (1994a). Non-cognitive factors in high road/low road learning: I. The modes of abstraction in adulthood. *Journal of Adult Development, 1,* 73–89.

Pascual Leone, J., & Irwin, R. R. (1994b). Non-cognitive factors in high road/low road learning: II. The will, the self, and modes of abstraction in adulthood. *Journal of Adult Development, 1,* 153–168.

Polkinghorne, D. E. (1988). *Narrative knowing and the human sciences.* Albany, NY: State University of New York Press.

Randall, W. L. (1995). *The stories we are: An essay on self-creation.* Toronto: University of Toronto Press.

Sarbin, T. R. (Ed.). (1986). *Narrative psychology: The storied nature of human conduct.* New York: Praeger.

Sogyal, R. (1993). *The Tibetan book of living and dying.* New York: HarperCollins.

Suzuki, S. (1970). *Zen mind, beginner's mind.* New York: Weatherhill.

Tappan, M. B., & Packer, M. J. (Eds.). (1991). *Narrative and storytelling: Implications for understanding moral development.* San Francisco: Jossey Bass.

Tart, C. T. (1994). *Living the mindful life.* Boston: Shambhala.

Trungpa, C. (1988a). *The myth of freedom and the way of meditation.* Boston: Shambhala.

Trungpa, C. (1988b). *Shambhala: The sacred path of the warrior.* Boston: Shambhala.

Trungpa, C. (1992). *Transcending madness: The experience of the six bardos.* Boston: Shambhala.

Trungpa, C. (1995). *The path is the goal: A basic handbook of Buddhist meditation.* Boston: Shambhala.

Varela, F. J., Thompson, E., & Rosch, E. (1991). *The embodied mind: Cognitive science and human experience.* Cambridge, MA: MIT Press.

Washburn, M. (1994). *Transpersonal psychology in psychoanalytic perspective.* Albany, NY: State University of New York Press.

Wilber, K. (1986a). The spectrum of development. In K. Wilber, J. Engler, & D. P. Brown (Eds.), *Transformations of consciousness: Conventional and contemplative perspectives on development* (pp. 65–105). Boston, MA: Shambhala.

Wilber, K. (1986b). The spectrum of psychopathology. In K. Wilber, J. Engler, & D. P. Brown (Eds.), *Transformations of consciousness: Conventional and contemplative perspectives on development* (pp. 107–126). Boston, MA: Shambhala.

Wilber, K. (1986c). Treatment modalities. In K. Wilber, J. Engler, & D. P. Brown (Eds.), *Transformations of consciousness: Conventional and contemplative perspectives on development* (pp. 127–159). Boston, MA: Shambhala.

Wilber, K. (1991). *Grace and grit: Spirituality and healing in the life and death of Treya Killam Wilber.* Boston: Shambhala.

Wilber, K. (1996). *A brief history of everything.* Boston: Shambhala.

12.

The Interplay of Object Relations and Cognitive Development: Implications for Spiritual Growth and the Transformation of Images

Melvin E. Miller

The varieties of religious and spiritual orientations are many—as diverse as, say, devoted evangelical Christianity, traditional Pure Land Buddhism, and staunch atheism. Each form of belief promotes a unique image of God, the good, or the ultimate. This vast range of images is remarkable and most intriguing. Are there so many different images of the ultimate simply because of the multitude of extant religious orientations? Or, is this tremendous heterogeneity a reflection of various personal choices and individual capacities for image making?

We can find no two descriptions of God that are identical—no matter whether the people in question belong to the same denomination, the same church, synagogue, temple, or the same family. One's image of God or the ultimate is as unique as one's personality. It is an amalgamation of cultural,

Acknowledgments. I would like to thank John McKenna, Loren Miller, and Alan West for their helpful comments and suggestions on earlier versions of this manuscript.

racial, and historical factors, one's personal religious training and experience, and deep-seated psychological dynamics. In light of such complexity, I am concerned in this chapter with how we, as social scientists, might make sense of these differences. I am particularly interested in investigating variations in religious content that have been learned, and in analyzing the introjected images from church, parents, family, village, and how these factors interface with the more ingrained psychological dynamics of the individual. I am also interested in how images of God and the ultimate might change over the life span.

An old friend and colleague often spoke of his early religious training during casual conversation. When he did, he spoke with contempt and anger. From Professor D:

> It was a hellfire-and-brimstone religion. My parents would drag us to church at least three times on Sunday, and who knows how many times during the middle of the week. This kind of religion and religious training ruined me. I hated it then, and I hate it even more now—upon reflection. It was ruinous. I am not a churchgoer; I loathe religion. It serves no purpose other than scaring the young, and ruining their minds through creating images of a cruel, malevolent God and nightmares of eternal punishment in hellfire. I want to keep me and my children away from, safe from, religion. It infuriates me to think of it, and what it did to me—what my parents did to me—as a child. I can never forgive them.

This man now denies subscribing to or buying into any image of God—none whatsoever. But, at the same time he acknowledges that the one forced upon him as a youngster was burnt into his psyche, and he cannot escape it. He forever loathes it and would like to obliterate it from his consciousness.

It may be difficult for some of us to imagine anyone taking such a negative stance toward religion and the ultimate. And, it is probably difficult for most of us to imagine the horrors this individual experienced as a youngster. Nonetheless, this vignette gives us much to reflect upon. How powerfully influential were these early god images in invading and structuring the mind of this individual? How formative are those formative years? It has been said: "Give us a child up to the age of 5 and he'll be a Catholic (Muslim, Jew, Buddhist) for the rest of his life."

Both conventional wisdom and the personal experience of Professor D attest to the likelihood that early religious experiences are intractable and remain with people throughout their lives. In this chapter, I will explore the feasibility of an individual moving beyond such early influences. I'll suggest that one's formative religious experiences are not unalterable—that they are not necessarily chiseled in stone, nor indelibly ingrained. I'll further suggest that images of God and the ultimate can, and sometimes do, change.

CONTEMPORARY THEORIES AND PERSPECTIVES

Lately, more psychologists have begun to discuss adult spiritual and religious development from the cognitive, emotional, psychodynamic, and object relational perspectives (e.g., Anderson & Hopkins, 1991; Jones, 1991; McDargh, 1983, 1997; Meissner, 1996; Rizzuto, 1976; Shafranske, 1996; Wulff, 1996).

James Fowler (1981, 1995, 1996) has been one of the most popular contemporary writers to address the development of faith and spirituality. His book, *Stages of Faith*, presents a hierarchical model similar to Kohlberg's (1981) stages of moral development. Fowler's approach, like Kohlberg's, is Piagetian in that successive stages arise from a fixed developmental sequence of changes in cognition. To some extent, his approach overlaps with both Perry's (1970) intellectual and ethical developmental stage theory, and Loevinger's (1976) ego development scheme. The ever-increasing cognitive complexity and life commitments of Fowler's stages closely parallel Perry's stages. Fowler's model is similar to Loevinger's theory in its emphasis on the continual evolution of both cognitive and imaginative complexity. For Fowler, these cognitive and imaginative gains are reflected in the levels of faith and images of God which emerge at higher stages of development. Fowler's stages are well-known:

#0-Primal Faith (Infancy): A prelanguage disposition of trust forms in the mutuality of one's relationships with parents and other caregivers to offset the anxiety that results from separations which occur during infant development.
#1-Intuitive-Projective Faith (Early Childhood): Imagination, stimulated by stories, gestures, and symbols, and not yet controlled by logical thinking, combines with perception and feelings to create long-lasting images that represent both the protective and threatening powers surrounding one's life.
#2-Mythic-Literal Faith (Childhood & beyond): The developing ability to think logically helps one order the world with categories of causality, space, and time; to enter into the perspectives of others; and to capture life meaning in stories.
#3-Synthetic-Conventional Faith (Adolescence & beyond): New cognitive abilities make mutual perspective-taking possible and enable one to integrate diverse self-images into a coherent identity. A personal and largely unreflective synthesis of beliefs and values evolves to support identity and to unite one in emotional solidarity with others.
#4-Individuative-Reflective Faith (Young Adulthood & beyond): Critical reflection upon one's beliefs and values, utilizing third-person perspective-taking; understanding of the self and others as part of a social system; the internalization of authority and the assumption of responsibility for making explicit choices of ideology and lifestyle open the way for critically self-aware commitments in relationships and vocation.
#5-Conjunctive Faith (Early Mid-life & beyond): The embrace of polarities in one's life, an alertness to paradox, and the need for multiple interpretations of reality mark this stage. Symbol and story, metaphor and myth (from one's own traditions and others') are newly appreciated (second, or willed naivete) as vehicles for expressing truth.
#6-Universalizing Faith (Mid-life & beyond): Beyond paradox and polarities, persons in this stage are grounded in a oneness with the power of being. Their visions and commitments free them for a passionate yet detached spending of the self in love, devoted to overcoming division, oppression and violence, and in effective anticipatory response to an inbreaking commonwealth of love and justice. (1996, p. 170)

From a Piagetian, cognitive perspective, these stages essentially move from preoperational levels—through concrete and formal—to postformal levels similar to those discussed by Commons (Commons & Richards, 1984) and Cook-Greuter (1994). Fowler speculates that any given person may experience and work through 3 to 6 stages over the life span. Moreover, Fowler (1996) makes the point that his approach, though structural, attempts to tie together both cognitive and emotional factors (p. 168). Fowler's perspective on faith development has obviously expanded from its inception to include a greater variety of formative variables, e.g., emotional, biological, and religio-cultural influences (1996, p. 169). To my mind, he has not yet gone far enough in privileging the emotional side of this interactive dyad, although his effort to include the affective component—to the degree that he has—is both noted and applauded. I would like to take such theorizing further in the direction of including emotion, affect, and related meanings.

In comparison to Fowler's scheme, Ana-Maria Rizzuto (1974, 1976, 1981) takes a more psychodynamic, object-relations, emotion-oriented (affect-laden) approach to the formation of individual images of God (God figures, faith, and ultimate points of reference). Instead of proffering a hierarchical stage theory, Rizzuto (1974) proposes that there are four categories of orientations to a God which are based on early object-relational experiences.[1] She believes that people typically take one of these four perspectives:

> (1) having a God with whom they relate in varied ways; (2) wondering whether to believe or not in a God whom they are

[1] Object-relation theorists such as Klein (1952), Fairbairn (1952), and Guntrip (1961) support the notion that it is the internal and partial representations of the important people in the individual's early environment that influence one's thoughts, feelings about self, and one's day-to-day relationships. From Greenberg and Mitchell (1983):

> [T]hese mental representations of others, shar[e] ... some of the characteristics of "real" people as well as some of their capacity to trigger behavioral response.... Such images go under various names in the psychoanalytic literature. In different theoretical systems they are called variously "internal objects," "illusory others," "introjects," "personifications," and the constituents of a "representational world." ... They may be understood as serving as a kind of loose anticipatory image of what is to be expected from people in the real world .. [T]hese internal images ... constitute a residue within the mind of relationships with important people in the individual's life. In some way crucial exchanges with others leave their mark; they are internalized and so come to shape subsequent attitudes, reactions, perceptions, and so on. (p. 11)

> not sure exists; (3) amazed, angered, or quietly surprised to see others deeply invested in a God who does not interest them, and (4) struggling with a demanding, harsh God they would like to get rid of if they were not convinced of his existence and power. These four positions can be epitomized in the sentences: "I have a God," "I might have a God," "I do not have a God," and "I have a God but I wish I did not." (1974, p. 88)

It is interesting to note the differences in approach taken by Rizzuto and Fowler. Fowler presents his categories in a hierarchy which is developmentally and structurally informed; Rizzuto simply presents four different categories—each hypothetically grounded in different early object relations.

AN INTEGRATED APPROACH: THE CONFLUENCE OF PSYCHOANALYTIC AND COGNITIVE-DEVELOPMENTAL THEORY

To present a more inclusive perspective, I would like to suggest a synthesis of these two orientations—the psychoanalytic and the cognitive-developmental—as represented in the writings of Rizzuto and Fowler. On the one hand, I acknowledge the possibility of a structural hierarchy similar to Fowler's for the development of faith, religious, and spiritual experience. On the other hand, I want to highlight the limitations inherent in placing any and all faith positions on a developmental hierarchy. I will suggest, consistent with Rizzuto and others (Jones, 1991; McDargh, 1983, 1997), that the quality of one's earliest object relations has the most formative impact in determining one's faith stance and one's images of the ultimate. Moreover, I will suggest that the impact of these early object relations is so influential that it will most likely override any allegedly "pure" cognitive elements involved.

I do not dispute Fowler's suggestion that spiritual development moves through a developmental progression. We must include an awareness of developmental processes in any dynamic description of faith. Empirical evidence illustrates that these progressions often unfold in a manner similar to the stage sequences outlined by Kohlberg and Piaget (Fowler, 1981, 1995, 1996). In addition to Fowler's own research program, DeNicola (1992) presents a meta-analysis of research conducted with faith development interviews on participants from various walks of life. Her results corroborate Fowler's findings and lend statistical support to both the internal coherence and the sequence of Fowler's faith development stages. Such engaging findings notwithstanding, I predict that we will derive more explanatory power for understanding the formation of individual God-images through an object-relations orientation. Moreover, our object relations strategy may help us understand better those individuals whose God-image choices seem to defy hierarchical placements. Such a theoretical formulation might also help us understand how some people can get stuck or fixated at certain (Fowler-type) Faith Stages (and, with certain religious content) even though their cognitive development might continue to progress. Let's turn to Rizzuto's basic hypothesis for a moment. Rizzuto (1974) contends that: "the elements unconsciously used to form the image of God originate in early object representations and interactions; and that these images—more or less integrated with the God provided by the environment—become an internalization with a life of its own" (p. 88). Rizzuto also leaves room for the possibility that these internalized images of God are not completely fixed, and implies that these God images always embody a "potential for change" (1974, p. 88).

My position on the formation of early images is fairly similar to Rizzuto's—especially as she emphasizes the degree to which these internalized objects become complexes or introjects with a "life of their own." As they take on the role or function of introjects and complexes, they serve as magnets or motivators for the specific images of God that are constructed. And, of course, within the context of transferential dynamics, these introjects serve as magnets for the kinds of interpersonal relationships an individual develops (see note 1.)

Rizzuto (1974) offers case studies to elucidate her particular object-relations approach to the development of God images. In one case (p. 92), a man develops an image of God based upon his early relations with strict and critical parents who demanded his obedience. Not surprisingly, the God he constructed was strict and critical; his God demanded obedience and did not tolerate anger or protestations. It was a God that he *had* to please—a God from whom he got a "happy feeling inside" when he obeyed Him. This man felt that he was obliged to love this God. He was not allowed to have any negative feelings toward Him, nor did he feel he had the right to rebel against Him. In talking about the interpersonal or relatedness aspect of this patient's experience with his image of the ultimate, Rizzuto notes that his feelings of closeness with his God do not reach the level of (true, interconnected) intimacy. He just feels a protective presence from this God, while the relationship remains distant and intellectual.

Rizzuto offers a very compelling formulation of this man's early object-relation experiences, and she explains how the parents' strict and demanding interactions, coupled with their limited affection and overcontrol, led to such a constricted adult image of God. This man worked hard to please both his parents and his God; he developed a passive dependency toward both; he tried to please both of these introjects, which had become internalized structures in their own right—that guided and directed his behavior. Rizzuto implies that this man's image of God is immature, and predicts that it would be very resistant to change.

DYNAMIC FORMULATIONS: CLINICAL ILLUSTRATIONS AND VIGNETTES

Religious and spiritual issues have emerged during the process of psychodynamic psychotherapy with many of my own patients.[2] I'll mention five of them here, summarizing selected aspects of their therapies to illustrate the formative impact early object-relations experiences have had upon their development. I also will look at the impact this early background has had

[2] Descriptive information pertaining to clients' background, age, family size, etc., has been altered to protect their confidentiality. Nonetheless, permission to include these vignettes was obtained.

upon the kinds of religious or spiritual experiences they either sought out or created. Certainly there were other issues and dynamics that were formative in their lives, but for now we are going to declare these early object-relations experiences as being most pivotal. Please note that we are not in a position to judge these people's lives nor be critical of their religious images or religious experiences; we'll simply note the dynamics that seemed to be present and attempt to respectfully understand the images of the ultimate they have created. Moreover, it is important to note that these are all highly intelligent people with intact cognitive development. Each performs well in the workaday world and is a fully functioning professional.

Clinical Illustration 1

Ms.Q is a single woman in her late 50s—a competent administrator and talented artist. She is the mother of five children. She describes her own parents as somewhat ineffectual. Being the oldest daughter, she believed she had to raise the rest of the children and hold the family together. She experienced pressure from both her parents to do the parenting in the family; she especially felt pressure from her father. It was pressure to do it well, to be the "perfect mother," and to function in place of the emotionally absent and sometimes cruel mother. My client attempted to do just what was expected of her, in spite of the messages declaring how "bad" she was. She attempted to live up to the expectations of a sometimes absent, yet demanding and intrusive father, and make up for the limitations of an ineffectual, cruel, and distant mother. Despite these attempts for perfection, she could never quite achieve it. She ended up feeling bad about herself. In her own words: "If all a kid gets is messages about how crappy she is, she'll take it in and eventually feel that way about herself all the time. Then she'll probably idolize others to perfection for a while, but then they too end up being placed in the dirt basket."[3]

[3] This client noted, at one point in the therapy, that this kind of thinking was a good example of splitting—a topic that will be subsequently addressed in greater detail.

These dynamics played themselves out in her own family, once she got married and had children of her own. They also appeared in other interpersonal relationships over time. And, more to the point of this project, they manifested themselves in her religious and spiritual searchings.

This woman describes herself as being an active spiritual seeker throughout most of her adult life. It was as if she were looking for something firm to hold onto, or seeking for something consistent, something where the expectations were clear. Not surprisingly, she gravitated to spiritual practices that demand a high level of involvement and activity (e.g., Transcendental Meditation, Sufism, Tai Chi, and Christian Science) and strict health regimens. These were all religions or practices that promote a kind of spiritual perfection. Thus, she would get involved in these activities, and strive for perfection. But, soon she would begin to feel imperfect in her strivings and move on. An impossible perfectionism in spiritual–religious practice seemed to be the outcome of her early object relations and her early role in the family system. Her efforts toward spiritual perfection notwithstanding, she always seemed to fall short of her self-imposed goals. The resultant self-condemnation and recrimination was most often extreme. She was left feeling "crappy" and bad about herself—reminiscent of not living up to the expectations of the demanding father and critical mother whom she had internalized.

Later in the therapeutic process she often talked about being less demanding of herself, a little "easier on herself," and, conversely, easier on others. Simultaneously, of course, the drive toward religious and spiritual perfection diminished considerably.

Clinical Illustration 2

Mr. R is a 49-year-old married man with four children. He is a skilled businessman, administrator, and artist. By his account, he was raised by distant and somewhat inadequate parents. He did not describe them as being mean nor overly intrusive, just distant and preoccupied, concerned with their own issues and problems. This client remembers being starved for their interest, attention, and affection; he vividly remembers never receiving any. He often mentioned throughout the course of therapy that his parents never seemed interested in his emotional problems; they were never interested in his inner life.

He became very religiously focused in his interests and pursuits very early in life. Throughout the years, Mr. R has tried out a handful of traditional religions and religious education experiences. He took up doctoral studies in theology after college, although he didn't complete them. Mr. R tended to be drawn toward very demanding and exacting religions—ones that included a sharp focus on what one *did*—on how one performed the intricacies of religious practice. Most recently he has been drawn to an especially conservative faith, one that has been extraordinarily demanding on him, the most demanding yet. He said that he looks for a "special intensity" with religious figures and religious experiences, a kind of intensity and connectedness that he never had with his parents. He seems to perceive the strict and challenging demands coming toward him from his newly chosen religion as "interest in him," or as "care." He experiences these demands (the intensity) as involvement—as an investment in him, even as affection. A demanding minister is an interested minister; a demanding God is an interested God. "Show me what to do, and I will do it. Tell me to work hard and I will work hard. I will work hard because I'll know what to do to get the right feedback and attention. The more intense it feels, the better." These demands for action (and his active, obedient responses) would usually leave him with a good feeling for a while, but they'd typically fall short of offering him the attention and care that he so deeply desired. He would then become frustrated and disillusioned with both the religion itself and its leaders. He would subsequently leave that religion and seek out a new one. He would keep trying to find and become involved with the "right" religion. The client also acknowledges being involved in similar dynamics with his wife and family members. His continuous wish for attention and care—and the cycle of disillusionment—has been played out vividly in both his religious life and his personal life.

Clinical Illustration 3

The third client that comes to mind is Ms. S, a single woman in her early 40s. As she recollects her childhood years, she remembers a mother who was intrusive and cruel, who would mock her and never take her seriously. She reports having a father who was critical and sometimes cruel, but who occasionally demonstrated some emotional warmth toward her. The mother was dogmatic in her religious beliefs and would readily shove her beliefs down Ms. S's throat. There was never any room made for Ms. S's own beliefs to be formulated or held, let alone expressed. Not surprisingly, Ms. S has taken an adamant stance against any formal or organized religion, and has especially eschewed any religion that appeared to be vaguely similar to her mother's. She reached a place where she was critical of almost any religious experience. She says she has her "own beliefs," but she wants to keep them extraordinarily private. "No one is going to take my beliefs away from me; no one is going to criticize them; no one is ever going to shove beliefs down my throat again." So, she plays it all very close to the vest.

Ms. S rebelled against her mother, against both parents, as if she were trying to get far away from the intrusiveness and cruelty. Yet she never got very far away from home. To this day, she continues to try to win them over—to fix them, to fix their marriage, and to fix how they relate to her. Meanwhile, she has tended to stay away from all intimate relationships. She seems to fear getting close to anyone; she seems to fear having someone intrude upon her again. She fears having someone not take her seriously again. She worries that the closer she gets to someone, the more likely it will be that these old patterns will be repeated.

Clinical Illustration 4

Mr. T is a single man in his late 40s. He had a father who was deferent and passive, and a mother who was intrusive and critical. His mother was especially intrusive with her religious beliefs and messages. Catholicism was forced upon him in no uncertain terms. He was sent to Catholic schools. He was pushed to be the perfect Catholic student; he was pushed to be perfectly behaved. He continuously experienced this pressure at home from his parents, and it was echoed repeatedly in school by the nuns. He worked diligently to comply with all their demands. The real (and introjected) parents and church authorities pushed him to perfection. Eventually, he could no longer take the pressure of attempting to live up to such perfectionistic demands—the demands to be the "perfect person." He began to rebel in the late high school years. His primary way of rebelling was to disavow all religions and all religious strivings, and to "officially" take up the cause of atheism. This client now alleges devout atheism. Although he uses many religious images and concepts in the therapeutic narrative, he stridently expresses steadfast atheism and wants nothing to do with any form of religion.

Mr. T's interpersonal relationships are strained. He has a very difficult time connecting in and committing to interpersonal relations. He expresses a fear of emotional attachments, while, at the same time, he voices a wish for some kind of permanent connection in relationship.

Clinical Illustration 5

Ms. U is a single woman in her early 40s. She is a competent professional and a talented musician. Ms. U was raised in a Catholic family and went to a Catholic college. She stated early on in therapy that "my Catholic upbringing was disastrous." Ms. U had an extremely intrusive mother who constantly reminded Ms. U just how much she did for her. Ms. U's mother frequently told her that she gave "over 150%" to her care every day of the year. This high "percentage of care" was frequently reiterated, despite Ms. U's nagging feeling that it was she who was always giving to her mother. Ms. U could never keep the dynamic straight in her mind. Perhaps this was partly so because she believed she could never break away from mother.

She believed she had to stand by her mother and take care of her.

Images of enmeshment, symbiosis, and entanglements would often appear in her dreams and drawings. Identification with religious images of Christ sacrificing himself on the cross also surfaced in dreams and artistic creations. Thoughts and fantasies of "redemption, salvation, and repentance" arose frequently during the sessions. Any thought of breaking away from mother was usually accompanied by the feeling that she was "evil, a sinner, and in need of punishment for her sins." Religious language and terms of this sort were used routinely in the psychotherapy. It was as if this was the only kind of language that could capture the powerful emotional depths and feelings that she experienced. Ms. U seemed to believe that if she sacrificed herself for her mother, her mother would be happy, and she (Ms. U) might be able to be "saved." She'd give anything to be "free at last." Despite the religious language, this client stated that she really could not believe in anything. She could not believe in anything ultimate, nor could she turn to any God or image of the ultimate for security or comfort. "I don't dare let myself imagine the presence of God or an image of God. I would like to think that religion or spirituality would help, but I'm afraid to turn to anything."

In all of these cases, religious themes often seemed to permeate the therapy hour and infiltrate the daily life of each client. Likewise, each client seemed to be engaged in a perplexing struggle with religious image making, religious expression, or the negation of religious experience. In most situations, it seemed that the espoused religious stance reflected the client's earlier relationships with parents—often in some unwitting, collusive, or interactive way. It is interesting to note at this point that the three patients with the most intrusive parents (3, 4, and 5) were the ones who said "no" to God imaging. In simple terms, it seemed that they declined to formulate or subscribe to images of the ultimate or the good. It appears that the present stance of these clients is a *reaction against* the religious position of a central parental figure or figures. Their religious "stances" (or opposition to taking a stance) and the accompanying restrictions in imaging the ultimate (God or sense of the good) were a direct response to the emotional intrusiveness and/or the dogmatic religiosity of the parent. They are saying through such a stance: "I will not let anyone in, and I will certainly not construct an image of God or the good in a manner similar to yours (i.e., the parents/the early objects). In the other cases (1 and 2), the patients' religious stances seemed to be a response to neglect and/or the disinterest of a parent or parents. This dynamic seemed to create a kind of anxiousness or anxious-attachment in clients that was reflected in their God-imaging.

Along these lines, it was also discovered that the present-day interpersonal experiences of some of these individuals revealed relational difficulties. It often appeared that a person's present-day interpersonal relations reflected central aspects of his or her religious upbringing. Put another way, the difficulties that people have with religion, the ultimate, or God—often mirror pivotal difficulties they have had in interpersonal relationships. This was not a universally detected phenomenon, but it occurred with enough frequency to be deemed noteworthy.

I am reluctant to place any of these people on Fowler's hierarchy of faith development. It could be done, and to do so might be quite informative. Nonetheless, it seems to me that (and this is a central point) the religious imaginings and religious stances of these people are not so much cognitive matters as they are emotional ones. Thus, to place any of them on Fowler's hierarchy would be a misguided effort. However, I do suspect that these individuals would move "upwards" on Fowler's scheme as their capacity for object relatedness improved (and the accompanying introjects and emotional states changed)—as their emotional issues and dynamics continued to be addressed.

In order to explore additional dynamics related to the development and transformation of images, and the occasional resistances to same, let's return to a further investigation of Rizzuto's client and Professor D.

OBSTACLES TO TRANSFORMATIVE EXPERIENCES

Both Rizzuto's patient and Professor D seem to be stymied in relation to religion and religious imaging. One is stuck trying to get the "correct" God image, and the other is stuck in an antagonistic stance against God-imaging and the ultimate. In the case of Rizzuto's patient, it was a situation of strict and demanding parents that seemed causative; it was the parents (the parent introjects) who had to be pleased at any cost. His attempts to please the parents stifled his passions, his creativity, and his spiritual development. These same introjects seemed to limit his capacity for God-imaging, and they led to interpersonal immaturity and dependency. Similar parental influences impacted Professor D—with the added intrusiveness of the parental religious focus. Both individuals, Rizzuto's patient and Professor D, became limited in their ways of thinking about the ultimate and their own change potential. Both floundered in limited and constricted relationships.

Although Rizzuto (1974) does not attempt to categorize her client according to Fowler's scheme, it strikes me that this individual would be placed at Fowler's Stage 1—the Intuitive-Projective Faith stage. Some of the Fowler Stage 1 attributes manifested by this client are: an egocentric blindness to others' interests; his moral categories are "good or bad"; he orients to size, power, or other concrete symbols of authority; relationships to authority are based on dependency upon primary caretakers, the desire to preserve this relationship, and the avoidance of punishment; world images are partial, fragmented and impressionistic; and symbols of the deity are most often anthropomorphic.

I will not classify Professor D in terms of Fowler's faith development model, but let's return to him again as an example of another kind of stasis that accompanies many forms of closed-mindedness. Professor D, our bright young, energetic college teacher, has been preoccupied with an antagonistic stance toward any form of religious imaging. He has become vehemently opposed to any kind of religious experience or expression. His dogmatism or closed-mindedness (Rokeach, 1960; Meissner, 1996, pp. 251–255) is as powerful as that of his parents—something for which he criticized them stridently. Although Professor D offers legitimate criticisms of the limitations and drawbacks imposed by early and extreme religious experiences (he can articulate the problem intellectually), he remains stunted in his ability to go beyond them, and limited in his ability (and inclination) to espouse any image of the good. He is either unwilling or unable to articulate any sense of the ultimate or an integrated ethical stance. In short, we could say that he is limited in this arena by the very same experiences that initially turned him away from God-imaging. He had to shut off (repress) imaging of the other, of God, and of the good. It was too painful to remain open to the other (to the parents in particular), and their religious messages. The messages were all too intrusive and too full of hellfire, etc. Emotional survival became almost an "all or none" affair. His primary psychological defense was a form of splitting. As might a child who had been severely traumatized, he had to create a world of all good vs. all bad in order to survive (see J. Rike's detailed explanation of the splitting dynamic in chapter 6).

Grotstein (1981) offers a commonly accepted explanation for the origins of splitting: "[A] patient may experience himself or herself to be fragmented (pathologically split) because of a failure to have acquired a sense of self from an empathically protective and supportive object(s)" (p. 5). From Grotstein again:

> Splitting involves separating experience, or the self which experiences the experience. Pathological splitting also alters the perception of the object by inappropriate divisions, by splintering and fragmentation. Splitting the perception of an object is also associated with a splitting of the self. (pp. 9–10)

Professor D split off the people, the relationships, and as a defense, retreated into a more impersonal world of ideas, a world devoid of people. Professor D had very strict and punitive God images thrust at him, coming in concert with additional strict and punitive messages from his parents. These messages and impending punishments made Professor D (as a child) defend himself against the hurt and shame. In reaction, he eschewed all religious images and contents in adulthood. All religion became "bad." One can perhaps now understand how he organized his inner experience and his world as he assumed what Klein (1952), Fairbairn (1952), and Guntrip (1961) have called the schizoid position—a defensive posture in which one retreats within self and emotionally distances oneself from others.

Here is Fairbairn's (1952) description of the schizoid position—a psychological defense that is sometimes found in the academician or scholar.

> Intellectual pursuits as such, whether literary, artistic, scientific or otherwise, appear to exercise a special attraction for individuals possessing schizoid characteristics to one degree or another.... the attraction would appear to depend upon the . . . individual's attitude of detachment, no less than upon his overvaluation of thought processes. (1952, p. 6)

Guntrip (1961) makes a similar point:

> The scientific attitude of complete unemotional detachment from the facts investigated is essentially schizoid. It is not a psychopathological state if it is an attitude of mind voluntarily adopted for the specific purpose of investigation. But schizoid intellectuals are bound to be attracted to science [and other intellectual pursuits] as an escape from the pressure of personal emotional relationships which the schizoid person finds difficult. (p. 249)

In short, Fairbairn and Guntrip describe bright, but wounded people as escaping into academics and science to avoid interpersonal relationships—perhaps any human contact. They then develop the resultant "wound" and its associated defenses into a worldview—into an ideology. To these individuals, science is good; intellectual pursuits and distance are good; relationships are bad. Science is rational and apersonal; religion is irrational and interpersonal. Again, we see the splitting that is so essential to maintaining this defensive, self-contained posture. Rizzuto's patient, Professor D, and some of my patients, the ones with the most intrusive parental objects, retreated from relationships into a distant, inner, and detached world. They seemed to have moved into a world that promises to be safer than the world of people and interpersonal relationships.

We can empathize with such a protective stance, and now understand the impact such a posture has had upon the religious image making of these individuals. If this defense is so fixed (in part because it was adopted so early on), we also must wonder what it will take to initiate or provoke change in them. We must assume that it will take a tremendous influence to enable these people to feel safe enough to return to the land of the relational, and to rekindle their capacities for care, kindness, and the desire for relational integrity. In like manner, I suspect that it will take some major life-transforming experience to jump start their imaginations, and make it safe for the conceptualization of possible goods, gods, and the ultimate.

THE POSSIBILITY OF TRANSFORMATION

Cognitive–developmental models and psychoanalytic theory are both based on assumptions of individual change and transformation. Principles from both approaches will be applied to help clarify the process of change and transformation in images of the ultimate.

A somewhat cursory explanation of spiritual growth from the standpoint of the cognitive–developmental model suggests that people will simply change automatically in some inexorable upward direction with the passage of time. From Fowler (1996):

> Faith-development theory is centered in the progressive movement of one stage to another. . . . My anthropology affirms that humans have evolved with prepotentiated capacities that underlie the structuring activities of faith and that equip people for their ontological callings to relatedness and partnership with God. (pp. 182–183)

By comparison, most psychoanalysts would argue that therapeutic change comes primarily through the relationship that develops between therapist and client. Over time, in a good frame analytically oriented therapy experience (e.g., regular meeting time, regular meeting place, ground rules, and certain protocols for the work), the patient develops a rather powerful transference relationship with the therapist (see Langs [1982, pp. 303–399] for a discussion of the psychoanalytic frame).[4] That is, the patient projects on to the therapist unresolved issues, dynamics, and ways of relating that have been central to his or her relationships with early formative objects (parents, siblings, teachers, etc.). Also, in this style of psychotherapy, an optimal "holding environment" is established—an environment (a place) in which the client is able to feel vulnerable, yet safe and contained. Good frame therapy, conducted in a good holding environment, comprise two variables that contribute to the flourishing of the transference.

According to Mitchell and Black (1995) and M. Stark (1996), the client's interpersonal and self deficiencies are remedied and restored through the creation of this safe environment coupled with the use of empathy, mirroring, and dynamic interpretations (Stark, 1996, pp. 238–239). Also, the therapist and her consulting room act as a transitional object or transitional space for the client, i.e., they offer the client "something to hold onto" while the gradual transformation takes place. Eventually, the client experiences safety and care in the presence of another person. This developing sense of trust and care—experienced in a context of mirroring and interpretation, in an environment of optimal support and optimal frustration—seem to be essential to the development of the client's inner structure and sense of self. With such a foundation in place, the client can accept the eventual frustrations in, and disappointments with, the therapist in a slow, gradual, step-by-step manner. Thus, the self structure continues to be built and supported, and not fragmented. These "new," safe, supportive, interrelational dynamics can help "jump start" the client into a relational way of being—away from the schizoid position and

---

[4] Although psychoanalytically oriented, psychodynamic psychotherapy remains the focus of this chapter, one could argue that similar transference and related dynamics would develop in almost any good frame psychotherapy, despite the name of the therapeutic modality and its espoused theoretical underpinnings.

into the depressed position—where the early losses can be mourned (not defended against), and from there into a relational and interpersonal space.

Thus, good-enough psychotherapy, experienced in a good-enough holding environment, where the early and current object relational dynamics are dealt with in the transference (where the transference and the working relationship are experienced, discussed, and interpreted), becomes the corrective antidote or remedy for both the splitting defense and the schizoid position. The patient begins to experience himself and the therapist in a more complex and yet integrated manner. And, as mentioned above, as a result of this new relationship, patients can now mourn the loss of the parents they never had, and gradually become open to new (ambivalent and complex) relations with multifaceted, complex, real-life people. This happens first with the therapist, then in other relationships. And, of course, if there is God-imaging, meaning making, and religious striving going on with this person, we would expect to witness changes in this arena as well.

This is an obvious oversimplification of the change process as it happens in a psychodynamic therapy. But there is much we can glean from this synopsis as we attempt to understand how "images of the ultimate" can actually change. For example, my patient 1, who had been seeking perfection in her religious or spiritual path, eventually began to realize that she was working with an imperfect therapist who perhaps was not demanding perfection from her. This perceived dynamic began to shift slowly over a period of time. This change in attributions and perceptions was also promoted through actually talking about this particular dynamic and its transference into the therapeutic relationship. As this shift in awareness slowly evolved, the client began to seek less perfection in herself, in others, and in her spiritual practice. In short, through the process of good frame, dynamic psychotherapy, the bad objects (bad introjects) were slowly altered or transfigured. Through this process, they did not necessarily become "good objects," but, more aptly so, became ambivalently held objects. The good traits, the bad traits, and the shades of gray that comprise the other (and likewise the self) were accepted more readily.

With these thoughts in mind, let us return to Fowler's model for a moment, and contemplate possible ways of reconceptualizing his stage progressions. I believe that we could take each stage of Fowler's scheme (with Rizzuto's help) and describe, with some degree of accuracy, the current level or quality of object-relatedness experienced by adults found at each stage of faith development. We also could analyze the level of openness and trust experienced by those at each stage. And, I think we could make a good guess at what some of the early object-relations were like for those at each Fowler stage.

For example, someone who scored (or placed) at a Fowler stage 3, Synthetic-Conventional faith, most likely would have had fairly sound (adequate; "good enough") early experiences in object-relatedness, or might have arrived at healthy object-relatedness through work in a therapeutic milieu (see Moseley, Jarvis, & Fowler [1986] for a scoring manual for faith development protocols). I would propose, based upon an understanding of object relations theory, that a good-enough degree of early trust in the other must be fostered (and experienced) in order for the individual to feel safe enough in self to take the position of the other. Mutual perspective taking is a state that is not easily achievable; one has to be emotionally secure to be able to risk letting go of one's own hard-won position or perspective in order to take the position of the other. If one has not experienced adequate early object relations, it would be unlikely that one would feel safe or secure despite the level of cognitive functioning (formal or postformal) that has been achieved. These individuals would not feel safe enough to experience the characteristic demands of this level of faith development and its concomitant religious or spiritual imaging. Acute or staunch psychological defenses would have to remain in operation to defend against the other, to defend against infringement or intrusion by the other. People without this early sense of safety and trust would be unlikely to go beyond stage 1 or 2, the Intuitive Projective or Mythic Literal stages. People who do reach the Synthetic-Conventional Stage would have both the cognitive and emotional complexity to appreciate a variety of religious images, God images, and spiritual perspectives.

This newfound appreciation of religious diversity notwithstanding, the God images at this stage tend to remain anthropomorphic and conventional.

Let us now jump ahead to Fowler's sixth stage, the stage of Universalizing Faith. Both a degree of postformal cognitive complexity and a solid foundation of emotional security would seem to be requisite for the faith dynamics or image-creating possibilities that might transpire here. It would seem to me that one would have to have had more-than-adequate early object-relations experiences as a foundation for this stage, or one would have to have arrived at this position through some form of a developmental reparative experience (perhaps through a good-enough psychotherapy process). Such a solid foundation would be essential to enable the individual to undergo the loss of self and loss of ego boundaries that seem to be consistently agreed upon characteristics of those reaching such advanced states (cf. Miller & Cook-Greuter, 1994). In addition, I think we would find the quality of their current interpersonal relations to be solid and well-formed. There would be much trust, care, and love exhibited in these relationships, directed toward both the other and the self. These are some of the essential ingredients that enable the individual to feel safe enough to "lose ego," to lose personal boundaries, and merge into an amorphous other—into a transcendental unknown, or state of unity consciousness (cf. Miller & Cook-Greuter, 1994, p. xxii). In addition, people at this stage would have less anthropocentric images of the ultimate. Likewise, they would be more respectful of the variety of religious ways, God-imaging, and image-creating activities experienced by others.

The narrative descriptions offered by those at Fowler's Universalizing Faith stage and those undergoing a unity consciousness or a transcendent experience are quite similar. In the following, we have a brief depiction of a universalizing and unity consciousness experience offered by one individual, a veteran meditator, who has achieved such a state.

> My perception of the environment has changed. I started to see and appreciate in all objects and events the subtlest fibers of creation which are vibrant with radiant light. It is very beautiful

> and brings me great bliss and joy. My attention has naturally turned to the author of this glorious creation, and I have begun to recognize the creator in everything. As I see the divine in everyone, all people have become very dear to me, and all interactions are filled with love. . . . (Alexander, Heaton, & Chandler, 1994, p. 49)

In the above passage, we see illustrated both the "advanced modes of perception" and the "spending of the self in love" —two attributes ascribed to stage 6 achievers in Fowler's scheme.

To offer complete descriptions of the postulated object-relations histories of those within each of Fowler's stages would be an ambitious undertaking—an enterprise that is not within the scope of this chapter. Nonetheless, it is provocative to think along these lines. Such a project would require bringing together ever more fully the clinical with the theological and spiritual aspects of development.

FURTHER EXPLORATIONS IN THE TRANSFORMATION OF IMAGES

In closing, I would like to leave the reader with some additional thoughts on how images of God and/or the ultimate might change. One thing that seems clear to me is: to get unstuck and/or to transform images of the ultimate one must "work on it." One must work on the change, on the transformation, both in therapy and outside of it. This sounds like such a simplistic notion, but I have found this to be so through my World View research project (1982, 1988, 1994; Miller & West, 1993), and through clinical experience. Moreover, there appears to be an attitudinal and motivational component to this process. If one wants to change a view of the world, theological constructs, or images of the ultimate, one must be inclined to and willing to work on *it* in addition to working on oneself. Working on change, consciously, does not rule out change through extraordinary experiences: e.g., heightened or peak experiences, traumas, conversions, epiphanies, psychotherapy, etc. I have certainly found through the World View Interview process (Miller, 1994) that unusual experiences do occur and can readily precipitate change. Nonetheless, I mainly have discovered, from both research and clinical practice, that thoughtful consideration and conscious effort, in addition to work in the therapeutic milieu, are the most predictable catalysts for personal change and transformation. Dedicated efforts in some form of meditation practice also have been demonstrated to augment change (Alexander et al., 1994, pp. 39–70). Through such efforts one becomes open to a broader range of images and a wider range of ways of relating to the other, to the ultimate. Additionally, one can learn to enter into dialogue and discussion with the other, and become more open to diverse points of view and a greater range of images of the ultimate. And, of course, this all seems to occur more readily in an atmosphere of trust and safety—where one is listened to and mirrored. Such prime, generative conditions for transformative experiences are not created easily.

In the following excerpt, Gordon Kaufman (1993) offers us an idea of what else might be done—the kind of work that needs to be done—to enhance development and the transformation of images of the ultimate—at both the individual level, and at the collective or community levels. I also hear, embedded in the Kaufman quote below, his effort to enlist our participation in such a project.

> [I]t is of fundamental importance—if we are truly to help bring about a more humane and just order in human affairs, and are to give proper attention to the ecosystem within which human life falls—for us men and women to think through carefully, in light of modern knowledges, the questions of who or what we humans are , what sort of world this is in which we find ourselves, which God [or Gods] must be served. Our concepts of God . . . must be reconceived with attention to our modern understandings of ourselves and of our universe, and to our new consciousness of the destructiveness we humans have worked on the world as well as on our fellow humans. (1993, p. xi)

Kaufman (1993) suggests elsewhere that:

> [T]he powers of the human imagination are the principal instruments which make . . . [this] work possible; and . . . the central theological ideas of God, humanity, and the world are . . . human imaginative constructs. Once this is understood . . . [our work] should become an activity of *deliberate* imaginative construction, carried out as self-consciously and responsibly as possible. (p. ix)

I am of the mind that the kind of active imagination that Kaufman promotes already occurs in some people, and that it is an ability that could be developed further in most. Furthermore, I propose that such imaginative activity is most likely essential for the future well-being of individuals, families, cultures, nations, and the entire globe. I suggest that this kind of creative image making will occur more readily in those who have worked at it and in those who do work at it. I also suspect that this capacity will be developed more readily in those who have worked through the limits to imagination imposed upon them by those early, formative experiences with disapproving, critical, and/or intrusive objects. Our individual and collective futures appear to require such transformative experiences. In this light, personal and collective transformations of our image-making capacities seem urgent.

Who knows where such developmental strides might ultimately lead. The development of new images might eventually lessen (or coincide with) a reduction in the anthropocentric focus of our current images, and perhaps obviate the need for anthropomorphic images and likenesses altogether. Some people might create new images of the ultimate and the good that will galvanize the imagination and foster humankind's indefatigable longing for improvement and refinement. These new images and ways of conceptualizing the ultimate could become magnets for the imagination that draw people toward more affirmative ways of relating, toward greater empathy and kindness. Such imaginative constructs also could help establish a universal ethic—a new ethos of stewardship and care—that will be displayed generously toward friends, neighbors, and strangers (at home and throughout the world), and toward the planet itself. These are merely hints, suggestions, or glimpses of the kinds of images that may be required for humankind's optimal future. Time for developing them seems to be limited. Perhaps we should work on it.

REFERENCES

Alexander, C. N., Heaton, D. P., & Chandler, H. M. (1994). Advanced human development in the vedic psychology of Maharishi Mahesh Yogi: Theory and research. In M. E. Miller & S. Cook-Greuter (Eds.), *Transcendence and mature thought in adulthood* (pp. 39–70). Lanham, MD: Rowman & Littlefield.

Anderson, R., & Hopkins, P. (1991). *The feminine face of God: The unfolding of the sacred in women.* New York: Bantam Books.

Commons, M. L., & Richards, F. A. (1984). A general model of stage theory. In M. L. Commons, F. A. Richards, & C. Armon (Eds.), *Beyond formal operations: Late adolescent and adult cognitive development* (pp. 120–140). New York: Praeger.

Cook-Greuter, S. R. (1994). Rare forms of self-understanding in mature adults. In M. E. Miller & S. Cook-Greuter (Eds.), *Transcendence and mature thought in adulthood* (pp. 119–146). Lanham, MD: Rowman & Littlefield.

DeNicola, K. B. (1992). *Formal operations thinking, stage 4, and practical knowing.* Paper presented at the Association of Practical Theology Conference.

Fairbairn, W. R. D. (1952). *Psychoanalytic studies of the personality.* New York: Basic Books.

Fowler, J. (1981). *Stages of faith: The psychology of human development and the quest for meaning.* New York: Harper & Row.

Fowler, J. (1995). Pluralism and oneness in religious experience: William James and faith development theory. *Psychology of Religion Newsletter, 19,* 1–10.

Fowler, J. (1996). Pluralism and oneness in religious experience: William James, faith development theory, and clinical practice. In E. P. Shafranske (Ed.), *Religion and the clinical practice of psychology* (pp. 165–186). Washington, DC: American Psychological Association.

Greenberg, J. R., & Mitchell, S. A. (1983). *Object relations in psychoanalytic theory.* Cambridge, MA: Harvard University Press.

Grotstein, J. S. (1981). *Splitting and projective identification.* New York: Jason Aronson.

Guntrip, H. (1961). *Personality structure and human interaction: The developing synthesis of psycho-dynamic theory.* New York: International Universities Press.

Jones, J. (1991). *Contemporary psychoanalysis and religion: Transference and transcendence.* New Haven, CT: Yale University Press.

Kaufman, G. D. (1993). *In face of mystery: A constructive theology.* Cambridge, MA: Harvard University Press.

Klein, M. (1952). Notes on some schizoid mechanisms. In M. Klein, P. Heimann, & J. Riviere (Eds.), *Developments in psycho-analysis* (pp. 271–291). London: Hogarth Press.

Kohlberg, L. C. (1981). *Essays in moral development: The philosophy of moral development* (Vol. 1). New York: Harper & Row.

Langs, R. (1982). *Psychotherapy: A basic text.* New York: Jason Aronson.

Loevinger, J. (1976). *Ego development: Conceptions and theories.* San Francisco: Jossey-Bass.

McDargh, J. (1983). *Psychoanalytic object relations theory and the study of religion: On faith and the imaging of God.* Lanham, MD: University Press of America.

McDargh, J. (1997). Creating a new research paradigm for the psychoanalytic study of religion: The pioneering work of Ana-Maria Rizzuto. In J. L. Jacobs & D. Capps (Eds.), *Religion, society, and psychoanalysis: Readings in contemporary theory* (pp. 181–199). Boulder, CO: Westview Press.

Meissner, W. W. (1996). The pathology of beliefs and the beliefs of pathology. In E. P. Shafranske (Ed.), *Religion and the clinical practice of psychology* (pp. 241–267). Washington, DC: American Psychological Association.

Miller, M. E. (1982). World views and ego development in adulthood. *Dissertation Abstracts International, 42,* 3459–3460.

Miller, M. E. (1988). Developing a world view: The universal and the particular. *The New England Psychological Association Newsletter, 5,* 3–4.

Miller, M. E. (1994). World views, ego development, and epistemological changes from the conventional to the postformal: A longitudinal perspective. In M. E. Miller & S. Cook-Greuter (Eds.), *Transcendence and mature thought in adulthood* (pp. 147–179). Lanham, MD: Rowman & Littlefield.

Miller, M. E., & Cook-Greuter, S. (Eds.). (1994). *Transcendence and mature thought in adulthood: The further reaches of adult development.* Lanham, MD: Rowman & Littlefield.

Miller, M. E., & West, A. N. (1993). Influences of world view on personality, epistemology, and choice of profession. In J. Demick & P. Miller (Eds.), *Development in the workplace* (pp. 3–19). Hillsdale, NJ: Lawrence Erlbaum.

Mitchell, S. A., & Black, M. J. (1995). *Freud and beyond: A history of modern psychoanalytic thought.* New York: Basic Books.

Mosley, R. M., Jarvis, D., & Fowler, J. (1986). *Manual for faith development research.* Atlanta, GA: Center for Research in Faith and Moral Development.

Perry, W. G. (1970). *Forms of ethical and intellectual development in the college years.* New York: Holt, Rinehart & Winston.

Rizzuto, A-M. (1974). Object relations and the formation of the image of God. *British Journal of Medical Psychology, 47,* 83–99.

Rizzuto, A-M. (1976). Freud, God, the devil and the theory of object representation. *International Review of Psycho-Analysis, 3,* 165–180.

Rizzuto, A-M. (1981). *The birth of the living God: A psychoanalytic study.* Chicago: University of Chicago Press.

Rokeach, M. (1960). *The open and closed mind.* New York: Basic Books.

Shafranske, E. P. (Ed.). (1996). *Religion and the clinical practice of psychology.* Washington, DC: American Psychological Association.

Stark, M. (1996). From structural conflict to relational conflict: A contemporary model of therapeutic action. In L. E. Lifson (Ed.), *Understanding therapeutic action: Psychodynamic concepts of cure* (pp. 237–252). Hillsdale, NJ: Analytic Press.

Wulff, D. M. (1996). The psychology of religion: An overview. In E. P. Shafranske (Ed.), *Religion and the clinical practice of psychology* (pp. 43–70). Washington, DC: American Psychological Association.

13.

Conversion and the Self

Kevin F. Ryan

Among the many sorts of changes an adult can experience, conversion is surely one of the more profound. A variety of phenomena can be subsumed under the label *conversion,* ranging from those mass conversions witnessed in movements such as the Christianization of Europe, to changes within or about an individual, such as the shift from one religious tradition to another (e.g., the Jew who converts to Christianity), or from one group to another within a particular tradition (e.g., the Catholic who is "born again" into Christian fundamentalism).

Virtually all discussions of conversion limit the phenomenon to specifically religious changes. But why should this be so? For what is striking is the structural similarity between religious conversion and other momentous life changes. While the term *conversion* may have had its genesis in religious discourse, the homology between major life changes and dramatic religious change is remarkable. One who comes to see himself as an alcoholic passes through much the same process as does one who becomes a Moonie or a born-again Christian. The fervent political activist resembles the religious convert in all but the specific language employed to describe one's transformation and new beliefs. In short, religious conversion shares key process characteristics with any significant personal transformation.

What then are the key features of conversion? What sort of change is involved and what is the mechanism of change? And what, exactly, changes? It is these questions that I address in what follows. In particular, I want to raise questions about the nature of the self that is involved in conversion and explore the implications of these questions for understanding the varieties of change. The attempt to develop a general theory inevitably ignores many nuances to which a more elaborated analysis would need to attend. I hint at some of these nuances in my concluding remarks.

THE LAYERED SELF

We can think of the "self" (as defined initially in Mead's [1934] symbolic interactionism) as composed of several layers, any one of which can change without alteration to the levels beneath it, though change in a deeper layer tends to bring with it change in more superficial layers. To put it metaphorically, the self is like an infinite onion, each layer peeling away to reveal further layers. In this view the self has no single core at the center of its being; it is, to modify the ancient proverb, layered all the way down.

Let me elaborate this formulation in two ways. First, the conception of the self as infinitely layered suggests that we have no reason to assume that any one description of the self we make is the real self. Rather, each description may merely be exposing a new and deeper layer of the self without ever arriving at the center. For all we can know, each probe deep inside a person to reveal ever deeper layers of the self fails to find the core, and so the idea of such a core is best set aside for now. Thus, no sense can be made of the claim that real change involves transformation of some deep core lying underneath the outer layers of the self; real change can take place at any of the layers of the self.

Further, we can profitably distinguish four features of the layered self: the self is (1) embodied, (2) becoming, (3) situational, and (4) reflexive (see Fontana, 1984, p. 11). One consequence of using the onion metaphor to describe the self, perhaps a consequence of the nature of language in general, is that it suggests that the self is a thing, a sort of brute reality or concrete thing, located at some ascertainable place within a person. There is something to this. The self is embodied; that is to say, the body of a person constitutes a sort of capsule for the self. The self receives stimuli from the body and is pressed to act on the basis of emotions and feelings flowing from the physical body.

But the self is not simply the interior dimension of a body. Rather, the self is best conceived not as a thing but as a process. The self is always unfolding, changing, developing in response to its changing perceptions of the world around it. Conversions, of course, represent momentous changes in the self. But the self is ever changing, in grand and small ways; it is always in the process of becoming.

A full appreciation of the self, however, requires more than a focus on the inner workings of the person. The embodied self acts, interacts, and changes in the world. Indeed, the self is part of the world and while the body constitutes a sort of barrier between self and world, that barrier is extraordinarily pervious. Research on the deviant self suggests the powerful influence of the features of the immediate situation the self enters, inhabits, and leaves (see Cullen, 1983; Katz, 1988; Luckenbill, 1977). The self always depends upon its immediate contexts for a sense of grounding and belonging. As a person moves from situation to situation, she is continually in the process of creating the self, developing and deploying self-images—definitions of one's self that fit or vary from one's self-concept, the relatively fixed notions one has of who one really is. As the situation changes, the extent to which one's presented image matches one's self-concept also changes. Each of us performs for a variety of audiences, presenting different performances for each audience. The self that appears before different audiences is a different self, and the differences may be noteworthy or minor.

The adaptation to the ever-changing situational stream demonstrates the reflexivity, the self-awareness, of the self. Conscious of its appearance, the self manages the impressions it gives. Further, a person forms notions about how others perceive her self and inevitably responds to those perceived impressions. Responses range from alterations in the face one presents to others, to narrative changes about who one is and why one acts as one does, to the adoption of a new frame and new self in response to the messages one receives from those in one's significant groups of others. The definitions, expectations, and evaluations of particular people or groups may be especially important: these are my significant others, those whose point of view I am most likely to adopt, whose role I am most likely to take, stepping into their place seeking to understand or anticipate their view of the situation. Of course, one's significant others may change over time, even from situation to situation. Thus, while at work I may adopt the perspective of my supervisors on some occasions, but drop that perspective once I am discussing work with my family, friends, or coworkers; with the latter groups, I take on a different viewpoint, in the process becoming a different self. I want to guard here against the implication that nothing about the self persists from moment to moment, situation to situation, for such a position would fly in the face of our common experience of ourselves and others. While it may be too strong to speak of the self in the process of becoming as a "structure," as do self psychologists (see Kohut, 1977; Wolf, 1988),[1] our experience does suggest some self-continuity. The self I presented to my students yesterday does not differ totally from the self I present today; nor does the self I present to my students differ entirely from the one I present at home.

What, then, persists? Here our standard linguistic tools fail us, for both the claim that some*thing* persists and the claim that no*thing* persists imply a core self. The claim that "something persists" tends to push us into the assumption that something solid lies at the heart of our self, something that resists the buffetings of our ever-changing environment. Likewise, the claim that nothing about the self persists across time assumes that something deep inside, some hard inner reality, shifts or

[1] As developed in the work of Ernest Wolf (1988), the notion of self as a structure loses much of its solid quality. Wolf speaks of the self as "elusive," and argues that "structure simply means stability over time" (p. 27)—much the same point I make in the text.

transmogrifies as we move from one situation to another. But if we cast aside the notion of a core self, how do we make sense of our experience of continuity? This dilemma points out the power of certain terminology over our thinking, for it seems that there is no way out of the box of foundationalist talk about a core self. Still, I believe a different kind of terminology can be employed, one that allows us to capture our intuitions of both change and continuity in the self.

I suggest that the self is *thickly constituted,* borrowing a term from the political theorist Michael Sandel (1982). Not only is the self responsive to the ever-changing situational environment; it is also rooted in the past situations through which it has come. It is in part a product of traditions, associations, and identifications that make up "where we have come from." When I say to a stranger that I am from Vermont, or from Colorado, I am gesturing to this important aspect of my self: something important about my self reflects my roots in those places; those places, and all that they held for me, have indeed helped constitute who I am. The self is richly put together with the expressive languages we have learned from a lifetime of interactions with significant others. Charles Taylor (1989) has described this as the dialogical character of human life. The reflexivity of the self means that we define ourselves in dialogue with others, perhaps even in struggle against the identities they would impose upon us.

Consequently, one dimension of the self that persists from moment to moment, that changes but continues, relates to the narrative lines we are developing in our lives. As we confront new situations, as we react to those who surround us, we work, often unconsciously, on the stories about ourselves we present to the world (and, reflexively, to ourselves). One's self is thickly constituted by these stories, many of which extend back into childhood. Most often, these narrative lines persist for years. But sometimes, as we shall see, they can change radically, old story lines can be dropped and new ones initiated.

My analysis of change and conversion seeks to unpack some of the ways in which a thickly constituted self, encapsulated in a body, self-aware, and caught up in an endless stream of situations, engages in the process of becoming. Conversions represent particularly startling periods of becoming, of self-transformation, of radical shifts in narrative lines, and they cast into high relief the characteristics of the layered self.

PSEUDOCHANGE

I want to begin to describe conversion by indicating what it is not. Some sorts of personal change, despite giving the appearance of transformation, present only a simulacrum of conversion. Such pseudochanges involve mere verbal or temporary behavioral shifts for the purpose of achieving particular goals. In pseudochange, persons more or less intentionally misrepresent themselves, pretending to have changed because they stand to profit or benefit from the appearance of change. Such persons play a role and do not identify with it, always maintaining a distinction between their "real" selves and their performances. Pseudochange, thus, entails a kind of impression management (Goffman, 1959), in which a person designs and presents a particular face to an audience; most often the presentation of this face involves telling a particular story about oneself. Of course, as Goffman has shown, all social actors engage in constant impression management; or as Peter Berger (1963, p. 135) expresses it, "in one way or another, we are all imposters." What distinguishes the impression management of pseudochangers is the conscious quality of their performance, a consciousness of presenting a particular self that differs from what they perceive to be their real self. Those caught up in the act of pseudochange provide the illusion of change; they consciously don the guise of change as the imposter dons the guise of the one imitated. Pseudochange, therefore, involves a reorganization of the outermost layer of the self—the layer we first present to others, the layer we consciously manipulate to serve our purposes.

Pseudochangers possess a stigma (the unreality of their change, the fact that they are only giving a performance) that could be discovered by their audience. Hence, such individuals are discreditable (Goffman, 1963), and while they carefully control the cues they give to their audience, they live in the consciousness that their bodies may give off cues that conflict with their performance and that will reveal them to be faking it. Further, pseudochangers are aware that their behavior "back stage" (Goffman, 1959), when they do not think they are "on," may contradict the cues given "front stage," as when the reformed alcoholic sneaks drinks, the reformed criminal commits a crime, or the minister of a conservative religion engages in some immoral act (e.g., hiring a prostitute or fraudulently garnering donations from the elderly).

Most often, individuals feigning positive change or alleging some kind of conversion have something to gain from the illusion of such transformations, and it is here that we see most clearly the reflexivity of the self. The drunk who alleges sobriety in Alcoholics Anonymous, or the felon who undergoes some form of miraculous transformation of behavior and personality through transcendental meditation, is sometimes up to mischief. Sometimes the deception is for conscious gain, and sometimes the deception is primarily self-deception. Indeed, a number of purposes may be served by presenting the face of a changed person. Such a presentation may be made in order to enable the person to get ahead, as when an inmate must seem to have changed in order to gain early release on parole or when one's social status depends upon having experienced conversion as it did in Puritan New England (Brauer, 1965). Alternatively, the mask of change may be donned simply for the thrill of "running a con" on some gullible victim. For example, many prison inmates tell visitors that they have "found Jesus" and turned their lives around, knowing full well that this is simply a line. Others may seek to seduce outsiders with their "sad tale" (Goffman, 1961), laughing later at the foolishness of their victims.

A more subtle, and less cynical, variation of the impression management of pseudochange involves a person's response to an immediate social environment in which everyone else in the social group claims to have achieved a rebirth or to have turned their lives around. Some persons appear to be what Snyder (1974) calls *high self-monitors,* who are quite sensitive to social cues and attuned to the behaviors demanded by particular situations. Rather than reveal a hidden stigma—she has not really turned her life around or been reborn, and hence is discreditable in her social group—the high self-monitor covers it up, seeking to "pass" (Goffman, 1963) by claiming a rebirth she knows has not occurred.

THE NATURE AND DYNAMICS OF CONVERSION

Personal change, however, does not always involve the conscious manipulation of the impressions one gives to others; not all those who profess to have changed are malingerers running a con on the system. Some persons experience a personal transformation that collapses the distinction between the role being played and "who one really is." These persons believe that they have turned themselves around, given up old and adopted new selves. In other words, these changes involve alteration of deeper layers of the self than were manipulated in pseudochange. We can speak of these transformations as conversions. Much can be learned about personal change from studying the momentous changes involved in conversions, whether these changes take on a religious character or whether they involve entering or exiting deviant and other self-defining roles.

The term *conversion* refers to a process of turning around or changing direction and involves a radical reorganization of identity, meaning, and life. All conversions entail a change in one's self-image, the view that one holds of one's own identity—a change in the self as self-understood. To change one's identity means to undergo the destruction of the old self and the construction of a new one. It means the transformation of the way one looks at oneself, of the terms within which one understands oneself, of the story one tells about oneself and one's place in the interactional world.

Additionally, conversion involves a tearing down of old cognitive frameworks and meaning systems, and a building up of new ones. As a result, one's understanding of the social and natural world changes significantly, though, as we shall see, this change sometimes may involve nothing more than a lateral shift of cognitive frameworks rather than any deeper revolution in psychological makeup. Finally, conversion entails a turning around of one's life, particularly in terms of external practices and ways of accounting for one's actions. Conversion brings with it dramatic change in one's speech and behavior; new patterns of everyday living come into existence for the convert, and for a time at least, the convert's existential reality is transformed.

As was asserted above, conversion refers not to a single, overwhelming event but to a *process* that occurs over time. For some the change may be experienced as abrupt and radical, and certainly many religious traditions describe conversion as a sudden transformation. Nevertheless, closer examination of these supposedly sudden changes reveals a preparatory process, a sequence of stages through which the convert progresses. The conversion process is characterized by shifts and oscillations (Adler & Adler, 1983), as the potential convert moves into and out of what can be referred to as a "sequence of uneasiness and solution" (see James, 1902/1958). In other words, the process is not a single smooth transition, but a series of forward jerks and backward slides. For example, conquering an addiction generally requires time, and importantly, the capacity to endure a string of failures. A positive relationship exists between both length of time in treatment and the number of separate courses of treatment, and the likelihood of success in treatment. Similar findings have become commonplace in criminal career research. Ending a career in crime, that is, converting to a conventional lifestyle, involves a process of phase-out, reentry, and repeated phase-out that can go on for years (e.g., Adler & Adler, 1983; Shover, 1985).

Caught up in the conversion sequence, perhaps seduced into it, the convert moves from a deeply felt crisis of self-doubt, to a surrender of the old self and old cognitive framework, to their replacement with a new self and new way of seeing things, to an attempt to carry the new vision of self and world into everyday life. I take up each of these stages in what follows.

Existential Crisis

In the first step of this sequence, the potential convert undergoes an existential crisis, in which she experiences a growing dissatisfaction with the self. This deep, existential dissatisfaction develops out of a felt discrepancy, either between what one's behavior suggests about one and the image one holds of oneself, or between what one perceives oneself to be and what one would like to be. The discrepancy may or may not be objectively real, but the potential convert experiences an acute tension that sets the stage for changes to come. Often the crisis is triggered by a deep "sense of sin" (James, 1902/1958, p. 198), in which one comes to experience one's immorality, crime, addiction, drunkenness, or class status as damnable. The sense of sin may be precipitated by immediate circumstances, as when one's drunken behavior lands one in jail or in a court-ordered treatment program. It is important to reiterate, however, that the crisis is usually the result of a growing unease, not a single, isolated event: while one may "hit bottom," one does so only after rolling down a long hill.

Crises can have many different sources and triggers. Persons seem susceptible to such deep-felt self-dissatisfaction at certain predictable moments in life, such as adolescent identity crises, midlife crises, periods of great change in one's external world (moving away from home, changing jobs, divorce, etc.). Of course because we develop our sense of self in interaction with others, because the self is reflexive, dialogical, and becoming, the growth of this feeling of unease may be fostered by significant others. The sense of sin that characterizes the existential crisis does not emerge fully articulated, but rather slowly grows in a symbiotic process: significant others begin to see one in a new and negative light, and communicate, haltingly, this altered perception; in response, one begins to doubt one's self, and so on.

Of course such crises of self-dissatisfaction may be dealt with through existing cognitive frames. One may, for example, cope with a growing feeling that one has a drinking problem by assuring oneself that nothing is wrong, that one drinks no more than anyone else, that the problem is only temporary, and so forth. In essence, this accounting behavior involves modifying the standard narrative one tells about oneself, tinkering with the wording while retaining the basic story line. Rather than give up the old interpretive frame, the convert seeks to modify it so as to make sense of the behavioral sources of increasing dis-ease.

Self-Surrender

Existential crises can vary in duration, intensity, and scope. After a time, however, it may no longer be possible to brush off the feelings of dissatisfaction through mere modification of one's old interpretive frame. When the old stories fail to account for one's changing perception of one's self, one enters the second stage of the conversion process: self-surrender, a giving up of one's old self (i.e., one's old conception of oneself). Unlike other scholars (e.g., Batson, Schoenrade, & Ventis, 1993), who have contended that self-surrender comes after one has reached a point of hopelessness and despair—what William James, borrowing a phrase from St. John of the Cross refers to as the "dark night of the soul"—I contend that the sense of sin involved in the crisis of self-dissatisfaction need not produce Kierkegaardian despair (though it might). The night is dark not because, or not entirely because, of the angst that pervades it, but also because it is no longer illumined by one's old frame and not yet lit up by the new one. Often all that is required to provoke a surrender of the old self is a sense of deep unease that seems unrelievable through less radical measures. The identification of oneself as a sinner slowly eats away at the attractiveness and utility of one's current life and current modes of understanding self and world, and makes surrender of that life and those meaning systems an increasingly attractive alternative.

Surely one critical influence prompting self-surrender comes from pressures outside of the self, particularly from influential, powerful, or valued persons and groups with whom one interacts. These pressures may be formalized. Goffman

(1961), for instance, has described how "total institutions" intentionally fashion the environment of the new inmate in such a way that the old self is broken down. Similarly, Garfinkel (1965) has examined the conditions under which "status degradation ceremonies" can be successful; that is, the circumstances under which others can successfully push the "denounced" into seeing the old self as a lower social type than had previously been thought. Generally, of course, the pressures from the surrounding environment are not this formal. Still, an analogous situation confronts any potential convert: the social environment pushes and pulls, sometimes compelling a dismantling of the old self.

Faced with inexorable pressures, from outside and from within, one can experience a deep emotional desire to strip off the old self. One longs to give up the old self and the old frame, and one parts with them with only an inkling of their replacements on the horizon. At this point one is very vulnerable, and very impressionable. It is here that intervention from others can push one into a new self, a new vision, a new frame through which to understand the world, one's self, and one's place in the world. The very availability of alternative story lines makes it easier to cast aside unraveling narratives about one's self. At this point one is ripe for conversion, a condition recognized by organizations seeking converts (particularly religious cults; e.g., Barker [1984]). These groups consciously look for persons in this highly susceptible state, or even seek to create this state of loss, recognizing intuitively the vulnerable reflexivity of the embryonic new self.

The New Self and Its Frame

Once the self has been surrendered the convert must adopt a new cognitive frame and build up (through interaction) a new self. I do not mean to imply here that the convert makes a conscious, calculated choice of cognitive frames or narrative lines. Instead, she "comes to tell her story this new way." She does not change roles in the way a person engaged in pseudochange would; the convert is not a performer, and there is a world of difference between the impression management of the pseudochanger and the unconscious and heart-felt narrative transformations undergone by the convert. The convert's new frame comes to replace, or perhaps, transcend, the old ways of thinking based on the old cognitive structure. Of course, the new frame may not transcend the old because one may stay on the same psychological ground, merely rearranging one's already existent cognitive furniture.

In any event, the adoption of the new frame permits a new way of seeing that will be understood as an insight. In specifically religious conversions, the insight seems to come from some transcendent realm. Even in conversions that are not religious in the traditional sense, such as conversions to the way of seeing espoused by 12-step recovery programs, transcendent power may be credited with the new insights into one's nature and one's place in the world (Alcoholics Anonymous, 1953). The new self emerges as a perceived recognition of who one really is, perhaps who one has always been. Thus, the new member of A.A. comes to see himself as, in essence, an alcoholic; the person with a newly discovered learning disability reinterprets her present and past life in terms of her "problem"; the person who has adopted a gay identity views homosexuality as the key to understanding who he is and has always been. Often, one learns to tell one's own story as one of decline and fall, a narrative move particularly characteristic of those diagnosed by authorities in the courtroom or the clinic. The shift in narrative line provides a psychologically helpful, retrospective reinterpretion of one's past life, an account of one's past behavior and one's transformation—for conversion is likely to be seen by one's previous associates, and perhaps by others in the outside world, as requiring an accounting. Indeed, one's old self would likely have seen the conversion as untoward and unjustifiable, if not beyond the pale.

Regardless, the situational reflexivity characteristic of the self means that this new vision is most often deeply affected by whom one is with, the members of one's primary reference group at the moment of the crisis. Dialogical selves respond to the interpretations of what is happening offered by significant others. It is their understanding of these changes that one most likely will come to share; further, it is their new definition of one's self that one is most likely to adopt. In total institutions, as Goffman (1961) points out, one receives the new cognitive frame, and the new self, through association or identification with the system that broke down the old self. Similar phenomena occur, and are meant to occur, in religious cults, military organizations, convents and seminaries, youth gangs, and many other settings. Indeed, something similar likely occurs in all conversions. Conversion experiences most often depend upon the existence of a group of others who can define for the convert the nature and meaning of the experience. Perhaps it is not too much to say that isolated conversion is very rare, if not impossible. Just as the novice user of psychoactive substances may need the help of experienced users in order to experience and appreciate the effects of a drug (Becker, 1967), so too the person who, prompted by "the deep sense of sin," has given up the old self and has entered a "state of temporary exhaustion" (James, 1902/1958, p. 208), relies on the interpretations of others to make sense of the whole process and to give content to the new cognitive frame.

The group's power in determining how one comes to redefine the self and reconstruct the cognitive frame is often (though not always) rooted in the development of a pattern of intensive interaction and the formation of close personal ties between the convert and the established members of the group (Barker, 1984; Lofland, 1966; Lofland and Stark, 1965). Many change programs, especially those seeking to break the hold of addictions over the lives of their clients, rely on the development of close bonds and regular, intense association between new participants and program veterans and staff. Further, identity shifts among criminals and drug users tend to be bound up with intense interaction with others in criminal or drug-using groups.

The Reconstruction of Life

In the fourth stage of conversion, the individual reconstructs her life in accordance with the vision contained in the new cognitive frame. Most frame shifts require dramatic changes in behavior as the new self becomes entrenched. This stage in the process is analogous to what labeling theorists have called "secondary deviance" (Lemert, 1951; Becker, 1963), where the identification of oneself as a new kind of person, both to oneself and publicly, leads to the adoption of the auxiliary traits associated with a convert of that sort. These auxiliary traits may include patterns of speech, styles of dress and grooming, and subsidiary habits of the established group members. The adoption of these traits, however, can drastically alter the nature of one's daily life, as one's old activities and associates are cast aside and new ones taken up.

One of the most noteworthy traits of the new convert is the deep sense of assurance that informs her interaction with others. The convert adopts a new outlook on everyday life, entailing both a loss of worry and a new sense of truth. The convert finds that the feeling of unease that triggered the conversion process withers away as the self-concerns that brought about the existential crisis disappear. One comes to feel that all is well, at least as long as one adheres to the path laid out in the new mental frame one has adopted. Thus, for example, those who take up transcendental meditation develop a sense of well-being and harmony, and this newfound peace is reflected in how TM practitioners score on psychological tests and in their decreased disciplinary problems and initially lower rates of recidivism (Abrams & Siegel, 1978; Alexander & Marks, 1982; Bleick & Abrams, 1987; Dillbeck & Abrams, 1987; Murray, 1991). Surely converts of other sorts experience similar feelings of peace and harmony with life.

In addition, converts become imbued with a new sense of truth, in which what was previously mysterious becomes lucid. The new cognitive frame adopted by the convert equips her with answers to the questions that once deeply troubled her: Why is the world this way? Why do I drink uncontrollably? Why do I commit crimes? Why am I so violent? Many change programs generate in their clients, at least for a time, a profound sense of certainty, an unshakable belief that they have discovered the Truth about themselves, about others, and about their world. The truths of which the convert is now so sure are, of course, very largely borrowed from the associational world in which the conversion took place. The new religious convert, for example, typically learns a new theology through interaction with established members of the group. In particular, one learns how this theology provides the answers to previously troubling questions—indeed provides answers (of some sort) to all questions—and, consequently, one is (for a time, at least) deeply imbued with a sense of the truth of one's new faith.

NARRATIVE CONVERSION

Of course, the same process can produce both deep change and lack of deep change or even regression. The conversion process may end in "a flight from everyday life into an otherworldly fantasy," emotional dependence through attachment to or infatuation with a religious leader or group, or the imposition of "rigid and arbitrary conceptualizations on one's experience in the form of dogmatic beliefs and rules for conduct" (Batson et al., 1993, p. 107). While the outer layers of the self may change, inner or deeper layers may remain the same, at least in the sense that even after conversion one deals with the world in ways that are structurally similar to the ways one has always dealt with the world.

Many, perhaps most, conversions are what I will call narrative conversions. Experienced by the convert as deep personal change of one's core being, narrative conversion does involve striking changes in the self. As with all conversions, and as opposed to the impression management and high self-monitoring of pseudochange, the convert takes on a new self-identity, changing her self-definition and adopting a new self-perception. She also presents herself differently to others and learns to talk about herself and her world in a new language. Any misrepresentation that occurs in the new story she tells about herself is unintentional, although cynical others may assume she is intentionally deceiving herself and others.

The person undergoing narrative conversion embraces her new way of being, sinking into or merging with what could have been a role. In conversion one loses the sense that one is presenting a self; indeed, the language of self-presentation (however applicable it may be in an external, coldly analytical sense) seems incongruous here. One feels as if one's old self has been transformed, has become a new "real self." Consequently, the convert no longer experiences the role distance characteristic of the person engaged in pseudochange, who is managing impressions in a more or less conscious way. It might be a mistake to think that the convert has somehow managed to integrate all self presentations into a single self—even the converted self remains layered and diversified and only the rare person interacts with all others in exactly the same way. Still, the dominant feature here is the convert's embrace of and identification with the new way of being. The new story told by the convert is a tale about what she believes to be her "real self"; certainly the convert herself does not, indeed cannot, experience this story as a mask donned for a performance. To the convert, there is no gap between the self as presented and the real self. From the perspective of the convert, conversion involves a collapsing of the distinction between front stage and back stage as the performance and the perceived real self converge. While the pseudochanger feels she is and must be "on," the convert does not—in the mind of the convert no role is being played and the world has ceased to be a stage.

Nevertheless, the structure of the new meaning system adopted by the convert often bears a remarkable similarity to the structure of the old, abandoned system. The cognitive change undergone by the narrative convert, what Berger and Luckmann (1966, p. 157) have labeled *alternation,* involves a shift from one cognitive organization to another, though often at essentially the same level of complexity. Someone may shift from unquestioning allegiance to the John Birch Society to unquestioning allegiance to a radical left-wing group, or from one religious cult to a drastically different one, without an increase in the differentiation or integration of one's cognitive structures (Miller, 1994). The narrative line has changed, but the shift has been horizontal: one has moved from one cognitive framework to another without altering the complexity of that framework; the number of organizing principles, the level of organization, and the interaction and interpenetration of existing principles remain the same.

Of course, it may be that some conversions involve something more than alternation (Travisano, 1975). Certainly all conversions involve an "Aha!" experience of "insight" as one's horizons drastically shift, and while this does not necessarily connote change at any deeper psychological level, such change cannot be ruled out altogether. Still, it seems to me that conversion entails both change and stability: at those layers of the self most susceptible to observation, where important narrative lines and behavior have indeed been transformed, one has changed (often significantly); at other layers of the self, however, the continuity can be striking. Often the complexity of one's frame has remained virtually the same, and even where more complex frames have emerged some story lines persist, though in an altered form to take account of one's conversion. It seems odd to suggest, for example, that St. Augustine was a totally new person after his conversion, for many narrative lines he had been pursuing (his intellectual interests, for instance) persisted into the new life fostered by his conversion.

To an extent, the narrative convert displays a reduced tendency to be consciously influenced by the expectations of others. Unlike the high self-monitor, who is concerned with the beneficial presentation of the proper face to others, the narrative convert believes deeply that the story she tells about herself is true. Nevertheless, much of that story has been drawn from the interactive web in which she has ensconced herself, so the attitudes and views of others still exert a good deal of power over the convert. There is room for much variation here. Those who enter into strong affective affiliation with a new group (such as converts to the Moonies) will be much more influenced by the understandings of the members of the group. Those whose affective affiliation with a new group is not as great will be influenced less by the group in developing their new narrative of self, and their stories will be more heavily influenced by individual personality or larger cultural variables.

Finally, while the person engaged in conscious impression management takes personal responsibility for her actions only because doing so puts up the right sort of verbal front, the narrative convert evinces a greater willingness to feel, and to assert, her responsibility for herself, her actions, and her effects on others. Still, the narrative convert tends to be bound by a sense that much about her and her world are out of her control or in the hands of a "higher power"—a feature of both religious transformations and conversions to more secular cognitive frames (e.g., Peele, 1989).

BEYOND NARRATIVE CONVERSION

Much more could be said concerning types and styles of conversion. Rambo (1993, pp. 12–14), for instance, distinguishes between five types of conversion based upon the extent to which someone moves socially and culturally. Lofland and Skonovd (1981) offer a theory of "conversion motifs," rooted in the sorts of defining experiences that distinguish between types of conversion. Certainly a complete theory of conversion must address such variations in the conversion process. Conversion is not, except in the most general sense, a single, universal process. Instead it takes on many different guises and themes depending on the full range of sociological, psychological, and historical factors influencing the convert's organization of experience.

On the present occasion, however, I want to close by briefly considering a different, indeed preliminary, issue: whether a justifiable distinction can be made between what I have here termed narrative conversion and some more genuine, some deeper or higher, sort of conversion. While this possibility remains open to empirical investigation, I confess to being skeptical that such a distinction can be grounded.

A Picture of Deep Change

What would more-than-narrative change look like? Such conversions would entail change on a different level than that involved in narrative conversion, requiring a movement into a more sophisticated order of thinking and being. While the narrative convert has learned new ways of talking about her self, the person undergoing deeper transformation would exhibit movement into and within ever-deeper layers of the self. Perhaps this would mean change not only of the story but also of cognitive and emotional structures and sensory/perceptual apparatus. Perhaps we could put this in Piagetian terms: while narrative conversion involves cognitive "assimilation," deeper structural transformation involves "accommodation"—an increase in the differentiation and integration of one's cognitive structures. Such a convert moves from a cognitive framework at one level of complexity to a new framework at a higher (or deeper) level, involving an increase in the number of organizing principles, the level of organization, and the interaction and interpenetration of existing principles. In addition, deep structural change may entail more than mere cognitive transformation, encompassing broader, more comprehensive, more holistic change, that is, changes in and across multiple structural domains.

Perhaps one could argue that one salient difference between narrative conversion and deeper change relates to the convert's openness to further transformation. Looked at in terms of the ideologies professed by narrative converts, narrative conversions tend to be closed to further change; indeed, they tend to foreclose it, locking the convert into an unshakable truth system. Where the new reality is dogmatic, one cannot imagine it being improved; hence, further development is discouraged. Nevertheless, it is often these dogmatic converts who are most likely to change, to shift to a new set of truths, a new interpretive frame, to undergo what we could call serial conversion (Balch & Taylor, 1977). Deeper transformation, on the other hand, ideologically invites further transformation (Batson et al., 1993, p. 107; Halpern, 1993); looked at in its own terms, such a transformation appears to be open-ended, reflexive, and tentative, recognizing the contingency of current understandings. In these hypothetical, deeper level changes, the door is left open for further development and transformation.

Epistemology and Real Change

Clinical practitioners tell us that they have witnessed change that appears to be more than narrative. Our measures of development seem to spot noteworthy differences between what I have termed narrative conversion and something else, something "deeper," something longer lasting. Some fascinating research has been done, for example, on the sorts of changes to be found in those whose lives have been "turned around" by TM (Abrams & Siegel, 1978; Alexander & Marks, 1982; Bleick & Abrams, 1987; Dillbeck & Abrams, 1987; Murray, 1991).

But caution is in order. Given the epistemological principles implied throughout my discussion, we should hesitate to leap from the observation that our measures seem to reveal something different and deeper than changes in the way we talk about ourselves and our world, to the claim that these measures are capturing something other than narrative changes. We tell the stories of our lives in many different ways. Virtually all of the measures we employ to explore personal change simply measure behavior or what one says. Physiological changes (such as those isolated by TM researchers) may simply be the product of the telling of new stories; feeling better about oneself, a common outcome of conversion, may produce less stress in one's life, but that does not necessarily mean that more-than-narrative change has occurred. Sophisticated personality inventories (such as the F-scale and similar measures of deep personality) may merely slip past high self-monitors, digging beneath the consciously managed impressions to reveal who one is "back stage"; in other words, they unearth deeper narratives but do not (as far as we can tell) get below all narratives to any real self within. Once we have given up the belief in some ghost in the machine lying at the center of our being, we must be cautious in assuming that our sophisticated measures capture anything other than ever-deeper sorts of narrative.

Of course, setting aside the view that real change can be contrasted with narrative change does not mean that important, profound, and valuable personal change does not take place. To suggest that most conversion is narrative is not meant to demean conversion or those who experience it. Quite the contrary. To begin to tell, with all the fervor of one witnessing to the truth, a new story about oneself is a momentous, life-changing experience. It is felt as profound by the convert because it is profound.

FUTURE DIRECTIONS

A range of avenues for future research are opened up by the analysis of the nature and dynamics of change I have presented. For one, we should continue the effort to develop measures to assess the different kinds of change I have described. This would involve the evaluation of existing measures of personal change and development and a revision of those measures found to achieve a modicum of success in distinguishing among the varieties of conversion. In addition, new measures could be developed to examine the varieties of narrative and the dimensions of narrative change involved in conversion.

Continued research needs to be conducted exploring the factors that influence the conversion process. These factors derive from a variety of contexts and sources. Social factors play a critical role in generating and structuring the conversion process. Such factors range from distal social factors (large-scale social and cultural factors), to factors in the convert's immediate social environment (subcultures, neighborhood characteristics, messages communicated by friends and other associates), to situational factors (the immediate interactive context in which action takes place). Likewise, personality factors undoubtedly exercise a powerful influence. Working from the notion of the layered self, or some similar conception, future research can explore more adequately these social and psychological factors that help define the nature and dynamics of conversion and the ontological characteristics of the self.

REFERENCES

Abrams, A. I., & Siegel, L. M. (1978). The Transcendental Meditation Program and rehabilitation at Folsom State Prison: A cross-validation study. *Criminal Justice and Behavior, 5,* 3–20.

Adler, P. A., & Adler, P. (1983). Shifts and oscillations in deviant careers: The case of upper-level drug dealers and smugglers. *Social Problems, 31,* 195–207.

Alcoholics Anonymous. (1953). *Twelve Steps and Twelve Traditions.* New York: Alcoholics Anonymous.

Alexander, C. N., & Marks, E. J. (1982). Ego development, personality and behavioral change in inmates practicing the Transcendental Meditation technique or participating in other programs: A summary of cross-sectional and longitudinal results. In D. Orme-Johnson & J. Farrow (Eds.), *Scientific research on the Transcendental Meditation Program: Collected papers* (Vol. 1, pp. 2127–2134). Rheinweiler, Germany: MERU Press.

Balch, R. W., & Taylor, D. (1977). Seekers and saucers. *American Behavioral Scientist, 20,* 839–860.

Barker, E. (1984). *The making of a Moonie: Brainwashing or choice?.* New York: Basil Blackwell.

Batson, C. D., Schoenrade, P., & Ventis, L. (1993). *Religion and the individual.* Oxford: Oxford University Press.

Becker, H. S. (1963). *Outsiders: Studies in the sociology of deviance.* New York: Free Press.

Becker, H. S. (1967). History, culture, and subjective experience: An exploration of the social bases of drug-induced experiences. *Journal of Health and Social Behavior, 8,* 163–176.

Berger, P. L. (1963). *Invitation to sociology: A humanistic perspective.* Garden City, NY: Doubleday.

Berger, P. L., & Luckmann, T. (1966). *The social construction of reality.* Garden City, NY: Doubleday.

Bleick, C. R., & Abrams, A. I. (1987). The Transcendental Meditation Program and criminal recidivism in California. *Journal of Criminal Justice, 15,* 211–230.

Brauer, J. C. (1965). *Protestantism in America: A narrative history.* Philadelphia: Westminster Press.

Cullen, F. T. (1983). *Rethinking crime and deviance theory: The emergence of a structuring tradition.* Totowa, NJ: Rowman & Allanheld.

Dillbeck, M. C., & Abrams, A. I. (1987). The application of the Transcendental Meditation Program to corrections. *International Journal of Comparative and Applied Criminal Justice, 11,* 111–132.

Fontana, A. (1984). Introduction: Existential sociology and the self. In J. A. Kotarba & A. Fontana (Eds.), *The existential self in society* (pp. 3–17). Chicago: University of Chicago Press.

Garfinkel, H. (1965). Conditions of successful degradation ceremonies. *American Journal of Sociology, 61,* 420–424.

Goffman, E. (1959). *The presentation of self in everyday life.* Garden City, NY: Doubleday.

Goffman, E. (1961). *Asylums: Essays on the social situation of mental patients and others.* Garden City, NY: Doubleday.

Goffman, E. (1963). *Stigma: Notes on the management of spoiled identity.* Englewood Cliffs, NJ: Prentice-Hall.

Halpern, M. (1993). *Transformation: Essays for a work in progress.* Unpublished manuscript, Princeton University, Department of Politics.

James, W. (1958). *The varieties of religious experience.* New York: Modern Library. (Original work published in 1902)

Katz, J. (1988). *Seductions of crime: Moral and sensual attractions in doing evil.* New York: Basic Books.

Kohut, H. (1977). *The restoration of the self.* New York: International Universities Press.

Lemert, E. M. (1951). *Social pathology.* New York: McGraw-Hill.

Lofland, J. (1966). *Doomsday cult.* Englewood Cliffs, NJ: Prentice-Hall.

Lofland, J., & Skonovd, N. (1981). Conversion motifs. *Journal for the Scientific Study of Religion, 20,* 372–385.

Lofland, J., & Stark, R. (1965). Becoming a world-saver: A theory of conversion to a deviant perspective. *American Sociological Review, 30,* 862–875.

Luckenbill, D. F. (1977). Criminal homicide as a situated transaction. *Social Problems, 25,* 176–186.

Mead, G. H. (1934). *Mind, self and society: From the standpoint of a social behaviorist.* Chicago: University of Chicago Press.

Miller, M. E. (1994). World views, ego development, and epistemological changes from the conventional to the postformal: A longitudinal perspective. In M. E. Miller & S. R. Cook-Greuter (Eds.), *Transcendence and mature thought in adulthood* (pp. 147–179). Lanham, MD: Rowman & Littlefield.

Murray, D. M. (1991). Transcendental Meditation can offer peaceful road to rehabilitation. *Corrections Today, 53,* 112–117.

Peele, S. (1989). *Diseasing of America: Addiction treatment out of control.* Lexington, MA: Lexington Books.

Rambo, L. R. (1993). *Understanding religious conversion.* New Haven, CT: Yale University Press.

Sandel, M. J. (1982). *Liberalism and the limits of justice.* Cambridge, U.K.: Cambridge University Press.

Shover, N. (1985). *Aging criminals.* Beverly Hills, CA: Sage.

Snyder, M. (1974). Self-monitoring of expressive behavior. *Journal of Personality and Social Psychology, 30,* 526–537.

Taylor, C. (1989). *Sources of the self.* Cambridge, MA: Harvard University Press.

Travisano, R. (1975). Alternation and conversion as qualitatively different transformations. In D. Brissett & C. Edgley (Eds.), *Life as theater* (pp. 91–103). Chicago: Aldine.

Wolf, E. (1988). *Treating the self: Elements of clinical self psychology.* New York: Guilford Press.

14.

Conversions across the Culture War Divide: Two Case Studies

Lene Arnett Jensen

On the basis of an analysis of public debates pertaining to issues such as abortion, sexuality, and family policy, the sociologist James Davison Hunter (1991, 1994) argues that contemporary America is experiencing a "culture war." The culture war pits groups that tend toward "orthodoxy" against groups that tend toward "progressivism." It is cultural in the sense that the two sides have markedly different moral conceptions. For example, those who are orthodox hold that moral precepts are revealed to humans by a transcendent authority, whereas those who are progressivist emphasize human agency in understanding and formulating moral precepts. It is a war in the sense that the two sides often engage in acrimonious exchanges.

In my research, I have found that the public division pointed out by Hunter between orthodox and progressivist outlooks also finds expression in ordinary Americans' moral evaluations and reasoning (Jensen, 1997a, 1998). In-depth interviews and questionnaires have shown that fundamentalist

This research was supported by a grant to Richard A. Shweder from the John D. and Catherine T. MacArthur Foundation Research Network on Successful Mid-Life Development, Gilbert Brim, Chair.

Baptists (representing the orthodox side) and mainline Baptists (representing the progressivist side) are markedly divided in their moral evaluations and reasoning on issues such as divorce and abortion. This division has been found within groups of young, midlife, and older adults.

The present aim is to explore the appeal of orthodoxy and progressivism, as well as the rejection of these worldviews. A phenomenological account will be given of two conversion experiences: one from orthodoxy to progressivism, and the other from progressivism to orthodoxy. Following sociologists such as Travisano (1970) and Heirich (1977), a conversion experience is understood as a radical change in identity and worldview. In McGuire's (1982) words, a conversion is a "transformation of self concurrent with a redefinition of one's central meaning system" (p. 49).

Here, the converts were two men. One was a highly conservative Southern Baptist minister who left his job and orthodox worldview behind. He now describes himself as "liberal," and is enrolled in a clinical psychology program. The other man was a self-described "atheist" with "rather liberal" views who went from trying to prove Christians wrong to himself adopting an orthodox worldview. He is now a member of a fundamentalist Baptist church. This chapter will provide an account of the men's conversion experiences in their own words—what the anthropologist Clifford Geertz (1983) calls "experience-near" concepts. Their accounts will also be related to the theories and observations of social scientists regarding religion, the culture war, and conversion experiences—what Geertz calls "experience-distant" concepts.

THE CULTURE WAR

James Davison Hunter's Analysis

Before turning to the two case studies in leaps of faith, I will review the literature on America's culture war. Hunter (1991, 1994) has examined the opposing political alliances that have been forged on a wide variety of current issues in American society, including those pertaining to abortion, sexuality, family policy, and the content of education and media (see also Bellah, 1987; Jensen, 1995; Neuhaus, 1990; Wuthnow, 1988, 1989). He has also examined the moral and political discourse of public figures. On the basis of his analyses, Hunter argues that the old lines between religious denominations have collapsed when it comes to moral and political issues. It is no longer the case that moral debates tend to divide different religious denominations, such as Protestants, Catholics, and Jews. Instead, according to Hunter, a new division has occurred within religious denominations and in American culture more generally. It is a division that is vividly seen in the political arena, but the political clashes reflect a deeper division over the sources of moral authority and the extent of individual autonomy. Hunter suggests that American people and groups are divided in terms of what he calls "the impulse toward orthodoxy" versus "the impulse toward progressivism" (p. 43).

Briefly described, those who are orthodox share a commitment to transcendent authority, an authority that is independent of, prior to, and more powerful than human experience. In the orthodox view, this transcendent authority originated a moral code and revealed it to human beings. Different religious traditions have different conceptions of the sources through which transcendence communicates its authority (for example, Jews look to the Torah and the community that upholds it; Protestants look to the Old and New Testaments). However, all orthodox regard moral precepts as given to humans by a transcendent being, and they regard these precepts as sufficient for all times and circumstances. Accordingly, moral precepts ought not to be altered to accommodate societal changes, or new human understandings, or individual differences. Rather, individuals and societies ought to adapt themselves in accordance with the moral precepts ordained by the transcendent authority.

In contrast to the orthodox, progressivists stress the importance of human agency in understanding and formulating moral precepts. They reject the view that a transcendent authority directly reveals itself and its will to humans. Instead moral (and spiritual) truths are expressed by humans. Progressivists vary in the basis on which they arrive at moral precepts. Some progressivists draw upon scientific evidence about the human condition. As pointed out by Hunter (1991), this approach is derived from the intellectual tradition of Enlightenment naturalism. Other progressivists draw upon their personal experiences. This approach is derived from the intellectual tradition of Enlightenment subjectivism. However, progressivists unite in a focus upon human understanding and formulation of moral precepts. Progressivists also unite in regarding moral precepts as changeable, because human and individual understandings evolve and societal circumstances change.

As should be clear, Hunter's categories of orthodoxy and progressivism are broad and a caveat is necessary. While American culture might show a marked division between impulses toward orthodoxy and progressivism, this should not be taken to mean that all political groups—let alone all individual Americans—can be classified neatly into two camps. The categories describe two general types, and it is recognized that some groups and individuals possess characteristics of each.

Ordinary Americans and the Culture War

In his writings, Hunter (1991, 1994) primarily focuses upon the views of publicly active figures and groups who are orthodox and progressivist. He does not analyze the moral reasoning of ordinary Americans who might tend toward orthodoxy and progressivism, respectively. In research with ordinary Americans, I have found that they also give voice to orthodox and progressivist moral outlooks (Jensen, 1997a, 1998). Next, I will provide a brief description of this research.

An interview study and a questionnaire study were carried out with fundamentalist Baptists, representing the orthodox side, and mainline Baptists, representing the progressivist side.[1]

[1] The interview study included 40 participants and the questionnaire study included 120 participants, with equal numbers in each group. The fundamentalist Baptists attended independent Baptist churches that self-identify as "fundamentalist." The mainline Baptists attended a church that has a dual affiliation with the American Baptist Churches/

The participants ranged in age from 19 to 84 years. The studies included only members of one religious tradition in order to capture the extent to which the division between orthodox and progressivist views is occurring within traditions, as Hunter (1991, 1994) describes it.

Results of the two studies showed that the orthodox and progressivist groups were markedly different in their moral evaluations of such practices as suicide, divorce, and abortion. Orthodox participants were generally more likely to evaluate these practices as morally wrong compared to progressivist participants.

The orthodox and progressivist groups also differed markedly in their moral reasoning. The participants' reasoning was analyzed in terms of Richard Shweder's (1990) three ethics of autonomy, community, and divinity. These three ethics entail different conceptions of the moral agent. Briefly, moral reasoning within the ethic of autonomy centers on the individual's rights and well-being. Within the ethic of community, the focus is on persons' obligations and relations to members of their social groups, such as family and nation. The focus of the ethic of divinity is a person's adherence to sacred guidelines and quest to connect with the divine.

In both the interview and questionnaire studies, progressivists reasoned more in terms of the ethic of autonomy than did orthodox participants. Orthodox participants reasoned more in terms of the ethic of divinity than did progressivists. However, progressivist and orthodox groups seldom differed significantly in their use of the ethic of community. These findings on the moral reasoning of orthodox and progressivist participants were consistent within groups of young, midlife, and older adults (Jensen, 1997a).

The results suggest that the public moral division detailed by Hunter also finds expression in ordinary Americans' moral thought. The orthodox and progressivist groups differed markedly in their moral evaluations of right and wrong, and in their moral reasoning. Orthodox participants repeatedly emphasized divine guidelines in explaining their moral views. In their

USA and the Southern Baptist Convention. The latter, affiliation, however, is regarded as historic.

view, God provides human beings with moral precepts. These precepts are given to humans in order that we may to the best of our abilities fulfill God's purposes for us. In the orthodox view, the moral precepts should serve to structure communal life and the lives of individuals. God has indicated that such practices as divorce, abortion, and ending one's life are morally wrong, except in a few particular circumstances. If individuals and communities allow these practices, they are defying God's will. Rather, individuals and communities ought to adhere to the divinely ordained moral precepts.

The progressivist participants focused considerably less on God's word, will, or agency in human affairs and the lives of individuals. Instead, they focused more upon the choices that we must make in life. In explaining the basis upon which choices are made, progressivists often referred to how individuals have the right to make choices. They also often referred to the outcomes of choices. For example, they considered whether the choices are useful and whether they lead to happiness for the self (and for others). The progressivists, then, emphasized that each individual to a large extent is free to make autonomous choices. Thus the progressivist participants were less willing to demand adherence to moral codes than the orthodox adults because they gave more consideration to individual inclinations. For example, they were less willing to set limits on the extent to which individuals might divorce, or have an abortion, or commit suicide.

Different Morals, Different Worldviews

As I have argued elsewhere, the division in moral evaluations and reasoning between the orthodox and progressivist groups has its basis in their different and more comprehensive worldviews (Jensen, 1997b). Typically, a worldview provides an account of what it means to be human, the nature of reality, and the reasons and remedies for human suffering (Walsh & Middleton, 1984; see also Berger, 1967; Luckmann, 1963).

Briefly, the orthodox participants' moral reasoning is based upon a worldview that regards humans as created by God, subject to God's authority, and striving to be in the presence of God in the next world. According to the orthodox worldview, we are living in a increasingly corrupt world where the inherent human propensity for sinful behavior is not kept properly in check. To overcome this state of affairs, we ought to follow God's guidelines. If we do this, according to the orthodox worldview, human suffering is alleviated in this world and we gain entry to God's heavenly realm.

In contrast, progressivist moral reasoning is based upon quite a different worldview. This worldview focuses upon this world, and upon individual rights and communal needs within it. It holds that every human being has considerable rights to self-determination and self-expression. What limits these rights are the responsibilities to others that come from living in society. In this world, human suffering is alleviated and progress occurs when we institute practices that respect individual rights and reduce social injustices.

TWO CASE STUDIES

Given the marked differences between the two worldviews, conversions from orthodoxy to progressivism and from progressivism to orthodoxy are striking experiences. They are also experiences that may offer insights into the appeal as well as the rejection of the worldviews. In the following, a case study in each of these two kinds of conversion experiences will be presented.

The case studies here are drawn from my interview study with mainline and fundamentalist Baptists (Jensen, 1998). As described above, participants in this study were asked to respond to general moral practices such as divorce and abortion. They were also asked to describe a memorable personal moral experience. In response to this request, two men recounted their conversion experiences.[2] Table 14.1 provides a demographic sketch of the two men.

[2] It might be noted that only 25% of the orthodox interviewees indicated that they had grown up attending a fundamentalist or evangelical church. Among the progressivist

TABLE 14.1
Demographic Profiles of John and Kyle

	From Orth. to Prog.	From Prog. to Orth.
Name	John Scott-Warner	Kyle Schultz
Childhood Religion	Southern Baptist	None
Present Religion	Mainline Baptist	Fundamentalist Baptist
Age	45	38
Race	Caucasian	Caucasian
Marital Status	Married	Married
No. of Children	0	5
Education	Postcollege	Postcollege
Occupation	Ph.D. Student	Professor in Mathematics
Salary	$36,000-50,000	Above $50,000

John Scott-Warner[3] grew up the son of a conservative Southern Baptist minister, and at the age of 23 became a Southern Baptist minister himself. However, in 1988 at the age of 37, he had become so dissatisfied with his position and the views that he was expected to preach that he decided to leave his job. Instead, he entered a Ph.D. program in clinical psychology. In the years that followed, John proceeded to leave his orthodox worldview further and further behind. He withdrew his membership from the Southern Baptist Convention and instead became a member of a mainline Baptist church. Today, he describes himself as "liberal" and liberated. In John's own words: "I identify so much with women's issues because I was kept in my place for such as long time. I was oppressed. . . . I'm one of the Virginia Slims commercials: 'You've come a long way baby!' "

Kyle Schultz has also experienced quite a change in his worldview, albeit a very different one. He describes it in the following way: "It's an amazing transformation. Because I was not only an atheist, I was also rather liberal. Now I'm a Christian and somewhat conservative. So the majority of my views have

interviewees, 80% indicated that they had grown up attending a mainline Protestant church.

[3] The names of the participants have been changed in order to protect their confidentiality. However, the names used here were chosen so as to resemble the men's own names in key respects. This was done in recognition of the fact that naming practices often reflect an underlying worldview. For example, in line with their own names, a biblical name was chosen for John but not for Kyle. Also, a hyphenated last name was chosen for John but not for Kyle.

changed a great deal." Kyle's mother came from a Mormon background and his father from an Episcopalian one. However, the family did not attend church when Kyle grew up and his parents wanted their children to decide independently upon their worldviews and spiritual beliefs. Explaining his parents' philosophy, Kyle said, "[They] didn't want to impose anything on us whatsoever. . . . The way I was raised was that everyone has their own choice and [that] you should be basically free to do anything you want. [We had] no religious training whatsoever." However, in the course of what Kyle estimates to be a 12-year process beginning shortly after college, he adopted an orthodox worldview. Today at age 38, Kyle is a member of a Baptist church that self-identifies as fundamentalist, and he and his wife are home schooling their five children in an effort to ensure that the children embrace the orthodox worldview.

Caveats

I have chosen to detail John and Kyle's conversion experiences because they speak to the appeal of orthodoxy and progressivism as well as their rejection. However, before proceeding, several caveats are necessary. First, John and Kyle's experiences may provide insights into the phenomena of conversion, orthodoxy, and progressivism. As with all case studies, however, their experiences cannot easily be generalized. In many respects, John and Kyle's conversions may be unique. When their individual accounts overlap with more general social science findings pertaining to conversion and religion, this will be pointed out.

Second, the two case studies detailed here pertain to persons whose conversion experiences have occurred within the specific religious and philosophical traditions of Baptism and atheism. Their conversions are described as switches from orthodoxy to progressivism and vice versa in line with Hunter's (1991) evidence that the commonalities within progressivist and orthodox outlooks (respectively) carry across different religious denominations and philosophical traditions. However, it should also be kept in mind that there are important differences in the theological and moral conceptions between different Protestant groups, as well as between Protestants and other religious and philosophical traditions.

Third, the case studies are limited to two men. It is possible that women and men differ in their conversion experiences, as well as in what they find attractive or objectionable about orthodoxy and progressivism. Recent research has examined the appeal of Orthodox Judaism to women who came from non-Orthodox backgrounds or who had fallen away from Orthodox Judaism (Davidman, 1991; Kaufman, 1991). Among other things, the women in this research recounted being strongly attracted to the clearly delineated gender roles within Orthodox Judaism, and to the high regard for the roles of wife and mother in the Orthodox Judaic community. The question of whether women and men differ in their conversion experiences to orthodoxy and progressivism is interesting, and one that research has yet to address.

Finally, John and Kyle's conversion experiences are striking because of the radical changes occurring in their worldviews and identities. However, the striking quality of their conversions should not be taken to mean that they are deviant. Sociologists have urged that conversions not be regarded as "odd experiences" (Heirich, 1977, p. 677) or as a "fringe" phenomenon (Greil & Rudy, 1983, p. 5), but rather as a fundamental, though not necessarily common, part of human experience. As Heirich (1977) suggests, a conversion can be regarded as an experience at the individual level akin to Thomas Kuhn's (1970) notion of a paradigm shift occurring at the group level—an occurrence that Kuhn also regards as fundamentally part of human history.

From Orthodoxy to Progressivism: John's Account

Let us now turn to the two conversion experiences, beginning with John's account. John's conversion was extended and gradual. He described it as "a decision that I made over a long term.

It wasn't very quickly done.'' Key events in John's conversion occurred many years apart. He resigned his position as a Southern Baptist minister in 1988 at the age of 37, but only 6 years later at the age of 43 did he withdraw his membership from the Southern Baptist Convention. Only by then did he entirely dissociate his views and identity from the Southern Baptist community. Only by then had he finally come to the view that, ''I am not one of these people. I can't in any way endorse what they're saying.''

The extended nature of John's conversion sets it apart from the mystical conversions that was the primary focus of scholars such as William James (1902/1936), Edwin Starbuck (1911), and E. T. Clark (1929) in the earlier part of this century. These conversions occurred suddenly and often dramatically in persons who experienced a loss of control and a sense of being subject to forces outside of themselves. Instead, John's conversion fits better with John Lofland and Norman Skonovd's (1981) notion of an ''experimental'' conversion. This kind of conversion involves a slow and tentative transformation of identity with behavioral changes often preceding gradual changes in beliefs (for examples of experimental conversions, see Davidman [1991]; Straus [1979]).

Since John's conversion took place over an extended period of time and involved several different events, it may be helpful to preview the key themes of John's account before turning to his own words. John began by describing his initial discontent with his job as a minister. Then followed an event that was pivotal to his resignation from his job. In the course of the next 6 years, John increasingly dissociated himself from the Southern Baptist Convention on matters of faith, morality, and politics until another pivotal issue led him to withdraw his membership from the convention. John ended his account by assessing his conversion as a process that has been conducive to his psychological health and sense of freedom. However, he also pointed out that his conversion has had negative consequences in that he has experienced an estrangement from his family and some of his friends.

Discontent and Tension

As just mentioned, John began by describing how he had become increasingly discontented with his job as a minister. His discontent went hand in hand with strong emotional tension. John explained:

> I grew up as a Southern Baptist and was a Southern Baptist minister. . . . I grew up in a minister's family. What I realized [was that] I lived in a glass house growing up, and I chose to live in a glass house even [as an adult]—always exposed to public view. What I realized was [that] living in a glass house is a very tentative kind of arrangement. It's very bounded and the freedoms are very, very limited. . . . In essence, I was really discovering that I couldn't have my own views. I could have them privately but I couldn't have them any other place, except in very limited ways. So, that began to be a very troubling thought.
>
> And I realized that *personally* and psychologically, it was very limiting as well. Because I kept feeling caged up and limited. Not that I wanted to go out and (laugh) paint the town red or anything, it's just that I felt constricted. I felt this noose tied around my neck.

John's description fits with the sociological theory that discontent and acute tension are key elements in the onset of the conversion process (Lofland & Stark, 1965). Sociologists studying conversions to such different worldviews as Orthodox Judaism (Davidman, 1991; Kaufman, 1991) and the Alcoholics Anonymous 12-step program (Greil & Rudy, 1983) have described stress and tension as important initial incentives toward conversion. However, Heirich (1977) has argued that converts may not experience more stress than nonconverts. When comparing a group of Catholics who converted to Pentecostalism and a control group of Catholics who did not convert, reports of stress-producing circumstances were high in both groups but did not distinguish them. Still, even if converts do not have more stress-producing circumstances in their lives than nonconverts, they may respond to the circumstances by experiencing more tension and discontent (Lofland & Stark, 1965).

A Pivotal Event

John's discontent with his job culminated with the occurrence of what he describes as a "pivotal" event:

> The pivotal event, I think, in all of this was a very strange staff meeting where I worked [at the state headquarters of the Southern Baptist Convention]. . . . One of the employees had just been promoted to a new position. [After his promotion, someone] had gone to the executive director who was the head of the staff [and had] said: "Did you know that this man that we've just given this job to . . . goes with his wife to [X City] and that they go to bars and they actually *dance* in these bars." So, at this very strange staff meeting all of this came to light. This man [who had just been promoted] basically had agreed that he had *repented* of doing this and he would not do it any more. He didn't [profess repentance] to us, but to the executive director.
>
> And I thought, there's something Mickey Mouse about this. And I think that was a real turning point. Because I grew up in a very strict environment where going to bars, much less drinking, and certainly dancing were all wrong. And, I saw this little parade come out, . . . this man keeping his job (laughs) by basically saying, "if it means my job, I won't do it any more." Because I couldn't imagine him *agreeing* to do it for any other reason. Because obviously, he didn't see it as being harmful or wrong. And yet, he had to do it in order to remain in the good graces of the organization. So that had some jarring effect on me right there, but I think it had much stronger effects later on. I see it now as a pivotal event. I just felt myself personally constricted and [I] had to do something to get out of that very constricting environment.

Following this event, John "shifted out of that denominational work and into counseling." He had become interested in clinical work through his wife's influence. According to John, she worked as a clinician and "enjoyed it very, very much. And I saw it as a very, very interesting and desirable option."

John's mention of his wife's influence and encouragement conforms to the observation that social support is often crucial to conversion experiences. Sometimes converts actively seek out encouragement, support, and affirmation of the changes they are undergoing (Straus, 1979). Organizations also often seek to promote conversions to their worldview by assigning mentors or guides to persons who are in the process of converting (Beckford, 1978; Davidman, 1991; Greil & Rudy, 1983). The attempt by organizations to foster a supportive and loving environment has been referred to as a "hooking" technique by Lofland (1978). When converts find themselves almost exclusively surrounded and supported by persons who are encouraging their conversion, Lofland (1978) describes the situation as one of "encapsulation."

Increasing Dissociation from the Old Worldview

In spite of having given up his position as a minister, John still sought to maintain some ties to the Southern Baptist Convention. However, over time "there were issues . . . that led me [to] say: 'I will not be a Southern Baptist anymore, and I will never *ever* be associated [with them] again.' " Thus John increasingly dissociated himself from his old worldview on issues of faith, morality, and politics. This dissociation came to a head over the stance of the Southern Baptist Convention toward gays and lesbians. John explained,

> [In] getting away from that Southern Baptist background, I think the pivotal point came . . . [when] a decision was made at the national level . . . that they would break ties with any church that either ordained a gay or lesbian person, or endorsed a union between . . . gay and lesbian people. I think it had been building with me for a long time. Because it seemed like every politically oriented decision that was made at that national level just grated against me—totally! They were all restrictive, oppressive, and notions of no choice. . . . [It] culminated for me in the gay and lesbian issue. . . . It was just a matter of saying, "I am not one of these people. I can't in any way endorse what they're saying." And yet, I don't have a *disdain* for those people. I just have a disdain for—uh—I just can't tolerate being a part of that kind of attitude. So for me that's been a real moral decision: It's not right for me to be a part of that.

At this point, it would seem that John had experienced a thorough transformation of his worldview and his identity. Most sociologists define such a complete transformation as a conversion (e.g., Heirich, 1977; McGuire, 1982; Travisano, 1970). However, Robert Balch (1980) has argued that some converts only act like believers. They use the prescribed language and engage in the prescribed behaviors, but have not experienced sweeping changes in their beliefs and personality. In the case of John, however, he described his conversion as a comprehensive transformation of his worldview and sense of self.

He regarded this transformation as a moral one. Many social science analyses of conversions include descriptions of converts framing their experience in moral terms. But the moral dimension of conversions has seldom been made explicit in the literature. A recent exception is Debra Kaufman's (1991) account of non-Orthodox women's embrace of Orthodox Judaism. She argues that their conversions represent a quest to "make moral sense of their lives" (p. 7). Greil and Rudy (1983) have also described how conversions to the worldview of Alcoholics Anonymous involves "taking moral inventories"(p. 19). It is possible that the present case studies highlight the moral dimension of conversions because the accounts were presented in the context of an interview pertaining to morality. Still, it may be useful in future research on conversions to explore their moral meaning in more detail.

Costs and Benefits

John ended his account of his conversion by assessing its costs and benefits. He explained that he has become estranged from his family and some of his friends.

> [My decision] has [had] a lot of implications for me, because my parents basically don't know too much about . . . my struggle. I'm not sure that they're ready to hear that now, or maybe ever will be. You know, I've kind of moved away from a whole set of friends, although I still have some friends—a very few—who I

> feel like I can talk openly with. . . . Some of the early contacts I had with former minister friends, just talking more openly than I'd ever talked before about issues, it scared the living daylights out of them (laughs). . . . A lot of people that we know, it's too difficult for them.

Many social scientists have described the estrangement from family and friends that accompanies conversions (e.g., Ammerman, 1987; Davidman, 1991; Kaufman, 1991). The convert's new ways of behaving and thinking make it difficult to interact with family and friends who maintain the old worldview. There is often a mutual distrust or outright disdain. One could describe this estrangement between the convert and her old community as the flip side of encapsulation. It is not only that the convert is embraced by a new community, it is also that an old community is left behind. The former experience is often joyful, but the latter can be very painful.

While John regretted his loss of intimacy with family and friends, he rejoiced in his new sense of freedom. He described how he felt liberated behaviorally and mentally.

> There certainly were constrictions about how a person is to act. One of the ironies of all of this—it's kind of amusing to me—is that my wife and I have *really* enjoyed taking dancing lessons (laughs). . . . One of the ministers that I knew in seminary . . . jok[ed] about pulling the shades down, turning the music on, and dancing. That's the kind of thing that people have to live by. There's just a restriction on *behavior*. But there was also a restriction on *thought*. . . . It somewhat stifled my development mentally, psychologically. It kept me in my place. . . . I was oppressed. I felt depressed.

John's understanding of the positive side of his conversion is framed in a progressivist discourse. Like many of the other members of his current church community who were interviewed for the study described above (Jensen, 1998), John makes frequent use of an ethic of autonomy. Thus, in explaining why his conversion has been for the better, John indicates that it has led to an improvement in his psychological health, allowed him more freedom of expression, and increased his opportunity for self-development. From this new progressivist stance, John regards his old worldview as confining and constricting.

From Progressivism to Orthodoxy: Kyle's Account

As is to be expected, Kyle Schultz's understanding of the virtues and vices of orthodoxy and progressivism differs markedly from John's. But many aspects of Kyle's conversion resemble John's: Kyle's conversion also spanned many years; its onset was marked by increasing disillusionment with the old worldview; social support was crucial to Kyle's identity and worldview transformation as were certain pivotal events; and Kyle regards his conversion to the new worldview as a source of relief.

As with John, Kyle's conversion in many ways conforms to Lofland and Skonovd's (1981) concept of an experimental conversion. Thus Kyle's identity transformation was gradual. With some sense of regret, he explained "early on after I became a Christian . . . I always felt I had been cheated or maybe I didn't do it right, because I didn't have a dramatic conversion. Lots of people can tell you the exact day and the time. I can't do that. It was a much more slow and gradual process." In fact, Kyle's conversion occurred over a long time period. He estimates that the "whole process . . . probably took 12 years."

In addition to its experimental quality, Kyle's conversion included elements of other types of conversions. As in mystical conversions (Clark, 1929; James, 1902/1936; Starbuck, 1911), Kyle had the sense of being subject to forces outside himself. He said, "at times I think I see God's providence and His hand in directing me to the point where I could make the decision for Him." Kyle's notion that his conversion was divinely preordained fits well with the emphasis upon God's will and agency within the orthodox worldview. In her study of conversions to Orthodox Judaism, Lynn Davidman (1991) also reported frequent references to preordination.

Kyle's conversion, furthermore, includes elements of what Lofland and Skonovd (1981) term an "intellectual conversion," where the person independently seeks out information about the new worldview from sources such as books and television. As will be described in more detail shortly, Kyle recounted how his conversion followed his decision to read the Bible and literature pertaining to biblical times. Lofland and Skonovd argue that intellectual conversions mostly are a recent phenomenon resulting from the increasingly privatized nature of contemporary religion (Bellah, Madsen, Sullivan, Swidler, & Tipton, 1985; Berger, 1967; Luckmann, 1963). Thus, Kyle initially read the Bible and related literature on his own rather than in the company of others.

Disillusionment and Discovery

Kyle's disillusionment with atheism and discovery of fundamentalism began in the context of his reading the Bible. Initially, he read the Bible not for religious inspiration but in order to prove to his Christian acquaintances how wrong they were.

> I'd always claimed to be an atheist, as early as I can remember. . . . I could see no reason why there had to be a God. I tended to always enjoy the sciences and mathematics, so it was easy to say: "Well, man can do all this stuff, so there is really no place for a God." But growing up I had run into a variety of [Christians], and most of them I had put off. But the thing that struck me was [that] I can *say* there's no God, but now they say there *is* a God. So when I argue[d] with them, they kept bringing up this Bible, . . . and I felt [that] in order to debate them appropriately and to show them that they were wrong, then I had to know what they were talking about.
>
> So I started studying the Bible to find out all the little things I could to trip them up, and make them look foolish, and to show them that they were absolutely wrong. And so early on I was able to find some little things here and there. . . . But then there was a guy, I guess when I was in high school, [who] knew the [Bible] inside and out, and I couldn't trip him up. . . . No matter what, he went back to the basic fact that it [was] his faith. So [I said to myself]: "Well, now I need some historical proof that this is not true. I can't argue with people using the Bible because that's all based on faith. They either believe it or they

> don't. So I need to find some historical proof to show that the Bible's obviously in error."
>
> And as I started trying to find things to show the Bible was in error, I could never find them. I kept trying to find evidence and the evidence I had kept pointing to the fact that this was true.

Kyle's account focuses upon his discovery of what was to become his new worldview. Compared to John, he is less overt about his disillusionment and discontent with his old worldview. Yet, it is evident that as Kyle began to consider the Bible to be God's true word, he was moving away from atheism. The tension that he seems to have experienced is suggested by some analogies that he applied to his conversion. He described it in terms of the head-splitting difficulties involved in solving a mathematical problem.

> I'm a mathematician and whenever you're trying to prove a theorem, it kind of works the same way. You knock your head on the wall and you try 400 different ways to prove this thing. Then one day you'll sit down and it'll just come to you. And Man! How stupid can I be? Why didn't I see that? Well it was kind of that same feeling.

Kyle also likened his experience with his old worldview to the frustrations of "paddling upstream." Apparently, he was beginning to feel exhausted and exasperated with his attempts to find truth in atheism and falsity in faith.

Social Support

Kyle's emerging notion of the Bible being God's true word received support from the woman who was to become his wife and from her pastor. Speaking of this time, shortly after his college years, Kyle said:

> During this time I had met Susan, and Susan was already a Christian. And she introduced me to her pastor, and I started

> talking to him. He was such a neat guy. He accepted me where I was. . . . . We'd have lots of discussions. And then on things I really thought should make a difference to Christians, things like abortion, evolution [and] a variety of different topics, he would say, "that's between you and God." He said, "really the only concern I ha[ve] is whether you are going to believe in Christ as your Savior or not. 'Cause I'm worried about your eternal soul." He said: "Once I have that taken care of, then I'll leave it up to God to convince you one way or the other on all these other aspects. They're minor as far as I'm concerned."
>
> Nobody had ever approached me that way before, because I could always get them to argue on the aspects, which really took away from the central message they were trying to get to me. So I guess I had never heard what the central message was, which was for my eternal life. And so he presented it that way, and tried to give me the evidence he felt would support it: [About] Christ being the Son of God, and why He died, and [the] fulfilling of all the prophecies, . . . and so on. So, I just couldn't conclude anything other than the fact that that had to be true. So I went ahead and made that . . . leap of faith. For me it was more a step than a leap at that point.

To Kyle, as to John, it was important to receive encouragement and affirmation from persons whom he felt close to and respected. For both men, such support was offered by their spouse or spouse-to-be, among others.

A Pivotal Event

While Kyle now considered himself a Christian in matters of faith, he still retained ties to his old worldview and identity. For example, he still maintained his old moral outlook on issues such as abortion for years after he had converted. According to Kyle, it was a pivotal event that finally made him change his outlook on the issue of abortion.

> After I first became a Christian, there were a lot of issues I felt: "Well, I'm really not sure about these. People tell me this is what God says, but I really don't know." And I just really tried

not to think about them too much. Then as you mature as a Christian you get closer to God, and you study His Word more, and He reveals more and more things to you.

In terms of abortion, I'd always viewed it like many pro-choice people do: "Well, it is better to [have an abortion] than [to] let [the child] grow up and be abused and so on and so forth." At one time I wanted to be a psychologist, and I had worked with some abused children. You could see how bad their lives were, and so it was easy to justify in my mind: "Okay, sure, it's better to be killed in the womb than born."

But then Susan and I had a miscarriage. Susan in essence gave birth to a 12-week old fetus. And when she miscarried, the doctor took it and he asked if we wanted to see it. And so, being scientifically oriented I said, "Sure, yeah, I want to see it." He put it in my hand, and at that point in time when I actually looked at it, I realized what that really was. That was my child. I guess from that point on . . . it really dawned on me that this is not just a fetus. This is not just some thing that's [been] hanging around in there and becomes viable at some point in time. This is a child, that died. You know, it made a big enough impact that from that point on I viewed abortion as wrong. . . . It would have been our fifth [child]. We actually already had four. [A] part of me knew [abortion] was wrong, but it had never really become totally concrete for me until that point.

Kyle, like John, described a situation involving a moral issue as pivotal to his complete identity and worldview transformation. However, unlike John, he again attributed some of his transformation to God's will rather than his own exclusive choice—an account consistent with his orthodox worldview.

Relief

Kyle did not discuss the costs of his conversion, as did John. However, like John, he discussed its positive implications.

[Becoming a Christian] was amazing to me because I never thought it would happen. It was very comforting. It was like a great burden was lifted, because I no longer had to disprove

> this thing. I could finally accept something that was actually true. . . . Now I could just accept what [God] had to give me, and now the journey was an enjoyable journey. Now it was just to know Him better, and to use what He is going to give me so that I could actually be more of what He wanted me to be.

Kyle frames his account of the positive implications of his conversion in an orthodox discourse. Like many of the members of his current church community (Jensen, 1998), he repeatedly invokes God's will. Thus Kyle sees his conversion as an opportunity put in his way by God, in order that he may fulfill God's purpose for him in this world. From this orthodox stance, Kyle's old worldview fails to lead in the direction of truth. Kyle's conception of the appeal of orthodoxy echoes the observations of Davidman (1991) and Kaufman (1991) who find that converts to Orthodox Judaism are attracted to its claims to clear and absolute truth.

CONCLUSION

In conclusion, the case studies of John and Kyle show many similarities in their conversion experiences, and many of these aspects have also been observed in other social science studies. Both men experienced discontent and frustration at the onset of their conversions. The progress of their conversions was significantly aided by the social support of persons to whom the men felt close. Also, both men specified events that were pivotal to the transformations in their worldviews and identities, and in both cases these events involved a moral issue. Finally, John and Kyle agreed that their conversions have afforded them a sense of relief.

But, of course, John and Kyle's conversions were also markedly different. John followed a path from orthodoxy to progressivism, whereas Kyle took the route from progressivism to orthodoxy. Thus the two men have markedly different understandings of the appealing and aversive characteristics of these two worldviews. To John orthodoxy with its claims to absolute truth is confining and constricting, whereas to Kyle it is affirming and assuring. To Kyle progressivism with its attention to individual autonomy is subject to the vagaries of time and individual desires, whereas to John it is a source of refreshing freedom.

REFERENCES

Ammerman, N. T. (1987). *Bible believers.* New Brunswick, NJ: Rutgers University Press.

Balch, R. W. (1980). Looking behind the scenes in a religious cult: Implications for the study of conversion. *Sociological Analysis, 41,* 137–143.

Beckford, J. A. (1978). Accounting for conversion. *British Journal of Sociology, 29,* 249–262.

Bellah, R. N. (1987). Conclusion: Competing visions of the role of religion in American society. In R. N. Bellah & F. E. Greenspahn (Eds.), *Uncivil religion: Interreligious hostility in America.* New York: Crossroad.

Bellah, R. N., Madsen, R., Sullivan, W. M., Swidler, A., & Tipton, S. M. (1985). *Habits of the heart.* New York: Harper & Row.

Berger, P. L. (1967). *The sacred canopy.* Garden City, NY: Anchor Books, Doubleday.

Clark, E. T. (1929). *The psychology of religious awakening.* New York: Macmillan.

Davidman, L. (1991). *Tradition in a rootless world: Women turn to Orthodox Judaism.* Berkeley: University of California Press.

Geertz, C. (1983). *Local knowledge: Further essays in interpretive anthropology.* New York: Basic Books.

Greil, A. L., & Rudy, D. R. (1983). Conversion to the world view of Alcoholic Anonymous: A refinement of conversion theory. *Qualitative Sociology, 6,* 5–28.

Heirich, M. (1977). Change of heart: A test of some widely held theories about religious conversion. *American Journal of Sociology, 83,* 653–680.

Hunter, J. D. (1991). *Culture wars: The struggle to define America.* New York: Basic Books.

Hunter, J. D. (1994). *Before the shooting begins: Searching for democracy in America's culture war.* New York: Free Press.

James, W. (1936). *The varieties of religious experience.* Garden City, NY: Doubleday. (Original work published 1902)

Jensen, L. A. (1995). The culture war and psychology: A review of Lifton's *The Protean Self. Culture and Psychology, 1,* 393–401.

Jensen, L. A. (1997a). Culture wars: American moral divisions across the adult lifespan. *Journal of Adult Development, 4,* 117–121.

Jensen, L. A. (1997b). Different worldviews, different morals: America's culture war divide. *Human Development, 40,* 325–344.

Jensen, L. A. (1998). Different habits, different hearts: The moral languages of the culture war. *The American Sociologist, 29,* 83–101.

Kaufman, D. R. (1991). *Rachel's daughters: Newly orthodox Jewish women.* New Brunswick, NJ: Rutgers University Press.

Kuhn, T. (1970). *The structure of scientific revolutions.* Chicago: University of Chicago Press.

Lofland, J. (1978). Becoming a world saver revisited. In J. T. Richardson (Ed.), *Conversion careers: In and out of the new religions.* Beverly Hills, CA: Sage.

Lofland, J., & Skonovd, N. (1981). Conversion motifs. *Journal for the Scientific Study of Religion, 20,* 373–385.

Lofland, J., & Stark, R. (1965). Becoming a world saver: A theory of conversion to a deviant perspective. *American Sciological Review, 30,* 862–874.

Luckmann, T. (1963). *The invisible religion.* New York: Macmillan.

McGuire, M. (1982). *Pentecostal Catholics: Power, charisma, and order in a religious movement.* Philadelphia: Temple University Press.

Neuhaus, R. J. (1990). Fundamentalism and the American polity. In N. J. Cohen (Ed.), *The fundamentalist phenomenon.* Grand Rapids, MI: William B. Eerdmans.

Shweder, R. A. (1990). In defense of moral realism: Reply to Gabennesch. *Child Development, 61,* 2060–2067.

Starbuck, E. D. (1911). *The psychology of religion.* New York: Scribners.

Straus, R. A. (1979). Religious conversion as a personal and collective accomplishment. *Sociological Analysis, 40,* 158–165.

Travisano, R. (1970). Alternation and conversion as qualitatively different transformations. In G. P. Stone & H. A. Farberman (Eds.), *Social psychology through symbolic interaction.* Waltham, MA: Ginn-Blaisdell.

Walsh, B. J., & Middleton, J. R. (1984). *The transforming vision: Shaping a Christian world view.* Downers Grove, IL: InterVarsity Press.

Wuthnow, R. (1988). *The restructuring of American religion.* Princeton, NJ: Princeton University Press.

Wuthnow, R. (1989). *The struggle for America's soul: Evangelicals, liberals, and secularism.* Grand Rapids, MI: William B. Eerdmans.

Name Index

Subject Index